# Classics In
# Child Development

# Classics In
# Child Development

*Advisory Editors*

**JUDITH KRIEGER GARDNER**
**HOWARD GARDNER**

*Editorial Board*

**Wayne Dennis**
**Jerome Kagan**
**Sheldon White**

# MENTAL EVOLUTION
# IN MAN

*ORIGIN OF HUMAN FACULTY*

BY

GEORGE JOHN ROMANES

## ARNO PRESS
A New York Times Company

New York — 1975

Reprint Edition 1975 by Arno Press Inc

Reprinted from a copy in
  The University of Illinois Library

Classics in Child Development
ISBN for complete set: 0-405-06450-0
See last pages of this volume for titles.

Manufactured in the United States of America

**Library of Congress Cataloging in Publication Data**

Romanes, George John, 1848-1894.
    Mental evolution in man.

    (Classics in child development)
    Reprint of the 1889 ed. published by  D. Appleton,
New York.
    Includes index.
    1.  Psychology, Comparative.  2.  Evolution.
I.  Title.  II.  Series.
BF671.R65  1975    156'.3      74-21426
ISBN 0-405-06475-6

# MENTAL EVOLUTION IN MAN

# MENTAL EVOLUTION
# IN MAN

*ORIGIN OF HUMAN FACULTY*

BY

## GEORGE JOHN ROMANES
M. A., LL. D., F. R. S.

AUTHOR OF "ANIMAL INTELLIGENCE," "MENTAL EVOLUTION IN ANIMALS"

NEW YORK
D. APPLETON AND COMPANY
1889

*Authorized Edition.*

# PREFACE.

IN now carrying my study of mental evolution into the province of human psychology, it is desirable that I should say a few words to indicate the scope and intention of this the major portion of my work. For it is evident that "Mental Evolution in Man" is a subject comprehending so enormous a field that, unless some lines of limitation are drawn within which its discussion is to be confined, no one writer could presume to deal with it.

The lines, then, which I have laid down for my own guidance are these. My object is to seek for the principles and causes of mental evolution in man, first as regards the origin of human faculty, and next as regards the several main branches into which faculties distinctively human afterwards ramified and developed. In order as far as possible to gain this object, it has appeared to me desirable to take large or general views, both of the main trunk itself, and also of its sundry branches. Therefore I have throughout avoided the temptation of following any of the branches into their smaller ramifications, or of going into the details of progressive development. These, I have felt, are matters to be dealt with by others who are severally better qualified for the task, whether their special studies have reference to language, archæology, technicology, science, literature, art, politics, morals, or religion. But, in so far as I shall subsequently have to deal with these subjects, I will do so with the purpose of arriving at general principles bearing upon mental evolution, rather than with that of collecting facts or opinions for the sake of their intrinsic interest from a purely historical point of view.

Finding that the labour required for the investigation, even as thus limited, is much greater than I originally anticipated, it appears to me undesirable to delay publication until the whole shall have been completed. I have therefore decided to publish the treatise in successive instalments, of which the present constitutes the first. As indicated by the title, it is concerned exclusively with the Origin of Human Faculty. Future instalments will deal with the Intellect, Emotions, Volition, Morals, and Religion. It will, however, be several years before I shall be in a position to publish these succeeding instalments, notwithstanding that some of them are already far advanced.

Touching the present instalment, it is only needful to remark that from a controversial point of view it is, perhaps, the most important. If once the genesis of conceptual thought from non-conceptual antecedents be rendered apparent, the great majority of competent readers at the present time would be prepared to allow that the psychological barrier between the brute and the man is shown to have been over-come. Consequently, I have allotted what might otherwise appear to be a disproportionate amount of space to my consideration of this the *origin* of human faculty—dis-proportionate, I mean, as compared with what has afterwards to be said touching the *development* of human faculty in its several branches already named. Moreover, in the present treatise I shall be concerned chiefly with the psychology of my subject—reserving for my next instalment a full con-sideration of the light which has been shed on the mental and social condition of early man by the study of his own remains on the one hand, and of existing savages on the other. Even as thus restricted, however, the subject-matter of the present treatise will be found more extensive than most persons would have been prepared to expect. For it does not appear to me that this subject-matter has hitherto received at the hands of psychologists any approach to the amount of analysis of which it is susceptible, and to which—in view of the general theory of evolution—it is unquestionably entitled. But I have everywhere endeavoured to avoid undue prolixity, trusting that the intelligence of any one who is likely to read the book will be able to appreciate the significance of important points, without the need of expatiation on the part of the writer. The only places, therefore, where I feel that I may be fairly open to the charge of unnecessary reiteration, are those in which I am endeavouring to render fully intelligible the newer features of my analysis. But even here I do not anticipate that readers of any class will complain of the efforts which are thus made to assist their understanding of a somewhat complicated matter.

As no one has previously gone into this matter, I have found myself obliged to coin a certain number of new terms, for the purpose at once of avoiding continuous circumlocution, and of rendering aid to the analytic inquiry. For my own part I regret this necessity, and therefore have not resorted to it save where I have found the force of circumstances imperative. In the result, I do not think that adverse criticism is likely to fasten upon any of these new terms as needless for the purposes of my inquiry. Every worker is free to choose his own instruments ; and when none are ready-made to suit his requirements, he has no alternative but to fashion those which may.

To any one who already accepts the general theory of evolution as applied to the human mind, it may well appear that the present instalment of my work is needlessly elaborate. Now, I can quite sympathize with any evolutionist who may thus feel that I have brought steam-engines to break butterflies ; but I must ask such a man to remember two things. First, that plain and obvious as the truth may seem to him, it is nevertheless a truth that is very far from having received general recognition, even among more intelligent members of the community : seeing, therefore, of how much importance it is to establish this truth as an integral part of the doctrine of descent, I cannot think that either time or energy is wasted in a serious endeavour to do so, even though to minds already persuaded it may seem unnecessary to have slain our opponents in a manner quite so mercilessly minute. Secondly, I must ask these friendly critics to take note that, although the discussion has everywhere been thrown into the form of an answer to objections, it really has a much wider scope: it aims not only at an overthrow of adversaries, but also, and even more, at an exposition of the principles which have probably been concerned in the " Origin of Human Faculty."

The Diagram which is reproduced from my previous work on " Mental Evolution in Animals," and which serves to represent the leading features of psychogenesis throughout the animal kingdom, will re-appear also in succeeding instalments of the work, when it will be continued so as to represent the principal stages of " Mental Evolution in Man."

18, CORNWALL TERRACE, REGENT'S PARK,
    *July*, 1888.

# CONTENTS.

# MENTAL EVOLUTION IN MAN.

## CHAPTER I.

### MAN AND BRUTE.

TAKING up the problems of psychogenesis where these were left in my previous work, I have in the present treatise to consider the whole scope of mental evolution in man. Clearly the topic thus presented is so large, that in one or other of its branches it might be taken to include the whole history of our species, together with our pre-historic development from lower forms of life, as already indicated in the Preface. However, it is not my intention to write a history of civilization, still less to develop any elaborate hypothesis of anthropogeny. My object is merely to carry into an investigation of human psychology a continuation of the principles which I have already applied to the attempted elucidation of animal psychology. I desire to show that in the one province, as in the other, the light which has been shed by the doctrine of evolution is of a magnitude which we are now only beginning to appreciate ; and that by adopting the theory of continuous development from the one order of mind to the other, we are able scientifically to explain the whole mental constitution of man, even in those parts of it which, to former generations, have appeared inexplicable.

In order to accomplish this purpose, it is not needful that I should seek to enter upon matters of detail in the application of those principles to the facts of history. On the contrary,

I think that any such endeavour—even were I qualified to make it—would tend only to obscure my exposition of those principles themselves. It is enough that I should trace the operation of such principles, as it were, in outline, and leave to the professed historian the task of applying them in special cases.

The present work being thus a treatise on human psychology in relation to the theory of descent, the first question which it must seek to attack is clearly that as to the evidence of the mind of man having been derived from mind as we meet with it in the lower animals. And here, I think, it is not too much to say that we approach a problem which is not merely the most interesting of those that have fallen within the scope of my own works ; but perhaps the most interesting that has ever been submitted to the contemplation of our race. If it is true that " the proper study of mankind is man," assuredly the study of nature has never before reached a territory of thought so important in all its aspects as that which in our own generation it is for the first time approaching. After centuries of intellectual conquest in all regions of the phenomenal universe, man has at last begun to find that he may apply in a new and most unexpected manner the adage of antiquity—*Know thyself.* For he has begun to perceive a strong probability, if not an actual certainty, that his own living nature is identical in kind with the nature of all other life, and that even the most amazing side of this his own nature—nay, the most amazing of all things within the reach of his knowledge—the human mind itself, is but the topmost inflorescence of one mighty growth, whose roots and stem and many branches are sunk in the abyss of planetary time Therefore, with Professor Huxley we may say :—" The importance of such an inquiry is indeed intuitively manifest. Brought face to face with these blurred copies of himself, the least thoughtful of men is conscious of a certain shock, due perhaps not so much to disgust at the aspect of what looks like an insulting caricature, as to the awaking of a sudden and profound mistrust of time-honoured theories and strongly rooted prejudices regarding his own position in nature, and his relations to the wider world of life; while that which remains a dim suspicion for the unthinking, becomes a vast argument, fraught with the deepest consequences, for all who are acquainted with the recent progress of anatomical and physiological sciences." *

The problem, then, which in this generation has for the first time been presented to human thought, is the problem of how this thought itself has come to be. A question of the deepest importance to every system of philosophy has been raised by the study of biology; and it is the question whether the mind of man is essentially the same as the mind of the lower animals, or, having had, either wholly or in part, some other mode of origin, is essentially distinct—differing not only in degree but in kind from all other types of psychical being. And forasmuch as upon his great and deeply interesting question opinions are still much divided—even among those most eminent in the walks of science who agree in accepting the principles of evolution as applied to explain the mental constitution of the lower animals,—it is evident that the question is neither a superficial nor an easy one. I shall however, endeavour to examine it with as little obscurity as possible, and also, I need hardly say, with all the impartiality of which I am capable. †

It will be remembered that in the introductory chapter of my previous work I have already briefly sketched the manner in which I propose to treat this question. Here, therefore, it is sufficient to remark that I began by assuming the truth of the general theory of descent so far as the animal kingdom

---

* *Man's Place in Nature*, p. 59.

† It is perhaps desirable to explain from the first that by the words " difference of kind," as used in the above paragraph and elsewhere throughout this treatise, I mean difference of *origin*. This is the only real distinction that can be drawn between the terms " difference of kind " and " difference of degree ; " and I should scarcely have deemed it worth while to give the definition, had it not been for the confused manner in which the terms are used by some writers—*e.g.* Professor Sayce, who says, while speaking of the development of languages from a common source, " differences of degree become in time differences of kind " (*Introduction to the Science of Language*, ii. 309).

is concerned, both with respect to bodily and to mental organization ; but in doing this I expressly excluded the mental organization of man, as being a department of comparative psychology with reference to which I did not feel entitled to assume the principles of evolution. The reason why I made this special exception, I sufficiently explained ; and I shall therefore now proceed, without further introduction, to a full consideration of the problem that is before us.

First, let us consider the question on purely *a priori* grounds. In accordance with our original hypothesis—upon which all naturalists of any standing are nowadays agreed— the process of organic and of mental evolution has been continuous throughout the whole region of life and of mind, with the one exception of the mind of man. On grounds of analogy, therefore, we should deem it antecedently improbable that the process of evolution, elsewhere so uniform and ubiquitous, should have been interrupted at its terminal phase. And looking to the very large extent of this analogy, the antecedent presumption which it raises is so considerable, that in my opinion it could only be counterbalanced by some very cogent and unmistakable facts, showing a difference between animal and human psychology so distinctive as to render it in the nature of the case virtually impossible that the one could ever have graduated into the other. This I posit as the first consideration.

Next, still restricting ourselves to an *a priori* view, it is unquestionable that human psychology, in the case of every individual human being, presents to actual observation a process of gradual development, or evolution, extending from infancy to manhood ; and that in this process, which begins at a zero level of mental life and may culminate in genius, there is nowhere and never observable a sudden leap of progress, such as the passage from one order of psychical being to another might reasonably be expected to show. Therefore, it is a matter of observable fact that, whether or not human intelligence differs from animal in kind, it certainly does admit of gradual development from a zero level. This I posit as the second consideration.

Again, so long as it is passing through the lower phases of its development, the human mind assuredly ascends through a scale of mental faculties which are parallel with those that are permanently presented by the psychological species of the animal kingdom. A glance at the Diagram which I have placed at the beginning of my previous work will serve to show in how strikingly quantitative, as well as qualitative, a manner the development of an individual human mind follows the order of mental evolution in the animal kingdom. And when we remember that, at all events up to the level where this parallel ends, the diagram in question is not an expression of any psychological theory, but of well-observed and undeniable psychological fact, I think every reasonable man must allow that, whatever the explanation of this remarkable coincidence may be, it certainly must admit of *some* explanation—*i.e.* cannot be ascribed to mere chance. But, if so, the only explanation available is that which is furnished by the theory of descent. These facts, which I present as a third consideration, tend still further—and, I think, most strongly—to increase the force of antecedent presumption against any hypothesis which supposes that the process of evolution can have been discontinuous in the region of mind.

Lastly, it is likewise a matter of observation, as I shall fully show in the next instalment of this work, that in the history of our race—as recorded in documents, traditions, antiquarian remains, and flint implements—the intelligence of the race has been subject to a steady process of gradual development. The force of this consideration lies in its proving, that if the process of mental evolution was suspended between the anthropoid apes and primitive man, it was again resumed with primitive man, and has since continued as un-interruptedly in the human species as it previously did in the animal species. Now, upon the face of these facts, or from a merely antecedent point of view, such appears to me, to say the least, a highly improbable supposition. At all events, it certainly is not the kind of supposition which men of science are disposed to regard with favour elsewhere ; for a long and arduous experience has taught us that the most paying kind of supposition which we can bring with us into our study of nature, is that which recognizes in nature the principle of *continuity*.

Taking, then, these several *a priori* considerations together, they must, in my opinion, be fairly held to make out a very strong *primâ facie* case in favour of the view that there has been no interruption of the developmental process in the course of psychological history ; but that the mind of man, like the mind of animals—and, indeed, like everything else in the domain of living nature—has been evolved. For these considerations show, not only that on analogical grounds any such interruption must be held as in itself improbable ; but also that there is nothing in the constitution of the human mind incompatible with the supposition of its having been slowly evolved, seeing that not only in the case of every individual life, but also during the whole history of our species, the human mind actually *does* undergo, and *has* undergone, the process in question.

In order to overturn so immense a presumption as is thus erected on *a priori* grounds, the psychologist must fairly be called upon to supply some very powerful considerations of an *a posteriori* kind, tending to show that there is something in the constitution of the human mind which renders it virtually impossible—or at all events exceedingly difficult to imagine—that it can have proceeded by way of genetic descent from mind of lower orders. I shall therefore proceed to consider, as carefully and as impartially as I can, the arguments which have been adduced in support of this thesis.

In the introductory chapter of my previous work I observed, that the question whether or not human intelligence has been evolved from animal intelligence can only be dealt with scientifically by comparing the one with the other, in order to ascertain the points wherein they agree and the points wherein they differ. I shall, therefore, here begin by briefly stating the points of agreement, and then proceed more carefully to consider all the more important views which have hitherto been propounded concerning the points of difference.

If we have regard to Emotions as these occur in the brute, we cannot fail to be struck by the broad fact that the area of psychology which they cover is so nearly co-extensive with that which is covered by the emotional faculties of man. In my previous works I have given what I consider unquestionable evidence of all the following emotions, which I here name in the order of their appearance through the psychological scale,—fear, surprise, affection, pugnacity, curiosity, jealousy, anger, play, sympathy, emulation, pride, resentment, emotion of the beautiful, grief, hate, cruelty, benevolence, revenge, rage, shame, regret, deceitfulness, emotion of the ludicrous.*

Now, this list exhausts all the human emotions, with the exception of those which refer to religion, moral sense, and perception of the sublime. Therefore I think we are fully entitled to conclude that, so far as emotions are concerned, it cannot be said that the facts of animal psychology raise any difficulties against the theory of descent. On the contrary, the emotional life of animals is so strikingly similar to the emotional life of man—and especially of young children— that I think the similarity ought fairly to be taken as direct evidence of a genetic continuity between them.

And so it is with regard to Instinct. Understanding this term in the sense previously defined,† it is unquestionably true that in man—especially during the periods of infancy and youth—sundry well-marked instincts are presented, which have reference chiefly to nutrition, self-preservation, reproduction, and the rearing of progeny. No one has

---

* See *Mental Evolution in Animals*, chapter on the Emotions.

† *Mental Evolution in Animals*, p. 159. "The term is a generic one, comprising all the faculties of mind which are concerned in conscious and adaptive action, antecedent to individual experience, without necessary knowledge of the relation between means employed and ends attained, but similarly performed under similar and frequently recurring circumstances by all individuals of the same species."

ventured to dispute that all these instincts are identical with those which we observe in the lower animals ; nor, on the other hand, has any one ventured to suggest that there is any instinct which can be said to be peculiar to man, unless the moral and religious sentiments are taken to be of the nature of instincts. And although it is true that instinct plays a larger part in the psychology of many animals than it does in the psychology of man, this fact is plainly of no importance in the present connection, where we are concerned only with identity of principle. If any one were childish enough to argue that the mind of a man differs in kind from that of a brute because it does not display any particular instinct— such, for example, as the spinning of webs, the building of nests, or the incubation of eggs,—the answer of course would be that, by parity of reasoning, the mind of a spider must be held to differ in kind from that of a bird. So far, then, as instincts and emotions are concerned, the parallel before us is much too close to admit of any argument on the opposite side.

With regard to Volition more will be said in a future instalment of this work. Here, therefore, it is enough to say, in general terms, that no one has seriously questioned the identity of kind between the animal and the human will, up to the point at which so-called freedom is supposed by some dissentients to supervene and characterize the latter. Now, of course, if the human will differs from the animal will in any important feature or attribute such as this, the fact must be duly taken into account during the course of our subsequent analysis. At present, however, we are only engaged upon a preliminary sketch of the points of resemblance between animal and human psychology. So far, therefore, as we are now concerned with the will, we have only to note that up to the point where the volitions of a man begin to surpass those of a brute in respect of complexity, refinement, and foresight, no one disputes identity of kind.

Lastly, the same remark applies to the faculties of Intellect.*

---

* Of course my opponents will not allow that this word can be properly applied to the psychology of any brute. But I am not now using it in a question-

Enormous as the difference undoubtedly is between these faculties in the two cases, the difference is conceded not to be one of kind *ab initio.* On the contrary, it is conceded that up to a certain point—namely, as far as the highest degree of intelligence to which an animal attains—there is not merely a similarity of kind, but an identity of correspondence. In other words, the parallel between animal and human intelligence which is presented in my Diagram, and to which allusion has already been made, is not disputed. The question, therefore, only arises with reference to those super-added faculties which are represented above the level marked 28, where the upward growth of animal intelligence ends, and the growth of distinctively human intelligence begins. But even at level 28 the human mind is already in possession of many of its most useful faculties, and these it does not afterwards shed, but carries them upwards with it in the course of its further development—as we well know by observing the psychogenesis of every child. Now, it belongs to the very essence of evolution, considered as a process, that when one order of existence passes on to higher grades of excellence, it does so upon the foundation already laid by the previous course of its progress ; so that when compared with any allied order of existence which has not been carried so far in this upward course, a more or less close parallel admits of being traced between the two, up to the point at which the one begins to distance the other, where all further comparison admittedly ends. Therefore, upon the face of them, the facts of comparative psychology now before us are, to say the least, strongly suggestive of the superadded powers of the human intellect having been due to a process of evolution.

Lest it should be thought that in this preliminary sketch of the resemblances between human and brute psychology I have been endeavouring to draw the lines with a biased hand,

begging sense : I am using it only to avoid the otherwise necessary expedient of coining a new term. Whatever view we may take as to the relations between human and animal psychology, we must in some way distinguish between the different ingredients of each, and so between the instinct, the emotion, and the intelligence of an animal. See *Mental Evolution in Animals,* p. 335, et seq.

I will here quote a short passage to show that I have not misrepresented the extent to which agreement prevails among adherents of otherwise opposite opinions. And for this purpose I select as spokesman a distinguished naturalist, who is also an able psychologist, and to whom, therefore, I shall afterwards have occasion frequently to refer, as on both these accounts the most competent as well as the most representative of my opponents. In his Presidential Address before the Biological Section of the British Association in 1879, Mr. Mivart is reported to have said :—

"I have no wish to ignore the marvellous powers of animals, or the resemblance of their actions to those of man. No one can reasonably deny that many of them have feelings, emotions, and sense-perceptions similar to our own ; that they exercise voluntary motion, and perform actions grouped in complex ways for definite ends ; that they to a certain extent learn by experience, and combine perceptions and reminiscences so as to draw practical inferences, directly apprehending objects standing in different relations one to another, so that, in a sense, they may be said to apprehend relations. They will show hesitation, ending apparently, after a conflict of desires, with what looks like choice or volition ; and such animals as the dog will not only exhibit the most marvellous fidelity and affection, but will also manifest evident signs of shame, which may seem the outcome of incipient moral perceptions. It is no great wonder, then, that so many persons, little given to patient and careful introspection, should fail to perceive any radical distinction between a nature thus gifted and the intellectual nature of man."

We may now turn to consider the points wherein human and brute psychology have been by various writers alleged to differ.

The theory that brutes are non-sentient machines need not detain us, as no one at the present day is likely to defend it.* Again, the distinction between human and brute

* If any one should be disposed to do so, I can only reply to him in the words of Professor Huxley, who puts the case tersely and well :—" What is the value of

psychology that has always been taken more or less for granted—namely, that the one is rational and the other irrational—may likewise be passed over after what has been said in the chapter on Reason in my previous work. For it is there shown that if we use the term Reason in its true, as distinguished from its traditional sense, there is no fact in animal psychosis more patent than that this psychosis is capable in no small degree of *ratiocination.* The source of the very prevalent doctrine that animals have no germ of reason is, I think, to be found in the fact that reason attains a much higher level of development in man than in animals, while instinct attains a higher development in animals than in man : popular phraseology, therefore, disregarding the points of similarity while exaggerating the more conspicuous points of difference, designates all the mental faculties of the animal instinctive, in contradistinction to those of man, which are termed rational. But unless we commit ourselves to an obvious reasoning in a circle, we must avoid assuming that all actions of animals are instinctive, and then arguing that, because they are instinctive, therefore they differ in kind from those actions of man which are rational. The question really lies in what is here assumed, and can only be answered by examining in what essential respect instinct differs from reason. This I have endeavoured to do in my previous work with as much precision as the nature of the subject permits ; and I think I have made it evident, in the first place, that there is no such immense distinction between instinct and reason as is generally assumed—the former often being

---

the evidence which leads one to believe that one's fellow-man feels ? The only evidence in this argument from analogy is the similarity of his structure and of his actions to one's own, and if that is good enough to prove that one's fellow-man feels, surely it is good enough to prove that an ape feels," etc. (*Critiques and Addresses*, p. 282). To this statement of the case Mr. Mivart offers, indeed, a criticism, but it is one of a singularly feeble character. He says, " Surely it is not by similarity of structure or actions, but by *language* that men are placed in communication with one another." To this it seems sufficient to ask, in the first place, whether language is not action ; and, in the next, whether, as expressive of *suffering*, articulate speech is regarded by us as more "eloquent" than inarticulate cries and gestures ?

blended with the latter, and. the latter as often becoming transmuted into the former,—and, in the next place, that all the higher animals manifest in various degrees the faculty of inferring. Now, *this is the faculty of reason, properly so called;* and although it is true that in no case does it attain in animal psychology to more than a rudimentary phase of development as contrasted with its prodigious growth in man, this is clearly quite another matter where the question before us is one concerning difference of kind.*

Again, the theological distinction between men and animals may be passed over, because it rests on a dogma with which the science of psychology has no legitimate point of contact. Whether or not the conscious part of man differs from the conscious part of animals in being immortal, and whether or not the "spirit" of man differs from the "soul" of animals in other particulars of kind, dogma itself would maintain that science has no voice in either affirming or denying. For, from the nature of the case, any information of a positive kind relating to these matters can only be expected to come by way of a Revelation ; and, therefore, however widely dogma and science may differ on other points, they are at least agreed upon this one—namely, if the conscious life of man differs thus from the conscious life of brutes, Christianity and Philosophy alike proclaim that only by a Gospel could its endowment of immortality have been brought to light.†

Another distinction between the man and the brute which we often find asserted is, that the latter shows no signs of

* Of course where the term Reason is intended to signify Introspective Thought, the above remarks do not apply, further than to indicate the misuse of the term.

† I here neglect to consider the view of Bishop Butler, and others who have followed him, that animals may have an immortal principle as well as man ; for, if this view is maintained, it serves to identify, not to separate, human and brute psychology. The dictum of Aristotle and Buffon, that animals differ from man in having no power of mental apprehension, may also be disregarded ; for it appears to be sufficiently disposed of by the following remark of Dureau de la Malle, which I here quote as presenting some historical interest in relation to the theory of natural selection. He says : "Si les animaux n'étaient pas suscéptibles d'apprendre les moyens de se conserver, les espèces se seraient anéanties."

mental progress in successive generations. On this alleged distinction I may remark, first of all, that it -begs the whole question of mental evolution in animals, and, therefore, is directly opposed to the whole body of facts presented in my work upon this subject. In the next place, I may remark that the alleged distinction comes with an ill grace from opponents of evolution, seeing that it depends upon a recognition of the principles of evolution in the history of mankind. But, leaving aside these considerations, I meet the alleged distinction with a plain denial of both the statements of fact on which it rests. That is to say, I deny on the one hand that mental progress from generation to generation is an invariable peculiarity of human intelligence ; and, on the other hand, I deny that such progress is never found to occur in the case of animal intelligence.

Taking these two points separately, I hold it to be a statement opposed to fact to say, or to imply, that all existing savages, when not brought into contact with civilized man, undergo intellectual development from generation to generation. On the contrary, one of the most generally applicable statements we can make with reference to the psychology of uncivilized man is that it shows, in a remarkable degree, what we may term a *vis inertiæ* as regards upward movement. Even so highly developed a type of mind as that of the Negro—submitted, too, as it has been in millions of individual cases to close contact with minds of the most progressive type, and enjoying as it has in many thousands of individual cases all the advantages of liberal education—has never, so far as I can ascertain, executed one single stroke of original work in any single department of intellectual activity.

Again, if we look to the whole history of man upon this planet as recorded by his remains, the feature which to my mind stands out in most marked prominence is the almost incredible slowness of his intellectual advance, during all the earlier millenniums of his existence. Allowing full weight to the consideration that " the Palæolithic age, referring as the phrase does to a stage of culture, and not to any chronological period, is something which has come and gone at very different dates in different parts of the world ; " * and that the same remark may be taken, in perhaps a smaller measure, to apply to the Neolithic age ; still, when we remember what enormous lapses of time these ages may be roughly taken to represent, I think it is a most remarkable fact that, during the many thousands of years occupied by the former, the human mind should have practically made no advance upon its primitive methods of chipping flints ; or that during the time occupied by the latter, this same mind should have been so slow in arriving, for example, at even so simple an invention as that of substituting horns for flints in the manufacture of weapons.   In my next volume, where I shall have to deal especially with the evidence of intellectual evolution, I shall have to give many instances, all tending to show its extra-ordinarily slow progress during these æons of prehistoric time. Indeed, it was not until the great step had been made of sub-stituting metals for both stones and horns, that mental evolution began to proceed at anything like a measurable rate.   Yet this was, as it were, but a matter of yesterday.   So that, upon the whole, if we have regard to the human species generally—whether over the surface of the earth at the present time, or in the records of geological history,—we can no longer maintain that a tendency to improvement in successive generations is here a leading characteristic.   On the contrary, any improvement of so rapid and continuous a kind as that which is really contemplated, is characteristic only of a small division of the human race during the last few hours, as it were, of its existence.

On the other hand, as I have said, it is not true that animal species never display any traces of intellectual improve-ment from generation to generation.   Were this the case, as already remarked, mental evolution could never have taken place in the brute creation, and so the phenomena of mind would have been wholly restricted to man : all animals would have required to present but a vegetative form of life.   But,

* John Fiske, *Excursions of an Evolutionist,* pp. 42, 43 (1884).

apart from this general consideration, we meet with many particular instances of mental improvement in successive generations of animals, taking place even within the limited periods over which human observations can extend. In my previous work numerous cases will be found (especially in the chapters on the plasticity and blended origin of instincts), showing that it is quite a usual thing for birds and mammals to change even the most strongly inherited of their instinctive habits, in order to improve the conditions of their life in relation to some change which has taken place in their environments. And if it should be said that in such a case "the animal still does not rise above the level of birdhood or of beasthood," the answer, of course, is, that neither does a Shakespeare or a Newton rise above the level of manhood.

On the whole, then, I cannot see that there is any valid distinction to be drawn between human and brute psychology with respect to improvement from generation to generation. Indeed, I should deem it almost more philosophical in any opponent of the theory of evolution, who happened to be acquainted with the facts bearing upon the subject, if he were to adopt the converse position, and argue that for the purposes of this theory there is *not a sufficient* distinction between human and brute psychology in this respect. For when we remember the great advance which, according to the theory of evolution, the mind of palæolithic man must already have made upon that of the higher apes, and when we remember that all races of existing men have the immense advantage of some form of language whereby to transmit to progeny the results of individual experience,—when we remember these things, the difficulty appears to me to lie on the side of explaining why, with such a start and with such advantages, the human species, both when it first appears upon the pages of geological history, and as it now appears in the great majority of its constituent races, should so far resemble animal species in the prolonged stagnation of its intellectual life.

I shall now pass on to consider the views of Mr. Wallace

and Mr. Mivart on the distinction between the mental endow-
ments of man and of brute.   Both these .authors are skilled
naturalists, and also professed evolutionists so far as the
animal world is concerned : moreover, they further agree in
maintaining that the principles of evolution cannot be held
to apply to man.   But it is curious that, so far as psychology
is concerned, they base their arguments in support of their
common conclusion on precisely opposite premisses.   For
while Mr. Mivart argues that human intelligence cannot be
the same in kind as animal intelligence, because the mind of
the lowest savage is incomparably superior to that of the
highest ape ; Mr. Wallace argues for the same conclusion on
the ground that the intelligence of savages is so little removed
from that of the higher apes, that the fact of their brains being
proportionately larger must be held to point prospectively
towards the needs of civilized life.   "A brain," he says,
"slightly larger than that of the gorilla would, according to
the evidence before us, fully have sufficed for the limited
mental development of the savage ; and we must therefore
admit that the large brain he actually possesses could never
have been developed solely by any of the laws of evolution." *

---

* *Natural Selection*, p. 343.   It will subsequently appear, as a general consequence of our investigation of savage psychology, that of these two opposite
opinions the one advocated by Mr. Mivart is best supported by facts.   But I may
here adduce one or two considerations of a more special nature bearing upon this
point.   First, as to cerebral *structure*, the case is thus summed up by Professor
Huxley :—" The difference in weight of brain between the highest and the lowest
man is far greater, both relatively and absolutely, than that between the lowest
man and the highest ape.   The latter, as has been seen, is represented by, say
12 ounces of cerebral substance absolutely, or by 32 : 20 relatively ; but, as the
largest recorded human brain weighed between 65 and 66 ounces, the former
difference is represented by more than 33 ounces absolutely, or by 65 : 32 relatively.
Regarded systematically, the cerebral differences of man and apes are not of more
than generic value—his family distinction resting chiefly on his dentition, his
pelves, and his lower limbs " (*Man's Place in Nature*, p. 103).· Next, concerning
cerebral *function*, Mr. Chauncey Wright well remarks :—"A psychological analysis
of the faculty of language shows that even the smallest proficiency in it might
require more brain power than the greatest proficiency in any other direction "
(*North American Review*, Oct. 1870, p. 295).   After quoting this, Mr. Darwin
observes of savage man, " He has invented and is able to use various weapons,
tools, traps, &c., with which he defends himself, kills or catches prey, and other-

Now, I have presented these two opinions side by side because I deem it an interesting, if not a suggestive circumstance, that the two leading dissenters in this country from the general school of evolutionists, although both holding the doctrine that man ought to be separated from the rest of the animal kingdom on psychological grounds, are nevertheless led to their common doctrine by directly opposite reasons.

The eminent French naturalist, Professor Quatrefages, also adopts the opinion that man should be separated from the rest of the animal kingdom as a being who, on psychological grounds, must be held to have had some different mode of origin. But he differs from both the English evolutionists in drawing his distinction somewhat more finely. For while Mivart and Wallace found their arguments upon the mind of man considered as a whole, Quatrefages expressly limits his ground to the faculties of conscience and religion. In other words, he allows—nay insists—that no valid distinction between man and brute can be drawn in respect of rationality or intellect. For instance, to take only one passage from his writings, he remarks :—" In the name of philosophy and psychology, I shall be accused of confounding certain intellectual attributes of the human reason with the exclusively sensitive faculties of animals. I shall presently endeavour to answer this criticism from the standpoint which should never be quitted by the naturalist, that, namely, of experiment and observation. I shall here confine myself to saying that, in my opinion, the animal is intelligent, and, although an (intellectually) rudimentary being, that its intelligence is nevertheless of the same nature as that of man." Later on he says :—" Psychologists attribute religion and morality to

wise obtains food. He has made rafts or canoes for fishing, or crossing over to neighbouring fertile islands. He has discovered the art of making fire. . . . These several inventions, by which man in the rudest state has become so pre-eminent, are the direct results of the development of his powers of observation, memory, curiosity, imagination, and reason. I cannot, therefore, understand how it is that Mr. Wallace maintains that ' natural selection could only have endowed the savage with a brain a little superior to that of an ape ' " (*Descent of Man*, pp. 48, 49).

the reason, and make the latter an attribute of man (to the exclusion of animals). But with the reason they connect the highest phenomena of the intelligence. In my opinion, in so doing they confound, and refer to a common origin, facts entirely different. Thus, since they are unable to recognize either morality or religion in animals, which in reality do not possess these two faculties, they are forced to refuse them intelligence also, although the same animals, in my opinion, give decisive proof of their possession of this faculty every moment."*

Touching these views I have only two things to observe. In the first place, they differ *toto cœlo* from those both of Mr. Wallace and Mr. Mivart ; and thus we now find that the *three* principal authorities who still stand out for a distinction of kind between man and brute on grounds of psychology, far from being in agreement, are really in fundamental opposition, seeing that they base their common conclusion on premisses which are all mutually exclusive of one another. In the next place, even if we were fully to agree with the opinion of the French anthropologist, or hold that a distinction of kind has to be drawn only at religion and morality, we should still be obliged to allow—although this is a point which he does not himself appear to have perceived—that the superiority of human intelligence is a necessary *condition* to both these attributes of the human mind. In other words, whether or not Quatrefages is right in his view that religion and morality betoken a difference of kind in the only animal species which presents them, at least it is certain that neither of these faculties could have occurred in that species, had it not also been gifted with a greatly superior order of intelligence. For even the most elementary forms of religion and morality depend upon ideas of a much more abstract, or intellectual, nature than are to be met with in any brute. Obviously, therefore, the first distinction that falls to be considered is the intellectual distinction. If analysis should show that the school represented by Quatrefages is right in regarding this

* *The Human Species*, English trans., p. 22.

distinction as one of degree—and, therefore, that the school represented by Mivart is wrong in regarding it as one of kind,— the time will then have arrived to consider, in the same con- nection, these special faculties of morality and religion. Such, therefore, is the method that I intend to adopt. The whole of the present volume will be devoted to a consideration of " the origin of human faculty " in the larger sense of this term, or in accordance with the view that distinctively human faculty begins with distinctively human ideation. When this matter has been thoroughly discussed, the ground will have been prepared for considering in subsequent volumes the more special faculties of Morality and Religion.*

---

* Sundry other and still more special distinctions of a psychological kind have been alleged by various writers as obtaining between man and the lower animals— such as making fire, employing barter, wearing clothes, using tools, and so forth. But as all these distinctions are merely particular instances, or detailed illustrations, of the more intelligent order of ideation which belongs to mankind, it is needless to occupy space with their discussion. Here, also, I may remark that in this work I am not concerned with the popular objection to Darwinism on account of " missing-links," or the absence of fossil remains structurally intermediate between those of man and the anthropoid apes. This is a subject that belongs to palæon- tology, and, therefore, its treatment would be out of place in these pages. Never- theless, I may here briefly remark that the supposed difficulty is not one of any magnitude. Although to the popular mind it seems almost self-evident that if there ever existed a long series of generations connecting the bodily structure of man with that of the higher apes, at least some few of their bones ought now to be forthcoming ; the geologist too well knows how little reliance can be placed on such merely negative testimony where the record of geology is in question. Countless other instances may now be quoted of connecting links having been but recently found between animal groups which are zoologically much more widely separated than are apes and men. Indeed, so destitute of force is this popular objection held to be by geologists, that it is not regarded by them as amounting to any objection at all. On the other hand, the close anatomical resemblance that subsists between man and the higher apes—every bone, muscle, nerve, vessel, etc., in the enormously complex structure of the one coinciding, each to each, with the no less enormously complex structure of the other—speaks so voluminously in favour of an uninterrupted continuity of descent, that, as before remarked, no one who is at all entitled to speak upon the subject has ventured to dispute this continuity so far as the corporeal structure is concerned. All the few naturalists who still withhold their assent from the theory of evolution in its reference to man, expressly base their opinion on those grounds of psychology which it is the object of the present treatise to investigate.

# CHAPTER II.

## IDEAS. *

I NOW pass on to consider the only distinction which in my opinion can be properly drawn between human and brute psychology. This is the great distinction which furnishes a full psychological explanation of all the many and immense differences that unquestionably do obtain between the mind of the highest ape and the mind of the lowest savage. It is, moreover, the distinction which is now universally recognized by psychologists of every school, from the Romanist to the agnostic in Religion, and from the idealist to the materialist in Philosophy.

The distinction has been clearly enunciated by many writers, from Aristotle downwards, but I may best render it in the words of Locke :—

"If it may be doubted, whether beasts compound and enlarge their ideas that way to any degree; this I think I may be positive in, that the power of abstracting is not at all in them ; and that the having of general ideas is that which puts a perfect distinction betwixt man and brutes, and is an excellency which the faculties of brutes do by no means attain

---

* In my previous work I devoted a chapter to "Imagination," in which I treated of the psychology of ideation so far as animals are concerned. It is now needful to consider ideation with reference to man ; and, in order to do this, it is further needful to revert in some measure to the ideation of animals. I will, however, try as far as possible to avoid repeating myself, and therefore in the three following chapters I will assume that the reader is already acquainted with my previous work. Indeed, the argument running through the three following chapters cannot be fully appreciated unless their perusal is preceded by that of chapters ix. and x. of *Mental Evolution in Animals.*

to. For it is evident we observe no footsteps in them of making use of general signs for universal ideas ; from which we have reason to imagine, that they have not the faculty of abstracting, or making general ideas, since they have no use of words, or any other general signs.

"Nor can it be imputed to their want of fit organs to frame articulate sounds that they have no use or knowledge of general words ; since many of them, we find, can fashion such sounds, and pronounce words distinctly enough, but never with any such application ; and, on the other side, men, who through some defect in the organs want words, yet fail not to express their universal ideas by signs, which serve them instead of general words ; a faculty which we see beasts come short in. And therefore I think we may suppose, that it is in this that the species of brutes are discriminated from men ; and it is that proper difference wherein they are wholly separated, and which at last widens to so vast a distance ; for if they have any ideas at all, and are not bare machines (as some would have them), we cannot deny them to have some reason. It seems evident to me, that they do some of them in certain instances reason, as that they have sense ; but it is only in particular ideas, just as they received them from their senses. They are the best of them tied up within those narrow bounds, and have not (as I think) the faculty to enlarge them by any kind of abstraction." *

* *Human Understanding*, bk. ii., chap. ii., 10, 11. To this passage Berkeley objected that it is impossible to form an abstract idea of quality as apart from any concrete idea of object ; *e.g.* an idea of motion distinct from that of any body moving. (See *Principles of Human Knowledge*, Introd. vii.–xix.). This is a point which I cannot fully treat without going into the philosophy of the great discussion on Nominalism, Realism, and Conceptualism—a matter which would take me beyond the strictly psychological limits within which I desire to confine my work. It will, therefore, be enough to point out that Berkeley's criticism here merely amounts to showing that Locke did not pursue sufficiently far his philosophy of Nominalism. What Locke did was to see, and to state, that a general or abstract idea embodies a perception of likeness between individuals of a kind while disregarding the differences ; what he failed to do was to take the further step of showing that such an idea is not an idea in the sense of being a mental image ; it is merely an intellectual symbol of an actually impossible existence, namely, of quality apart from object. Intellectual symbolism of this

Here, then, we have stated, with all the common-sense lucidity of this great writer, what we may term the initial or basal distinction of which we are in search : it is that "proper difference" which, narrow at first as the space included between two lines of rails at their point of divergence, "at last widens to so vast a distance" as to end almost at the opposite pòles of mind.   For, by a continuous advance along the same line of development, the human mind is enabled to think about abstractions of its own making, which are more and more remote from the sensuous perception of concrete objects ; it can unite these abstractions into an endless variety of ideal combinations ; these, in turn, may become elaborated into ideal constructions of a more and more complex character ; and so on until we arrive at the full powers of introspective thought with which we are each one of us directly cognisant.

We now approach what is at once a matter of refined analysis, and a set of questions which are of fundamental importance to the whole superstructure of the present work. I mean the nature of abstraction, and the classification of ideas.   No small amount of ambiguity still hangs about these important subjects, and in treating of them it is impossible to employ terms the meanings of which are agreed upon by all psychologists.   But I will carefully define the meanings which I attach to these terms myself, and which I think are the meanings that they ought to bear.   Moreover, I will end by adopting a classification which is to some extent novel, and by fully giving my reasons for so doing.

Psychologists are agreed that what they call particular

kind is performed mainly through the agency of verbal or other conventional signs (as we shall see later on), and it is owing to a clearer understanding of this process that Realism was gradually vanquished by Nominalism.   The only difference, then, between Locke and Berkeley here is, that the nominalism of the former was not so complete or thorough as that of the latter.   I may remark that if in the following discussion I appear to fail in distinctly setting forth the doctrine of nominalism, I do so only in order that my investigation may avoid needless collision with conceptualism.   For myself I am a nominalist, and agree with Mill that to say we think in concepts is only another way of saying that we think in class names.

ideas, or ideas of particular objects, are of the nature of mental images, or memories of such objects—as when the sound of a friend's voice brings before my mind the idea of that particular man. Psychologists are further agreed that what they term general ideas arise out of an assemblage of particular ideas, as when from my repeated observation of numerous individual men I form the idea of Man, or of an abstract being who comprises the resemblances between all these individual men, without regard to their individual differences. Hence, particular ideas answer to percepts, while general ideas answer to concepts: an individual preception (or its repetition) gives rise to its mnemonic equivalent as a particular idea; while a group of similar, though not altogether similar perceptions, gives rise to its mnemonic equivalent as a conception, which, therefore, is but another name for a general idea, thus *generated* by an assemblage of particular ideas. Just as Mr. Galton's method of superimposing on the same sensitive plate a number of individual images gives rise to a blended photograph, wherein each of the individual constituents is partially and proportionally represented; so in the sensitive tablet of memory, numerous images of previous perceptions are fused together into a single conception, which then stands as a composite picture, or class-representation, of these its constituent images. Moreover, in the case of a sensitive plate it is only those particular images which present more or less numerous points of resemblance that admit of being thus blended into a distinct photograph; and so in the case of the mind, it is only those particular ideas which admit of being run together in a class that can go to constitute a clear concept.*

So much, then, for ideas as particular and general. Next, the term abstract has been used by different psychologists in different senses. For my own part, I will adhere to the usage of Locke in the passage above quoted, which is the usage adopted by the majority of modern writers upon these subjects. According to this usage, the term "abstract

---

* This simile has been previously used by Mr. Galton himself, and also by Mr. Huxley in his work on Hume.

idea" is practically synonymous with the term "general idea." For the process of abstraction consists in mentally analysing the complex which is presented by any given object of perception, and ideally extracting those features or qualities upon which the attention is for the time being directed. Even the most individual of objects cannot fail to present an assemblage of qualities, and although it is true that such an object could not be divided into all its constituent qualities actually, it does admit of being so divided ideally. The individual man whom I know as John Smith could not be disintegrated into so much heat, flesh, bone, blood, colour, &c., without ceasing to be a man at all ; but this does not hinder that I may ideally abstract his heat (by thinking of him as a corpse), his flesh, bones, and blood (by thinking of him as a dissected " subject "), his white colour of skin, his black colour of hair, and so forth. Now, it is evident that in the last resort our power of forming general ideas, or concepts, is dependent on this power of abstraction, or the power of ideally separating one or more of the qualities presented by percepts, *i.e.* by objects of particular ideas. My general idea of heat has only been rendered possible on account of my having ideally abstracted the quality of heat from sundry heated bodies, in most of which it has co-existed with numberless different associations of other qualities. But this does not hinder that, wherever I meet with that one quality, I recognize it as the same ; and hence I arrive at a general or abstract idea of heat, apart from any other quality with which in particular cases it may happen to be associated.*

This faculty of ideal abstraction furnishes the *conditio sine*

* Hence, the only valid distinction that can be drawn between abstraction and generalization is that which has been drawn by Hamilton, as follows : " Abstraction consists in concentration of attention upon a particular object, or particular quality of an object, and diversion of it from everything else. The notion of the *figure* of the desk before me is an abstract idea—an idea that makes part of the total notion of that body, and on which I have concentrated my attention, in order to consider it exclusively. This idea is abstract, but it is at the same time individual : it represents the figure of this particular desk, and not the figure of any other body." Generalization, on the other hand, consists in an ideal

*quâ non* to all grades in the development of thought ; for by
it alone can we compare idea with idea, and thus reach ever
onwards to higher and higher levels, as well as to more and
more complex structures of ideation. As to the history of
this development we shall have more to say presently.
Meanwhile I desire only to remark two things in connection
with it. The first is that throughout this history the development is a *development:* the faculty of abstraction is everywhere the same in *kind.* And the next thing is that this
development is everywhere dependent on the faculty of
*language.* A great deal will require to be said on both these
points in subsequent chapters ; but it is needful to state the
facts thus early—and they are facts which psychologists of
all schools now accept,—in order to render intelligible the
next step which I am about to make in my classification of
ideas. This step is to distinguish between the faculty of
abstraction where it is not dependent upon language, and
where it is so dependent. I have just said that the faculty
of abstraction is *everywhere* the same in kind ; but, as I
immediately proceeded to affirm that the *development* of
abstraction is dependent upon language, I have thus far left
the question open whether or not there can be any
rudimentary abstraction without language. It is to this
question, therefore, that we must next address ourselves.

compounding of abstractions, " when, comparing a number of objects, we seize on
their resemblances ; when we concentrate our attention on these points of
similarity. . . . The general notion is thus one which makes us know a quality,
property, power, notion, relation, in short, any point of view under which we
recognize a plurality of objects as a unity." Thus, there may be abstraction
without generalization ; but inasmuch as abstraction has then to do only with
particulars, this phase of it is disregarded by most writers on psychology, who
therefore employ abstraction and generalization as convertible terms. Mill says,
" By *abstract* I shall always, in Logic proper, mean the opposite of *concrete ;* by an
abstract name the name of an attribute ; by a concrete name, the name of an
object " (*Logic,* i. § 4). Such limitation, however, is arbitrary—it being the same
kind of mental act to " concentrate attention upon a particular *object,*" as it is to
do so upon any "particular *quality* of an object." Of course in this usage Mill is
following the schoolmen, and he expressly objects to the change first introduced
(apparently) by Locke, and since generally adopted. But it is of little consequence
in which of the two senses now explained a writer chooses to employ the word
"abstract," provided he is consistent in his own usage.

On the one hand it may be argued that by restricting the term abstract to ideas which can only be formed by the aid of language, we are drawing an arbitrary line—fixing upon one degree in the continuous scale of a faculty which is throughout the same in kind. For, say some psychologists, it is evident that in our own case most of our more simple abstract or general ideas are not dependent for their existence upon words. Or, if this be disputed, these psychologists are able to point to infants, and even to the lower animals, in proof of their assertion. For an infant undoubtedly exhibits the possession of simple general ideas prior to the possession of any articulate language ; and after it begins to use such language it does so by spontaneously widening the generality of signification attaching to its original words. In proof of both these statements numberless observations might be quoted, and further on will be quoted ; but here I need only wait to give one in proof of each. As regards the first, Professor Preyer tells us that at eight months old,[*] and therefore long before it was able to speak, his child was able to classify all glass bottles as resembling—or belonging to the order of—a feeding-bottle.[†] As regards the second, M. Taine tells us of a little girl eighteen months old, who was amused by her mother hiding in play behind a piece of furniture, and saying "Coucou." Again, when her food was too hot, when she went too near the fire or candle, and when the sun was warm, she was told "Ça brûle." One day, on seeing the sun disappear behind a hill, she exclaimed, "'A b'ûle coucou," thereby showing both the formation and combination of general ideas, "not only expressed by words which we do not employ (and, therefore, not by any other words that she can have previously employed), but also corresponding to ideas, *consequently to classes*

---

[*] The age here mentioned closely corresponds with that which is given by M. Perez, who says :—"At seven months he compares better than at three ; and he appears at this age to have visual perceptions associated with ideas of *kind:* for instance, he connects the different flavours of a piece of bread, of a cake, of fruit, with their different forms and colours" (*First Three Years of Childhood*, English trans., p. 31).

[†] *Die Seele des Kindes*, s. 87.

*of objects and general characters* which in our cases have disappeared. The hot soup, the fire on the hearth, the flame of the candle, the noonday heat in the garden, and last of all, the sun, make up one of these classes. The figure of the nurse or mother disappearing behind a hill, form the other class." *

Coming next to the case of brutes, and to begin with the simplest kind of illustrations, all the higher animals have general ideas of "Good-for-eating," and "Not-good-for-eating," quite apart from any particular objects of which either of these qualities happens to be characteristic. For, if we give any of the higher animals a morsel of food of a kind which it has never before met with, the animal does not immediately snap it up, nor does it immediately reject our offer ; but it subjects the morsel to a careful examination before consigning it to the mouth. This proves, if anything can, that such an animal has a general or abstract idea of sweet, bitter, hot, or, in general, Good-for-eating and Not-good-for-eating—the motives of the examination clearly being to ascertain which of these two general ideas of kind is appropriate to the particular object examined. When we ourselves select something which we suppose will prove good to eat, we do not require to call to our aid any of that higher class of abstract ideas for which we are indebted to our powers of language : it is enough to determine our decision if the particular appearance, smell, or taste of the food makes us feel that it probably conforms to our general idea of Good-for-eating. And, therefore, when we see animals determining between similar alternatives by precisely similar methods, we cannot reasonably doubt that the psychological processes are similar ; for, as we know that these processes in ourselves do not involve any of the higher powers of our minds, there is no reason to doubt that the processes, which in their manifestations appear so similar, really are what they appear to be—the same. Again, if I see a fox prowling about a farm-yard, I infer that he has been led by hunger to go where he has a general idea that there are a good many eatable things to be fallen in with—just

* Taine, *Intelligence*, p. 18.

as I myself am led by a similar impulse to visit a restaurant. Similarly, if I say to my dog the word "Cat," I arouse in his mind an idea, not of any cat in particular—for he sees so many cats,—but of a Cat in general. Or when this same dog accidentally crosses the track of a strange dog, the scent of this strange dog makes him stiffen his tail and erect the hair on his back in preparation for a fight; yet the scent of an unknown dog must arouse in his mind, not the idea of any dog in particular, but an idea of the animal Dog in general.

Thus far, it will be remembered, I have been presenting evidence in favour of the view that both infants and animals show themselves capable of forming general ideas of a simple order, and, therefore, that to the formation of such ideas the use of language is not essential. I will next consider what has to be said on the other side of the question; for, as previously remarked, many.—I may say most—psychologists repudiate this kind of evidence *in toto*, as not germain to the subject of debate. First, therefore, I will consider their objections to this kind of evidence; next I will sum up the whole question; and, lastly, I will suggest a classification of ideas which in my opinion ought to be accepted by both sides as constituting a common ground of reconciliation.

To begin with another quotation from Locke, "How far brutes partake in this faculty [*i.e.* that of comparing ideas] is not easy to determine; I imagine they have it not in any great degree: for though they probably have several ideas distinct enough, yet it seems to me to be the prerogative of human understanding, when it has sufficiently distinguished any ideas, so as to perceive them to be perfectly different, and so consequently two, to cast about and consider in what circumstances they are capable to be compared: and therefore I think beasts compare not their ideas further than some sensible circumstances annexed to the objects themselves. The other power of comparing, which may be observed in men, belonging to general ideas, and useful only to abstract reasonings, we may probably conjecture beasts have not.

"The next operation we may observe in the mind about

its ideas, is composition ; whereby it puts together several of those simple ones it has received from sensation and reflection, and combines them into complex ones.  Under this head of composition may be reckoned also that of enlarging ; wherein, though the composition does not so much appear as in more complex ones, yet it is nevertheless a putting several ideas together, though of the same kind.  Thus, by adding several units together, we make the idea of a dozen ; and by putting together the repeated ideas of several perches, we frame that of a furlong.

" In this, also, I suppose, brutes come far short of men ; for though they take in, and retain together several combinations of simple ideas, as possibly the shape, smell, and voice of his master make up the complex idea a dog has of him, or rather are so many distinct marks whereby he knows him ; yet I do not think they do of themselves ever compound them, and make complex ideas.  And perhaps even where we think they have complex ideas, it is only one simple one that directs them in the knowledge of several things, which possibly they distinguish less by sight than we imagine ; for I have been credibly informed that a bitch will nurse, play with, and be fond of young foxes, as much as, and in place of, her puppies ; if you can but get them once to suck her so long, that her milk may go through them.  And those animals, which have a numerous brood of young ones at once, appear not to have any knowledge of their number : for though they are mightily concerned for any of their young that are taken from them whilst they are in sight or hearing ; yet if one or two be stolen from them in their absence, or without noise, they appear not to miss them, or have any sense that their number is lessened." *

Now, from the whole of this passage, it is apparent that the " comparing," " compounding," and " enlarging " of ideas which Locke has in view, is the *conscious* or *intentional* comparing, compounding, and enlarging that belongs only to the province of reflection, or thought.  He in no way concerns

* *Human Understanding*, bk. ii., ch. ii., §§ 5–7.

himself with such powers of " comparing and compounding of ideas " as he allows that animals present, unless it can be shown that animals are able to " cast about and consider in what circumstances they are capable to be compared." And then he adds, " Therefore, I think, beasts compare not their ideas *further than some sensible circumstances annexed to the objects themselves.* The *other* power of comparing, which may be observed in men, *belonging to general ideas, and useful only to abstract reasonings*, we may probably conjecture beasts have not." So far, then, it seems perfectly obvious that Locke believed animals to present the power of " comparing and compounding " " simple ideas," up to the point where such comparison and composition begins to be assisted by the power of reflective thought. Therefore, when he immediately afterwards proceeds to explain abstraction thus : " The same colour being observed to-day in chalk or snow, which the mind yesterday received from milk, it considers that appearance alone, makes it a representative of all of that kind ; and having given it the name whiteness, it by that sound signifies the same quality, wheresoever it be imagined or met with ; and thus universals, whether ideas or terms, are made "—when he thus proceeds to explain abstraction, we can have no doubt that what he means by abstraction is the power of *ideally contemplating qualities as separated from objects*, or, as he expresses it, "*considering* appearances alone." Therefore I conclude, without further discussion, that in the terminology of Locke the word abstraction is applied only to those higher developments of the faculty which are rendered possible by reflection.

Now, on what does this power of reflection depend? As we shall see more fully later on, it depends on Language, or on the power of affixing names to abstract and general ideas. So far as I am aware, psychologists of all existing schools are in agreement upon this point, or in holding that the power of affixing names to abstractions is at once the condition to reflective thought, and the explanation of the difference between man and brute in respect of ideation.

It seems needless to dwell upon a matter where all are agreed, and concerning which a great deal more will require to be said in subsequent chapters.  At present I am only endeavoûring to ascertain the ground of difference between those psychologists who attribute, and those who deny to animals the faculty of abstraction.  And I think I am now in a position to render this point perfectly clear.  As we have already seen, and we shall frequently see again, it is allowed on all hands that animals in their ideation are not shut up ᵗo the special imaging (or remembering) of particular perceptions ; but that they do present the power, as Locke phrases it, of "taking in and retaining together several combinations of simple ideas." *  The only question, then, really is whether or not this power is the power of abstraction. In the opinion of some psychologists it is : in the opinion of other psychologists it is not.  Now, on what does an answer to this question depend ?  Clearly it depends on whether we hold it essential to an abstract or general idea that it should be incarnate as a word.  Under one point of view, to "take in and retain together several combinations of simple ideas," is to form a general concept of so many percepts.  But, under another point of view, such a combination of simple ideas is only then entitled to be regarded as a concept, when it has been conceived by the mind *as* a concept, or when, in virtue of having been bodied forth in a name, it stands before the mind as a distinct and organic offspring of mind—so becoming an object as well as a product of ideation.  For then only can the abstract idea be known *as* abstract, and then only can it be available as a definite creation of thought, capable of being built into any further and more elaborate structure of ideation. Or, to quote M. Taine, who advocates this view with great lucidity, " Of our numerous experiences [*i.e.* individual perceptions of a show of araucarias] there remain on the following

---

* If required, proof of this fact is to be found in abundance in the chapter on "Imagination," *Mental Evolution in Animals*, pp. 142–158.  It is there shown that imagination in animals is not dependent only on associations aroused by sensuous impressions from without, but reaches the level of carrying on a train of mental imagery *per se.*

day four or five more or less distinct recollections, which obliterated themselves, leave behind in us a simple, colourless, vague representation, into which enter as components various reviving sensations, in an utterly feeble, incomplete, and abortive state. But this representation is not the general or abstract idea. It is but its accompaniment, and, if I may say so, the one from which it is extracted. For the representation, though badly sketched, is a sketch, the sensible sketch of a distinct individual ; in fact, if I make it persist and dwell upon it, it repeats some special visual sensation ; I see mentally some outline which corresponds only to some particular araucaria, and, therefore, cannot correspond to the whole class : now, my abstract idea corresponds to the whole class ; it differs, then, from the representation of an individual. Moreover, my abstract idea is perfectly clear and determinate ; now that I possess it, I never fail to recognize an araucaria among the various plants I may be shown ; it differs, then, from the con-fused and floating representation I have of some particular araucaria. What is there, then, within me so clear and determinate, corresponding to the abstract character, corre-sponding to all araucarias, and corresponding to it alone ? A class-name, the name araucaria. . . . Thus we conceive the abstract characters of things by means of abstract names which *are* our abstract ideas, and the formation of our abstract ideas is nothing more than the formation of names." *

The real issue, then, is as to what we are to understand by this term abstraction, or its equivalents. If we are to limit the term to the faculty of " taking in and retaining together several combinations of simple ideas," *plus* the faculty of giving a name to the resulting compound, then

---

* *Loc. cit.*, pp. 397-399. Allusion may also be here conveniently made to an interesting and suggestive work by another French writer, M. Binet (*La Psychologie du Raisonnement*, 1886). His object is to show that all processes of reasoning are fundamentally identical with those of perception. In order to do this he gives a detailed exposition of the general fact that processes of both kinds depend on " fusions " of states of consciousness. In the case of perception the elements thus fused are sensations, while in the case of reasoning they are perceptions—in both cases the principle of association being alike concerned.

undoubtedly animals differ from men in not presenting the faculty of abstraction ; for this is no more than to say that animals have not the faculty of speech. But if the term in question be not thus limited—if it be taken to mean the first of the above-named processes irrespective of the second,— then, no less undoubtedly, animals resemble men in presenting the faculty of abstraction. In accordance with the former definition, it necessarily follows that " we conceive the abstract characters of things *by means of abstract names which* ARE *our abstract ideas ;* " and, therefore, that " the formation of our abstract ideas is nothing more than the formation of names." But, in accordance with the latter view, great as may be the importance of affixing a name to a compound of simple ideas for the purpose of giving that compound greater clearness and stability, the essence of abstraction consists in the act of compounding, or in the blending together of particular ideas into a general idea of the class to which the individual things belong. The act of bestowing upon this compound idea a class-name is quite a distinct act, and one which is necessarily subsequent to the previous act of com- pounding : why then, it may be asked, should we deny that such a compound idea is a general or abstract idea, only because it is not followed up by the artifice of giving it a name ?

In my opinion so much has to be said in favour of both of these views that I am not going to pronounce against either. What I have hitherto been endeavouring to do is to reveal clearly that the question whether or not there is any difference between the brute and the man in respect of abstraction, is nothing more than a question of terminology. The real question will arise only when we come to treat of the faculty of language : the question before us now is merely a question of psychological classification, or of the nomenclature of ideas. Now, it appears to me that this question admits of being definitely settled, and a great deal of needless misunder- standing removed, by a slight re-adjustment and a closer definition of terms. For it must be on all hands admitted that, whether or not we choose to denominate by the word abstraction the faculty of compounding simple ideas without the faculty of naming the compounds, at the place where this additional faculty of naming supervenes, so immense an accession to the previous faculty is furnished, that any system of psychological nomenclature must be highly imperfect if it be destitute of terms whereby to recognize the difference.  For even if it were conceded by psychologists of the opposite school that the essence of abstraction consists in the compounding of simple ideas, and not at all in the subsequent process of naming the compounds ; still the effect of this subsequent process—or additional faculty—is so prodigious, that the higher degrees of abstraction which by it are rendered possible, certainly require to be marked off, or to be distinguished from, the lower degrees.  Without, therefore, in any way prejudicing the question as to whether we have here a difference of degree or a difference of kind, I will submit a classification of ideas which, while not open to objection from either side of this question, will greatly help us in our subsequent treatment of the question itself.

The word " Idea " I will use in the sense defined in my previous work—namely, as a generic term to signify indifferently any product of imagination, from the mere memory of a sensuous impression up to the result of the most abstruse generalization.*

By " Simple Idea," " Particular Idea," or " Concrete Idea," I understand the mere memory of a particular sensuous perception.

By " Compound Idea," " Complex Idea," or " Mixed Idea," I understand the combination of simple, particular, or concrete ideas into that kind of composite idea which is possible without the aid of language.

Lastly, by " General Idea," " Abstract Idea," " Concept," or " Notion," I understand that kind of composite idea which is rendered possible only by the aid of language, or by the process of naming abstractions as abstractions.

* *Mental Evolution in Animals*, p. 118.

Now in this classification, notwithstanding that it is needful to quote at least ten distinct terms which are either now in use among psychologists or have been used by classical English writers upon these topics, we may observe that there are really but three separate classes to be distinguished. Moreover, it will be noticed that, for the sake of definition, I restrict the first three terms to denote memories of particular sensuous perceptions—refusing, therefore, to apply them to those blended memories of many sensuous perceptions which enable animals and infants (as well as ourselves) to form compound ideas of kind or class without the aid of language. Again, the first division of this threefold classification has to do only with what are termed percepts, while the last has to do only with what are termed concepts. Now there does not exist any equivalent word to meet the middle division. And this fact in itself shows most forcibly the state of ambiguous confusion into which the classification of ideas has been wrought. Psychologists of both the schools that we are considering— namely, those who maintain and those who deny that there is any difference of kind between the ideation of men and animals—are equally forced to allow that there is a great difference between what I have called a simple idea and what I have called a compound idea. In other words, it is a matter of obvious fact that the only distinction between ideas is *not* that between the memory of a particular percept and the formation of a named concept; for between these two classes of ideas there obviously lies another class, in virtue of which even animals and infants are able to distinguish individual objects as belonging to a sort or kind. Yet this large and important territory of ideation, lying between the other two, is, so to speak, unnamed ground. Even the words "compound idea," "complex idea," and "mixed idea," are by me restricted to it without the sanction of previous usage; for, as above remarked, so completely has the existence of this intermediate land been ignored, that we have no word at all which is applicable to it in the same way that Percept

and Concept are applicable to the lands on either side of it.
The consequence is that psychologists of the one school
invade this intermediate province of ideation with terms that
are applicable only to the lower province, while psychologists
of the other school invade it with terms which are applicable
only to the higher : the one matter upon which they all
appear to agree being that of ignoring the wide area which
this intermediate territory covers—and, consequently, also
ignoring the great distance by which the territories on either
side of it are separated.

In addition, then, to the terms Percept and Concept, I
coin the word *Recept*. This is a term which seems exactly to
meet the requirements of the case. For as perception literally
means a *taking wholly*, and conception a *taking together*,
reception means a *taking again*. Consequently, a recept is
that which is taken again, or a *re-cognition* of things
previously *cognized*. Now, it belongs to the essence of what
I have defined as compound ideas (recepts), that they arise
in the mind out of a repetition of more or less similar
percepts. Having seen a number of araucarias, the mind
*receives* from the whole mass of individuals which it *perceives*
a composite idea of Araucaria, or of a class comprising all
individuals of that kind—an idea which differs from a general
or abstract idea only in not being consciously fixed and
signed as an idea by means of an abstract name. Compound
ideas, therefore, can only arise out of a *repetition* of more or
less similar percepts ; and hence the appropriateness of
designating them recepts. Moreover, the associations which
we have with the cognate words, Receive, Reception, &c., are
all of the *passive* kind, as the associations which we have
with the words Conceive, Conception, &c., are of the *active*
kind. Now, here again, the use of the word recept is seen to
be appropriate to the class of ideas in question, because in
receiving such ideas the mind is passive, as in conceiving
abstract ideas the mind is active. In order to form a
concept, the mind must intentionally bring together its
percepts (or the memories of them), for the purpose of

binding them up as a bundle of similars, and labelling the bundle with a name. But in order to form a recept, the mind need perform no such intentional actions: the similarities among the percepts with which alone this order of ideation is concerned, are so marked, so conspicuous, and so frequently *repeated* in observation, that in the very moment of perception they sort themselves, and, as it were, fall into their appropriate classes spontaneously, or without any conscious effort on the part of the percipient. We do not require to name stones to distinguish them from loaves, nor fish to distinguish them from scorpions. Class distinctions of this kind are conveyed in the very act of perception—*e.g.* the case of the infant with the glass bottles,—and, as we shall subsequently see, in the case of the higher animals admit of being carried to a wonderful pitch of discriminative perfection. Recepts, then, are *spontaneous associations, formed unintentionally* as what may be termed *unperceived abstractions.**

---

* In this connection I may quote the following very lucid statements from a paper by the Secretary of the Victoria Institute, which is directed against the general doctrine that I am endeavouring to advance, *i.e.* that there is no distinction of kind between brute and human psychology.

"Abstraction and generalization only become intellectual when they are utilized by the intellect. A bull is irritated by a red colour, and not by the object of which redness is a property; but it would be absurd to say that the bull voluntarily abstracts the phenomenon of redness from these objects. The process is essentially one of abstraction, and yet at the same time it is essentially automatic." And with reference to the ideation of brutes in general, he continues :—"Certain qualities of an object engage his attention to the exclusion of other qualities, which are disregarded; and thus he abstracts automatically. The image of an object having been imprinted on his memory, the feelings which it excited are also imprinted on his memory, and on the reproduction of the image these feelings and the actions resulting therefrom are reproduced, likewise automatically : thus he acts from experience, automatically still. The image may be the image of the same object, or the image of another object of the same species, but the effect is the same, and thus he generalizes, automatically also." Lastly, speaking of inference, he says :—"This method is common to man and brute, and, like the faculties of abstraction, &c., it only becomes intellectual when we choose to make it so." {E. J. Morshead, in an essay on *Comparative Psychology, Journ. Vic. Inst.*, vol. v., pp. 303, 304, 1870.) In the work of M. Binet already alluded to, the distinction in question is also recognized. For he says that the "fusion" of sensations which takes place in an act of perception is performed automatically (*i.e.* is receptual); while the "fusion" of perceptions which are concerned in an act of reason is performed intentionally (*i.e.* is conceptual).

One further remark remains to be added before our nomenclature of ideas can be regarded as complete. It will have been noticed that the term "general idea" is equally appropriate to ideas of class or kind, whether or not such ideas are named. The ideas Good-for-eating and Not-good-for-eating are as general to an animal as they are to a man, and have in each case been formed in the same way—namely, by an accumulation of particular experiences spontaneously assorted in consciousness. General ideas of this kind, however, have not been contemplated by previous writers while dealing with the psychology of generalization : hence the term "general," like the term "abstract," has by usage become restricted to those higher products of ideation which depend on the faculty of language. And the only words that I can find to have been used by any previous writers to designate the ideas concerned in that lower kind of generalization which does not depend on language, are the words above given—namely, Complex, Compound, and Mixed. Now, none of these words are so good as the word General, because none of them express the notion of *genus* or *class ;* and the great distinction between the idea which an animal or an infant has, say of an individual man and of men in general, is not that the one idea is simple, and the other complex, compound, or mixed ; but that the one idea is *particular* and the other *general.* Therefore consistency would dictate that the term "general" should be applied to *all* ideas of class or kind, as distinguished from ideas of particulars or individuals—irrespective of the *degree* of generality, and irrespective, therefore, of the accident whether or not, *quâ* general, such ideas are dependent on language. Nevertheless, as the term has been through previous usage restricted to ideas of the higher order of generality, I will not introduce confusion by extending its use to the lower order, or by speaking of an animal as capable of generalizing. A parallel term, however, is needed ; and, therefore, I will speak of the general or class ideas which are formed without the aid of language as *generic.* This word has the double advantage of retaining a verbal as well as a substantial analogy with the allied term *general.* It also serves to indicate that generic ideas, or recepts, are not only ideas of class or kind, but have been *generated* from the intermixture of individual ideas—*i.e.* from the blended memories of particular percepts.

My nomenclature of ideas, therefore, may be presented in a tabular form thus :—

IDEAS
{
General, Abstract, or Notional  = Concepts.
Complex, Compound, or Mixed = Recepts, or Generic Ideas.
Simple, Particular, or Concrete = Memories of Percepts.*
}

* The more elaborate analysis of German psychologists has yielded five orders instead of three ; namely, *Wahrnehmung, Anschauung, Vorstellungen, Erfahrungsbegriff,* and *Verstandesbegriff.* But for the purposes of this treatise it is needless to go into these finer distinctions.

4

# CHAPTER III.

## LOGIC OF RECEPTS.

WE have seen that the great border-land, or *terra media*, lying between particular ideas and general ideas has been strangely neglected by psychologists, and we may now be prepared to find that a careful exploration of this border-land is a matter of the highest importance for the purposes of our inquiry. I will, therefore, devote the present chapter to a full consideration of what I have termed generic ideas, or recepts.

It has already been remarked that, in order to form any of these generic ideas, the mind does not require to combine *intentionally* the particular ideas which go to construct it: a recept differs from a concept in that it is *received*, not *conceived*. The percepts out of which a recept is composed are of so comparatively *simple* a character, are so frequently *repeated* in observation, and present among themselves resemblances or analogies so *obvious*, that the mental images of them run together, as it were, spontaneously, or in accordance with the primary laws of merely sensuous association, without requiring any conscious act of comparison. This is a truth which has been noticed by several previous writers. For instance, I have in this connection already quoted a passage from M. Taine, and, if necessary, could quote another, wherein he very aptly likens what I have called recepts to the unelaborated ore out of which the metal of a concept is afterwards smelted. And still more to the purpose is the following passage, which I take from Mr. Sully:—" The more *concrete* concepts, or *generic* images, are formed to a large extent by a *passive* process of *assimilation*. The likeness among dogs, for example, is so great and striking that when a child, already familiar with one of these animals, sees a second, he recognizes it as identical with the first in certain obvious respects. The representation of the first combines with the representation of the second, bringing into distinct relief the common dog features, more particularly the canine form. In this way the images of different dogs come to overlap, so to speak, giving rise to a typical image of dog. Here there is very little of *active* direction of the mind from one thing to another in order to discover where the resemblance lies: *the resemblance forces itself upon the mind.* When, however, the resemblance is less striking, as in the case of more abstract concepts, a *distinct operation of active comparison is involved."* *

Similarly, M. Perez remarks, " the necessity which children are under of seeing in a detached and scrappy manner in order to see well, makes them continually practise that kind of abstraction by which we separate qualities from objects. From those objects which the child has already distinguished as individual, there come to him at different moments particularly vivid impressions. . . . Dominant sensations of this kind, by their energy or frequency, tend to efface the idea of the objects from which they proceed, *to separate or abstract them-selves.* . . . The flame of a candle is not always equally bright or flickering ; tactile, sapid, olfactory, and auditive impressions do not always strike the child's sensorium with the same intensity, nor during the same length of time. This is why the recollections of individual forms, although strongly graven on their intelligence, lose by degrees their first precision, so that the idea of a tree, for instance, furnished by direct and perfectly distinct memories, comes back to the mind in a vague and indistinct form, which might be taken for a general idea." †

Again, in the opinion of John Stuart Mill, " It is the doctrine of one of the most fertile thinkers of modern times,

---

* *Outlines of Psychology,* p. 342. The italics are mine. It will be observed hat Mr. Sully here uses the term " generic " in exactly the sense which I propose.

† *First Three Years of Childhood,* English trans., pp. 180–182.

Auguste Comte, that besides the logic of signs, there is a logic of images, and a logic of feelings. In many of the familiar processes of thought, and especially in uncultured minds, a visual image serves instead of a word. Our visual sensations, perhaps only because they are almost always present along with the impressions of our other senses, have a facility of becoming associated with them. Hence, the characteristic visual appearance of an object easily gathers round it, by association, the ideas of all other peculiarities which have, in frequent experience, co-existed with that appearance ; and, summoning up these with a strength and certainty far surpassing that of merely casual associations which it may also raise, it concentrates the attention on them. This is an image serving for a sign—the logic of images. The same function may be fulfilled by a feeling. Any strong and highly interesting feeling, connected with one attribute of a group, spontaneously classifies all objects according as they possess, or do not possess, that attribute. We may be tolerably certain that the things capable of satisfying hunger form a perfectly distinct class in the mind of any of the more intelligent animals ; quite as much as if they were able to use or understand the word food. We here see in a strong light the important truth that hardly anything universal can be affirmed in psychology except the laws of association." *

Furthermore, Mansel tersely conveys the truth which I am endeavouring to present, thus :—" The mind recognizes the impression which a tree makes on the retina of the eye : this is presentative consciousness. It then depicts it. From many such pictures it forms a general notion, and to that notion it at last appropriates a name." † Almost in identical language

---

* *Examination of Hamilton's Philosophy*, p. 403.

† To this, Max Müller objects on account of its veiled conceptualism—seeing that it represents the " notion " as chronologically prior to the " name " (*Science of Thought*, p. 268). With this criticism, however, I am not concerned. Whether " the many pictures " which the mind thus forms, and blends together into what Locke terms a " compound idea," deserve, when so blended, to be called " a general notion " or a " concept "—this is a question of terminology of which I steer clear, by assigning to such compound ideas the term recepts, and reserving the term notions, or concepts, for compound ideas *after they have been named.*

the same distinction is conveyed by Noiré thus :—"All trees hitherto seen by me may leave in my imagination a mixed image, a kind of ideal representation of trees. Quite different from this is the concept, which is never an image." *

And, not to overburden the argument with quotations, I will furnish but one more, which serves if possible with still greater clearness to convey exactly what it is that I mean by a recept. Professor Huxley writes :—"An anatomist who occupies himself intently with the examination of several specimens of some new kind of animal, in course of time acquires so vivid a conception of its form and structure, that the idea may take visible shape and become a sort of waking dream." †

Although the use of the word " conception " here is unfortunate in one way, I regard it as fortunate in another : it shows how desperate is the need for the word which I have coined.

The above quotations, then, may be held sufficient to show that the distinction which I have drawn has not been devised merely to suit my own purposes. All that I have endeavoured so far to do is to bring this distinction into greater clearness, by assigning to each of its parts a separate name. And in doing this I have not assumed that the two orders of generalization comprised under recepts and concepts are the same in kind. So far I have left the question open as to whether a mind which can only attain to recepts differs in degree or in kind from the intellect which is able to go on to the formation of concepts. Had I said, with Sully, "When the resemblance is less striking, as in the case of more abstract

---

* *Logos*, p. 175, quoted by Max Müller, who adds :—" The followers of Hume might possibly look upon the faded images of our memory as abstract ideas. Our memory, or, what is often equally important, our oblivescence, seems to them able to do what abstraction, as Berkeley shows, never can do ; and under its silent sway many an idea, or cluster of ideas, might seem to melt away till nothing is left but a mere shadow. These shadows, however, though they may become very vague, remain percepts ; they are not concepts " (*Science of Thought*, p. 453). Now, I say it is equally evident that these shadows are *not* percepts : they are the result of the *fusion* of percepts, no one of which corresponds to their generic sum. Seeing, then, that they are neither percepts nor concepts, and yet such highly important elements in ideation, I coin for them the distinctive name of recepts.

† *Life of Hume*, p. 96.

concepts, a distinct operation of active comparison is involved,"
I should have been assuming that there is only a difference
of degree between a recept and a concept : designating both
by the same term, and therefore implying that they differ only
in their level of abstraction, I should have assumed that what
he calls the "passive process of assimilation," whereby an
infant or an animal recognizes an individual man as belonging
to a class, is really the same kind of psychological process as
that which is involved "in the case of more abstract concepts,"
where the individual man is designated by a proper name, while
the class to which he belongs is designated by a common name.
Similarly, if I had said, with Thomas Brown, that in the process
of generalization there is, " in the first place, the perception
of two or more objects [percept] ; in the second place, the
feeling of their resemblance [recept] ; and, lastly, the expression of this common relative feeling by a name, afterwards
used as a general name [concept] ; "—if I had spoken thus,
I should have virtually begged the question as to the universal
continuity of ideation, both in brutes and men.  Of course
this is the conclusion towards which I am working ; but my
endeavour in doing so is to proceed in the  proof step by step,
without anywhere prejudging my case.  These passages,
therefore, I have quoted merely because they recognize more
clearly than others which I have happened to meet with what
I conceive to be the true psychological classification of ideas ;
and although, with the exception of that quoted from Mill,
no one of the passages shows that its writer had before his
mind the case of animal intelligence—or perceived the
immense importance of his statements in relation to the
question which we have to consider,—this only renders of more
value their independent testimony to the soundness of my
classification.*

* Steinthal and Lazarus, however, in dealing with the problem touching the
origin of speech, present in an adumbrated fashion this doctrine of receptual
ideation with special reference to animals.  For instance, Lazarus says, " Es gibt
in der gewöhnlichen Erfahrung kein so einfaches Ding von einfacher Beschaffen-
heit, dass wir es durch *eine* Sinnesempfindung wahrnehmen könnten ; erst aus
der Sammlung seiner Eigenschaften, d. h. erst aus der *Verbindung* der mehreren

The question, then, which we have to consider is whether there is a difference of kind, or only a difference of degree, between a recept and a concept. This is really the question with which the whole of the present volume will be concerned, and as its adequate treatment will necessitate somewhat

Empfindungen ergibt sich *die Wahrnehmung eines Dinges:* erst indem wir die weisse Farbe sehen, die Härte fühlen und den süssen Geschmack empfinden, erkennen wir ein Stück Zucker" (*Das Leben der Seele* (1857), 8, ii. 66). This and other passages in the same work follow the teaching of Steinthal ; *e.g.* "Die Anschauung von einem Dinge ist der Complex der sämmtlichen Empfindungser-kenntnisse, die wir von einem Dinge haben .· . . die Anschauung ist eine Synthesis, aber eine unmittelbare, die durch die Einheit der Seele gegeben ist." And, following both these writers, Friedrich Müller says, "Diese Sammlung und Einigung der verschiedenen Empfindungen gemäss der in den Dingen verbun-denen Eigenschaften heisst Anschauung" (*Grundriss der Sprachwissenschaft*, i. 26). On the other hand, their brother philologist, Geiger, strongly objects to this use of the term *Anschauung*, under which, he says, "wird theils etwas von der Sinneswahrnehmung gar nicht Unterschiedenes verstanden, theils auch ein dunkles Etwas, welches, ohne dass die Bedingungen und Ursachen zu erkennen sind, die Einheit der Wahrnehmungen zu kleineren und grössern Complexen bewirken soll. . . . ·So dass ich eine solche ' Synthesis ' nicht auch bei dem Thiere ganz ebenso wie bei dem Menschen voraussetze : ich glaube im Gegentheile, dass es sich mit der Sprache erst entwickelt" (*Ursprung der Sprache*, 177, 178). Now, I have quoted these various passages because they serve to render, in a brief and instructive form, the different views which may be taken on a comparatively simple matter owing to the want of well-defined terms. No doubt the use of the term *Anschauung* by the above writers is unfortunate ; but by it they appear to me clearly to indicate a nascent idea of what I mean by a recept. They all three fail to bring out this idea in its fulness, inasmuch as they restrict the powers of non-conceptual "synthesis" to a grouping of simple perceptions furnished by different sense-organs, instead of extending it to a synthesis of syntheses of perceptions, whether furnished by the same or also by different senses. But these three philologists are all on the right psychological track, and their critic Geiger is quite wrong in saying that there can be no synthesis of (non-conceptual) ideas without the aid of speech. As a matter of fact the *dunkles Etwas* which he complains of his predecessors as importing into the ideation of animals, is an *Etwas* which, when brought out into clearer light, is fraught with the highest importance. For, as we shall subsequently see, it is nothing less than the needful psychological condition to the subsequent development both of speech and thought. The term *Apperception* as used by some German psychologists is also inclusive of what I mean by receptual ideation. But as it is also inclusive of conceptual, nothing would here be gained by its adoption. Indeed F. Müller expressly restricts its meaning to conceptual ideation, for he says, "Alle psychischen Processe bis einschliesslich zur Perception lassen sich ohne Sprache ausführen und voll-kommen begreifen, die Apperception dagegen lässt sich nur an der Hand der Sprache denken" (*loc. cit.* i., 29).

laborious inquiries in several directions, I will endeavour to keep the various issues distinct by fully working out each branch of the subject before entering upon the next.

First of all I will show, by means of illustrations, the highest levels of ideation that are attained within the domain of recepts ; and, in order to do this, I will adduce my evidence from animals alone, seeing that here there can be no suspicion —as there might be in the case of infants—that the logic of recepts is assisted by any nascent growth of concepts. But, before proceeding to state this evidence, it seems desirable to say a few words on what I mean by the term just used, namely, Logic of Recepts.

As argued in my previous work, all mental processes of an adaptive kind are, in their last resort, processes of classification : they consist in discriminating between differences and resemblances. An act of simple perception is an act of noticing resemblances and differences between the objects of such perception ; and, similarly, an act of conception is the taking together—or the intentional *putting* together—of ideas which are recognized as analogous. Hence abstraction has to do with the abstracting of analogous qualities ; reason is ratiocination, or the comparison of ratios ; and thus the highest operations of thought, like the simplest acts of perception, are concerned with the grouping or co-ordination of resemblances, previously distinguished from differences.* Consequently, the middle ground of ideation, or the territory occupied by recepts, is concerned with this same process on a plane higher than that which is occupied by percepts, though lower than that which is occupied by concepts. In short, the object or use, and therefore the method or *logic*, of all ideation is the same. It is, indeed, customary to restrict the latter term to the higher plane of ideation, or to that which has to do with concepts. But, as Comte has shown, there is no reason why, for purposes of special exposition, this term should not be extended so as to embrace all operations of the mind, in so

* As stated in a previous foot-note, this truth is well exhibited by M. Binet, *loc. cit.*

far as these are operations of an orderly kind. For in so far
as they are orderly or adaptive—and not merely sentient or
indifferent—such operations all consist, as we have just seen,
in processes of ideal grouping, or *binding together.** And
therefore I see no impropriety in using the word Logic for the
special purpose of emphasizing the fundamental identity of all
ideation—so far, that is, as its method is concerned. I object,
however, to the terms "Logic of Feelings" and "Logic of
Signs." For, on the one hand, "Feelings," have to do primarily
with the sentient and emotional side of mental life, as distinguished from the intellectual or ideational. And, on the
other hand, "Signs" are the *expressions* of ideas ; not the ideas
themselves. Hence, whatever method, or meaning, they may
present is but a reflection of the order, or grouping, among
the ideas which they are used to express. The logic, therefore, is neither in the feelings nor in the signs ; but in the ideas.
On this account I have substituted for the above terms what
I take to be more accurate designations—namely, the Logic
of Recepts, and the Logic of Concepts.†

In the present chapter we have only to consider the logic
of recepts, and, in order to do so efficiently, we may first of
all briefly note that even within the region of percepts we
meet with a process of spontaneous grouping of like with like,
which, in turn, leads us downwards to the purely unconscious
or mechanical grouping of stimuli in the lower nerve-centres.
So that, as fully argued out in my previous work, on its
objective face the method has everywhere been the same :

---

* The word Logic is derived from λόγος, which in turn is derived from λέγω, to
arrange, to lay in order, to pick up, to bind together.

† The terms Logic of Feelings and Logic of Signs were first introduced and
extensively employed by Comte. Afterwards they were adopted, and still more
extensively employed by Lewes, who, however, seems to have thought that he so
employed them in some different sense. To me it appears that in this Lewes was
mistaken. Save that Comte is here, as elsewhere, intoxicated with theology, I
think that the ideas he intended to set forth under these terms are the same as
those which are advocated by Lewes—although his incoherency justifies the remark
of his follower :—" Being unable to understand this, I do not criticize it " (*Probs.
of Life and Mind*, iii., p. 239). The terms in question are also sanctioned by
Mill, as shown by the above quotation (p. 42).

whether in the case of reflex action, of sensation, perception, reception, conception, or reflection, on the side of the nervous system, the method of evolution has been uniform : " it has everywhere consisted in a progressive development of the power of discriminating between stimuli, joined with the complementary power of adaptive response." * But although this is a most important truth to recognize (as it appears to have been implicitly recognized—or, rather, accidentally implied—by using a variant of the same term to designate the lowest and the highest members of the above-named series of faculties), for the purposes of psychological as distinguished from physiological inquiry, it is convenient to disregard the objective side of this continuous process, and therefore to take up our analysis at the place where it is attended by a subjective counterpart—that is, at Perception.

So much has already been written on what is termed the " unconscious judgments" or " intuitive judgments " incidental to all our acts of perception, that I feel it is needless to occupy space by dwelling at any length upon this subject. The familiar illustration of looking straight into a polished bowl, and alternately perceiving it as a bowl and a sphere, is enough to show that here we *do* have a logic of feelings : without any act of ideation, but simply in virtue of an automatic grouping of former percepts, the mind spontaneously infers—or unconsciously judges—that an object, which *must either* be a bowl or a sphere, is now one and now the other.† From which we

---

* *Mental Evolution in Animals*, p. 62.

† Special attention, however, may be drawn to the fact that the term " unconscious judgment " is not metaphorical, but serves to convey in a technical sense what appears to be the precise psychology of the process. For the distinguishing element of a judgment, in its technical sense, is that it involves an element of *belief*. Now, as Mill remarks, " when a stone lies before me, I am conscious of certain sensations which I receive from it ; but if I say that these sensations come to me from an external object which I perceive, the meaning of these words is, that receiving the sensations, I intuitively believe that an external cause of those sensations exists " (*Logic*, i., p. 58). In cases, such as that mentioned in the text, where the " unconscious judgment " is wrong—*i.e.* the perception illusory—it may, of course, be over-ridden by judgment of a higher order, and thus we do not end by believing that the bowl is a sphere. Nevertheless, so far as it is dependent on the testimony of our senses, the mind judges

gather that all our visual perceptions are thus of the nature of automatic inferences, based upon previous correspondencies between them and perceptions of touch. From which, again, we gather that perceptions of every kind depend upon previous grouping, whether between those supplied by the same sense only, or also in combination with those supplied by other senses.

Now, if this is so well known to be the case with percepts, obviously it must also be the case with recepts. If we thus find by experiment that all our perceptions are dependent on sub-conscious co-ordination wholly automatic, much more may we be prepared to find that the simplest of our ideas are dependent on spontaneous co-ordinations almost equally automatic. Accordingly, it requires but a slight analysis of our ordinary mental processes to prove that all our simpler ideas are group-arrangements, which have been formed as I say spontaneously, or without any of that intentionally comparing, sifting, and combining process which is required in the higher departments of ideational activity. The comparing, sifting, and combining is here done, as it were, *for* the conscious agent ; not *by* him. Recepts are *received :* it is only concepts that require to be *conceived.* For a recept is that kind of idea the constituent parts of which—be they but the memories of percepts, or already more or less elaborated as recepts—unite spontaneously as soon as they are brought together. It matters not whether this readiness to unite is due to obvious similarity, or to frequent repetition : the point is that there is so strong an *affinity* between the elementary constituents, that the compound is formed as a consequence

---

erroneously in perceiving the bowl as a sphere. In his work on *Illusions,* Mr. Sully has shown that illusions of perception arise through the mental "application of a rule, valid for the majority of cases, to an exceptional case." In other words, an erroneous judgment is made by the non-conceptual faculties of perception—this judgment being formed upon the analogies supplied by past experience. Of course, such an act of merely perceptual inference is not a judgment, strictly so called ; but it is clearly *allied* to judgment, and convenience is consulted by following established custom in designating it "unconscious," "intuitive," or "perceptual judgment."

of their mere apposition in consciousness. If I am crossing a street and hear behind me a sudden shout, I do not require to wait in order to predicate to myself that there is probably a hansom cab just about to run me down : a cry of this kind, and in those circumstances, is so intimately associated in my mind with its purpose, that the idea which it arouses need not rise above the level of a recept ; and the adaptive movements on my part which that idea immediately prompts, are performed without any intelligent reflection. Yet, on the other hand, they are neither reflex actions nor instinctive actions : they are what may be termed receptual actions, or actions depending on recepts.

This, of course, is an exceedingly simple illustration, and I have used it in order to make the further remark that actions depending on recepts, although they often thus lie near to reflex actions, are by no means bound to do so. On the contrary, as we shall immediately find, actions depending on recepts are often so highly "intelligent," that in our own case it is impossible to draw the line between them and actions depending on concepts. That is to say, in our own case there is a large border-land where introspection is unable to determine whether adjustive action is due to recepts or to concepts ; and hence it is only in the case of animals that we can be certain as to the limits of intelligent adjustment which are possible under the operation of recepts alone. The question therefore, now arises,—How far can this process of spontaneous or unintentional comparing, sifting, and combining go without the intentional co-operation of the conscious agent ? To what level of ideation can recepts attain without the aid of concepts ? We have seen in the last chapter that animals display generic or receptual ideas of Good-for-eating, Not-good-for-eating, &c. ; and we know that in our own case we "instinctively" avoid placing our hands in a flame, without requiring to formulate any proposition upon the properties of flame. How far, then, can this kind of unnamed or non-conceptional ideation extend ? Or, in other words, how far can mind travel without the vehicle of Language ? For the reasons already given, I will answer this question by fastening attention exclusively on the mind of brutes.

To lead off with a few instances which have been already selected for substantially the same purpose by Mr. Darwin :—

"Houzeau relates that, while crossing a wide and arid plain in Texas, his two dogs suffered greatly from thirst, and that between thirty and forty times they rushed down the hollows to search for water. These hollows were not valleys, and there were no trees in them, or any other difference in the vegetation ; and as they were absolutely dry, there could have been no smell of damp earth. The dogs behaved as if they knew that a dip in the ground offered them the best chance of finding water, and Houzeau has often witnessed the same behaviour in other animals." *

I have myself frequently observed this association of ideas between hollow ground and probability of finding water in the case of setter-dogs, which require much water while working ; and it is evident that the ideas associated are of a character highly generic.

Further, Mr. Darwin writes :—" I have seen, as I dare say have others, that when a small object is thrown on the ground beyond the reach of one of the elephants in the Zoological Gardens, he blows through his trunk on the ground beyond the object, so that the current reflected on all sides may drive the object within his reach. Again, a well-known ethnologist, Mr. Westropp, informs me that he observed in Vienna a bear deliberately making with his paw a current in some water, which was close to the bars of his cage, so as to draw a piece of floating bread within his reach." *

In *Animal Intelligence* it will be seen that both these observations are independently confirmed by letters which I have received from correspondents ; so that the facts must be accepted. And they imply a faculty of forming generic ideas of a high order of complexity. Indeed, these are not unlike the generic ideas of intelligent water-dogs with reference to

* *Descent of Man,* p. 76.

water-currents, which induce the animals to make allowance for the force of the current by running in the opposite direction to its flow before entering the water.  Dogs accustomed to tidal rivers, or to swimming in the sea, acquire a still further generic idea of uncertainty as to the direction of the flow at any given time ; and therefore some of the more intelligent of these dogs first ascertain the direction in which the tide is running by placing their fore-paws in the stream, and then proceed to make their allowance for drift-way accordingly. *

Lastly, Mr. Darwin writes :—" When I say to my terrier in an eager voice (and I have made the trial many times), ' Hi, hi, where is it ? ' she at once takes it as a sign that something is to be hunted, and generally first looks quickly all around, and then rushes into the nearest thicket, to scout for any game, but finding nothing, she looks up into any neighbouring tree for a squirrel.  Now, do not these actions clearly show that she had in her mind a general idea, or concept, that some animal is to be discovered and hunted ? " †

From the many instances which I have already given in *Animal Intelligence* of the high receptual capabilities of ants, it will here be sufficient to re-state the following, which is quoted from Mr. Belt, whose competency as an observer no one can dispute.

" A nest was made near one of our tramways, and to get to the trees the ants had to cross the rails, over which the waggons were continually passing and re-passing.  Every time they came along a number of ants were crushed to death.  They persevered in crossing for some time, but at last set to work and tunnelled underneath each rail.  One day, when the waggons were not running, I stopped up the tunnels with stones ; but although great numbers carrying leaves were thus cut off from the nest, they would not cross the rails, but set to work making fresh tunnels underneath them."

* See *Animal Intelligence*, pp. 465, 466.
† Of course the words "general idea" and "concept" here are open to that psychological objection for the avoidance of which I have coined the terms generic dea and recept.

These facts cannot be ascribed to "instinct," seeing that tram-cars could not have been objects of previous experience to the ancestors of the ants; and therefore the degree of receptual intelligence, or "practical inference," which was displayed is highly remarkable. Clearly, the insects must have appreciated the nature of these repeated catastrophes, and correctly reasoned out the only way by which they could be avoided.

As this is an important branch of my subject, I will add a few more illustrations drawn from vertebrated animals, beginning with some from the writings of Leroy, who had more opportunity than most men of studying the habits of animals in a state of nature.*

He says of the wolf :—"When he scents a flock within its fold, memory recalls to him the impression of the shepherd and his dog, and balances that of the immediate neighbourhood of the sheep; he measures the height of the fence, compares it with his own strength, takes into account the additional difficulty of jumping it when burdened with his prey, and thence concludes the uselessness of the attempt. Yet he will seize one of a flock scattered over a field, under the very eyes of the shepherd, especially if there be a wood near enough to offer him a hope of shelter. He will resist the most tempting morsel when accompanied by this alarming accessory [the smell of man]; and even when it is divested of it, he is long in overcoming his suspicions. In this case the wolf can only have an abstract idea of danger—the precise nature of the trap laid for him being unknown. . . . Several nights are hardly sufficient to give him confidence. Though the cause of his suspicions may no longer exist, it is reproduced by memory, and the suspicion is unremoved. The idea of man is connected with that of an unknown danger, and makes him distrustful of the fairest appearances." †

Leroy also well observes :—"Animals, like ourselves, are

---

* In my previous works I have already quoted facts of animal intelligence narrated by this author, but not any of those which I am now about to use.

† *Intelligence of Animals*, English trans., p. 20.

*forced* to make abstractions. A dog which has lost his master runs towards a group of men, by virtue of a general abstract idea, which represents to him the qualities possessed in common with these men by his master. He then experiences in succession several less general, but still abstract ideas of sensation, until he meets the particular sensation which he seeks." *

Again, with regard to the stag, this author writes :—" He exhausts every variety and every design of which the action of flight consists. He has perceived that in thickets, where the passage of his body leaves a strong trace, the dogs follow him ardently, and without any checks ; he therefore leaves the thicket and plunges into the forests where there is no underwood, or else skirts the high-road. Sometimes he leaves that part of the country altogether, and depends wholly on his speed for escape. But even when out of hearing of the dogs, he knows that they will soon come up with him ; and, instead of giving himself up to false security, he avails himself of this respite to invent new artifices to throw them out. He takes a straight course, returns on his steps, and bounding from the earth many times consecutively, throws out the sagacity of the dogs. . . . When hard pressed he will often drop down in the hope that their ardour will carry them beyond the track, and should it do so he retraces his steps. Often he seeks the company of others of his species, and when his friend is sufficiently heated to share the peril with, he leaves him to his fate and escapes by rapid flight. Frequently the quarry is thus changed, and this artifice is one the success of which is most certain." †

" Often (when not being hunted at all), instead of returning home in confidence and straightway lying down to rest, he will wander round the spot ; he enters the wood, leaves it,

---

* *Ibid.*, p. 107. This identical illustration appears to have occurred independently both to Mr. Darwin and Mr. Leslie Stephen. All these writers use the terms "abstract" and "general" as above ; but, of course, as shown in my last chapter, this is merely a matter of terminology—in my opinion, however, objectionable, because appearing to assume, without analysis, that the ideation of brutes and of men is identical in kind.

† *Ibid.*, pp. 43, 44.

goes and returns on his steps many times. Without having any immediate cause for his uneasiness, he employs the same artifices which he would have employed to throw out the dogs, if he were pursued by them. This foresight is an evidence of remembered facts, and of a series of ideas and suppositions resulting from those facts." *

It is remarkable enough that an animal should seek to confuse its trail by such devices, even when it knows that the hounds are actually in pursuit; but it is still more so when the devices are resorted to in order to confuse *imaginary* hounds which may *possibly* be on the scent. Perhaps to some persons it may appear that such facts argue on the part of the animals which exhibit them some powers of representative thought, or some kind of reflection conducted without the aid of language. Be it remembered, therefore, I am not maintaining that they do not: I am merely conceding that the evidence is inadequate to justify the conclusion that they do; and all I am now concerned with is to make it certain that in animals there is a *logic*, be it a logic of recepts only, or likewise what I shall afterwards explain as a logic of *pre-concepts.*

Again, Leroy says of the fox :—" He smells the iron of the trap, and this sensation has become so terrible to him, that it prevails over every other. If he perceives that the snares become more numerous, he departs to seek a safe neighbourhood. But sometimes, grown bold by a nearer and oft-repeated examination, and guided by his unerring scent, he manages, without hurt to himself, to draw the bait adroitly out of the trap. . . . If all the outlets of his den are guarded by traps, the animal scents them, recognizes them, and will suffer the most acute hunger rather than attempt to pass them. I have known foxes keep their dens a whole fortnight, and only then make up their minds to come out because hunger left them no choice but as to the mode of death. . . . There is nothing he will not attempt in order to save himself. He will dig till he has worn away his claws to effect his exit by a

* *Ibid.*, p. 39.

fresh opening, and thus not unfrequently escapes the snares of the sportsman. If a rabbit imprisoned with him gets caught in one of the snares, or if by any other means one should go off, he infers that the machine has done its duty, and walks boldly and securely over it." *

Lastly, this author gives the case, which has since been largely quoted—although its source is seldom given—of crows which it is desired to shoot upon their nests, in order to destroy birds and eggs at the same time. The crows will not return to their nests during daylight, if they see any one waiting to shoot them. If, to lull suspicion, a hut is made below the

---

* *Ibid.*, p. 30. In the present connection, also, I may refer to the chapter on Imagination in my previous work, where sundry illustrations are given of this faculty as it occurs in animals ; for wherever imagination leads to appropriate action, there is evidence of a Logic of Recepts, which in the higher levels of imagination, characteristic of man, passes into a Logic of Concepts.

Since publishing the chapter just alluded to, I have received an additional and curious illustration of the imaginative faculty in animals, which I think deserves to be published for its own sake. Of course we may see in a general way that dogs and cats resemble children in their play of "pretending" that inanimate objects are alive, and this betokens a comparatively high level of the imaginative faculty. The case which I am about to quote, however, appears to show that this kind of imaginative play may extend in animals, as in children, to the still higher level of not only pretending that inanimate objects are alive, but of "peopling space with fancy's airy forms." I shall quote the facts in the words of my correspondent, who is Miss Bramston, the authoress.

" *Watch* is a collie dog belonging to the Archbishop of Canterbury ; but lives with me a good deal, as Lambeth does not suit him. He is a very remarkable dog in many ways, which I will not inflict on you. He is very intelligent, understands many words, and can perform tricks. What I mention him for, however, is that he is the only dog I ever met with a dramatic faculty. His favourite drama is chasing imaginary pigs. He used now and then to be sent to chase real pigs out of the field, and after a time it became a custom for Miss Benson to open the door for him after dinner in the evening, and say, ' Pigs !' when he always ran about, wildly chasing imaginary pigs. If no one opened the door, he went to it himself wagging his tail, asking for his customary drama. He now reaches a furthur stage, for as soon as we get up after our last meal he begins to bark violently, and if the door is open he rushes out to chase imaginary pigs with no one saying the word ' pigs ' at all. He usually used to be sent out to chase pigs after prayers in the evening, and when he came to my small house it was amusing to see that he recognized the function of prayers, performed with totally different accompaniments, to be the same as prayers performed in an episcopal chapel, so far as he expected ' Pigs ' to be the end of both. The word ' Pigs,' uttered in any tone, will always set him off playing the same drama."

rookery and a man conceal himself in it with a gun, he waits in vain if the bird has ever before been shot at in a similar manner. "She knows that fire will issue from the cave into which she saw a man enter." Leroy then goes on to say :—"To deceive this suspicious bird, the plan was hit upon of sending two men into the watch-house, one of whom passed on while the other remained ; but the crow counted and kept her distance. The next day three went, and again she perceived that only two returned. In fine it was found necessary to send five or six men to the watch-house in order to put her out of her calculation."

Now, as Leroy is not a random writer, and as his life's work was that of Ranger at Versailles, we must not lightly set aside this statement as incredible, more especially as he adds that the "phenomenon is always to be repeated when the attempt is made," and so is to be regarded as "among the very commonest instances of the sagacity of animals."* If it is once granted that a bird has sagacity enough to infer that where she has observed two men pass in and only one come out, therefore the second man remains behind, it is only a matter of degree how far the differential perception may extend. Of course it would be absurd to suppose that the bird counts out the men by any process of notation, but we know that for simple ideas of number no symbolism in the way of figures is necessary. If we were to see three men pass into a building and only two come out, we should not require to calculate $3 - 2 = 1$ ; the contrast between the simultaneous sense-perception of $A + B + C$, when receptually compared with the subsequently serial perceptions of A and B, would be sufficient for the spontaneous inference that C must still be in the building. And this process would in our own case continue possible up to the point at which the simultaneous perception was not composed of too many parts to be afterwards receptually analysed into its constituents.†

---

* *Ibid.,* pp. 125, 126.

† Professor Preyer has ascertained experimentally the number of objects (such as shot-corns, pins, or dots on a piece of paper), which admit of being simul-

In this connection also I may state that, with the assistance of the keeper, I have succeeded in teaching the Chimpanzee now at the Zoological Gardens to count correctly as far as five. The method adopted is to ask her for one straw, two straws, three straws, four straws, or five straws—of course without observing any order in the succession of such requests. If more than one straw is asked for, the ape has been taught to hold the others in her mouth until the sum is completed, so that she may deliver all the straws simultaneously. For instance, if she is asked for four straws, she successively picks up three straws and puts them in her mouth : then she picks up the fourth, and hands over all the four together. This method prevents any possible error arising from her interpretation of vocal tones, which might well arise if each straw were asked for separately. Thus there can be no doubt that the animal is able to distinguish receptually between the numbers 1, 2, 3, 4, 5, and understands the name for each. Further than this I have not attempted to take her. I may add that her performance has been witnessed by the officers of the Zoological Society and also by other naturalists, who will be satisfied with the accuracy of the above account. But the ape is capricious, and, unless she happens to be in a favourable mood at the time, visitors must not be disappointed if they fail to be entertained by an exhibition of her learning.

The great physiologist Müller and the great philosopher Hegel are quoted by Mr. Mivart as maintaining, that " to form abstract conceptions of such operations as of something common to many under the notion of cause and effect, is a perfect impossibility to them " (animals *) ; and no doubt many other illustrious names might be quoted in support of the same statement. But it seems to me that needless

taneously estimated with accuracy. (*Sitzungs berichten der Gesellschaft für Medicin und Naturwissenshaft*, 29 Juli, 1881.) The number admits of being largely increased by practice, until, with an exposure to view of one second's duration, the estimate admits of being correctly made up to between twenty and thirty objects. (See also *Mental Evolution in Animals*, p. 138.)

* *Lessons from Nature*, pp. 219, 220.

obscurity is imported into this matter, by not considering in what our own idea of causality consists. It is clear that to attain a *general* idea of causality as universal, &c., demands higher powers of abstract thought than are possessed by any animals, or even by the great majority of men ; but it is no less clear that all men and most animals have a *generic* idea of causality, in the sense of expecting uniform experience under uniform conditions. A cat sees a man knock at the knocker of a door, and observes that the door is afterwards opened : remembering this, when she herself wants to get in at that door, she jumps at the knocker, and waits for the door to be opened.* Now, can it be denied that in this act of inference, or imitation, or whatever name we choose to call it, the cat perceives such an association between the knocking and the opening as to feel that the former as antecedent was in some way required to determine the latter as consequent? And what is this but such a perception of causal relation as is shown by a child who blows upon a watch to open the case— thinking this to be the cause of the opening from the uniform deception practised by its parent,—or of the savage who plants nails and gunpowder to make them grow? And endless illustrations of such a perception of causality might be drawn from the everyday life of civilized man : indeed, how seldom does any one of us wait to construct a general proposition about causality in the abstract before we act on our practical knowledge of it. And that this practical knowledge in the case of animals enables them to form a generic idea, or recept, of the *equivalency* between causes and effects—such that a perceived equivalency is recognized by them as an *explanation*—would appear to be rendered evident by the following fact, which I carefully observed for the express purpose of testing the question. I quote the incident from an already-published lecture, which was given before the British Association at Dublin, in 1878.

" I had a setter dog which was greatly afraid of thunder. One day a number of apples were being shot upon the

* See *Animal Intelligence,* pp. 422–424.

wooden floor of an apple-room, and, as each bag of apples was shot, it produced through the rest of the house a noise resembling that of distant thunder. My dog became terror-stricken at the sound ; but as soon as I brought him to the apple-room and showed him the true *cause* of the noise, he became again buoyant and cheerful as usual." *

The importance of clearly perceiving that animals have a generic, as distinguished from an abstract, idea of causation —and, indeed, *must* have such an idea if they are in any way at all to adjust their actions to their circumstances—the importance of clearly perceiving this is, that it carries with it a proof of the logic of recepts being able to reach generic ideas of *principles*, as well as of objects, qualities, and actions. In order to prove this important fact still more unquestionably, I will here quote a passage from the biography of the cebus which I kept for the express purpose of observing his intelligence.

" To-day he obtained possession of a hearth-brush, one of the kind which has the handle screwed into the brush. He soon found the way to unscrew the handle, and, having done that, he immediately began to try to find out the way to screw it in again. This he in time accomplished. At first he put the wrong end of the handle into the hole, but turned it round and round the right way for screwing. Finding it did not hold, he turned the other end of the handle, carefully stuck it into the hole, and began again to turn it the right way. It was, of course, a very difficult feat for him to perform, for he required both his hands to hold the handle in the proper position, and to turn it between his hands in order to screw it in ; and the long bristles of the brush prevented it from remaining steady, or with the right side up. He held the

---

* I may here observe that the earliest age in the infant at which I have observed such appreciation of causality to occur is during the sixth month. With my own children at that age I noticed that if I made a knocking sound with my concealed foot, they would look round and round the room with an obvious desire to ascertain the cause that was producing the sound. Compare, also, *Mental Evolution in Animals*, pp. 156–158, on emotions aroused in brutes by sense of the *mysterious—i.e.* the *unexplained*.

brush with his hind hands, but even so it was very difficult for him to get the first turn of the screw to fit into the thread ; he worked at it, however, with the most unwearying perseverance until he got the first turn of the screw to catch, and he then quickly turned it round and round until it was screwed up to the end. The most remarkable thing was that, however often he was disappointed in the beginning, he never was induced to try turning the handle the wrong way ; he always screwed it from right to left. As soon as he had accomplished his wish, he unscrewed it again, and then screwed it on again the second time rather more easily than the first, and so on many times."

The above is extracted from the diary kept by my sister. I did not myself witness the progress of this research with the hearth-brush, as I did so many of the other investigations successfully pursued by that wonderful animal. But I have a perfect confidence in the accuracy of my sister's observation, as well as in the fidelity of her account; and, moreover, the point with which I am about to be concerned has reference to what followed subsequently, as to which I had abundant opportunities for close and repeated observations. For the point is that, after having thus discovered the mechanical *principle* of the screw in that one particular case, the monkey forthwith proceeded to *generalize*, or to apply his newly gained knowledge to every other case where it was at all probable that the mechanical principle in question was to be met with. The consequence was that the animal became a nuisance in the house by incessantly unscrewing the tops of fire-irons, bell-handles, &c., &c., which he was by no means careful always to replace. Here, therefore, I think we have unquestionable evidence of intelligent recognition of a principle, which in the first instance was discovered by "the most unwearying perseverance" in the way of experiment, and afterwards sought for in multitudes of wholly dissimilar objects.*

* The reader is referred to the whole biography of this monkey (*Animal Intelligence*, pp. 484–498) for a number of other facts serving to show to how high a level of intelligent grouping—or of "logic"—recepts may attain without the aid

To these numerous facts I will now add one other, which is sufficiently remarkable to deserve republication for its own sake. I quote the account from the journal *Science*, in which it appeared anonymously. But finding on inquiry that the observer was Mr. S. P. Langley, the well-known astronomer, and being personally assured by him that he is certain there is no mistake about the observation, I will now give the latter in his own words.

"The interesting description by Mr. Larkin (*Science*, No. 58) of the lifting by a spider of a large beetle to its nest, reminds me of quite another device by which I once saw a minute spider (hardly larger than the head of a pin) lift a house-fly, which must have been more than twenty times its weight, through a distance of over a foot. The fly dangled by a single strand from the cross-bar of a window-sash, and, when it first caught my attention, was being raised through successive small distances of something like a tenth of an inch each ; the lifts following each other so fast, that the ascent seemed almost continuous. It was evident that the weight must have been quite beyond the spider's power to stir by a ' dead lift ; ' but his motions were so quick, that at first it was difficult to see how this apparently impossible task was being accomplished. I shall have to resort to an illustration to explain it ; for the complexity of the scheme seems to belong less to what we ordinarily call instinct than to intelligence, and that in a degree we cannot all boast ourselves.

"The little spider proceeded as follows :—

"*a b* is a portion of the window-bar, to which level the fly was to be lifted, from his original position at F vertically beneath *a;* the spider's first act was to descend halfway to the fly (to *d*), and there fasten one end of an almost invisible thread ; his second to ascend to the bar and run out to *b*, where he made fast the other end, and hauled on his guy

of concepts. In the same connection I may refer to the chapter on "Imagination" in *Mental Evolution in Animals*, and also to the following pages in *Animal Intelligence:*—128–40 ; 181–97, 219–222, 233, 311–335, 337, 338, 340, 348–352, 377–385, 397–410, 413–425, 426–436, 445–470, 478–498.

with all his might. Evidently the previously straight line must yield somewhat in the middle, whatever the weight of the fly, who was, in fact, thereby brought into position F′, to the right of the first one and a little higher. Beyond this point, it might seem, he could not be lifted ; but the guy being left fast at *b*, the spider now went to an intermediate point *c* directly over his victim's new position, and thus spun a new vertical line from *c*, which was made fast at the bend at *d′*, after which *a d* was cast off, so that the fly now hung vertically below *c*, as before below *a*, but a little higher.

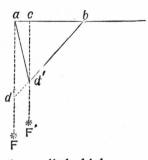

"The same operation was repeated again and again, a new guy being occasionally spun, but the spider never descending more than about halfway down the cord, whose elasticity was in no way involved in the process. All was done with surprising rapidity. I watched it for some five minutes (during which the fly was lifted perhaps six inches), and then was called away."

Without further burdening the argument with illustrative proof, it must now be evident that the "ore" out of which concepts are formed is highly metalliferous : it is not merely a dull earth which bears no resemblance to the shining substance smelted from it in the furnace of Language ; it is already sparkling to such an extent that we may well feel there is no need of analysis to show it charged with that substance in its pure form—that what we see in the ore is the same kind of material as we take from the melting-pot, and differs from it only in the degree of its agglomeration. Nevertheless, I will not yet assume that such is the case. Before we can be perfectly sure that two things which seem to the eye of common sense so similar are really the same, we must submit them to a scientific analysis. Even though it be certain that the one is extracted from the other, there still remains a possibility that in the melting-pot some further ingredient may have been added. Human intelligence is undoubtedly derived from human experience, in the same way as animal intelligence is derived from animal experience; but this does not prove that the ideation which we have in common with brutes is not supplemented by ideation of some other order, or kind. Presently I shall consider the arguments which are adduced to prove that it has been, and then it will become apparent that the supplement, if any, must have been added in the smelting-fire of Language—a fact, be it observed, which is conceded by all modern writers who deny the genetic continuity of mind in animal and human intelligence. Thus far, then, I have attempted nothing more than a preliminary clearing of the ground—first by carefully defining my terms and impartially explaining the psychology of ideation; next by indicating the nature of the question which has presently to be considered; and, lastly, by showing the level to which intelligence attains under the logic of recepts, without any possibility of assistance from the logic of concepts.

Only one other topic remains to be dealt with in the present chapter. We continually find it assumed, and confidently stated as if the statement did not admit of question, that the simplest or most primitive order of ideation is that which is concerned only with particulars, or with special objects of perception. The nascent ideas of an infant are supposed to crystallize around the nuclei furnished by individual percepts; the less intelligent animals—if not, indeed, animals in general —are supposed, as Locke says, to deal "only in particular ideas, just as they receive them from the senses." Now, I fully assent to this, if it is only meant (as I understand Locke to mean) that infants and animals are not able consciously, intentionally, or, as he says, "*of themselves*, to compound and make complex ideas." In order thus intentionally, or of themselves, to compound their ideas, they would require to *think* about their ideas *as* ideas, or consciously to set one idea before another as two distinct objects of thought, *and for the known purpose of composition.* To do this requires powers of introspective reflection ; therefore it is a kind of mental activity impossible to infants or animals, since it has to do with concepts as distinguished from recepts. But, as we have now so fully seen, it does not follow that because ideas cannot be thus compounded by infants or animals *intentionally*, therefore they cannot be ccmpounded *at all.* Locke is very clear in recognizing that animals do " take in and retain together several combinations of simple ideas to make up a complex idea : " he only denies that animals " do *of themselves* ever compound them and make complex ideas." Thus, Locke plainly teaches my doctrine of recepts as distinguished from concepts ; and I do not think that any modern psychologist—more especially in view of the foregoing evidence—will so far dispute this doctrine. But the point now is that, in my opinion, many psychologists have gone astray by assuming that the most primitive order of ideation is concerned only with particulars, or that in chronological order the memory of percepts precedes the occurrence of recepts. It appears to me that a very little thought on the one hand, and a very little observation on the other, is enough to make it certain that so soon as ideas of any kind begin to be formed at all, they are formed, not only as memories of particular percepts, but also as rudimentary recepts ; and that in the subsequent development of ideation the genesis of recepts everywhere proceeds *pari passu* with that of percepts. I say that a very little thought is enough to show that this *must* be so, while a very little observation is enough to show that it *is* so. For, *a priori*, the more unformed the powers of perception, the less able must they be to take cognizance of particulars. The development of these powers consists in the ever-increasing efficiency of their analysis, or *cognition* of smaller and smaller differences of detail ; and, consequently, of their *recognition* of these differences in different combinations. Hence, the feebler the powers of perception, the more must they occupy themselves with the larger or class distinctions between objects of sensuous experience, and the less with the smaller

or more individual distinctions.  Or, if we like, what afterwards become class distinctions, are at earlier stages of
ideation the *only* distinctions ; and, therefore, all the same as
what are afterwards individual distinctions.  But what follows ?
Surely that—be it in the individual or the race—when these
originally individual distinctions begin to grow into class
distinctions, they leave in the mind an indelible impress of
their first nativity : they were the original recepts of memory ;
and if they are afterwards slowly differentiated as they slowly
become organized into many particular parts, this does not
hinder that throughout the process they never lose their
organic unity : the mind must always continue to recognize
that the parts which it subsequently perceived as successively,
unfolding from what at first was known only as a whole, are
parts which belong to that whole—or, in other words, that the
more newly observed particulars are members of what is now
perceived as a class.  Therefore, I say, on merely *a priori*
grounds we might banish the gratuitous statement that the
lower the order of ideation the more it is concerned with
particular distinctions, or the less with class distinctions.  The
truth must be that the more primitive the recepts the larger
are the class distinctions with which they are concerned—
provided, of course, that this statement is not taken to apply
beyond the region of sensuous perception.

Accordingly we find, as a matter of fact, both in infants
and in animals, that the lower the grade of intelligence, the
more is that intelligence shut up to a perception of class
distinctions.  "We pronounce the word *Papa* before a child
in its cradle, at the same time pointing to his father.  After a
little, he in turn lisps the word, and we imagine that he understands it in the same sense that we do, or that his father's
presence only will recall the word.  Not at all.  When another
person—that is, one similar in appearance, with a long coat,
a beard, and loud voice—enters the room, he calls him also
*Papa*.  The name was individual ; he has made it general.
In our case it is applicable to one person only ; in his, to a
class. . . .  A little boy, a year old, had travelled a good deal

by railway. The engine, with its hissing sound and smoke, and the great noise of the train, struck his attention, and the first word he learned to pronounce was *Fefer* (chemin de fer). Then afterwards, a steam-boat, a coffee-pot with spirit lamp— everything that hissed or smoked was a *Fefer.**

Now, I have quoted such familiar instances from this author because he adduces them as proof of the statement that "here there appears a delicacy of impression which is special to man." Without waiting to inquire whether this statement is justified by the evidence adduced, or even whether the infant has personally distinguished his father from among other men at the time when he first calls all men by the same name; it is enough for my present purposes to observe the single fact, that when a child is first able to show us the nature of its ideation by means of speech, it furnishes us with ample evidence that this ideation is what I have termed generic. The dress, the beard, and the voice go to form a recept to which all men are perceived to correspond: the most striking peculiarities of a locomotive are vividly impressed upon the memory, so that when anything resembling them is met with elsewhere, it is receptually classified as belonging to an object of analogous character. Only much later, when the analytic powers of perception have greatly developed, does the child begin to draw its distinctions with sufficient "refinement" to perceive that this classification is too crude— that the resemblances which most struck its infant imagination were but accidental, and that they have to be disregarded in favour of less striking resemblances which were originally altogether unnoticed. But although the process of classification is thus perpetually undergoing improvement with advancing intelligence, from the very first it has been *classification*—although, of course, thus far only within the region of sensuous perception. And similarly with regard to animals, it is sufficiently evident from such facts as those already instanced, that the imagery on which their adaptive action depends is in large measure generic.

* Taine, *On Intelligence*, pp. 16, 17.

Therefore, without in any way prejudging the question as to whether or not there is any radical distinction between a mind thus far gifted and the conceptual thought of man, I may take it for granted that the ideation of infants is from the first generic; and hence that those psychologists are greatly mistaken who thoughtlessly assume that the formation of class-ideas is a prerogative of more advanced intelligence. No doubt their view of the matter seems plausible at first sight, because within the region of conceptual thought we know that progress is marked by increasing powers of *generalization*—that it is the easiest steps which have to do with the cognition of particulars; the more difficult which have to do with abstractions. But this is to confuse recepts with concepts, and so to overlook a distinction between the two orders of generalization which it is of the first importance to be clear about. A *generic* idea is generic because the particular ideas of which it is composed present such *obvious* points of resemblance that they spontaneously fuse together in consciousness; but a *general* idea is general for precisely the opposite reason—namely, because the points of resemblance which it has seized are *obscured* from immediate perception, and therefore could never have fused together in consciousness but for the aid of intentional abstraction, or of the power of a mind knowingly to deal with its own ideas as ideas. In other words, the kind of classification with which recepts are concerned is that which lies nearest to the kind of classification with which all processes of so-called "intuitive inference" depend—such as mistaking a bowl for a sphere. But the kind of classification with which concepts are concerned is that which lies furthest from this purely automatic grouping of perceptions. Classification there doubtless is in both cases; but the one order is due to the closeness of resemblances in an act of perception, while in the other order it is an expression of their remoteness from merely perceptual associations.

Or, to put the matter in yet another light, if we think it sounds less paradoxical to speak of the process of classification as everywhere the same in kind, we must conclude that the groupings of recepts stand to those of concepts in much the same relation as the groupings of percepts do to those of recepts. In each case it is the lower order of grouping which furnishes material for the higher: and the object of this chapter has been to show, first, that the unintentional grouping which is distinctive of recepts may be carried to a wonderful pitch of perfection without any aid from the intentional grouping which is distinctive of concepts; and, second, that from the very beginning conscious ideation has been concerned with *grouping*. Not only, or not even chiefly, has it had to do with the registration in memory of particular percepts; but much more has it had to do with the spontaneous sorting of such percepts, with the spontaneous arrangement of them in ideal (or imagery) systems, and, consequently, with the *spontaneous reflection in consciousness* of many among the less complex *relations*—or the less abstruse *principles*—which have been uniformly encountered by the mind in its converse with an orderly world.

# CHAPTER IV.

### LOGIC OF CONCEPTS.

THE device of applying symbols to stand for ideas, and then using the symbols as ideas, operates to the formation of more highly abstract ideas in a manner that is easily seen. For instance, because we observe that a great many objects present a certain quality in common, such as redness, we find it convenient to give this quality a name; and, having done so, we speak of redness in the abstract, or as standing apart from any particular object. Our word "redness" then serves as a sign or symbol of a quality, apart from any particular object of which it may happen to be a quality; and having made this symbolic abstraction in the case of a simple quality, such as redness, we can afterwards compound it with other symbolic abstractions, and so on till we arrive at verbal symbols of more and more abstract or general qualities, as well as qualities further and further removed from immediate perception. Thus, seeing that many other objects agree in being yellow, others blue, and so on, we combine all these abstractions into a still more general concept of Colour, which, *quâ* more abstract, is further removed from immediate perception—it being impossible that we can ever have a percept answering to the amalgamated concept of *colour*, although we have many percepts answering to the constituent concepts of *colours*.

So in the analogous case of objects. The proper names Peter, Paul, John, &c., stand in my mind as marks of my individual concepts: the term Man serves to sum up all the points of agreement between them—and also between all other individuals of their kind—without regard to their points of disagreement : the word Animal takes a still wider range, and so with nearly all words denoting objects. Like words connoting qualities, they may be arranged in rank above rank according to the range of their generality : and it is obvious that the wider this range the further is their meaning withdrawn from anything that can ever have been an object of immediate perception.

We shall afterwards find it is of the highest importance to note that these remarks apply quite as much to actions and states as they do to objects and qualities. Verbs, like nouns and adjectives, may be merely the names of simple recepts, or they may be compounds of other concepts—in either case differing from nouns and adjectives only in that they have to do with actions and states. To sow, to dig, to spin, &c., are names of particular actions ; to labour is the name of a more general action ; to live is the symbol of a concept yet more general. And it is obvious that here, as previously, the more general concepts are built out of the more special.

Later on I will adduce evidence to show that, whether we look to the growing infant or to the history of mankind as newly unearthed by the researches of the philologist, we alike find that no one of these divisions of simple concepts— namely, nouns, adjectives, and verbs—appears to present priority over the others. Or, if there is any evidence of such priority, it appears to incline in favour of nouns and verbs. But the point on which I desire to fasten attention at present is the enormous leverage which is furnished to the faculty of ideation by thus using words as the mental equivalents of ideas. For by the help of these symbols we climb into higher and higher regions of abstraction : by thinking in verbal signs we think, as it were, with the semblance of ideas : we dispense altogether with the necessity of actual images, whether of percepts or of recepts : we quit the sphere of sense, and rise to that of thought.

6

Take, for example, another type of abstract ideation, and one which not only serves better than most to show the importance of signs as substitutes for ideas, but also best illustrates the extraordinary results to which such symbolism may lead when carried out persistently. I refer to mathematics. Of course, before the idea of number or of relation can arise at all, the faculty of conception must have made great advances; but let us take this faculty at the point where the artifice of substituting signs for ideas has gone as far as to enable a mind to count by means of simple notation. It would clearly be impossible to conduct the least intricate trains of reasoning which invoke any ideas of number or proportion, were we deprived of the power of attaching particular signs to particular ideas of number. We could not even tell whether a clock had struck eleven or twelve, unless we were able to mark off each successive stroke with some distinctive sign ; so that when it is said, as it often is, that an animal cannot count, we must remember that neither could a senior wrangler count if deprived of his symbols. "Man begins by counting things, grouping them visibly [*i.e.* by the Logic of Recepts]. He then learns to count simply the numbers, in the absence of things, using his fingers and toes for symbols. He then substitutes abstract signs, and Arithmetic begins. From this he passes to Algebra, the signs of which are not merely abstract but general ; and now he calculates numerical relations, not numbers. From this he passes to the higher calculus of relations."

And just as in mathematics the symbols that are employed contain in an easily manipulated form enormous bodies of meaning—possibly, indeed, the entire meaning of a long calculation,—so in all other kinds of abstract ideation, the symbols which we employ—whether in gesture, speech, or writing—contain more or less condensed masses of signification. Or, to take another illustration, which, like the last example, I quote from Lewes, "It is the same with the development of commerce. Men begin by exchanging things.

They pass to the exchange of values. First money, then notes or bills, is the symbol of value. Finally men simply debit and credit one another, so that immense transactions are effected by means of this equation of equations. The complicated processes of sowing, reaping, collecting, shipping, and delivering a quantity of wheat, are condensed into the entry of a few words in a ledger."

Thus, without further treatment, it must be obvious that it is impossible for us to over-estimate the importance of Language as the handmaid of Thought. "A sign," as Sir William Hamilton says, "is necessary to give stability to our intellectual progress—to establish each step in our advance as a new starting-point for our advance to another beyond. . . . Words are the fortresses of thought. They enable us to make every intellectual conquest the basis of operations for others still beyond." Moreover, thought and language act and react upon one another; so that, to adopt a happy metaphor from Professor Max Müller, the growth of thought and language is coral-like. Each shell is the product of life, but becomes in turn the support of new life. In the same manner each word is the product of thought, but becomes in turn a new support for the growth of thought.

It seems needless to say more in order to show the immense importance of sign-making to the development of ideation—the fact being one of universal recognition by writers of every school. I will, therefore, now pass on to the theme of the present chapter, which is that of tracing in further detail the *logic* of this faculty, or the *method* of its development.

From what I have already said, it may have been gathered that the simplest concepts are merely the names of recepts ; while concepts of a higher order are the names of other concepts. Just as recepts may be either memories of particular percepts, or the results of many percepts (*i.e.* sundry other recepts) grouped as a class; so concepts may be either names of particular recepts, or the results of many named recepts (*i.e.* sundry other concepts) grouped as a class. The word "red," for example, is my name for a particular recept ; but the word "colour" is my name for a whole group of named recepts. And similarly with words signifying objects, states, and actions. Hence, we may broadly distinguish between concepts as of two orders—namely, those which have to do with recepts, and those which have to do with other concepts. For a concept is a concept even though it be nothing more than a named recept ; and it is still a concept, even though it stands for the highest generalization of thought. I will make this distinction yet more clear by means of better illustrations.

Water-fowl adopt a somewhat different mode of alighting upon land, or even upon ice, from that which they adopt when alighting upon water ; and those kinds which dive from a height (such as terns and gannets) never do so upon land or upon ice. These facts prove that the animals have one recept answering to a solid substance, and another answering to a fluid. Similarly, a man will not dive from a height over hard ground or over ice, nor will he jump into water in the same way as he jumps upon dry land. In other words, like the water-fowl, he has two distinct recepts, one of which answers to solid ground, and the other to an unresisting fluid. But, unlike the water-fowl, he is able to bestow upon each of these recepts a name, and thus to raise them both to the level of concepts. So far as the practical purposes of locomotion are concerned, it is of course immaterial whether or not he thus raises his recepts into concepts ; but, as we have seen, for many other purposes it is of the highest importance that he is able to do this. Now, in order to do it, he must be able to set his recept before his own mind as an object of his own thought : before he can bestow upon these generic ideas the names of "solid" and "fluid," he must have *cognized* them *as* ideas. Prior to this act of cognition, these ideas differed in no respect from the recepts of a water-fowl ; neither for the ordinary requirements of his locomotion is it needful that they should : therefore, in so far as these requirements are

concerned, the man makes no call upon his higher faculties of
ideation. But, in virtue of this act of cognition, whereby he
assigns a name to an idea known as such, he has created
for himself—and for purposes other than locomotion—a
priceless possession : he has formed a concept.

Nevertheless, the concept which he has formed is an
extremely simple one—amounting, in fact, to nothing more
than the naming of one among the most habitual of his
recepts. But it is of the nature of concepts that, when once
formed, they admit of being intentionally compared ; and thus
there arises a new possibility in the way of grouping ideas—
namely, no longer by means of sensuous associations, but by
means of symbolic representations. The names of recepts
now serve as symbols of the recepts themselves, and so admit
of being grouped without reference to the sensuous perceptions out of which they originally sprang. No longer
restricted to time, place, circumstance, or occasion, ideas may
now be called up and manipulated at pleasure ; for in this
new method of ideation the mind has, as it were, acquired an
*algebra of recepts :* it is no longer necessary that the actual
recepts themselves should be present to sensuous perception,
or even to representative imagination. And as concepts are
thus symbols of recepts, they admit, as I have said, of being
compared and combined without reference to the recepts
which they serve to symbolize. Thus we become able, as it
were, to calculate in concepts in a way and to an extent that
would be quite impossible in the merely perceptual medium
of recepts. Now, it is in this algebra of the imagination that
all the higher work of ideation is accomplished ; and as the
result of long and elaborate syntheses of concepts we turn out
mental products of enormous intricacy—which, nevertheless,
may be embodied in single words. Such words, for example,
as Virtue, Government, Mechanical Equivalent, stand for
immensely more elaborated concepts than the words Solid
or Fluid—seeing that to the former there are no possible
equivalents in the way of recepts.

Hence I say we must begin by recognizing the great reach

of intellectual territory which is covered by what are called concepts. At the lowest level they are nothing more than named recepts ; beyond that level they become the names of other concepts ; and eventually they become the named products of the highest and most complex co-ordinations of concepts which have been achieved by the human mind. By the term *Lower Concepts*, then, I will understand those which are nothing more than named recepts, while by the term *Higher Concepts* I will understand those which are compounded of other concepts.

The next thing I wish to make clear is that concepts of the lower order of which I speak, notwithstanding that they are the simplest kind of concepts possible, are already something more than the names of *particular* ideas : they are the names of what I have called *generic* ideas, or recepts. We may search through the whole dictionary of any language and not find a single word which stands as a name for a truly particular idea—*i.e.* for the memory of a particular percept. Proper names are those which most nearly approach this character ; but even proper names are really names of recepts (as distinguished from particular percepts), seeing that every object to which they are applied is a highly complex object, presenting many and diverse qualities, all of which require to be registered in memory as appertaining to that object if it is again to be recognized as the same.

Names, then, are not concerned with particular ideas, strictly so called : concepts, even of the lowest order, have to do with generic ideas. Furthermore, the generic ideas with which they have to do are for the most part highly generic : even before a recept is old enough to be baptized—or sufficiently far developed to be admitted as a member of the body conceptual,—it is already a highly organized product of ideation. We have seen in the last chapter how wonderfully far the combining power of imagination is able to go without the aid of language ; and the consequence of this is, that before the advent of language mind is already stored with a rich accumulation of orderly ideas, grouped together in many systems of logical coherency. When, therefore, the advent of language does take place, it is needless that this work of logical grouping should be recommenced *ab initio*. What language does is to take up the work of grouping where it has been left by generic ideation ; and if it is found expedient to name any generic ideas, it is the more generic as well as the less generic that are selected for the purpose. In short, immense as is the organizing power of the Logos, it does not come upon the scene of its creative power to find only that which is without form and void : rather does it find a fair structure of no mean order of system, shaped by prior influences, and, so far as thus shaped, a veritable cosmos.

Again, all concepts in their last resort depend on receipts, just as in their turn recepts depend on percepts. This fact admits of being abundantly proved, not only by general considerations but also by the etymological derivation of abstract terms. The most highly abstract terms are derived from terms less abstract, and these from others still less abstract, until, by two or three such steps at the most, we are in all cases led directly back to their origin in a " lower concept "—*i.e.* in the name of a recept. As I will prove later on, there is no abstract word or general term in any language which, if its origin admits of being traced at all, is not found to have its root in the name of a recept. Concepts, therefore, are originally nothing more than named recepts ; and hence it is *a priori* impossible that any concept can be formed unless it does eventually rest upon the basis of recepts. Owing to the elaboration which it subsequently undergoes in the region of symbolism, it may, indeed, so far cease to bear any likeness to its parentage that it is only the philologist who can trace its lineage. When we speak of Virtue, we need no longer think about a man, nor need we make any conscious reference to the steering of a ship when we use the word Government. But it is none the less obvious that both these highly abstract words have originated in the naming of recepts (the one of an object, the other of an action) ; and that their subsequent elevation in the

scale of generality has been due to a progressive widening
of conceptual significance at the hands of symbolical thought
In other words, and to revert to my previous terminology,
" higher concepts " can in no case originate *de novo :* they can
only be born of " lower concepts," which, in turn, are the
progeny of recepts.

I must now recur to a point with which we were concerned at the close of the last chapter.   I there showed that
the kind of classification, or mental grouping of ideas, which
goes to constitute the logic of recepts, differs from the mental
grouping of ideas which constitutes the logic of concepts, in
that while the former has to do with similarities which are
most obvious to perception, and therefore with analogies
which most obtrude themselves upon attention, the latter have
to do with similarities which are least obvious to perception,
and therefore with analogies which are least readily apparent
to the senses.   Classification there is in both cases ; but while
in the one it depends on the closeness of the resemblances in
an act of perception, in the other it is expressive of their
remoteness.   Now, from this it follows that the more conceptual the classification, the less obvious to immediate perception are the similarities between the things classified ; and,
consequently, the higher a generalization the greater must be
the distance by which it is removed from the merely automatic groupings of receptual ideation.
For example, the earliest classification of the animal kingdom with which we are acquainted, grouped together, under
the common designation of " creeping things," articulata,
mollusca, reptiles, amphibia, and even certain mammals, such
as weasels, &c.   Here, it is evident, the classification reposed
only on the very superficial resemblances which are exhibited
by these various creatures in their modes of locomotion.   As
yet conceptual thought had not been directed to the anatomy
of animals ; and, therefore, when it undertook a classification
of animals, in the first instance it went no further than to note
the most obvious differences as to external form and move-

ment. In other words, this earliest conceptual classification was little more than the verbal statement of a receptual classification. But when the science of comparative anatomy was inaugurated by the Greeks, a much more conceptual classification of animals emerged—although the importance of anything like a systematic arrangement of the animal kingdom as a whole was so little appreciated that it does not appear to have been attempted, even by Aristotle. For, marvellous as is the advance of conceptual grouping here displayed by him, he confined himself to drawing anatomical comparisons between one group of animals and another ; he neither had any idea of group subordinate to group which afterwards constituted the leading principle of taxonomic research, nor does he anywhere give a tabular statement of his own results, such as he could scarcely have failed to give had he appreciated the importance of classifying the animal kingdom as a systematic whole. Lastly, since the time of Ray the best thought of the best naturalists has been bestowed upon this work, with the result that conceptual ideation has continuously ascended through wider and wider generalizations, or generalizations more and more chastened by the intentional and combined accumulations of knowledge. How enormous, then, is the contrast between the first simple attempt at classification as made by the early Jews, and the elaborate body of abstract thought which is presented by the taxonomic science of to-day.

Similar illustrations might be drawn from any of the other departments of conceptual evolution, because everywhere such evolution essentially consists in the achievement of ideal integrations further and further removed from simple perceptions. Or, as Sir W. Hamilton puts it, " by a first generalization we have obtained a number of classes of resembling individuals. But these classes we can compare together, observe their similarities, abstract from their differences, and bestow on their common circumstance a common name. On the second classes we can again perform the same operation, and thus, ascending through the scale of general notions, throwing out of view always a greater number of differences, and seizing always on fewer similarities in the formation of our classes, we arrive at length at the limit of our ascent in the notion of being or existence." *

Now, the point on which I wish to be perfectly clear about is, that this process of conceptual ideation, whereby ideas become general, must be carefully distinguished from the processes of receptual ideation, whereby ideas become generic. For these latter processes consist in particular ideas, which are given immediately in sense perception, becoming by association of similarity or contiguity automatically fused together ; so that out of a number of such associated percepts there is formed a recept, without the need of any intentional co-operation of the mind in the matter. On the other hand, a general idea, or concept, can only be formed by the mind itself intentionally classifying its recepts known as such—or, in the case of creating "higher concepts," performing the same process with its already acquired general ideas, for the purpose of constructing ideas still more general. A generic idea, then, is generalized in the sense that a naturalist speaks of a lowly organism as generalized—*i.e.* as not yet differentiated into the groups of higher and more specialized structures that subsequently emanate therefrom. But a general idea is generalized in the sense of comprising a group of such higher and more specialized structures, already formed and named under a common designation with reference to their points of resemblance. Classification there is in all cases ; but in the receptual order it is automatic, while in the conceptual order it is introspective.

So far as my analysis has hitherto gone, I do not anticipate criticism or dissent from any psychologist, to whatever school he may belong. But there is one matter of subordinate importance which I may here most conveniently dispose of, although my views with regard to it may not meet with universal assent.

* *Lectures*, vol. ii., p. 290.

It appears to me an obvious feature of our introspective life that we are able to carry on elaborate processes of ideation without the aid of words—or, to put it paradoxically, that we are able to conceive without concepts. I am, of course, aware that this apparently obvious power of being able to think without any mental rehearsal of verbal signs (the *verbum mentale* of scholasticism) is denied by several writers of good standing—notably, for instance, by Professor Max Müller, who seeks with much elaboration to prove that " not only to a considerable extent, but always and altogether, we think by means of names." * Now this statement appears to me either a truism or untrue : it is either tautological in expression, or erroneous in fact. If we restrict the term " thought " to the operation of naming, it is merely a truism to say that there can be no thought without language ; for this is merely to say that there can be no naming without names. But if the term "thought " is taken to cover all processes of ideation which we do not share with brutes, I hold that the statement is opposed to obvious fact ; and, therefore, I agree with the long array of logicians and philosophers whom Professor Max Müller quotes as showing what he calls " hesitation " in accepting a doctrine which in his opinion is the inevitable conclusion of Nominalism. For to me it appears evident that within the region of concepts, the frequent handling of those with which the mind is familiar enables the mind to deal with them in somewhat the same automatic manner as, on a lower plane of co-ordinated action, the pianist deals with his chords and phrases. Whereas at first it required intentional and laborious effort to perform these many varied and complex adjustments, by practice their performance passes more and more out of the range of conscious effort, until they come to be executed in a manner well-nigh mechanical. So in the case of purely mental operations, even of the highest order. At first every link in the chain of ideation requires to be separately fastened to attention by means of a word : every step in a process of

* *Science of Thought*, p. 35. For his whole argument, see pp. 30–64.

reasoning requires to be taken on the solid basis of a pro-position. But by frequent habit the thinking faculty ceases to be thus restricted : it passes, so to speak, from one end of the chain to the other without requiring to pause at every link : for its original stepping-stones it has substituted a bridge, over which it can pass almost at a bound. Or, again, to change the metaphor, there arises a method of short-hand thinking, wherein even the symbols of ideas (concepts) need no longer appear in consciousness: judgment follows judgment in logical sequence, yet without any articulate expression by the *verbum mentale.* This, I say, is a matter of fact which it appears to me a very small amount of introspection is enough to verify. On reading a letter, for instance, we may instan-taneously decide upon our answer, and yet have to pause before we are able to frame the propositions needed to express that answer. Or, while writing an essay, how often does one feel, so to speak, that a certain truth stands to be stated, although it is a truth which we cannot immediately put into words. We know, in a general way, that a truth is *there,* but we cannot supply the vehicle which is to bring it *here ;* and it is not until we have tried many devices, each of which involve long trains of sequent propositions, that we begin to find the satisfaction of rendering explicit in language what was previously implicit in thought. Again, in playing a game of chess we require to take cognizance of many and complex relations, actual and contingent ; so that to play the game as it deserves to be played, we must make a heavy demand on our powers of abstract thinking. Yet in doing this we do not require to preach a silent monologue as to all that we might do, and all that may be done by our opponent. Lastly, to give only one other illustration, in some forms of aphasia the patient has lost every trace of verbal memory, and yet his faculties of thought for all the practical purposes of life are not materially impaired.

On the whole, therefore, I conclude that, although language is a needful condition to the *original construction* of con-ceptional thought, when once the building has been completed, the scaffolding may be withdrawn, and yet leave the edifice as stable as before. In this way familiar concepts become, as it were, degraded into recepts, but recepts of a degree of complexity and organization which would not have been possible but for their conceptional parentage. With Geiger we may say, "So ist denn überall die Sprache primar, der Begriff entsteht durch das Wort." * Yet this does not hinder that with Friedrich Müller we should add, "Sprechen ist nicht Denken, sondern es ist nur Ausdruck des Denkens." †

With the exception of the last paragraph, my analysis, as already observed, will probably not be impugned by any living psychologist, either of the evolutionary or non-evolutionary schools ; for, with the exception of this paragraph, I have purposely arranged my argument so as thus far to avoid debatable questions. And it will be observed that even this paragraph has really nothing to do with the issue which lies before us ; seeing that the question with which it deals is concerned only with intellectual processes exclusively human. But now, after having thus fully prepared the way by a somewhat lengthy clearing of preliminary ground, we have to proceed to the question whether it is conceivable that the faculty of speech, with all the elaborate structure of ideation to which it has led, can have arisen by way of a natural

---

\* *Ursprung der Sprache,* s. 91.

† *Grundriss der Sprachwissenshaft,* i., s. 16.　It will be observed that there is an obvious analogy between the process above described, whereby conceptual ideation becomes degraded into receptual, and that whereby, on a lower plane of mental evolution, intelligence becomes degraded into instinct.　In my former work I devoted many pages to a consideration of this subject, and showed that the condition to intelligent adjustments thus becoming instinctive is invariably to be found in frequency of repetition.　Instincts of this kind (" secondary instincts ") may be termed degraded recepts, just as the recepts spoken of in the text are degraded concepts ; neither could be what it now is, but for its higher parentage.　Any one who is specially interested in the question whether there can be thought without words, may consult the correspondence between Prof. Max Müller, Mr. Francis Galton, myself, and others, in *Nature,* May and June, 1887 (since published in a separate form) ; between the former and Mr. Mivart, in *Nature,* March, 1888. Also an article by Mr. Justice Stephen in the *Nineteenth Century,* April, 1888. Prof. Whitney has some excellent remarks on this subject in his *Language and the Study of Language,* pp. 405-411.

genesis from the lower faculties of mind. As we have now seen, it is on all hands agreed that the one and only distinction between human and animal psychology consists in the former presenting this faculty which, otherwise stated, means, as we have likewise seen, the power of translating ideas into symbols, and using these symbols in the stead of ideas.

This, I say, is the one distinction upon which all are agreed; the only question is as to whether it is a distinction of kind or of degree. Since the time when the ancient Greeks applied the same word to denote the faculty of language and the faculty of thought, the philosophical propriety of the identification has become more and more apparent. Obscured as the truth may have become for a time through the fogs of Realism, discussion of centuries has fully cleared the philosophical atmosphere so far as this matter is concerned. Hence, in these latter days, the only question here presented to the evolutionist is—Why has no mere brute ever learnt to communicate with its fellows? Why has man alone of animals been gifted with the Logos? To answer this question we must undertake a somewhat laborious investigation of the philosophy of Language.

# CHAPTER V.

ETYMOLOGICALLY the word Language means sign-making by means of the tongue, *i.e.* articulate speech. But in a wider sense the word is habitually used to designate sign-making in general, as when we speak of the "finger-language" of the deaf-and-dumb, the "language of flowers," &c. Or, as Professor Broca says, "there are several kinds of language ; every system of signs which gives expression to ideas in a manner more or less intelligible, more or less perfect, or more or less rapid, is a language in the general sense of the word. Thus speech, gesture, dactylology, writing both hieroglyphic and phonetic, are all so many kinds of language. There is, then, a general faculty of language which presides over all these modes of expression, and which may be defined—the faculty of establishing a constant relation between an idea and a sign, be this a sound a gesture, a figure, or a drawing of any kind."

The best classification of the sundry exhibitions of sign-making faculty which I have met with, is one that is given by Mr. Mivart in his *Lessons from Nature* (p. 83). This classification, therefore, I will render in his own words.

"We may altogether distinguish six different kinds of language :—

"1. Sounds which are neither articulate nor rational, such as cries of pain, or the murmur of a mother to her infant.

"2. Sounds which are articulate but not rational, such as the talk of parrots, or of certain idiots, who will repeat, without comprehending, every phrase they hear.

" 3. Sounds which are rational but not articulate, ejaculations by which we sometimes express assent to, or dissent from, given propositions.

" 4. Sounds which are both rational and articulate, constituting true speech.

" 5. Gestures which do not answer to rational conceptions, but are merely the manifestations of emotions and feelings.

" 6. Gestures which do answer to rational conceptions, and are therefore 'external,' but not oral manifestations of the *verbum mentale.*"

To this list of the "Categories of Language" a seventh must be added, to contain all kinds of written signs; but with such obvious addition I assent to the classification, as including all the species that can possibly be included under the genus Language, and therefore as excluding none.

Now the first thing to be noticed is, that the signs made may be made either intentionally or unintentionally; and the next is, that the division of intentional signs may be conveniently subdivided into two classes—namely, intentional signs which are natural, and intentional signs which are conventional.

The subdivision of conventional signs may further be split into those which are due to past associations, and those which are due to inferences from present experience. A dog which "begs" for food, or a parrot which puts down its head to be scratched, may do so merely because past experience has taught the animal that by so doing it receives the gratification it desires; here is no need for reason—*i.e.* inference—to come into play. But if the animal has had no such previous experience, and therefore could not know by special association that such a particular gesture, or sign, would lead to such a particular consequence, and if under such circumstances a dog should see another dog beg, and should imitate the gesture on observing the result to which it led ; or if under such analogous circumstances a parrot should spontaneously depress its head for the purpose of making an expressive gesture,—then the sign might strictly be termed a rational one.

But it is evident that rational signs admit of almost numberless degrees of complexity and elaboration ; so that reason itself does not present a greater variety of manifestations in this respect than does the symbolism whereby it is expressed : an algebraical formula is included in the same category of sign-making as the simplest gesture whereby we intentionally communicate the simplest idea. Rational signs, therefore, may be made by gesture, by tone, by articulation, or by writing — using each of these words in its largest sense.*

The following schema may serve to show this classification in a diagrammatic form—*i.e.* the classification which I have myself arrived at, and which follows closely the one given by Mr. Mivart. Indeed, there is no difference at all between the two, save that I have endeavoured to express the distinction between signs as intentional, unintentional, natural, conventional, emotional, and intellectual. The subdivision of the latter into denotative, connotative, denominative, and predicative, will be explained in Chapter VIII.

---

* From this it will be seen that by using such terms as "inference," "reason," "rational," &c., in alluding to mental processes of the lower animals, I am in no way prejudicing the question as to the distinction between man and brute. In the higher region of recepts both the man and the brute attain in no small degree to a perception of analogies or relations : this is inference or ratiocination in its most direct form, and differs from the process as it takes place in the sphere of conceptual thought only in that it is not itself an object of knowledge. But, considered as a process of inference or ratiocination, I do not see that it should make any difference in our terminology whether or not it happens to be itself an object of knowledge. Therefore I do not follow those numerous writers who restrict such terms to the higher exhibitions of the process, or to the ratiocination which is concerned only with introspective thought. It may be a matter of straw-splitting, but I think it is best to draw our distinctions where the distinctions occur ; and I cannot see that it modifies the process of inference, as inference, whether or not the mind, in virtue of a superadded faculty, is able to think about the process as a process—not any more, for instance, than the process of association is altered by its becoming itself an object of knowledge. Therefore, I hope I have made it clear that in maintaining the rationality of brutes I am not arguing for anything more than that they have the power, as Mr. Mivart himself allows, of drawing "practical inferences." Hitherto, then, my difference with Mr. Mivart—and, so far as I know, with all other modern writers who maintain the irrationality of brutes—is only one of terminology.

## LANGUAGE, OR SIGN-MAKING.

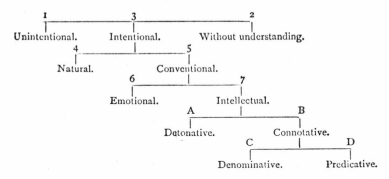

Or, neglecting the unintentional and merely imitative signs as not, properly speaking, signs at all, every kind of intentional sign may be represented diagrammatically as in the illustration opposite.

Now, thus far we have been dealing with matters of fact concerning which I do not think there can be any question. That is to say, no one can deny any of the statements which this schema serves to express ; a difference of opinion can only arise when it is asked whether the sundry faculties (or cases) presented by the schema are developmentally continuous with one another. To this topic, therefore, we shall now address ourselves.

First let it be observed that there can be no dispute about one point, namely, that all the faculties or cases presented by the schema, with the single exception of the last (No. 7), are common to animals and men. Therefore we may begin by taking as beyond the reach of question the important fact that animals do present, in an unmistakable manner, a *germ* of the sign-making faculty. But this fact is so important in its relation to our subject, that I shall here pause to consider the modes and degrees in which the faculty is exhibited by animals.

Huber says that when one wasp finds a store of honey,

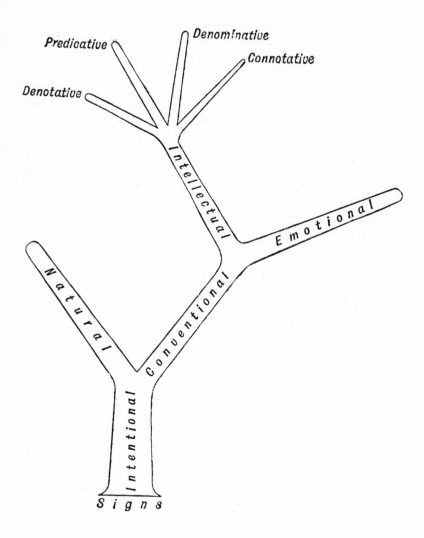

"it returns to the nest and brings off in a short time a
hundred other wasps;" and this statement is confirmed by
Dujardin. Again, the very able observer, F. Müller, writes,
in one of his letters to Mr. Darwin, that he observed a queen
bee depositing her eggs in a nest of 47 cells. In the process
she overlooked four of the cells, and when she had filled
the other 43, supposing her work to have been completed,
prepared to retire. "But as she had overlooked the four
cells of the new comb, the workers ran impatiently from this
part to the queen, pushing her in an odd manner with their
heads, as they did also the other workers they met with.
In consequence, the queen began again to go round on the
two older combs; but, as she did not find any cell wanting
an egg, she tried to descend, yet everywhere she was pushed
back by the workers. This contest lasted rather a long while,
till the queen escaped without having completed her work.
Thus the workers knew how to advise the queen that something was yet to be done; but they knew not how to show
her where it had to be done."

According to De Fravière, Landois, and some other
observers, bees have a number of different notes, or tones,
whereby they communicate information to one another; [*]
but there seems to be little doubt that the means chiefly
employed are gestures made with the antennæ. For example,
Huber divided a hive into two chambers by means of a
partition: great excitement prevailed in the half of the hive
deprived of the queen, and the bees set to work to build royal
cells for the creation of a new queen. Huber then divided
a hive in exactly the same manner, with the difference only
that the screen, or partition, was made of trellis work, through
the openings of which the bees on either side could pass
their antennæ. Under these circumstances the bees in the
queenless half of the hive exhibited no disturbance, nor did
they construct any royal cells: the bees in the other, or
separated, half of the hive were able to inform them that the
queen was safe.

[*] See *Animal Intelligence*, p. 158.

Turning now to ants, the extent to which the power of communicating by signs is here carried cannot fail to strike us as highly remarkable. In my work on *Animal Intelligence* I have given many observations by different naturalists on this head, the general results of which I will here render.

When we consider the high degree to which ants carry the principle of co-operation, it is evident that they must have some means of intercommunication. This is especially true of the Ecitons, which so strangely mimic the tactics of military organization. "The army marches in the form of a rather broad and regular column, hundreds of yards in length. The object of the march is the capture and plunder of other insects, &c., for food ; and as the well-organized host advances, its devastating legions set all other terrestrial life at defiance. From the main column there are sent out smaller lateral columns, the component individuals of which play the part of scouts, branching off in various directions, and searching about with the utmost activity for insects, grubs, &c., over every log, under every fallen leaf, and in every nook and cranny where there is any chance of finding prey. When their errand is completed, they return into the main column. If the prey found is sufficiently small for the scouts themselves to manage, it is immediately seized, and carried back to the main column ; but if the amount is too large for the scouts to deal with alone, messengers are sent back to the main column, whence there is immediately despatched a detachment large enough to cope with the requirements. . . . On either side of the main column there are constantly running up and down a few individuals of smaller size and lighter colour than the other ants, which seem to play the part of officers ; for they never leave their stations, and while running up and down the outsides of the column, they every now and again stop to touch antennæ with some member of the rank and file, as if to give instructions. When the scouts discover a wasps'-nest in a tree, a strong force is sent out from the main army, the nest is pulled to pieces, and all the larvæ carried to the rear of the army, while the wasps fly around defenceless against the

invading multitude. Or, if the nest of any other species of
ant is found, a similarly strong force—or perhaps the whole
army—is deflected towards it, and with the utmost energy the
innumerable insects set to work to sink shafts and dig mines
till the whole nest is rifled of its contents. In these mining
operations the ants work with an extraordinary display of
organized co-operation; for those low down in the shafts do
not lose time by carrying up the earth which they excavate,
but pass the pellets to those above; and the ants on the surface, when they receive the pellets, carry them—with an
appearance of forethought which quite staggered Mr. Bates—
only just far enough to insure that they shall not roll back
again into the shaft, and, after depositing them, immediately
hurry back for more. But there is not a rigid (or merely
mechanical) division of labour : the work seems to be performed
by intelligent co-operation amongst a host of eager little
creatures; for some of them act at one time as carriers of
pellets, and at another as miners, while all shortly afterwards
assume the office of conveyers of the spoil." *

Mr. Belt writes :—" The Ecitons and most other ants
follow each other by scent, and I believe they can communicate the presence of danger, of booty, or other intelligence to
a distance by the different intensity or qualities of the odours
given off. I one day saw a column running along the foot of
a nearly perpendicular tramway cutting, the side of which
was about six feet high. At one point I noticed a sort of
assembly of about a dozen individuals that appeared in
consultation. Suddenly one ant left the conclave, and ran
with great speed up the perpendicular face of the cutting
without stopping. . . . On gaining the top of the cutting,
the ants entered some brushwood suitable for hunting. In a
very short time the information was communicated to the
ants below, and a dense column rushed up in search of prey."

Again, Mr. Bates writes :—" When I interfered with the
column, or abstracted an individual from it, news of the
disturbance was quickly communicated to a distance of several

* *Animal Intelligence*, pp. 114-116.

yards to the rear, and the column at that point commenced retreating."

On arriving at a stream of water, the marching column first endeavours to find some natural bridge whereby to cross it. Should no such bridge be found, " they travel along the bank of the river until they arrive at a flat sandy shore. Each ant now seizes a bit of dry wood, pulls it into the water and mounts thereon. The hinder rows push the front ones farther out, holding on to the wood with their feet and to their comrades with their jaws. In a short time the water is covered with ants, and when the raft has grown too large to be held together by the small creatures' strength, a part breaks itself off, and begins the journey across, while the ants left on the bank pull the bits of wood into the water, and work at enlarging the ferry-boat until it breaks again. This is repeated as long as an ant remains on shore." *

So much, then, to give a general idea of the extent to which co-operation is exhibited by Ecitons—a fact which must be taken to depend upon some system of signs. Turning next to still more definite evidence of communication, Mr. Hague, the geologist, writing to Mr. Darwin from South America, says that on the mantel-shelf of his sitting-room there were three vases habitually filled with fresh flowers. A nest of red ants discovered these flowers, and formed a line to them, constantly passing upwards and downwards between the mantel-shelf and the floor, and also between the mantel-shelf and the ceiling. For several days in succession Mr. Hague frequently brushed the ants in great numbers from the wall to the floor, but, as they were not killed, the line again reformed. One day, however, he killed with his finger some of the ants upon the mantel-shelf. "The effect of this was immediate and unexpected. As soon as those ants which were approaching arrived near to where their fellows lay dead and suffering, they turned and fled with all possible haste. In half an hour the wall above the mantel-shelf was cleared of ants. During the space of an hour or two the colony from below continued

---

* Kreplin, quoted by Büchner.

to ascend until reaching the lower bevelled edge of the shelf,
at which point the more timid individuals, although unable
to see the vase, somehow became aware of the trouble, and
turned without further investigation ; while the more daring
advanced hesitatingly just to the upper edge of the shelf,
when, extending their antennæ and stretching their necks,
they seemed to peep cautiously over the edge until they beheld
their suffering companions, when they too turned and followed
the others, expressing by their behaviour great excitement
and terror.  An hour or two later the path or trail leading
from the lower colony to the vase was entirely free from ants.
. . .  A curious and invariable feature of their behaviour was
that when an ant, returning in fright, met another approaching, the two would always communicate ; but each would
pursue its own way, the second ant continuing its journey to
the spot where the first ant had turned about, and then
following that example.  For some days after this there were
no ants visible on the wall, either above or below the shelf.
Then a few ants from the lower colony began to reappear ; but
instead of visiting the vase, which had been the scene of the
disaster, they avoided it altogether, and, following the lower
front edge of the shelf to the tumbler standing near the middle,
made their attack upon that with precisely the same result."

Lastly, Sir John Lubbock made some experiments with
the express purpose of testing the power of communication
by ants.  He found that if an ant discovered a deposit of
larvæ outside the nest, she would return to the nest, and,
even though she might have no larvæ to show, was able to
communicate her need of assistance—a number of friends
proceeding to follow her as a guide to the heap of larvæ
which she had found.

In one very instructive experiment Sir John arranged
three parallel pieces of tape, each about two and a half feet
long : one end of each piece of tape was attached to the nest,
and the other dipped into a glass vessel.  In the glass at the
end of one of the tapes he placed a considerable number of
larvæ (300 to 600) : in the glass at the end of another of the

pieces he put only two or three larvæ, while the third glass he left empty. The object of the empty glass was to see whether any of the ants would come to the glass under such circumstances by mere accident. He then took two ants, one of which he placed in the glass with the many larvæ, and the other in the glass with the few. Each ant took a larva, carried it to the nest, then returned for more, and so on. After each journey he put another larva in the glass with the few larvæ, in order to replace the one which had been removed. The result of the experiment was that during 47½ hours the ants which had gone to the glass containing numerous larvæ brought 257 friends to their assistance, while during 53 hours those which had gone to the glass containing only two or three larvæ brought only 82 friends ; and no single ant came to the glass which contained no larva. Now, as all the glasses were exposed to similar conditions, and as the roads to the first two must, in the first instance at all events, have been equally scented by the passage of ants over them, these results appear very conclusive as proving some power of definite communication, not only that larvæ are to be found, but even where the largest store is to be met with.

As to the means of communication, or method of sign-making, there can be no doubt that this in ants, as in bees, is mainly gestures made by the antennæ ; but that gestures of other kinds are also employed is sufficiently well proved by the following observation of the Rev. Dr. M'Cook. " I have seen an ant kneel down before another and thrust forward the head, drooping quite under in fact, and lie there motionless, thus expressing as plainly as sign-language could, her desire to be cleansed. I at once understood the gesture, and so did the supplicated ant, for she at once went to work."

So much, then, for the power of sign-making displayed by the Hymenoptera. As I have not much evidence of sign-making in any of the other Invertebrata,* I shall pass on at once to the Vertebrata.

---

* The best instances of sign-making among Invertebrata other than the Hymenoptera which I have met with is one that I have myself observed and

Ray observed the different tones used by the common hen, and found them uniformly significant of different ideas, or emotional states; therefore we may properly regard this as a system of language, though of a very rudimentary form. He distinguishes altogether nine or ten distinct tones, which are severally significant of as many distinct emotions and ideas—namely, brooding, leading forth the brood, finding food, alarm, seeking shelter, anger, pain, fear, joy or pride in having laid an egg. Houzeau, who independently observed this matter, says that the hen utters at least twelve significant sounds.*

Many other cases could be given among Birds, and a still greater number among Mammals, of vocal tones being used as intentionally significant of states of feeling and of definite ideas; but to save space I will only render a few facts in a condensed form.

"In Paraquay, the *Cebus azaræ* when excited utters at least six distinct sounds, which excite in other monkeys similar emotions (Rengger). . . . It is a more remarkable fact that the dog, since being domesticated, has learned to bark in at least four or five distinct tones : . . . the bark of eagerness, as in the chase ; that of anger, as well as growling ; the yelp, or howl of despair, when shut up ; the baying at night ; the bark of joy when starting on a walk with his master ; and the very distinct one of demand or supplication, as when wishing for a door or window to be opened." †

I may next briefly add allusions to those instances of the

already recorded in *Mental Evolution in Animals* (p. 343, note). The animal is the processional caterpillar. These larvæ migrate in the form of a long line, crawling Indian file, with the head of the one touching the tail of the next in the series. If one member of the series be removed, the next member in advance immediately stops and begins to wag its head in a peculiar manner from side to side. This serves as a signal for the next member also to stop and wag his head, and so on till all the members in front of the interruption are at a standstill, all wagging their heads. But as soon as the interval is closed up by the advance of the rear of the column, the front again begins to move forward, when the head-wagging ceases.

* *Fac. Ment. des Animaux,* tom. ii., p. 348.
† Darwin, *Descent of Man,* pp. 84, 85.

use of signs by mammals which are fully detailed in *Animal Intelligence.*

Mr. S. Goodbehere tells me of a pony which used to push back the inside bolt of a gate in its paddock, and neigh for an ass which was loose in the yard beyond ; the ass would then come and push up the outside latch, thus opening the gate and releasing the pony (p. 333).

With respect to gestures, Mrs. K. Addison wrote me of her jackdaw—which lived in a garden, and which she usually supplied with a bath—reminding her that she had forgotten to place the bath, by coming before her and going through the movements of ablution upon the ground (p. 316).

Youatt gives the case of a pig which was trained to point game with great precision (pp. 339, 340), and this, as in the case of the dog, implies a high development of the sign-making faculty. Every sportsman must know how well a setter understands its own pointing, *and also the pointing of other dogs*, as gesture-signs. As regards its own pointing, if at any distance from the sportsman, the animal will look back to see if the "point" has been noticed ; and, if it has, the point will be much more "steady" and prolonged than if the animal sees that it has not been observed. As regards the pointing of other dogs, the "backing" of one by another means that as soon as one dog sees another dog point he also stands and points, whether or not he is in a position to scent the game. In my previous work, while treating of artificial instincts, I have shown (as Mr. Darwin had previously remarked) that in well-bred sporting dogs a tendency to "back," more or less pronounced, is intuitive. But I have also observed among my own setters that even in cases where a young dog does not show any innate disposition to "back," by working him with other dogs for a short time he soon acquires the habit, without any other instruction than that which is supplied by his own observation. I have also noticed that all sporting dogs are liable to be deceived by the attitude which their companions strike when defæcating ; but this is probably due to their line of sight being so much lower than that of a man, that slight differences of attitude are not so perceptible to them as to ourselves.

Major Skinner writes of a large wild elephant which he saw on a moonlight night coming out of a wood that skirted some water. Cautiously advancing across the open ground to within a hundred yards of the water, the animal stood perfectly motionless—the rest of the herd, still concealed in the wood, being all the while so quiet and motionless that not the least sound proceeded from them. Gradually, after three successive advances, halting some minutes after each, he moved up to the water's edge, in which however he did not think proper to quench his thirst, but remained for several minutes listening in perfect stillness. He then returned cautiously and slowly to the point at which he had issued from the wood, whence he came back with five other elephants, with which he proceeded, somewhat less slowly than before, to within a few yards of the tank, where he posted them as patrols. He then re-entered the wood and collected the whole herd, which must have amounted to between eighty and a hundred, and led them across the open ground, with the most extraordinary composure and quiet, till they came up to the five sentinels, when he left them for a moment and again made a reconnaissance at the edge of the tank. At last, being apparently satisfied that all was safe, he turned back, and obviously gave the order to advance ; "for in a moment," says Major Skinner, "the whole herd rushed to the water, with a degree of unreserved confidence so opposite to the caution and timidity which had marked their previous movements, that nothing will ever persuade me that there was not rational and preconcerted co-operation throughout the whole party "—and so, of course, some definite communication by signs (p. 401).

With regard to the use of gesture-signs by cats, I have given such cases as those of their imitating the begging of a terrier on observing that the terrier received food in answer to this gesture (p. 414) ; making a peculiar noise on desiring to have a door opened, which, if not attended to, was followed up by "pulling one's dress with its claws, and then, having succeeded in attracting the desired attention, it would walk to the street door and stop there, making the same cry until let out" (p. 414); also of a cat which, on seeing her friend the parrot "flapping its wings and struggling violently up to its knees in dough," ran upstairs after the cook to inform her of the catastrophe—"mewing and making what signs she could for her to go down," till at last "she jumped up, seized her apron, and tried to drag her down," so that the cook did go down in time to save the bird from being smothered. This gesture-sign of pulling at clothing, in order to induce one to visit a scene of catastrophe, is of frequent occurrence both in cats and dogs. Several instances are likewise given of cats jumping on chairs and looking at bells when they want milk (this being intended as a sign that they desire the bell pulled to call the servant who brings the milk), placing their paws upon the bell as a still more emphatic sign, or even themselves ringing the bell (p. 416).

Concerning gesture-signs made by dogs (other than pointing), I may allude to a terrier which I had, and which when thirsty used to signify his desire for water by begging before a wash-stand, or any other object where he knew that water was habitually kept. And Sir John Lefroy, F.R.S., gave me a similar, though still more striking, case of his terrier, which it was the duty of a maid-servant to supply with milk. One morning this servant was engaged on some needlework, and did not supply the milk. "The dog endeavoured in every possible way to attract her attention and draw her forth, and at last pushed aside the curtain of a closet, and, although never having been taught to fetch or carry, took between his teeth the cup she habitually used, and brought it to her feet" (p. 466). Another case somewhat similar is given on the same page.

Again, Mr. A. H. Browning wrote me:—"My attention was called to my dog appearing in a great state of excitement, not barking (he seldom barks) but whining, and performing all sorts of antics (in a human subject I should have said *gesticulating*). The herdmen and myself returned to the sty; we caught but one pig, and put him back; no sooner had we done so, than the dog ran after each pig in succession, brought him back to the sty by the ear, and then went after another, until the whole number were again housed " (p. 450).

Further, I give an observation of my own (p. 445) on one terrier making a gesture-sign to another. Terrier A being asleep in my house, and terrier B lying on a wall outside, a strange dog, C, ran along below the wall on the public road following a dog-cart. Immediately on seeing C, B jumped off the wall, ran upstairs to where A was asleep, woke him up by poking him with his nose in a determined and suggestive manner, which A at once understood as a sign: he jumped over the wall and pursued the dog C, although C was by that time far out of sight, round a bend in the road.

On page 447 I give, on the authority of Dr. Beattie, the case of a dog which saved his master's life (who had fallen through the ice, and was supporting himself with a gun placed across the opening), by running into a neighbouring village, and pulling a man by the coat in so significant a manner that he followed the animal and rescued the gentleman. Many cases more or less similar to this one are recorded in the anecdote books.

Concerning the use of gesture-signs by monkeys, I give on page 472 the remarkable case recorded by James Forbes, F.R.S., of a male monkey begging the body of a female which had just been shot. " The animal," says Forbes, " came to the door of the tent, and, finding threats of no avail, began a lamentable moaning, and by the most expressive gestures seemed to beg for the dead body. It was given him; he took it sorrowfully in his arms and bore it away to his expecting companions. They who were witnesses of this extraordinary scene resolved never again to fire at one of the monkey race."

Again, Captain Johnson writes of a monkey which he shot upon a tree, and which then, as he says, " instantly ran down to the lowest branch of a tree, as if he were going to fly at me stopped suddenly, and coolly put his paw to the part wounded covered with blood, and held it out for me to see. I was so much hurt at the time that it has left an impression never to be effaced, and I have never since fired a gun at any of the tribe. Almost immediately on my return to the party, before I had fully described what had passed, a Syer came to inform us that the monkey was dead. We ordered the Syer to bring it to us ; but by the time he returned the other monkeys had carried the dead one off, and none of them could anywhere be seen " (p. 475).

And Sir William Hoste records a closely similar case. One of his officers, coming home after a long day's shooting, saw a female monkey running along the rocks, with her young one in her arms. He immediately fired, and the animal fell. On his coming up, she grasped her little one close to her breast, and with her other hand pointed to the wound which the ball had made, and which had entered above her breast. Dipping her finger in the blood and holding it up, she seemed to reproach him with having been the cause of her pain, and also of that of the young one, to which she frequently pointed. " I never," says Sir William, " felt so much as when I heard the story, and I determined never to shoot one of these animals as long as I lived " (p. 476).

Lastly, as proof that the more intelligent of the lower animals admit of being *taught the use of signs of the most conventional character* (or most remote from any natural expression of their feelings and ideas), I may allude to the recent experiments by Sir John Lubbock on "teaching animals to converse." These experiments consisted in writing on separate and similar cards such words as " bone," " water," "out," " pet me," &c., and teaching a dog to bring a card bearing the word expressive of his want at the time of bringing it. In this way an association of ideas was established between the appearance of a certain number and form of written signs, and the meaning which they severally betokened. Sir John Lubbock found that his dog learnt the correct use of those signs.* Of course in these experiments marks of

* *Nature*, April 10, 1884, pp. 547, 548.

any other kind would have served as well as written words ; for it clearly would be absurd to suppose that the dog could read the letters, so as mentally to construct them into the equivalent of a spoken word, in any such way as a child would spell b-o-n-e, bone. But, all the same, these experiments are of great interest as showing that it falls within the mental capacity of the more intelligent animals to appreciate the use of signs so conventional as those which constitute a stage of writing *above* the drawing of pictures, and *below* the employment of an alphabet.

Enough has now been said to prove incontestably that animals present what I have called the germ of the sign-making faculty. As the main object of these chapters is to estimate the probability of human language having arisen by way of a continuous development from this germ, we may next turn to take a general survey of human language in its largest sense, or as comprising all the manifestations of the sign-making faculty.

Referring again to the schema (page 88), it is needless to consider cases 1 and 2, for evidently these are on a psychological level in man and animals. Case 3, also, especially in the direction of its branch 4, is to a large extent psychologically equivalent in men and animals: so far as there is any difference it depends on the higher psychical nature of man being much more rich in ideas which find their natural expression in gestures or tones, and which, therefore, are impossible in brutes. But it will be conceded that here there is nothing to explain. The fact that man has a mind more richly endowed with ideas carries with it, as a matter of course, the fact that their natural expression is more multiplex.

The case, however, is different when we arrive at conventional signs ; for these attain so enormous a development in man as compared with animals, that the question whether they do not really depend on some additional mental faculty, distinct in kind, becomes fully admissible.

The first thing, then, we have to notice with regard to conventional signs as used by man is, that no line of strict demarcation can be drawn between them and natural signs; the latter shade off into the former by gradations, which it becomes impossible to detect over large numbers of individual cases. With respect to tones, for example, it cannot be said, in many instances, whether this and that modulation, which is now recognized as expressive of a certain state of feeling, has always been thus expressive, or has only become so by conventional habit; although, if we consider the different tones by which different races of mankind express some of their similar feelings, we may be sure that in these cases one or other of the differences must be due to conventional habit—just as in the converse cases, in which all mankind use the same tones to express the same feelings, we may be sure that this mode of expression is natural. And so with gestures. Many which at first sight we should, judging from our own feelings alone, suppose to be natural—such, for instance, as kissing—are shown by observation of primitive races to be conventional; while others which we should probably regard as conventional —such, for instance, as shrugging the shoulders—are shown by the same means to be natural.*

But for our present purposes it is clearly a matter of no consequence that we should be able to classify all signs as natural or conventional. For it is certain that animals employ both; and hence no distinction between the brute and the man can be raised on the question of the kind of signs which they severally employ as natural or conventional. This distinction, therefore, may in future be disregarded, and natural and conventional signs, *if made intentionally as signs*, I shall consider as identical. For the sake of method, however, I shall treat the sign-making faculty as exhibited by man in the order of its probable evolution ; and this means that I shall begin with the most natural, or least conventional, of the systems. This is the language of tone and gesture.

* For information on all these points, see Darwin, *Expression of the Emotions.*

8

# CHAPTER VI.

### TONE AND GESTURE.

TONE and Gesture, considered as means of communication, may be dealt with simultaneously. For while it cannot be said that either historically or psychologically one is prior to the other, no more can it be said that in the earliest phases of their development one is more expressive than the other. All the more intelligent of the lower animals employ both ; and the hissings, spittings, growlings, screamings, gruntings, cooings, &c., which in different species accompany as many different kinds of gesture, are assuredly not less expressive of the various kinds of feelings which are expressed. Again, in our own species, tone is quite as general, and, within certain limits, quite as expressive as gesture. Nay, even in fully developed speech, rational meaning is largely dependent for its conveyance upon slight differences of intonation. The five hundred words which go to constitute the Chinese language are raised to three times that number by the use of significant intonation ; and even in the most highly developed languages shades of meaning admit of being rendered in this way which could not be rendered in any other.

Nevertheless, the language of tone, like the language of gesture, clearly lies nearer to, and is more immediately expressive of the logic of recepts, than is the language of articulation. This is easily proved by all the facts at our disposal. We know that an infant makes considerable advance in the language of tone and gesture before it begins to speak; and, according to Dr. Scott, who has had a large experience

in the instruction of idiotic children, "those to whom there is
no hope of teaching more than the merest rudiments of speech,
are yet capable of receiving a considerable amount of knowledge by means of signs, and of expressing themselves by
them." * Lastly, among savages, it is notorious that tone,
gesticulation, and grimace play a much larger part in conversation than they do among ourselves. Indeed, we have
some, though not undisputed, evidence to show that in the
case of many savages gesticulation is so far a necessary aid
to articulation, that the latter without the former is but very
imperfectly intelligible. For example, "those who, like the
Arapahos, possess a very scanty vocabulary, pronounced in a
quasi-intelligible way, can hardly converse with one another
in the dark." † And, as Mr. Tylor says, "the array of
evidence in favour of the existence of tribes whose language
is incomplete without the help of gesture-signs, even for
things of ordinary import, is very remarkable." ‡ A fact
which, as he very properly adds, "constitutes a telling
argument in favour of the theory that the gesture-language
is the original utterance of mankind [as it is ontogenetically
in the individual man], out of which speech has developed
itself more or less fully among different tribes." ‡

In support of the same general conclusions I may here
also quote the following excellent remarks from Colonel
Mallery's laborious work on Gesture-language :— §

"The wishes and emotions of very young children are
conveyed in a small number of sounds, but in a great variety
of gestures and facial expressions. A child's gestures are intelligent long in advance of speech ; although very early and
persistent attempts are made to give it instruction in the
latter but none in the former, from the time when it begins
*risu cognoscere matrem.* It learns words only as they are

---

* Quoted by Tylor, *Early History of Mankind*, p. 80.
† Burton, *City of the Saints*, p. 151.
‡ *Loc. cit.*, p. 78.
§ *Sign-language among the North American Indians, &c.*, by Lieut.-Col. Garrick
Mallery (*First Annual Report of the Bureau of Ethnology, Washington*, 1881).

taught, and learns them through the medium of signs which are not expressly taught. Long after familiarity with speech, it consults the gestures and facial expressions of its parents and nurses, as if seeking thus to translate or explain their words. These facts are important in reference to the biologic law that the order of development of the individual is the same as that of the species. . . . The insane understand and obey gestures when they have no knowledge whatever of words. It is also found that semi-idiotic children who cannot be taught more than the merest rudiments of speech can receive a considerable amount of information through signs, and can express themselves by them. Sufferers from aphasia continue to use appropriate gestures. A stammerer, too, works his arms and features as if determined to get his thoughts out, in a manner not only suggestive of the physical struggle, but of the use of gestures as a hereditary expedient."

Words, then, in so far as they are not intentionally imitative of other sounds, and so approximate to gestures, are essentially more conventional than are tones immediately expressive of emotions, or bodily actions which appeal to the eye, and which, in so far as they are intentionally significant, are made, as far as possible, intentionally pictorial. Therefore, either to make or to understand these more conventional signs requires a higher order of mental evolution ; and on this account it is that we everywhere find the language of tone and gesture preceding that of articulate speech, as at once the more simple, more natural, and therefore more *primitive* means of conveying receptual ideas.

We find the same general truth exemplified in the fact that the language of tone and gesture is always resorted to by men who do not understand each others' articulate speech ; and although among the races in which gesture-language has been carried to its highest degree of elaboration most of the signs employed have become more or less conventional, in the main they are still pictorial. This is directly proved, without the need of special analysis, by the fact that the members of such races are able to communicate with one another in a manner so singularly complete that to an onlooker the result seems almost magical.

Thus "the Indians who have been shown over the civilized East have often succeeded in holding intercourse by means of their invention and application of principles, in what may be called the voiceless mother utterance, with white deaf-mutes, who surely have no semiotic code more nearly connected with that attributed to the Indians than is derived from their common humanity. They showed the greatest pleasure in meeting deaf-mutes, precisely as travellers in a foreign country are rejoiced to meet persons speaking their language." *

Again, Tylor says, "Gesture-language is substantially the same all the world over," and Mallery confirms this by the remark that "the writer's study not only sustains it, but shows a surprising number of signs for the same idea which are substantially identical, not only among savage tribes, but among all peoples that use gesture-signs with any freedom. Men, in groping for a mode of communication with each other, and using the same general methods, have been under many varying conditions and circumstances which have determined differently many conceptions and their semiotic execution, but there have also been many of both which were similar."

Such being the case, it is a matter of interest to determine the syntax of this language ; for we may be sure that by so doing we are at work upon the root-principles of the sign-making faculty where it arises out of the logic of recepts, and not upon the developed ramifications of this faculty where we find it wrought up into the more highly conventional logic of concepts characteristic of speech. But before I enter upon this branch of our subject, I shall say a few words to show to what a high degree of perfection gesture-language admits of being developed.

---

* Mallery, *loc. cit.*, p. 320. The author gives several very interesting records of such conversations, and adds that the mutes show more aptitude in understanding the Indians than *vice versa*, because to them "the 'action, action, action,' of Demosthenes is their only oratory, and not a heightening of it, however valuable."

Tylor observes :—"As a means of communication, there is no doubt that the Indian pantomime is not merely capable of expressing a few simple and ordinary notions, but that to the uncultured savage, with his few and material ideas, it is a very fair substitute for his scanty vocabulary." * And Colonel Mallery, in the admirable treatise already referred to, shows in detail to what a surprising extent this " Indian pantomime " is thus available as a substitute for speech. The following may be selected from among the numerous dialogues and discourses which he gives, and which all present the same general character. It is communicated by Mr. Ivan Pehoff, who took notes of the conversation at the time. The two conversers were Indians of different tribes.

"(1) *Kenaitze.*—Left hand raised to height of eye, palm outward, moved several times from right to left rapidly ; fingers extended and closed ; pointing to strangers with left hand. Right hand describes a curve from north to east.— 'Which of the north-eastern tribes is yours ? '

"(2) *Tennanal.*—Right hand, hollowed, lifted to mouth, then extended and describing waving line gradually descending from right to left. Left hand describing mountainous outline, apparently one peak rising above the other. Said by Chalidoolts to mean, 'Tenan-tnu-kohtana, Mountain-river-men.'

"(3) *K.*—Left hand raised to height of eye, palm outward, moved from right to left, fingers extended. Left index describes curve from east to west. Outline of mountain and river as in preceding sign.—'How many days from Mountain-river ? '

"(4) *T.*—Right hand raised towards index, and thumb forming first crescent and then ring. This repeated three times.—'Moon, new and full three times.'

"(5) Right hand raised, palm to front, index raised and lowered at regular intervals—'Walked.' Both hands imitating paddling of canoe, alternately right and left.—'Travelled three months on foot and by canoe.'

* *Loc. cit.*, p. 39.

"(6) Both arms crossed over breast, simulating shivering. —'Cold, winter.'

"(7) Right index pointing toward speaker.—'I'; left hand pointing to the west—'travelled westward.'

"(8) Right hand lifted cup-shaped to mouth—'Water.' Right hand describing waving line from right to left gradually descending, pointing to the west.—'River running westward.'

"(9) Right hand gradually pushed forward, palm upward, from height of breast. Left hand shading eyes; looking at great distance.—'Very wide.'

"(10) Left and right hands put together in shape of sloping shelter.—'Lodge, camp.'

"(11) Both hands lifted height of eye, palm inward, fingers spread.—'Many times.'

"(12) Both hands closed, palm outward, height of hips.—'Surprised.'

"(13) Index pointing from eye forward.—'See.'

"(14) Right hand held up, height of shoulder, three fingers extended, left hand pointing to me.—'Three white men.'

"(15) *K.*—Right hand pointing to me, left hand held up, three fingers extended.—'Three white men.'

"(16) Making Russian sign of cross—'Russians.'—'Were the three white men Russians?'

"(17) *T.*—Left hand raised, palm inward, two fingers extended sign of cross with right.—'Two Russians.'

"(18) Right hand extended, height of eye, palm outward, moved outward a little to right.—'No.'

"(19) One finger of left hand raised.—'One.'

"(20) Sign of cross with right.—'Russian.'

"(21) Right hand, height of eye, fingers closed and extended, palm outward a little to right.—'Yes.'

"(22) Right hand carried across chest, hand extended, palm upward, fingers and thumb closed as if holding something. Left hand in same position carried across the right, palm downward.—'Trade.'

"(23) Left hand upholding one finger, right pointing to me.—'One white man.'

"(24) Right hand held horizontally, palm downward, about four feet from ground.—'Small.'

"(25) Forming rings before eyes with index and thumb.— 'Eye-glasses.'

"(26) Right hand clinched, palm upward, in front of chest, thumb pointing inward.—'Gave one.'

"(27) Forming cup with right hand, simulating drinking. —'Drink.'

"(28) Right hand grasping chest repeatedly, fingers curved and spread.—'Strong.'

"(29) Both hands pressed to temple, and head moved from side to side.—'Drunk, headache.'

"(30) Both index fingers placed together extended, pointing forward.—'Together.'

"(31) Fingers interlaced repeatedly.—'Build.'

"(32) Left hand extended, fingers closed, placed slopingly against left.—'Camp.'

"(33) Both wrists placed against temples, hands curved upward and outward, fingers spread.—'Horns.'

"(34) Both hands horizontally lifted to height of shoulder, right arm extended gradually full length, hand drooping a little at the end.—'Long back, moose.'

"(35) Both hands upright, palm outward, fingers extended and spread, placing one before the other alternately.—'Trees, dense forest.'

"(36) Sign of cross.—'Russian.'

"(37) Motions of shooting again.—'Shot.'

"(38) Sign for moose (Nos. 33, 34); showing two fingers of left hand.—'Two.'

"(39) Sign for camp as before (No. 10).—'Camp.'

"(40) Right hand describing curve from east to west, twice.—'Two days.'

"(41) Left hand lifted height of mouth, back outward, fingers closed as if holding something; right hand simulating motion of tearing off, and placing in mouth.—'Eating moose meat.'

"(42) Right hand placed horizontally against heart;

fingers closed, moved forward a little and raised a little several times.—'Glad at heart.'

"(43) Fingers of left hand and index of right hand extended and placed together horizontally, pointing forward height of chest. Hands separated, right pointing eastward, and left westward.—'Three men and speaker parted, going west and east.'"

And so on, the conversation continuing up to 116 paragraphs. No doubt some of these gestures appear conventional, and such is undoubtedly the case with a great many which Colonel Mallery gives in his *Dictionary of Indian Signs*. But this only shows that no system of signs can be developed in any high degree without becoming more or less conventional. The point I desire to be noticed is, that gesture-language continues as far as possible—or as long as possible—to be the natural expression of the logic of recepts. As Mallery elsewhere observes, "the result of the studies, so far as presented is, that that which is called the sign-language of Indians is not, properly speaking, one language; but that it, and the gesture-systems of deaf-mutes, and of all peoples, constitute together one language—the gesture-speech of mankind—of which each system is a dialect." As showing this, and at the same time to give other instances of the perfection of gesture-language, I may quote one instance of the employment of such language by other nations, and one of its employment by deaf-mutes. The first which I select is recorded by Alexander Dumas.

"Six weeks after this, I saw a second example of this faculty of mute communication. This was at Naples. I was walking with a young man of Syracuse. We passed by a sentinel. The soldier and my companion exchanged two or three grimaces, which at another time I should not even have noticed; but the instances I had before seen led me to give attention. 'Poor fellow!' sighed my companion. 'What did he say to you?' I asked. 'Well,' said he, 'I thought that I recognized him as a Sicilian, and I learned from him, as we passed, from what place he came; he said he was from

Syracuse, and that he knew me well. Then I asked him how he liked the Neapolitan service; he said he did not like it at all, and if his officers did not treat him better he should certainly end by deserting. I then signified to him that if he ever should be reduced to that extremity, he might rely upon me, and that I would aid him all in my power. The poor fellow thanked me with all his heart, and I have no doubt that one day or other I shall see him come.' Three days after I was at the quarters of my Syracusan friend, when he was told that a man asked to see him who would not give his name; he went out and left me nearly ten minutes. 'Well,' said he on returning, 'just as I said.' 'What?' said I. 'That the poor fellow would desert.'"

The instance which I select of gesture-language as employed by a deaf-mute occurred in the National Deaf-Mute College at Washington, to which Colonel Mallery took seven Uta Indians on March 6, 1880.

"Another deaf-mute gestured to tell us that, when he was a boy, he went to a melon-field, tapped several melons, finding them to be green or unripe: finally, reaching a good one, he took his knife, cut a slice and ate it. A man made his appearance on horseback, entered the patch on foot, found the cut melon, and, detecting the thief, threw the melon towards him, hitting him in the back, whereupon he ran away crying. The man mounted and rode off in an opposite direction.

"All of these signs were readily comprehended, although some of the Indians varied very slightly in their translation. When the Indians were asked whether, if they (the deaf-mutes) were to come to the Uta country, they would be scalped, the answer was given, 'Nothing would be done to you; but we would be friends,' as follows :—

"The palm of the right hand was brushed toward the right over that of the left ('nothing'), and the right made to grasp the palm of the left, thumbs extended over, and lying upon the back of the opposing hand ('friends').

"This was readily understood by the deaf-mutes. Deaf-mute sign of milking a cow and drinking the milk was fully and quickly understood.

"The narrative of a boy going to an apple tree, hunting for ripe fruit, and filling his pockets, being surprised by the owner and hit upon the head with a stone, was much appreciated by the Indians and completely understood."

Innumerable other instances of the same kind might be given ;* but I have now said enough to establish the only points with which I am here concerned—namely, that gesture-language admits of being developed to a degree which renders it a fair substitute for spoken language, where the ideas to be conveyed are not highly abstract ; and that it admits of being so developed without departing further from a direct or natural expression of ideation (as distinguished from a conventional or artificial) than allows it to be readily understood by the sign-talkers, without any preconcerted agreement as to the meanings to be attached to the particular signs employed.

Such being the case, it is of importance next to note that, as all the existing races of mankind are a word-speaking race, we are not now able to eliminate this factor, and to say how far the sign-making faculty, as exhibited in the gesture-language of man, is indebted to the elaborating influence produced by the constant and parallel employment of spoken language. We can scarcely, however, entertain any doubt that the reflex influence of speech upon gesture must have been considerable, if not immense. Even the case of the deaf-mutes proves nothing to the contrary ; for these unfortunate individuals, although not able themselves to speak, nevertheless inherit in their human brains the psychological structure which has been built up by means of speech ; their sign-making *faculty* is as well developed as in other men, though, from a physiological accident, they are deprived of the ordinary means of displaying it. Therefore we have

* See especially Tylor, *loc. cit.*, pp. 28–30, where an interesting account is given of the elaborate and yet self-speaking signs whereby an adult deaf-mute gave directions for the drawing up of his will.

no evidence to show to what level of excellence the sign-making faculty of man would have attained, if the race had been destitute of the faculty of speech. I shall have to return to this consideration in the next chapter, and only mention it here to avoid an undue estimate being prematurely formed of the importance of gesture as a means of thought-formation, or distinct from that of thought-expression.

I shall now proceed to analyze in some detail the syntax of gesture-language. And here again I must depend for my facts upon the two writers who have best studied this kind of language in a properly scientific manner.

Mr. Tylor says :—" The gesture-language has no grammar, properly so called ; it knows no inflections of any kind, any more than the Chinese. The same sign stands for ' walk,' ' walkest,' ' walking,' ' walked,' ' walker.' Adjectives and verbs are not easily distinguished by the deaf and dumb. ' Horse, black, handsome, trot, canter,' would be the rough translation of the signs by which a deaf-mute would state that a black handsome horse trots and canters. Indeed, our elaborate system of parts of speech is but little applicable to the gesture-language, though, as will be more fully said in another chapter, it may perhaps be possible to trace in spoken language a Dualism, in some measure resembling that of the Gesture-language, with its two constituent parts, the bringing forward objects and actions in actual fact, and the mere suggestion of them by imitation. . . . It has, however, a syn-tax which is worthy of careful examination. The syntax of speaking man differs according to the language he may learn, ' equus niger,' ' a black horse ; ' ' hominem amo,' ' j'aime l'homme.' But the deaf-mute strings together the signs of the various ideas he wishes to connect, in what appears to be the natural order in which they follow one another in his mind, for it is the same among the mutes in different countries, and is wholly independent of the syntax which may happen to belong to the language of their speaking friends. For instance, their usual construction is not ' Black horse,' but ' Horse black ; ' not ' Bring a black hat,' but ' Hat black bring ; '

not 'I am hungry, give me bread,' but 'Hungry me, bread give.' . . .

"The fundamental principle which regulates the order of the deaf-mutes' signs, seems to be that enunciated by Schmalz: that which seems to him the most important he always acts before the rest, and that which seems to him superfluous he leaves out. For instance, to say, 'My father gave me an apple,' he makes the sign for 'apple,' then that for 'father,' and then that for 'I,' without adding that for 'give.' The following remarks, sent to me by Dr. Scott, seem to agree with this view: With regard to the two sentences you give (I struck Tom with a stick—Tom struck me with a stick), the sequence in the introduction of the particular parts would in some measure depend on the part that most attention was wished to be drawn towards. If a mere telling of the fact was required, my opinion is that it would be arranged so, 'I-Tom-struck-a-stick,' and the passive form in a similar manner with the change of 'Tom,' first.

"Both these sentences are not generally said by the deaf-and-dumb without their having been interested in the fact, and then, in coming to tell of them, they first give that part they are most anxious to impress on their hearer. Thus, if a boy had struck another boy, and the injured party came to tell us, if he was desirous to acquaint us with the idea that a particular boy did it, he would point to the boy first. But if he was anxious to draw attention to his own suffering, rather than to the person by whom it was caused, he would point to himself and make the act of striking, and then point to the boy; or if he was wishful to draw attention to the cause of his suffering, he might sign the striking first, and then tell us afterwards by whom it was done.

"Dr. Scott is, so far as I know, the only person who has attempted to lay down a set of distinct rules for the syntax of the gesture-language. 'The subject comes before the attribute, the object before the action.' A third construction is common, though not necessary, 'the modifier after the modified.' The first construction, by which the 'horse' is put before the 'black,' enables the deaf-mute to make his syntax supply, to some extent, the distinction between adjectives and substantives, which his imitative signs do not themselves express.

"The other two are well exemplified by a remark of the Abbé Sicard's : A pupil to whom I one day put this question, 'Who made God ?' and who replied, 'God made nothing,' left me in no doubt as to this kind of inversion, usual to the deaf-and-dumb, when I went on to ask him, 'Who made the shoe ?' and he answered, 'The shoe made the shoemaker.' So when Laura Bridgman, who was blind as well as deaf-and-dumb, had learnt to communicate ideas by spelling words on her fingers, she would say, 'Shut door,' 'Give book ;' no doubt because she had learnt these sentences whole, but when she made sentences for herself, she would go back to the natural deaf-and-dumb syntax, and spell out 'Laura bread give,' to ask for bread to be given her, and 'Water drink Laura,' to express that she wanted to drink water. . . .

"A look of inquiry converts an assertion into a question, and fully seems to make the difference between 'The master is come,' and 'Is the master come ?' The interrogative pronouns 'Who ?' 'What ?' are made by looking or pointing about in an inquiring manner ; in fact, by a number of unsuccessful attempts to say, 'he,' 'that.' The deaf-and-dumb child's way of asking, 'Who has beaten you ?' would be, 'You beaten ; who was it ?' Though it is possible to render a great mass of simple statements and questions, almost gesture for word, the concretism of thought which belongs to the deaf-mute, whose mind has not been much developed by the use of written language, and even to the educated one when he is thinking and uttering his thoughts in his native signs, commonly requires more complex phrases to be recast. A question so common amongst us as, 'What is the matter with you ?' would be put, 'You crying ? You have been beaten ?' and so on. The deaf-and-dumb child does not ask, 'What did you have for dinner yesterday ?' but 'Did you have soup ? Did you have porridge ?' and so forth. A con-

junctive sentence he expresses by an alternative or contrast ;
'I should be punished if I were lazy and naughty,' would be
put, 'I lazy, naughty, no!—lazy, naughty, I punished, yes!'
Obligation may be expressed in a similar way ; 'I must love
and honour my teacher,' may be put, 'Teacher, I beat, deceive,
scold, no!—I love, honour, yes!' As Steinthal says in his
admirable essay, it is only the certainty which speech gives to
a man's mind in holding fast ideas in all their relations,
which brings him to the shorter course of expressing only the
positive side of the idea, and dropping the negative. . . .

"To 'make' is too abstract an idea for the deaf-mute ; to
show that the tailor makes the coat, or that the carpenter
makes the table, he would represent the tailor sewing the
coat, and the carpenter sawing and planing the table. Such
a proposition as 'Rain makes the land fruitful,' would not
come into his way of thinking: 'rain fall, plants grow,'
would be his pictorial expression. . . . The order of the signs
by which the Lord's Prayer is rendered is much as follows : —
'Father our, heaven in—name Thy hallowed—kingdom Thy
come—will Thy done—earth on, heaven in, as. Bread give us
daily—trespasses our forgive us, them trespass against us,
forgive as. Temptation lead not—but evil deliver from—
Kingdom power glory thine for ever.'" *

I shall now add some quotations from Colonel Mallery on
the same subject.

"The reader will understand without explanation that
there is in sign-language no organized sentence such as is in
the language of civilization, and that he must not look for
articles or particles, or passive voice or case or grammatic
gender, or even what appears in those languages as a
substantive or a verb, as a subject or a predicate, or as
qualifiers or inflexions. The sign radicals, without being
specifically any of our parts of speech, may be all of them in
turn. Sign-language cannot show by inflection the reciprocal
dependence of words and sentences. Degrees of motion
corresponding with vocal intonations are only used rhetori-

* *Early History of Mankind*, pp. 24–32.

cally, or for degrees of comparison, The relations of ideas and objects are therefore expressed by placement, and their connection is established when necessary by the abstraction of ideas. The sign-talker is an artist, grouping persons and things so as to show the relations, and the effect is that which is seen in a picture. But though the artist has the advantage in presenting in a permanent connected scene the result of several transient signs, he can only present it as it appears at a single moment. The sign-talker has the succession of time at his disposal, and his scenes move and act, are localized and animated, and their arrangement is therefore more varied and significant." *

The following is the order in which the parable of the Prodigal Son would be translated by a cultivated sign-talker, with Colonel Mallery's remarks thereon :—

"'Once, man one, sons two. Son younger say, Father property your divide : part my, me give. Father so.—Son each, part his give. Days few after, son younger money all take, country far go, money spend, wine drink, food nice eat. Money by and by gone all. Country everywhere food little : son hungry very. Go seek man any, me hire. Gentleman meet. Gentleman son send field swine feed. Son swine husks eat, see—self husks eat want—cannot—husks him give nobody. Son thinks, say, father my, servants many, bread enough, part give away can—I none—starve, die. I decide : Father I go to; say I bad, God disobey, you disobey—name my hereafter *son*, no—I unworthy. You me work give servant like. So son begin go. Father far look : son see, pity, run, meet, embrace. Son father say, I bad, you disobey, God disobey— name my hereafter *son*, no—I unworthy. But father servants call, command robe best bring, son put on, ring finger put on, shoes feet put on, calf fat bring, kill. We all eat, merry. Why? Son this my formerly dead, now alive: formerly lost, now found : rejoice.'

"It may be remarked, not only from this example, but from general study, that the verb 'to be' as a copula or

* *Loc. cit.*, p. 54.

predicant does not have any place in sign-language. It is
shown, however, among deaf-mutes as an assertion of presence
or existence by a sign of stretching the arms and hands
forward and then adding the sign of affirmation. *Time* as
referred to in the conjunctions *when* and *then* is not gestured.
Instead of the form, 'When I have had a sleep I will go to
the river,' or 'After sleeping I will go to the river,' both deaf-
mutes and Indians would express the intention by 'Sleep done,
I river go.' Though time present, past, and future is readily
expressed in signs, it is done once for all in the connection to
which it belongs, and once established is not repeated by any
subsequent intimation, as is commonly the case in oral speech.
Inversion, by which the object is placed before the action, is
a striking feature of the language of deaf-mutes, and it
appears to follow the natural method by which objects and
actions enter into the mental conception. In striking a rock
the natural conception is not first of the abstract idea of
striking or of sending a stroke into vacancy, seeing nothing
and having no intention of striking anything in particular,
when suddenly a rock rises up to the mental vision and
receives the blow; the order is that the man sees the rock,
has the intention to strike it, and does so; therefore he
gestures, 'I rock strike.' For further illustration of this
subject, a deaf-mute boy, giving in signs the compound action
of a man shooting a bird from a tree, first represented the
tree, then the bird as alighting upon it, then a hunter coming
toward and looking at it, taking aim with a gun, then the
report of the latter and the falling and the dying gasps of
the bird. These are undoubtedly the successive steps that an
artist would have taken in drawing the picture, or rather
successive pictures, to illustrate the story. . . . Degrees of
comparison are frequently expressed, both by deaf-mutes and
by Indians, by adding to the generic or descriptive sign that
for 'big' or 'little.' *Damp* would be 'wet—little'; *cool*, 'cold
—little'; *hot*, 'warm—much.' The amount or force of motion
also often indicates corresponding diminution or augmenta-
tion, but sometimes expresses a different shade of meaning,

9

as is reported by Dr. Matthews with reference to the sign for *bad* and *contempt.* This change in degree of motion is, however, often used for emphasis only, as is the raising of the voice in speech or italicizing and capitalizing in print. The Prince of Wied gives an instance of a comparison in his sign for *excessively hard,* first giving that for *hard,* viz. : Open the left hand, and strike against it several times with the right (with the backs of the fingers). Afterwards he gives *hard, excessively,* as follows : Sign for *hard,* then place the left index finger upon the right shoulder, at the same time extend and raise the right arm high, extending the index finger upward, perpendicularly."

I have entered thus at some length into the syntax of gesture-language because this language is, as I have before remarked, the most natural or immediate mode of giving expression to the logic of recepts ; it is the least symbolic or conventional phase of the sign-making faculty, and therefore a study of its method is of importance in such a general survey of this faculty as we are endeavouring to take. The points in the above analysis to which I would draw attention as the most important are, the absence of the copula and of many other "parts of speech," the order in which ideas are expressed, the pictorial devices by which the ideas are presented in as concrete a form as possible, and the fact that no ideas of any high abstraction are ever expressed at all.*

---

* Further information of a kind corroborating what has been given in the foregoing chapter concerning gesture-language may be found in Long's *Expedition to the Rocky Mountains,* and Kleinpaul's paper in *Völkerpsychologie, &c.,* vi. 352–375. The subject was first dealt with in a philosophical manner by Leibnitz, in 1717, *Collectanea Etymologia,* ch. ix.

# CHAPTER VII.

## ARTICULATION.

IT will be my aim in this chapter to take a broad view of Articulation as a special development of the general faculty of sign-making, reserving for subsequent chapters a consideration of the philosophy of Speech.

On the threshold of articulate language, then, we have four several cases to distinguish: first, articulation by way of meaningless imitation; second, meaningless articulation by way of a spontaneous or instinctive exercise of the organs of speech; third, understanding of the signification of articulate sounds, or words; and fourth, articulation with an intentional attribution of the meaning understood as attaching to the words. I shall consider each of these cases separately.

The meaningless imitation of articulate sounds occurs in talking birds, young children, not unfrequently in savages, in idiots, and in the mentally deranged. The faculty of such meaningless imitation, however, need not detain us; for it is evident that the mere re-echoing of a verbal sound is of no further psychological significance than is the mimicking of any other sound.

Meaningless articulation of a spontaneous or instinctive kind occurs in young children, in uneducated deaf-mutes, and also in idiots.* Infants usually (though not invariably) begin

---

* For meaningless articulation by idiots, see Scott's *Remarks on Education of Idiots*. The fact is alluded to by most writers on idiot psychology, and I have frequently observed it myself. But the case of uneducated deaf-mutes is here more

with such syllables as "alla," "tata," "mama," and "papa' (with or without the reduplication) before they understand the meaning of any word.　One of my own children could say all these syllables very distinctly at the age of eight months and a half; and I could detect no evidence at that time of his understanding words, or of his having learnt these syllabic utterances by imitation.　Another child of mine, which was very long in beginning to speak, at fourteen and a half months old said once, and only once, but very distinctly "Ego."　This was certainly not said in imitation of any one having uttered the word in her presence, and therefore I mention the incident to show that meaningless articulation in young children is spontaneous or instinctive, as well as intentionally imitative ; for at that age the only other syllables which this child had uttered were those having the long *ā*, as above mentioned.　Were it necessary, I could give many other instances of this fact ; but, as it is generally recognized by writers on infant psychology, I need not wait to do so.

We now come to the third of our divisions, or the understanding of articulate sounds.　And this is an important matter for us, because it is evident that the faculty of appreciating the meaning of words betokens a considerable advance in the general faculty of language.　As we have before seen, tone and gesture, being the natural expression of the logic of recepts—and so even in their most elaborated forms being intentionally pictorial,—are as little as possible conventional ;

to the purpose.　I will, therefore, furnish one quotation in evidence of the above statement.　" It is a very notable fact bearing upon the problem of the Origin of Language, that even born-mutes, who never heard a word spoken, do of their own accord and without any teaching make vocal sounds more or less articulate, to which they attach a definite meaning, and which, when once made, they go on using afterwards in the same unvarying sense.　Though these sounds are often capable of being written down more or less accurately with our ordinary alphabets, this effect on those who make them can, of course, have nothing to do with the sense of hearing, but must consist only in particular ways of breathing, combined with particular positions of the vocal organs " (Tylor, *Early History of Mankind,* p. 72, where see for evidence).　The instinctive articulations of Laura Bridgman (who was blind as well as deaf) are in this connection even still more conclusive (see *ibid.,* pp. 74, 75).

but words, being coined expressly for the subservience of concepts, are always less graphic, and usually arbitrary. Therefore, although it would of course be wrong to say that a higher faculty is required to learn the arbitrary association between a particular verbal sound and a particular act or phenomenon, than is required to depict an abstract idea in gesture; this only shows that where higher faculties are present, they are able to display themselves in gesture as well as in speech. The consideration which I now wish to present is that understanding a word implies (other things equal, or supposing the gesture not to be so purely conventional as a word) a higher development of the sign-making faculty than does the understanding of a tone or gesture—so that, for instance, if an animal were to understand the word "Whip," it would show itself more intelligent in appreciating signs than it would by understanding the gesture of threatening as with a whip.

Now, the higher animals unquestionably do understand the meanings of words; idiots too low in the scale themselves to speak are in the same position; and infants learn the signification of many articulate sounds long before they begin themselves to utter them.* In all these cases it is of course important to distinguish between the understanding of words and the understanding of tones; for, as already observed, both in the animal kingdom and in the growing child it is evident that the former represents a much higher grade of mental evolution than does the latter—a fact so obvious to common observation that I need not wait to give illustrations. But although the fact is obvious, it is no easy matter to distinguish in particular cases whether the understanding is due to an appreciation of words, to that of tones, or to both combined.

---

* Writers on infant psychology differ as to the time when words are first understood by infants. Doubtless it varies in individual cases, and is always more or less difficult to determine with accuracy. But all observers agree—and every mother or nurse could corroborate—that the understanding of many words and sentences is unmistakable long before the child itself begins to speak. Mr. Darwin's observations showed that in the case of his children the understanding of words and sentences was unmistakable between the tenth and twelfth months.

We may be sure, however, that words are never understood unless tones are likewise so, and that understanding of words may be assisted by understanding of the tones in which they are uttered. Therefore, the only method of ascertaining where words as such are first understood, is to find where they are first understood irrespective of the tones in which they are uttered. This criterion—so far, at least, as my evidence goes —excludes all cases of animals obeying commands, answering to their names, &c., with the exception of the higher mammalia. That is to say, while the understanding of certain tones of the human voice extends at least through the entire vertebrated series,* and occurs in infants only a few weeks old ; the understanding of words without the assistance of tones appears to occur only in a few of the higher mammalia, and first dawns in the growing child during the second year.†

The fact that the more intelligent Mammalia are able to understand words irrespective of tones is, as I have said, important ; and therefore I shall devote a few sentences to prove it.

My friend Professor Gerald Yeo had a terrier, which was taught to keep a morsel of food on its snout till it received the verbal signal " Paid for ; " and it was of no consequence in what tones these words were uttered. For even if they were introduced in an ordinary stream of conversation, the dog distinguished them, and immediately tossed the food into his mouth. Seeing this, I thought it worth while to try whether the animal would be able to distinguish the words " Paid for " from others presenting a close similarity of sound ;

---

* See *Animal Intelligence :* for Fish, p. 250 ; for Frogs and Toads, p. 225 ; for Snakes, p. 261 ; for Birds and Mammals in various parts of the chapters devoted to these animals.  The case quoted on the authority of Bingley regarding the tame bees of Mr. Wildman, which he had taught to obey words of command (p. 189), would, if corroborated, carry the faculty in question into the invertebrate series.

† Although the ages at which talking proper begins varies much in different children, it may be taken as a universal rule—as stated in the last foot-note— that words, and even sentences, are understood long before they are intelligently articulated ; although, as previously remarked, even before any words are *understood* meaningless syllables may be spontaneously or instinctively articulated.

and, therefore, while he was expecting the signal, I said "Pinafore;" the dog gave a start, and very nearly threw the food off his nose; but immediately arrested the movement, evidently perceiving his mistake. This experiment was repeated many times with these two closely similar verbal sounds, and always with the same result: the dog clearly distinguished between them. I have more recently repeated this experiment on another terrier, which had been taught the same trick, and obtained exactly the same results.

The well-known anecdote told of the poet Hogg may be fitly alluded to in this connection. A Scotch collie was able to understand many things that his master said to him, and, as proof of his ability, his master, while in the shepherd's cottage, said in as calm and natural tone as possible, "I'm thinking the cow's in the potatoes." Immediately the dog, which had been lying half asleep on the floor, jumped up, ran into the potato-field, round the house, and up the roof to take a survey; but finding no cow in the potatoes, returned and lay down again. Some little time afterwards his master said as quietly as before, "I'm sure the cow's in the potatoes," when the same scene was repeated. But on trying it a third time, the dog only wagged his tail. Similarly, Sir Walter Scott, among other anecdotes of his bull terrier, says:—"The servant at Ashestiel, when laying the cloth for dinner, would say to the dog as he lay on the mat by the fire, 'Camp, my good fellow, the sheriff's coming home by the ford,' or 'by the hill;' and the poor animal would immediately go forth to welcome his master, advancing as far and as fast as he was able in the direction indicated by the words addressed to him." And numberless other anecdotes of the same kind might be quoted.*

But the most remarkable display of the faculty in question on the part of a brute which has happened to fall under my own observation, is that which many other English naturalists must have noticed in the case of the chimpanzee now in the

---

* See, for instance, Watson's *Reasoning Power in Animals*, pp. 137–149, and Meunier's *Les Animaux Perfectibles*, ch. xii.

Zoologica, Gardens. This ape has learnt from her keeper the meanings of so many words and phrases, that in this respect she resembles a child shortly before it begins to speak. Moreover, it is not only particular words and particular phrases which she has thus learnt to understand; she also understands, to a large extent, the combination of these words and phrases in sentences, so that the keeper is able to explain to the animal what it is that he requests her to do. For example, she will push a straw through any particular meshes in the network of her cage which he may choose successively to indicate by such phrases as—" The one nearest your foot; now the one next the key-hole; now the one above the bar," &c., &c. Of course there is no pointing to the places thus verbally designated, nor is any order observed in the designation. The animal understands what is meant by the words alone, and this even when a particular mesh is named by the keeper remarking to her the accident of its having a piece of straw already hanging through it.

In connection with the subject of the present treatise it appears to me difficult to overrate the significance of these facts. The more that my opponents maintain the fundamental nature of the connection between speech and thought, the greater becomes the importance of the consideration that the higher animals are able in so surprising a degree to participate with ourselves in the understanding of words. From the analogy of the growing child we well know that the understanding of words precedes the utterance of them, and therefore that the condition to the attainment of conceptual ideation is given in this higher product of receptual ideation. Surely, then, the fact that not a few among the lower animals (especially elephants, dogs, and monkeys) demonstrably share with the human infant this higher excellence of receptual capacity, is a fact of the largest significance. For it proves at least that these animals share with an infant those qualities of mind, which in the latter are immediately destined to serve as the vehicle for elevating ideation from the receptual to the conceptual sphere : the faculty of understanding words in so considerable a degree brings us to the very borders of the faculty of using words with an intelligent appreciation of their meaning.

Familiarity with the facts now before us is apt to blunt this their extraordinary significance ; and therefore I invite my opponents to reflect how differently my case would have stood, supposing that none of the lower animals had happened to have been sufficiently intelligent thus to understand the meanings of words. How much greater would then have been the argumentative advantage of any one who undertook to prove the distinctively human prerogative of the Logos. No mere brute, it might have been urged, has ever displayed so much as the first step in approaching to this faculty : from its commencement to its termination the faculty belongs exclusively to mankind. But, as matters actually stand, this cannot be urged : the lower animals share with us the order of ideation which is concerned in the understanding of words— and words, moreover, so definite and particular in meaning as is involved in explaining the particular mesh in a large piece of wire-netting through which it is required that a straw shall be protruded. While watching this most remark- able performance on the part of the chimpanzee, I felt more than ever disposed to agree with the great philologist Geiger, where he says " there is scarcely a more wonderful relation- ship upon the earth than this accession [*i.e.* the understanding of words] by the intelligence of animals to that of man."*

I take it then, as certainly proved, that the germ of the sign-making faculty which is present in the higher animals is so far developed as to enable these animals to understand not merely conventional gestures, but even articulate sounds, irrespective of the tones in which they are uttered. There- fore, in view of this fact, together with the fact previously established that these same animals frequently make use of conventional gesture-signs themselves, I think we are justified in concluding *a priori*, that if these animals were able to articulate, they would employ simple words to express simple

* *Ursprung der Sprache,* p. 122.

ideas. I do not say, nor do I think, that they would form propositions ; but it seems to me little less than certain that they would use articulate sounds, as they now use natural or conventional tones and gestures, to express such ideas as they now express in either of these ways. For instance, it would involve the exercise of no higher psychical faculty to say the word " Come," than it does to pull at a dress or a coat to convey the same idea ; or to utter the word " Open," instead of mewing in a conventional manner before a closed door; or, yet again, to utter the word " Bone," than to select and carry a card with the word written upon it. If this is so, we must conclude that the only reason why the higher Mammalia do not employ simple words to convey simple ideas, is that which we may term an accidental reason, so far as their psychology is concerned ; it is an anatomical reason, depending merely on the structure of their vocal organs not admitting of articulation.*

Of course at this point my attention will be called to the case of talking birds ; for it is evident that in them we have the anatomical conditions required for speech, though assuredly occurring at a most unlikely place in the animal series ; and therefore these animals may be properly

* Some cases are on record of dogs having been taught to articulate. Thus the thoughtful Leibnitz vouches for the fact (which he communicated to the *Académie Royale* at Paris, and which that body said they would have doubted had it not been observed by so eminent a man), that he had heard a peasant's dog distinctly articulate thirty words, which it had been taught to say by the peasant's son. The *Dumfries Journal*, January, 1829, mentions a dog as then living in that town, who uttered distinctly the word " William," which was the name of a person to whom he was attached. Again, Colonel Mallery writes :—" Some recent experiments of Prof. A. Graham Bell, no less eminent from his work in artificial speech than in telephones, shows that animals are more physically capable of pronouncing articulate sounds than has been supposed. He informed the writer that he recently succeeded by manipulation in causing an English terrier to form a number of the sounds of our letters, and particularly brought out from it the words 'How are you, grandmama,' with distinctness." As I believe that the barrier to articulation in dogs is anatomical and not psychological, I regard it as merely a question of observation whether this barrier may not in some cases be partly overcome ; but, as far as the evidence goes, I think it is safer to conclude that the instances mentioned consisted in the animals so modulating the tones of their voices as to resemble the sounds of certain words.

adduced to test the validity of my *a priori* inference—namely, that if the more intelligent brutes could articulate, they would make a proper use of simple verbal signs. Let it, however, be here remembered that birds are lower in the psychological scale than dogs, or cats, or monkeys ; and, therefore, that the inference which I drew touching the latter need not necessarily be held as applying also to the former. Nevertheless, it so happens that even in the case of these psychologically inferior animals the evidence, such as it is, is not opposed to my inference : on the contrary, there is no small body of facts which goes to support it in a very satisfactory manner. A consideration of this evidence will now serve to introduce us to the fourth and last case presented in the programme at the beginning of this chapter, or the case of articulation with attribution of the meaning understood as attaching to the words.

Taking, first, the case of proper names, it is unquestionable that many parrots know perfectly well that certain names belong to certain persons, and that the way to call these persons is to call their appropriate names. I knew a parrot which used thus to call its mistress as intelligently as any other member of the household ; and if she went from home for a day, the bird became a positive nuisance from its incessant calling for her to come.

And in a similar manner talking birds often learn correctly to assign the names of other pet animals kept in the same house, or even the names of inanimate objects. There can thus be no question as to the use by talking birds of proper names and noun-substantives.

With respect to adjectives, Houzeau very properly remarks that the apposite manner in which some parrots habitually use certain words shows an aptitude correctly to perceive and to name qualities as well as objects. Nor is this anything more than we might expect, seeing, on the one hand, as already shown, that animals possess generic ideas of many qualities, and, on the other, that an obvious quality is as much a matter of immediate observation—and so of sensuous association—as is the object of which it may happen to be a quality.

Again, it is no less certain that many parrots will understand the meaning of active and passive verbs, whether as uttered by others or by themselves. The request to " Scratch Poll " or the anouncement " Poll is thirsty," when intentionally used as signs, show as true an appreciation of the meaning of verbs—or rather, let us say, of verbal signs indicative of actions and states—as is shown by the gesture-sign of a dog or a cat in pulling one's dress to indicate " come," or mewing before an open door to signify " open."

But not only may talking birds attach appropriate significations to nouns, adjectives, and verbs ; they may even use short sentences in a way serving to show that they appreciate —not, indeed, their grammatical structure—but their applicability as a whole to particular circumstances.* But this again is not a matter to excite surprise. For all such

---

* Mr. Darwin writes :—"It is certain that some parrots, which have been taught to speak, connect unerringly words with things, and persons with events. I have received several detailed accounts to this effect. Admiral Sir J. Sullivan, whom I know to be a careful observer, assures me that an African parrot, long kept in his father's house, invariably called certain persons of the household, as well as visitors, by their names. He said ' Good morning ' to every one at breakfast, and ' Good night ' to each as they left the room at night, and never reversed these salutations. To Sir J. Sullivan's father he used to add to the ' good morning ' a short sentence, which was never repeated after his father's death. He scolded violently a strange dog which came into the room through an open window, and he scolded another parrot (saying, ' You naughty polly ! '), which had got out of its cage, and was eating apples on the kitchen table. Dr. A. Moschkan informs me that he knew a starling which never made a mistake in saying in German ' good morning ' to persons arriving, and ' good-bye, old fellow ' to those departing. I could add several other cases " (*Descent of Man*, p. 85). Similarly Houzeau gives some instances of nearly the same kind (*Fac. Ment. des Anim.*, tom. ii., p. 309, *et seq.*) ; and Mrs. Lee, in her *Anecdotes* records several still more remarkable cases (which are quoted by Houzeau), as does also M. Meunier in his recently published work on *Les Animaux Perfectibles*. In my own correspondence I have received numerous letters detailing similar facts, and from these I gather that parrots often use comical phrases when they desire to excite laughter, pitiable phrases when they desire to excite compassion, and so on ; although it does not follow from this that the birds understand the meanings of these phrases, further than that they are as a whole appropriate to excite the feelings which it is desired to excite. I have myself kept selected parrots, and can fully corroborate all the above statements from my own observations.

instances of the apposite use of words or phrases by talking birds are found on inquiry to be due, as antecedently we should expect that they must, to the principle of association. The bird hears a proper name applied to a person, and so, on learning to say the name, henceforth associates it with that person. And similarly with phrases. These with talking birds are mere vocal gestures, which in themselves present but little more psychological significance than muscular gestures. The verbal petition, " Scratch poor poll," does not in itself display any further psychological development than the significant gesture already alluded to of depressing the head against the bars of the cage; and similarly with all cases of the appropriate use of longer phrases. Thus, supposing it to be due to association alone, a verbal sign of any kind is not much more remarkable, or indicative of intelligence, than is a gesture sign, or a vocal sign of any other kind. The only respect in which it differs from such other signs is in the fact that it is wholly arbitrary or conventional; and although, as I have previously said, I do consider this an important point of difference, I am not at all surprised that even the intelligence of a bird admits of such special associations being formed, or that a wholly arbitrary sign of any kind should here be acquired by this means, and afterwards used as a sign.

And that the verbal signs used by talking birds are due to association, and association only, all the evidence I have met with goes to prove. As showing how association acts in this case, I may quote the following remarks of Dr. Samuel Wilks, F.R.S., on his own parrot, which he carefully observed. He says that when alone this bird used to " utter a long catalogue of its sayings, more especially if it heard talking at a distance, as if wishing to join in the conversation, but at other times a particular word or phrase is only spoken when suggested by a person or object. Thus, certain friends who have addressed the bird frequently by some peculiar expression, or the whistling of an air, will always be welcomed by the same words or tune, and as regards myself, when I enter the house—for my footstep is recognized—the bird will repeat one of my sayings. If the servants enter the room Poll will be ready with one of their expressions, and in their own tone of voice. It is clear that there is a close association in the bird's mind between certain phrases and certain persons or objects, for their presence or voice at once suggests some special word. For instance, my coachman, when coming for orders, has so often been told half-past two, that no sooner does he come to the door than Poll exclaims, ' Half-past two.' Again, having at night found her awake, and having said, 'Go to sleep,' if I have approached the cage after dark the same words have been repeated. Then, as regards objects, if certain words have been spoken in connection with them, these are ever afterwards associated together. For example, at dinner time the parrot, having been accustomed to have savory morsels given to her, I taught her to say, ' Give me a bit.' This she now constantly repeats, but only and appropriately at dinner-time. The bird associates the expression with something to eat, but, of course, knows no more than the infant the derivation of the words she is using. Again, being very fond of cheese, she easily picked up the word, and always asks for cheese towards the end of the dinner course, and at no other time. Whether the bird attaches the word to the true substance or not I cannot say, but the time of asking for it is always correct. She is also fond of nuts, and when these are on the table she utters a peculiar squeak ; this she has not been taught, but it is Poll's own name for nuts, for the sound is never heard until the fruit is in sight. Some noises which she utters have been obtained from the objects themselves, as that of a cork-screw at the sight of a bottle of wine, or the noise of water poured into a tumbler on seeing a bottle of water. The passage of the servant down the hall to open the front door suggests a noise of moving hinges, followed by a loud whistle for a cab."*

Concerning the accuracy of these observations I have no doubt, and I could corroborate most of them were it necessary.

* *Journal of Mental Science,* July, 1879.

It appears, then, first, that talking birds may learn to associate certain words with certain objects and qualities, certain other words or phrases with the satisfaction of particular desires and the observation of particular actions ; words so used we may term vocal-gestures. Second, that they may invent sounds of their own contriving, to be used in the same way ; and that these sounds may be either imitative of the objects designated, as the sound of running fluid for " Water," or arbitrary, as the " particular squeak " that designated " Nuts." Third, but that in a much greater number of cases the sounds (verbal or otherwise) uttered by talking birds are imitative only, without the animals attaching to them any particular meaning. The third division, therefore, we may neglect as presenting no psychological import ; but the first and second divisions require closer consideration.

In designating as "vocal gestures " * the correct use (acquired by direct association) of proper names, noun-substantives, adjectives, verbs, and short phrases, I do not mean to disparage the faculty which is displayed. On the contrary, I think this faculty is precisely the same as that whereby children first learn to talk ; for, like the parrot, the infant learns by direct association the meanings of certain words (or sounds) as denotative of certain objects, connotative of certain qualities, expressive of certain desires, actions, and so on. The only difference is that, in a few months after its first commencement in the child, this faculty develops into proportions far surpassing those which it presents in the bird, so that the vocabulary becomes much larger and more discriminative. But the important thing to attend to is that at first, and for several months after its commencement, the vocabulary of a child is always designative of particular objects, qualities, actions, or desires, and is acquired by direct association. The distinctive peculiarity of human speech, which elevates it above the region of animal gesticulation, is of later growth—the peculiarity, I mean, of using words, no

---

* This term has been previously used by some philologists to signify ejaculation by man. It will be observed that I use it in a more extended sense.

longer as stereotyped in the framework of special and direct association, but as movable types to be arranged in any order that the meaning before the mind may dictate. When this stage is reached, we have the faculty of predication, or of the grammatical formation of sentences which are no longer of the nature of vocal gestures, designative of particular objects, qualities, actions, or states of mind : but vehicles for the conveyance of ever-changing thoughts.

We shall presently see that this distinction between the naming and the predicating phases of language is of the highest importance in relation to the subject of the present treatise ; but meanwhile all we have to note is that the naming phase of spoken language occurs—in a rudimentary form, indeed, but still unquestionably—in the animal kingdom ; and that the fact of its doing so is not surprising, if we remember that in this stage language is nothing more than vocal gesticulation. Psychologically considered, there is nothing more remarkable in the fact that a bird which is able to utter an articulate sound should learn by association to use that sound as a conventional sign, than there is that it should learn by association similarly to use a muscular action, as it does in the act of depressing its head as a sign to have it scratched. Therefore we may now, I think, take the position as established *a posteriori* as well as *a priori*, that it is, so to speak, a mere accident of anatomy that all the higher animals are not able thus far to talk ; and that, if dogs or monkeys were able to do so, we have no reason to doubt that their use of words and phrases would be even more extensive and striking than that which occurs in birds. Or as Professor Huxley observes, " a race of dumb men, deprived of all communication with those who could speak, would be little indeed removed from the brutes. The moral and intellectual differences between them and ourselves would be practically infinite, though the naturalist should not be able to find a single shadow even of specific structural difference.*

* *Man's Place in Nature,* p. 52. I may here appropriately allude to a paper which elicited a good deal of discussion some years ago. It was read before the

We must next briefly consider the remaining feature in the psychology of talking birds to which Dr. Wilks has drawn attention, namely, that of inventing sounds of their own contrivance to be used as designative of objects and qualities,

Victoria Institute in March, 1872, by Dr. Frederick Bateman, under the title "Darwinism tested by Recent Researches in Language;" and its object was to argue that the faculty of articulate speech constitutes a difference of kind between the psychology of man and that of the lower animals. This argument Dr. Bateman sought to establish, first on the usual grounds that no animals are capable of using words with any degree of understanding, and, second, on grounds of a purely anatomical kind. In the text I fully deal with the first allegation: as a matter of fact, many of the lower animals understand the meanings of many words, while those of them which are alone capable of imitating our articulate sounds not unfrequently display a correct appreciation of their use as signs. But what I have here especially to consider is the anatomical branch of Dr. Bateman's argument. He says :—"As the remarkable similarity between the brain of man and that of the ape cannot be disputed, if the seat of human speech could be positively traced to any particular part of the brain, the Darwinian could say that, although the ape could not speak, he possessed the germ of that faculty, and that in subsequent generations, by the process of evolution, the 'speech centre' would become more developed, and the ape would then speak. . . . If the scalpel of the anatomist has failed to discover a *material locus habitandi* for man's proud prerogative—the faculty of Articulate Language ; if science has failed to trace speech to a 'material centre,' has failed thus to connect matter with mind, I submit that speech is the barrier between men and animals, establishing between them a difference not only of degree but of kind ; the Darwinian analogy between the brain of man and that of his reputed ancestor, the ape, loses all its force, whilst the common belief in the Mosaic account of the origin of man is strengthened." Now, I will not wait to present the evidence which has fully satisfied all living physiologists that "the faculty of Articulate Language" has "a *material locus habitandi ;*" for the point on which I desire to insist is that it cannot make one iota of difference to "the Darwinian analogy" whether this faculty is restricted to a particular "speech-centre," or has its anatomical "seat" distributed over any wider area of the cerebral cortex. Such a "seat" there must be in either case, if it be allowed (as Dr. Bateman allows) that the cerebral cortex "is undoubtedly the instrument by which this attribute becomes externally manifested." The question whether "the material organ of speech" is large or small cannot possibly affect the question on which we are engaged. Since Dr. Bateman wrote, a new era has arisen in the localization of cerebral functions ; so that, if there were any soundness in his argument, one would now be in a position immensely to strengthen "the Darwinian analogy;" seeing that physiologists now habitually utilize the brains of monkeys for the purpose of analogically localizing the "motor centres" in the brain of man. In other words, "the Darwinian analogy" has been found to extend in physiological, as well as in anatomical detail, throughout the entire area of the cortex. But, as I have shown, there is no soundness in his argument ; and therefore I do not avail myself of these recent and most wonderfully suggestive results of physiological research.

10

or expressive of desires—sounds which may be either imitative
of the things designated, or wholly arbitrary.   And this, I
think, is a most important feature ; for it serves still more
closely to connect the faculty of vocal sign-making in animals
with the faculty of speech in man.   Thus, turning first to the
case of a child beginning to speak, as Dr. Wilks points out—
and nearly all writers on the philosophy of language have
noticed—"baby talk" is to a large extent onomatopoetic.
And although this is in part due to an inheritance of "nursery
language," the very fact that nursery language has come to
contain so large an element of onomatopœia is additional
proof, were any required, that this kind of word-invention
appeals with ready ease to the infant understanding.   But, on
the other hand, no one can have attended to the early
vocabulary of any child without having observed a fertile
tendency to the invention of words wholly arbitrary.   As this
spontaneous invention of arbitrary words by young children
will be found of importance in later stages of my exposition,
I will conclude the present chapter by presenting evidence to
show the extent to which, under favourable circumstances, it
may proceed.   Meanwhile, however, I desire to point out that
all such cases of the invention of arbitrary vocal signs by
young children differ from the analogous cases furnished by
parrots only in that the former are usually articulate, while
the latter are usually not so.   But this difference is easily
explained when we remember that hereditary tendency makes
as strongly in the direction of inarticulate sounds in the case
of the bird, as in the case of the infant it makes in the
direction of articulate.

There still remains one feature in the psychology of talking birds to which I must now draw prominent attention.   So
far as I can ascertain it has not been mentioned by any
previous writer, although I should think it is one that can
scarcely have escaped the notice of any attentive observer of
these animals.   I allude to the aptitude which intelligent
parrots display of extending their articulate signs from one
object, quality, or action, to another which happens to be

strikingly similar in kind. For example, one of the parrots which I kept under observation in my own house learnt to imitate the barking of a terrier, which also lived in the house. After a time this barking was used by the parrot as a denotative sound, or proper name, for the terrier—*i.e.* whenever the bird saw the dog it used to bark, whether or not the dog did so. Next, the parrot ceased to apply this denotative name to that particular dog, but invariably did so to any other, or unfamiliar, dog which visited the house. Now, the fact that the parrot ceased to bark when it saw my terrier after it had begun to bark when it saw other dogs, clearly showed that it distinguished between individual dogs, while receptually perceiving their class resemblance. In other words, the parrot's name for an individual dog became extended into a generic name for all dogs. Observations of this kind might no doubt have been largely multiplied, if observers had thought it worth while to record such apparently trivial facts.

In this general survey of articulate language, then, we have reached these conclusions, all of which I take to be established by the evidence of direct and adequate observation.

There are four divisions of the faculty of articulate sign-making to be distinguished :—namely, meaningless imitation, instinctive articulation, understanding words irrespective of tones, and intentional use of words as signs. Cases falling under the first division do not require consideration. Cases belonging to the second, being due to hereditary influence, occur only in infants, uneducated deaf-mutes and idiots. Understanding of words is shown by animals and idiots as well as by infants, and implies, *per se*, a higher development of the sign-making faculty than does the understanding of tones, or gestures—unless, of course, the latter happen to be of as purely conventional a character as words. And, lastly, concerning the intentional use of words as signs, we have noticed the following facts.

Talking birds—which happen to be the only animals whose vocal organs admit of uttering articulate sounds—show themselves capable of correctly using proper names, noun-substantives, adjectives, verbs, and appropriate phrases, although they do so by association alone, or without appreciation of grammatical structure. Words are to them vocal gestures, as immediately expressive of the logic of recepts as any other signs would be. Nevertheless, it is important to observe that this faculty of vocal gesticulation is the first phase of articulate speech in a growing child, is the last to disappear in the descending scale of idiocy, and is exhibited by talking birds in so considerable a degree that the animals even invent names (whether by making distinctive sounds, as a particular squeak for " nuts," or by applying words to designate objects, as "half-past-two" for the name of the coachman)—such invention often clearly having an onomatopoetic origin, though likewise often wholly arbitrary.

I will now conclude this chapter by detailing evidence to show the extent to which, under favourable circumstances, young children will thus likewise invent arbitrary signs, which, however, for reasons already mentioned, are here almost invariably of an articulate kind. It would be easy to draw this evidence from sundry writers on the psychogenesis of children ; but it will be sufficient to give a few quotations from an able writer who has already taken the trouble to collect the more remarkable instances which have been recorded of the fact in question. The writer to whom I allude is Mr. Horatio Hale, and the paper from which I quote is published in the *Proceedings of the American Association for the Advancement of Science*, vol. xxxv., 1886.

" In the year 1860 two children, twin boys, were born in a respectable family residing in a suburb of Boston. They were in part of German descent, their mother's father having come from Germany to America at the age of seventeen ; but the German language, we are told, was never spoken in the household. The children were so closely alike that their grandmother, who often came to see them, could only distinguish them by some coloured string or ribbon tied around the arm. As often happens in such cases, an intense affection existed between them, and they were constantly together. The remainder of their interesting story will be best told in the words of the writer, to whose enlightened zeal for science we are indebted for our knowledge of the facts.

" At the usual age these twins began to talk, but, strange to say, not their 'mother-tongue.' They had a language of their own, and no pains could induce them to speak anything else. It was in vain that a little sister, five years older than they, tried to make them speak their native language—as it would have been. They persistently refused to utter a syllable of English. Not even the usual first words, ' papa,' ' mamma,' ' father,' ' mother,' it is said, did they ever speak; and, said the lady who gave this information to the writer,— who was an aunt of the children, and whose home was with them,—they were never known during this interval to call their mother by that name. They had their own name for her, but never the English. In fact, though they had the usual affections, were rejoiced to see their father at his re- turning home each night, playing with him, &c., they would seem to have been otherwise completely taken up, absorbed with each other. . . . The children had not yet been to school ; for, not being able to speak their ' own English,' it seemed impossible to send them from home. They thus passed the days, playing and talking together in their own speech, with all the liveliness and volubility of common children. Their accent was German—as it seemed to the family. They had regular words, a few of which the family learned sometimes to distinguish ; as that, for example, for carriage, which, on hear- ing one pass in the street, they would exclaim out, and run to the window. This word for carriage, we are told in another place, was ' ni-si-boo-a,' of which, it is added, the syllables were sometimes so repeated that they made a much longer word."

The next case is quoted by Mr. Hale from Dr. E. R.

Hun, who recorded it in the *Monthly Journal of Psychological Medicine*, 1868.

"The subject of this observation is a girl aged four and a half years, sprightly, intelligent, and in good health. The mother observed, when she was two years old, that she was backward in speaking, and only used the words 'papa' and 'mamma.' After that she began to use words of her own invention, and though she understood readily what she said, never employed the words used by others. Gradually she enlarged her vocabulary until it has reached the extent described below. She has a brother eighteen months younger than herself, who has learned her language, so that they can talk freely together. He, however, seems to have adopted it only because he has more intercourse with her than the others ; and in some instances he will use a proper word with his mother, and his sister's word with her. She, however, persists in using only her own words, though her parents, who are uneasy about her peculiarity of speech, make great efforts to induce her to use proper words. As to the possibility of her having learned these words from others, it is proper to state that her parents are persons of cultivation, who use only the English language. The mother has learned French, but never uses the language in conversation. The domestics, as well as the nurses, speak English without any peculiarities, and the child has heard even less than usual of what is called baby-talk. Some of the words and phrases have a resemblance to the French ; but it is certain that no person using that language has frequented the house, and it is doubtful whether the child has on any occasion heard it spoken. There seems to be no difficulty about the vocal organs. She uses her language readily and freely, and when she is with her brother they converse with great rapidity and fluency.

"Dr. Hun then gives the vocabulary, which, he states, was such as he had 'been able at different times to compile from the child herself, and especially from the report of her mother.' From this statement we may infer that the list probably did not include the whole number of words in this child-language.

It comprises, in fact, only twenty-one distinct words, though many of these were used in a great variety of acceptations, indicated by the order in which they were arranged, or by compounding them in various ways. . . .

"Three or four of the words, as Dr. Hun remarks, bear an evident resemblance to the French, and others might, by a slight change, be traced to that language. He was unable, it will be seen, to say positively that the girl had never heard the language spoken ; and it seems not unlikely that, if not among the domestics, at least among the persons who visited them, there may have been one who amused herself, innocently enough, by teaching the child a few words of that tongue. It is, indeed, by no means improbable that the peculiar linguistic instinct may thus have been first aroused in the mind of the girl, when just beginning to speak. Among the words show-ing this resemblance are *feu* (pronounced, we are expressly told, like the French word), used to signify 'fire, light, cigar, sun ;' *too* (the French 'tout'), meaning 'all, everything ;' and *ne pa* (whether pronounced as in French, or otherwise, we are not told), signifying 'not.' *Petee-petee*, the name given to the boy by his sister, is apparently the French 'petit,' little ; and *ma*, 'I,' may be from the French 'moi,' 'me.' If, however, the child was really able to catch and remember so readily these foreign sounds at such an early age, and to interweave them into a speech of her own, it would merely show how readily and strongly in her case the language-making faculty was developed.

"Of words formed by imitation of sounds, the language shows barely a trace. The mewing of the cat evidently sug-gested the word *mea*, which signified both 'cat' and 'furs.' For the other vocables which make up this speech, no origin can be conjectured. We can merely notice that in some of the words the liking which children and some races of men have for the repetition of sounds is apparent. Thus we have *migno-migno*, signifying 'water, wash, bath ;' *go-go*, 'delicacies, as sugar, candy, or dessert,' and *waia-waiar*, 'black, darkness, or a negro.' There is, as will be seen from these examples, no special tendency to the monosyllabic form. *Gummigar*, we are told, signifies 'all the substantials of the table, such as bread, meat, vegetables, &c. ; ' and the same word is used to designate the cook. The boy, it is added, does not use this word, but uses *gna-migna*, which the girl considers as a mistake. From which we may gather that even at their tender age the form of their language had become with them an object of thought ; and we may infer, moreover, that the language was not invented solely by the girl, but that both the children contributed to frame it.

"Of miscellaneous words may be mentioned *gar*, 'horse ;' *deer*, 'money of any kind ;' *beer*, 'literature, books, or school ; ' *peer*, 'ball ;' *bau*, 'soldier, music ;' *odo*, 'to send for, to go out, to take away ;' *keh*, 'to soil ;' *pa-ma*, 'to go to sleep, pillow, bed.' The variety of acceptations which each word was capable of receiving is exemplified in many ways. Thus *feu* might become an adjective, as *ne-pa-feu*, 'not warm.' The verb *odo* had many meanings, according to its position or the words which accompanied it. *Ma odo*, 'I (want to) go out ;' *gar odo*, 'send for the horse ;' *too odo*, 'all gone.' *Gaan* signified God ; and we are told—When it rains, the children often run to the window, and call out, *Gaan odo migno-migno, feu odo*, which means, 'God take away the rain, and send the sun ' —*odo* before the object meaning 'to take away,' and after the object, 'to send.' From this remark and example we learn, not merely that the language had—as all real languages must have—its rules of construction, but that these were sometimes different from the English rules. This also appears in the form *mea waia-waiaw*, 'dark furs' (literally, 'furs dark'), where the adjective follows its substantive.

"The odd and unexpected associations which in all languages govern the meaning of words are apparent in this brief vocabulary. We can gather from it that the parents were Catholics, and punctual in church observances. The words *papa* and *mamma* were used separately in their ordinary sense ; but when linked together in the compound term *papa-mamma*, they signified (according to the connection, we may presume), 'church,' 'prayer-book,' 'cross,' 'priest,' 'to say their prayers.' *Bau* was 'soldier;' but, we are told, from seeing the bishop in his mitre and vestments, thinking he was a soldier, they applied the word *bau* to him. *Gar odo* properly signified 'send for the horse;' but as the children frequently saw their father, when a carriage was wanted, write an order and send it to the stable, they came to use the same expression (*gar odo*) for pencil and paper.

"There is no appearance of inflection, properly speaking, in the language; and this is only what might be expected. Very young children rarely use inflected forms in any language. The English child of three or four years says, 'Mary cup,' for 'Mary's cup;' and 'Dog bite Harry' will represent every tense and mood. It is by no means improbable that, if the children had continued to use their own language for a few years longer, inflections would have been developed in it, as we see that peculiar forms of construction and novel compounds—which are the germs of inflection—had already made their appearance.

"These two recorded instances of child-languages have led to further inquiries, which, though pursued only for a brief period, and in a limited field, have shown that cases of this sort are by no means uncommon."

The author then proceeds to furnish other corroborative instances; but the above quotations are, I think, sufficient for my purposes.* For they show (1) that the spontaneous and

* I may, however, add the following corroborative observations, as they have not been previously published. I owe them to the kindness of my friend Mr. A. E. Street, who kept a diary of his children's psychogenesis. When about two years of age one of these children possessed the following vocabulary :—

Af-ta (in imitation of the sound which the nurse used to make when pretending to drink) = *drinking* or a *drink, drinking-vessel,* and hence a *glass* of any kind.
Vy = a *fly.*
Vy-'ta = *window, i.e.* the 'ta or af-ta (*glass*) on which a fly walks.
Blow = *candle.*
Blow-hattie = a *lamp, i.e.* candle with a hat or shade.
'Nell = a *flower, i.e.* smell.

These words are clearly all of imitative origin. The following, however, seem to have been purely arbitrary :—

to all appearances arbitrary word-making, which is more or less observable in all children when first beginning to speak, may, under favourable circumstances, proceed to an astonishing degree of fulness and efficiency ; (2) that although the words, or articulate signs, thus invented are sometimes of a plainly onomatopoetic origin, as a general rule they are not so ; (3) that the words are far from being always monosyllabic ; (4) that they admit of becoming sufficiently numerous and varied to constitute a not inefficient language, without as yet having advanced to the inflexional stage ; and (5) that the syntax of this language presents obvious points of resemblance to that of the gesture-languages of mankind previously considered.

Numby = *food* of any kind (onomatopoetic).

Nunny = *dress* of any kind.

Milly = *dressing*, and any article used in dressing, *e.g.* a pin.

Lee = *the name for her nurse*, though no one else called the woman by any other name than nurse.

Diddle-iddle = *a hole ;* hence *a thimble ;* hence *a finger.*

Wasky = *the sea.*

Bilu-bilu = *the printed character* " &, " invented on learning the first letters of her alphabet, and always afterwards used.

# CHAPTER VIII.

WE have already seen that spoken language differs from the
language of tone and gesture in being, as a system of signs,
more purely conventional. This means that for semiotic
purposes articulation is a higher product of mental evolution
than either gesticulation or intonation. It also means that as
an instrument of such evolution articulate speech is more
efficient. The latter point is an important one, so I shall
proceed to deal with it at some length.

As noticed in a previous chapter, our system of coinage,
bank-notes, and bills of sale is a more convenient system of
signifying value of labour or of property, than is the more
primitive and less conventional system of actually exchanging
the labour or bartering the property ; and our system of
arithmetic is similarly more convenient for the purpose of
calculation than is the more natural system of counting on the
fingers. But not only are these more conventional systems
more convenient ; they are likewise conducive to a higher
development of business transactions on the one hand, and of
calculation on the other. In the absence of such an improved
system of signs, it would be impossible to conduct as many or
such intricate transactions and calculations as we do conduct.
Similarly with speech as distinguished from gesture. Words,
like gestures, are signs of thoughts and feelings ; but in being
more conventional they are more pure as signs, and so admit
of being wrought up into a much more convenient or
efficient system, while at the same time they become more
constructive in their influence upon ideation. The great

superiority of words over gestures in both these respects may most easily be shown by the use of a few examples.

I open Colonel Mallery's book at random, and find the following as the sign for a barking dog : —

" Pass the arched hand forward from the lower part of the face, to illustrate elongated nose and mouth ; then, with both forefingers extended, remaining fingers and thumbs closed, place them upon either side of the lower jaw, pointing upwards, to show lower canines, at the same time accompanying the gesture with an expression of withdrawing the lips so as to show the teeth snarling ; then, with the fingers of the right hand extended and separated throw them quickly forward and slightly upward (voice or talking)."

Here, be it observed, how elaborate is this pictorial method of designating a dog barking as compared with the use of two words ; and after all it is not so efficient, for the signs were misunderstood by the Indians to whom they were shown—the meaning assigned to them being that of a growling bear. What a large expenditure of thought is required for the devising and the interpretation of such ideograms ! and, when they are formed and understood, how cumbersome do they appear if contrasted with words ! Colonel Mallery, indeed, says of gesture-language that, " when highly cultivated, its rapidity on familiar subjects exceeds that of speech, and approaches to that of thought itself ; " but, besides the important limitation " on familiar subjects," he adds,—" at the same time it must be admitted that great increase in rapidity is chiefly obtained by the system of preconcerted abbreviations before explained, and by the adoption of arbitrary forms, in which naturalness is sacrificed and conventionality established." *

But besides being cumbersome, gesture-language labours

---

* Touching the comparative rapidity with which signs admit of being made to the eye and ear respectively, it may be pointed out that there is a physiological reason why the latter should have the advantage ; for while the ear can distinguish successive sensations separated only by an interval of ·016 sec., the eye cannot do so unless the interval is more than ·047 sec. (Wundt).

under the more serious defect of not being so precise, and the still more serious defect of not being so serviceable as spoken language in the development of abstraction. We have previously seen how words, being more or less purely conventional as signs, are not tied down, as it were, to material objects; although they have doubtless all originated as expressive of sensuous perceptions, not being necessarily ideographic, they may easily pass into signs of general ideas, and end by becoming expressive of the highest abstractions. "Words are thus the easily manipulated counters of thought," and so, to change the metaphor, are the progeny of generalization. But gestures, in being always more or less ideographic, are much more closely chained to sensuous perceptions; and, therefore, it is only when exercised on "familiar subjects" that they can fairly be said to rival words as a means of expression, while they can never soar into the thinner medium of high abstraction. No sign-talker, with any amount of time at his disposal, could translate into the language of gesture a page of Kant.

Let it be observed that I am here speaking of gesture-language as we actually find it. What the latent capabilities of such language may be is another question, and one with reference to which speculation is scarcely calculated to prove profitable. Nevertheless, as the subject is not altogether without importance in the present connection, I may quote the following brief passage from a recent essay by Professor Whitney. After remarking that "the voice has won to itself the chief and almost exclusive part in communication," he adds : —

"This is not in the least because of any closer connection of the thinking apparatus with the muscles that act to produce audible sounds than with those that act to produce visible motions ; not because there are natural uttered names for conceptions, any more than natural gestured names. It is simply a case of 'survival of the fittest,' or analogous to the process by which iron has become the exclusive material of swords, and gold and silver for money : because, namely, experience has shown this to be the material best adapted to this special use. The advantages of the voice are numerous and obvious. There is first its economy, as employing a mechanism that is available for little else, and leaving free for other purposes those indispensable instruments, the hands. Then there is its superior perceptibleness ; its nice differences impress themselves upon the sense at a distance at which visible motions become indistinct ; they are not hidden by intervening objects ; they allow the eyes of the listeners as well as the hands of the speaker to be employed in other useful work ; they are as plain in the dark as in the light ; and they are able to catch and command the attention of one who is not to be reached in any other way." *

To these advantages we may add that words, in being as we have seen less essentially ideographic than gestures, must always have been more available for purposes of abstract expression. We must remember how greatly gesture-language, as it now appears in its most elaborate form, is indebted to the psychologically constructing influence of spoken language ; and, thus viewed, it is a significant fact that even now gesture language is not able to convey ideas of any high degree of abstraction. Still, I doubt not it would be possible to construct a wholly conventional system of gestures which should answer to, or correspond with, all the abstract words and inflections of a spoken language ; and that then the one sign-system might replace the other—just as the sign-system of writing is able similarly to replace that of speech. This, however, is a widely different thing from supposing that such a perfect system of gesture-signs could have grown by a process of natural development ; and, looking to the essentially ideographic character of such signs, I greatly question whether, even under circumstances of the strongest necessity (such as would have arisen if man, or his progenitors, had been unable to articulate), the language of gesture could have been developed into anything approaching a substitute for the language of words.

* *Encyclop. Brit.*, 9th ed., art. *Philology.*

It may tend to throw some light on this hypothetical question—which is of some importance for us—if we consider briefly the psychological *status* of wholly uneducated deaf-mutes ; for although it is true that their case is not fairly parallel to that of a human race destitute of the faculty of speech (seeing that the individual deaf-mute does not find any elaborate system of signs prepared for him by the exertions of dumb ancestors, as would doubtless have been the case under the circumstances supposed), still, on the other hand, and as a compensating consideration, we must remember that the individual deaf-mute not only inherits a human brain, the structure of which has been elaborated by the speech of his ancestors, but is also surrounded by a society the whole structure of whose ideation is dependent upon speech.  So far, therefore, as the complex conditions of the question admit of being disentangled, the case of uneducated deaf-mutes living in a society of speaking persons affords the best criterion we can obtain of the prospect which gesture-language would have had as a means of thought-formation in the human race, supposing this race to have been destitute of the faculty of speech.  To show, therefore, the psychological condition of an individual thus circumstanced, I will quote a brief passage from a lecture of my own, which was given before the British Association in 1878.

" It often happens that deaf and dumb children of poor parents are so far neglected that they are never taught finger-language, or any other system of signs, whereby to converse with their fellow-creatures.  The consequence, of course, is that these unfortunate children grow up in a state of intellectual isolation, which is almost as complete as that of any of the lower animals.  Now, when such a child grows up and falls into the hands of some competent teacher, it may of course be educated, and is then in a position to record its experiences when in its state of intellectual isolation.  I have therefore obtained all the evidence I can as to the mental condition of such persons, and I find that their testimony is perfectly uniform.  In the absence of language, the mind is able to think in the logic of feelings; but can never rise to any ideas of higher abstraction than those which the logic of feelings supplies. The uneducated deaf-mutes have the same notions of right and wrong, cause and effect, and so on, as we have already seen that animals and idiots possess. They always think in the most concrete forms, as shown by their telling us (when educated) that so long as they were uneducated they always thought in pictures. Moreover, that they cannot attain to ideas of even the lowest degree of abstraction, is shown by the fact that in no one instance have I been able to find evidence of a deaf-mute who, prior to education, had evolved for himself any form of supernaturalism. And this, I think, is remarkable, not only because we might fairly suppose that some rude form of fetishism, or ghost-worship, would not be too abstract a system for the unaided mind of a civilized man to elaborate; but also because the mind in this case is *not* wholly unaided. On the contrary, the friends of the deaf-mute usually do their utmost to communicate to his mind some idea of whatever form of religion they may happen to possess. Yet it is uniformly found that, in the absence of language, no idea of this kind can be communicated. For instance, the Rev. S. Smith tells me that one of his pupils, previous to education, supposed the Bible to have been printed by a printing-press in the sky, which was worked by printers of enormous strength—this being the only interpretation the deaf-mute could assign to the gestures whereby his parents had sought to make him understand, that they believed the Bible to contain a revelation from a God of power who lives in heaven. Similarly, Mr. Graham Bell informs me of another, though similar case, in which the deaf-mute supposed the object of going to church to be that of doing obeisance to the clergy."

To the same effect Mr. Tylor says, in the passage already quoted, that deaf-mutes cannot form ideas of any save the lowest degree of abstraction, and further on he gives some interesting illustrations of the fact. Thus, for instance, a deaf-mute who had been educated said that before his instruction his fingers had taught him his numbers, and that when the number was over ten, he made notches on a piece of wood. Here we see the inherited capability of numerical computation united with the crudest form of numerical notation, or symbolism. And so in all other cases of deaf-mutes before instruction ; they present an inherited capacity of abstract ideation, and yet do not find their sign-language of much service in assisting them to develop this capacity : it is too essentially pictorial to go far beyond the region of sensuous perception.

Thus, on the whole, although I deem it profitless to speculate on what the language of gestures might have become in the absence of speech, I think it is highly questionable whether it would have reached any considerable level of excellence ; and I think it is not improbable that, in the absence of articulation, the human race would not have made much psychological advance upon the anthropoid apes. For we must never forget the important fact that thought is quite as much the effect as it is the cause of language, whether of speech or of gesture ; and seeing how inferior gesture is to speech as a system of language, especially in regard to precision and abstraction, I do not think it probable that, in the absence of speech, gesture alone would have supplied the exact and delicate conditions which are essential to the growth of any highly elaborate ideation.

The next point which I desire to consider is that, although gesture language is not in my opinion so efficient a means of developing abstract ideation as is spoken language, it must nevertheless have been of much service in assisting the growth of the latter, and so must have been of much service in laying the foundation of the whole mental fabric which has been constructed by the faculty of speech. Whether we look to young children, to savages, or in a lesser degree to idiots, we find that gesture plays an important part in assisting speech ; and in all cases where a vocabulary is scanty or imperfect, gesture is sure to be employed as the natural means of supplementing speech. Therefore, supposing

11

speech to have had a natural mode of genesis, it is, in my opinion, perfectly certain that its origin and development must have been greatly assisted by gesture. In subsequent chapters I will adduce direct evidence upon this head. At present I wish to draw attention to another point. This is, that although gesture psychologically precedes speech, when once articulate sounds have been devised for the expression of ideas, the faculty of using these articulate sounds as signs of their corresponding ideas does not involve the presence of a higher psychological development than does the faculty of using tones and gestures for the conveyance of similar ideas.

As already shown, it is a matter of observable fact that the only animals which are able to articulate are able to employ nouns, adjectives, and verbs, as expressive of concrete ideas; while animals which are not able to articulate similarly employ tones, and in many cases are able to understand words. Therefore, it is a matter of observable fact that the psychological level required for using tones as vocal gestures, understanding words as expressive of simple ideas, and even uttering words with a correct appreciation of their meaning, is a level not higher than that which obtains in some existing animals.

If we turn from animals to man, we find the same truth exemplified. For in the descending grade of human intelligence as exhibited by idiots, we see that while the use of simple gestures as signs occurs in idiots somewhat too low in the scale to utter any articulate words, nevertheless the interval between such an idiot and one capable of uttering the simplest words is a short interval. Again, in the ascending grade of human intelligence, as exhibited by the growing child, we find the same observation to apply; although, on account of some children requiring a longer time than others to develop the *mechanique* of articulation, we might by considering their cases alone over-estimate the psychological interval which separates gesticulation from speech. *

* It will be remembered that in a previous chapter I argued the impossibility

Thus all the evidence at our disposal goes to show that, while the language of tone and gesture is distinctive, in its least-developed form, of a comparatively low grade of mental evolution, in all but its least-developed form it is not thus distinctive ; for as soon as the language of gesture becomes in the smallest degree conventional, so soon is the psychological level sufficiently high to admit of the use of articulate sounds, vocal gestures, or words expressive of concrete ideas—always supposing that these are already supplied by the psychological environment. Whether or not articulate sounds are then actually made depends, of course, on conditions of a purely anatomical kind.

And here it may be as well to remember the point previously mentioned, namely, that although no existing quadrumanous animal has shown itself able to articulate, we may be quite sure that this fact depends on anatomical as distinguished from psychological conditions ; for not only are the higher monkeys much more intelligent than talking birds, but they are likewise much more imitative of human gestures ; and for both these reasons they are the animals which, more than any others, would be psychologically apt to learn the use of words from man, were it not for some accident of anatomy which stands in the way of their uttering them. And in this connection it is worth while to bear in mind the remark of Professor Huxley, that an imperceptibly small difference of innervation, or other anatomical character of the parts concerned, might determine or prevent the faculty of making articulate sounds.

Looking to the direction in which my argument is tending, this appears to be the most convenient place to dispose of a

of estimating the reflex influence of speech upon gesture, in the case of the high development attained by the latter in man. In the text I am now considering the converse influence of gesture upon speech, and find that it is no more easy precisely to estimate. There can be no doubt, however, that the reciprocal influence must have been great in both directions, and that it must have proceeded from gesture to speech in the first instance, and afterwards, when the latter had become well developed as a system of auditory signs, from speech to gesture. More will require to be said upon this point in a future chapter.

criticism that is not unlikely to arise.  It may be suggested, by way of objection to my views, that if all the foregoing discussion is accepted as paving the way to the conclusion that human intelligence has been developed from animal intelligence, the discussion itself is proving too much.  For, if animals possess in so conspicuous a degree the germ of the sign-making faculty, why, it may be asked, has this germ been developed only in the case of our own ancestors?

In answer to this question I must begin by reminding the reader, that during the course of the present chapter I have endeavoured to make good the following positions.  First, that in the absence of articulation, or of the power of forming verbal signs, the faculty of language is not likely to have made much advance in the animal kingdom.  Second, seeing that words are essentially less ideographic, as well as more precise than gestures—and, therefore, more available for the purpose both of expressing and constructing abstract ideas,— I do not think it is probable that in the absence of articulation the human race would have made much psychological advance upon the anthropoid apes.  Third, that although gesture language is not so efficient a means of developing abstract ideation as is articulate language, it must nevertheless have been of much service in assisting the growth of the latter ; so that where the power of articulation was present, both systems of sign-making would have co-operated in the development of abstract thought : in the presence of articulation, gestures would themselves gain additional influence in this respect.

From these data there follows the important consequence that only from some species of ape which possessed the requisite anatomical conditions could the human mind have taken its origin.  In other words, the above considerations are adduced to show the futility of arguing that, if the human mind has been developed in virtue of the sign-making faculty as this is exemplified in speech, we might therefore have expected that from the same starting-point (namely, the anthropoid apes) some comparably well-elaborated mind should have been developed in virtue of the sign-making faculty as this is exemplified in gesture. I maintain that we can see very good reason why (even if we suppose all the other conditions parallel) the branch of the Primates which presented the power—or the potentiality—of articulation should have been able to rise in the psychological scale, as we evolutionists believe that it has risen ; while all the companion branches, being restricted in their language to gesture, should have remained in their original condition.

To this it may be answered that the talking birds might be looked to as the possible—or even probable—rivals of articulating mammals in respect of potential intelligence ; and, therefore, that according to the views which I am advocating, it might have been expected that there should now be existing upon the earth some race of bird-like creatures ready to dispute the supremacy of man.

This, however, would be a very shallow criticism. The veriest tyro in natural science is aware that, if there is any truth at all in the general theory of descent, we are every-where compelled to see that the conditions which determine the development of a species in any direction are always of a complex character. Why one species should remain constant through inconceivably enormous lapses of geological time, while others pass through a rich and varied history of upward change—why this should be so in any case we cannot say. We can only say, in general terms, that the conditions which in any case determine upward growth or stationary type are too numerous and complex to admit of our unravelling them in detail. Now, if this is the case even as between the structures of allied types—where there may be nothing to indicate the difference of the conditions which have led to the difference of results,—much more must it be the case between animals so unlike as a parrot and an ape. I think he would be a bold man who would affirm that even if the orang-outang had been able to articulate, this ape would necessarily, or probably, have become the progenitor of another human race. Absurd, then, it is to argue that, if the human race sprang from some other species of man-like creature, and became human in virtue of the power of articulation *plus* all the other conditions external and internal, therefore the talking birds ought to have developed some similar progeny, merely because they happen to satisfy one of these conditions.

Take a fair analogy. Flying is no doubt a very useful faculty to all animals which present it, and it is shown to be mechanically possible in animals so unlike one another as Insects, Reptiles, Birds, and Mammals. We might therefore suppose that, from the fact of bats being able to fly, many other mammals should have acquired the art. But, as they have not done so, we can only say that the reason is because the complex conditions leading to the growth of this faculty have been satisfied in the bats alone. Similarly "the flight of thought" is a most useful faculty, and it has only been developed in man. One of the conditions required for its development—power of articulation—occurs also in a few birds. But to argue from this that these birds ought to have developed the faculty of thought, would be just as unwarrantable as to argue that some other mammals ought to have developed the faculty of flight, seeing that they all present the most important of the needful conditions—to wit, bones and muscles actuated by nerves. Indeed, the argument would be even more unwarranted than this ; for we can see plainly enough that the most important conditions required for the development of thought are of a psychological and social kind—those which are merely anatomical being but of secondary value, even though, as I have endeavoured to indicate, they are none the less indispensable.

In short, I am not endeavouring to argue that the influence of articulation on the development of thought is in any way *magical.* Therefore, the mere fact that certain birds are able to make articulate sounds in itself furnishes no more difficulty to my argument than the fact that they are able to imitate a variety of other sounds. For the *psychological* use of articulate sounds can only be developed in the presence of many other and highly complex conditions, few if any of which can be shown to obtain among birds. If any existing species of anthropoid ape had proved itself capable of imitating articulate sounds, there might have been a little more force in the apparent difficulty ; though even in that case the argument would not have been so strong as in the above parallel with regard to the great exception furnished by bats in the matter of flight.

So far, then, as we have yet gone, I do not anticipate that opponents will find it prudent to take a stand. Seeing that monkeys use their voices more freely than any other animals in the way of intentionally expressive intonation ; that all the higher animals make use of gesture signs ; that denotative words are (psychologically considered) nothing more than vocal gestures ; that, if there is any psychological interval between simple gesticulation and denotative articulation, the interval is demonstrably bridged in the case alike of talking birds, infants, and idiots ;—seeing all these things, it is evident that opponents of the doctrine of mental evolution must take their stand, not on the faculty of *articulation*, but on that of *speech*. They must maintain that the mere power of using denotative words implies no real advance upon the power of using denotative gestures ; that it therefore establishes nothing to prove the possibility, or even the probability, of articulation arising out of gesticulation ; that their position can only be attacked by showing how a sign-making faculty, whether expressed in gesticulation or in articulation, can have become developed into the faculty of predication ; that, in short, the fortress of their argument consists, not in the power which man displays of using denotative words, but in his power of constructing predicative propositions. This central position, therefore, we must next attack. But, before doing so, I will close the present chapter by clearly defining the exact meanings of certain terms as they will afterwards be used by me.

By the *indicative* stage of language, or sign-making, I will understand the earliest stage that is exhibited by intentional sign-making. This stage corresponds to the divisions marked four and six in my representative scheme (p. 88), and, as we have now so fully seen, is common to animals and human beings. Indicative signs, then, whether in the form of gestures, tones, or words, are intentionally significant. For the most part they are expressive of emotional states, and simple desires. When, for example, an infant holds out its arms to be taken by the nurse, or points to objects in order to be taken to them, it cannot be said to be *naming* anything ; yet it is clearly *indicating* its wants. Infants also cry *intentionally*, or as a partly conventional sign to show discomfort, whether bodily or mental.* They will likewise at an early age learn wholly conventional signs whereby to indicate—though not yet to name—particular feelings, objects, qualities, and actions. My son, for instance, was taught by his nurse to shake his head for " No," nod it for " Yes," and wave his hand for " Ta-ta," or leave-taking : all these indicative gestures he performed well and appropriately when eight and a half months old. This indicative stage of language, or sign-making, is universally exhibited by all the more intelligent animals, although not to so great an extent as in infants. The parrot which depresses its head to invite a scratching, the dog which begs before a wash-stand, the cat which pulls one's clothes to solicit help for her kittens in distress—all these animals are making what I call *indicative* signs.

Following upon the indicative stage of language there is what I have called *denotative* (7 A in the scheme on p. 88). This likewise occurs both in animals and in children when first beginning to speak—talking birds, for instance, being able to learn and correctly use names as *notæ*, or marks, of particular

---

* " The remark made by Tiedemann on the imperative intention of tears, is confirmed by similar observations of Charles Darwin's. At the age of eleven weeks, in the case of one of his children, a little sooner in another, the nature of their crying changed according to whether it was produced by hunger or suffering. And this means of communication appeared to be very early placed at the service of the will. The child seemed to have learnt to cry when he wished, and to contract his features according to the occasion, so as to make known that he wanted something. This development of the will takes place towards the end of the third month." (Perez, *First Three Years of Childhood*, English trans., p. 101.)

objects, qualities, and actions. Yet such *notæ*—be they verbal or otherwise—thus learned by special association, are not, strictly speaking, *names*. By the use of such a sign the talking bird merely affixes a vocal mark to a particular object, quality, or action : it does not *extend* the sign to any other similar objects, qualities, or actions of the same class ; and, therefore, by its use of that sign does not really *connote* anything of the particular object, quality, or action which it *denotes*.

So much, then, for signs as *denotative*. By signs as *connotative*, I mean signs which are in any measure *attributive*. If we call a dog Jack, that is a denotative name : it does not attribute any quality as belonging to that dog. But if we call the animal " Smut," or " Swift," or by any other word serving to imply some quality which is distinctive of that dog, we are thereby connoting of the dog the fact of his presenting such a quality. Connotative names, therefore, differ from denotative, in that they are not merely *notæ* or marks of the things named, but also imply some character, or characters, as belonging to those things. And the character, or characters, which they thus imply, by the mere fact of implication, assign the things named to a *group :* hence these connotative names are *con-notæ*, or the marking of one thing *along with* another—*i.e.* express an act of nominative *classification*. This is an important fact to remember, because, as we shall afterwards find, all connotative terms arise from the need which we experience of thus verbally classifying our perceptions of likeness or analogy. Moreover, it is of even still more importance to note that such verbal classification may be either receptual or conceptual. For instance, the first word (after *Mamma, Papa*, &c.) that one of my children learnt to say was the word *Star*. Soon after having acquired this word, she extended its signification to other brightly shining objects, such as candles, gas-lights, &c. Here there was plainly a perception of likeness or analogy, and hence the term *Star*, from having been originally denotative, began to be also connotative. But this connotative extension of the term must evidently have been what I term receptual. For it is impossible to suppose that at that tender age the child was capable of thinking about the term *as* a term, or of setting the term before the mind as an object of thought, distinct from the object which it served to name. Therefore, we can only suppose that the extension of this originally denotative name (whereby it began to be connotative) resembled the case of a similar extension mentioned in the last chapter, where my parrot raised its originally denotative sign for a particular dog to an incipiently connotative value, by applying that sign to all other dogs. That is to say, both in the case of the child and the bird, connotation within these moderate limits was rendered possible by means of receptual ideation alone. But, with advancing age and developing powers, the human mind attains to conceptual ideation ; and it is then in a position to constitute the names which it uses *themselves objects of thought*. The consequence is that connotation may then no longer represent the merely spontaneous expression of likeness receptually perceived : it may become the intentional expression of likeness conceptually thought out. In the mind of an astronomer the word *Star* presents a very different mass of connotative meaning from that which it presented to the child, who first extended it from a bright point in the sky to a candle shining in a room. And the reason of this great difference is, that the conceptual thought of the astronomer, besides having greatly *added* to the connotation, has also greatly *improved* it. The only common quality which the name served to connote when used by the child was that of brightness ; but, although the astronomer is not blind to this point of resemblance between a star and a candle, he disregards it in the presence of fuller knowledge, and will not apply the term even to objects so much more closely resembling a star as a comet or a meteor. Now, this greater *accuracy* of connotation, quite as much as the greater *mass* of it, has been reached by the astronomer in virtue of his powers of conceptual thought. It is because he has thought about his names *as* names that he has thus been able with so much accuracy to define their meanings—*i.e.* to limit their connotations in some directions, as well as to extend them in others.

Obviously, therefore, we are here in the presence of a great distinction, and one which needs itself to be in some way connoted. It is, indeed, but a special exhibition of the one great distinction which I have carried through the whole course of this work—namely, that between ideation as receptal and conceptual. But it is none the less important to designate this special exhibition of it by means of well-defined terms ; and I can only express surprise that such should not already have been done by logicians. The terms which I shall use are the following.

By a connotative name I will understand the connotative extension of a denotative name, whether such extension be great or small, and, therefore, whether it be extended receptually or conceptually. But for the *exclusively conceptual* extension of a name I will reserve the convenient term *denomination*. This term, like those previously defined, was introduced by the schoolmen, and by them was used as synonymous with connotation. But it is evident that they (and all subsequent writers) only had before their minds the case of conceptual connotation, and hence they felt no need of the distinction which for present purposes it is obviously imperative to draw. Now, I do not think that any two more appropriate words could be found whereby to express this distinction than are these words *connotation* and *denomination*, if for the purposes of my own subsequent analysis I am allowed to define them in accordance with their etymology. For, when so defined, a connotative sign will mean a *classificatory* sign, whether conferred receptually or conceptually ; while a denominative sign will mean a connotative sign which has been conferred as such *with a truly conceptual intention*—*i.e.* with an introspective appreciation of its function as all that logicians understand by a *name*.

I will now sum up these sundry definitions.

By an *indicative* sign I will understand a significant tone or gesture intentionally expressive of a mental state ; but yet not in any sense of the word denominative.

By a *denotative* sign I will understand the receptual marking of particular objects, qualities, actions, &c.

By a *connotative* sign I will understand the classificatory attribution of qualities to objects named by the sign, whether such attribution be due to receptual or to conceptual operations of the mind.

By a *denominative* sign I will understand a connotative sign consciously bestowed as such, or with a full conceptual appreciation of its office and purpose as a name.

By a *predicative* sign I will mean a proposition, or the conceptual apposition of two denominative terms, expressive of the speaker's intention to connote something of the one by means of the other.

# CHAPTER IX.

## SPEECH.

We are now coming to close quarters with our subject. All the foregoing chapters have been arranged with a view to preparing the way for what is hereafter to follow ; and, therefore, as already remarked, I have thus far presented material over which I do not think it is possible that any dispute can arise. But now we come to that particular exhibition of the sign-making faculty which not only appears to be peculiar to man, but which obviously presents so great an advance upon all the lower phases hitherto considered, that it is the place where my opponents have chosen to take their stand. When a man maintains that there is a difference of kind between animal and human intelligence, he naturally feels himself under some obligation to indicate the point where this difference obtains. To say that it obtains with the appearance of language, in the sense of sign-making, is obviously too wide a statement ; for, as we have now so fully seen, language, in this widest sense, demonstrably obtains among the lower animals. Consequently, the line must be drawn, not at language or sign-making, but at that particular kind of sign-making which we understand by Speech. Now the distinctive peculiarity of this kind of sign-making—and one, therefore, which does not occur in any other kind—consists in predication, or the using of signs as movable types for the purpose of making propositions. It does not signify whether or not the signs thus used are words. The gestures of Indians and deaf-mutes admit, as we have seen, of being wrought up into a machinery of predication which, for all purposes of practical life, is almost as efficient as speech. The distinction, therefore, resides in the intellectual powers ; not in the symbols thereof. So that a man *means*, it matters not by what system of signs he expresses his meaning : the distinction between him and the brute consists in his being able to *mean a proposition.* Now, the kind of mental act whereby a man is thus enabled to mean a proposition is called by psychologists an act of Judgment. Predication, or the making of a proposition, is nothing more nor less than the expression of a judgment ; and a judgment is nothing more nor less than the apprehension of whatever meaning it may be that a proposition serves to set forth. Therefore, it belongs to the very essence of predication that it should involve a judgment ; and it belongs to the very essence of a judgment that it should admit of being stated in the form of a proposition.*

* Several writers of repute have habitually used the word "Judgment" in a most unwarrantable manner—Lewes, for instance, making it stand indifferently for an act of sensuous determination and an act of conceptual thought. I may, therefore, here remark that in the following analysis I shall not be concerned with any such gratuitous abuses of the term, but will understand it in the technical sense which it bears in logic and psychology. The extraordinary views which Mr. Huxley has published upon this subject I can only take to be ironical. For instance, he says :—"Ratiocination is resolvable into predication, and predication consists in marking in some way the existence, the co-existence, the succession, the likeness and unlikeness, of things or their ideas. Whatever does this, reasons ; and I see no more ground for denying to it reasoning power, because it is unconscious, than I see for refusing Mr. Babbage's engine the title of a calculating machine on the same grounds" (*Critiques and Addresses*, p. 281). If this statement were taken seriously, of course the answer would be that Mr. Babbage's engine is called a calculating machine only in a metaphorical sense, seeing that it does not evolve its results by any process at all resembling, or in any way analogous to, those of a human mind. It would be an absurd misstatement to say that a machine either reasons or predicates, *only* because it "marks in some way the existence, the co-existence, the succession, and the likeness and unlikeness of things." A rising barometer or a striking clock do not predicate, any more than a piece of wood, shrieking beneath a circular saw, feels. To denominate purely mechanical or unconscious action—even though it should take place in a living agent and be perfectly adjustive—reason or predication, would be to confuse physical phenomena with psychical ; and, as I have shown in my previous work, even if it be supposed that the latter are mere "indices" or "shadows" of the former, *still the fact of their existence must be recognized ;* and the processes in question have reference to them, not to their physical counterparts. It is, therefore, just as incorrect to

Lastly, just as this is the place where my opponents take a stand, so, as they freely allow, it is the only place where they *can* take a stand. If once this chasm of speech were bridged, there would be no further chasm to cross. From the simplest judgment which it is possible to make, and therefore from the simplest proposition which it is possible to construct, it is on all hands admitted that human intelligence displays an otherwise uniform or uninterrupted ascent through all the grades of excellence which it afterwards presents. Here, then, and here alone, we have what Professor Max Müller calls the Rubicon of Mind, which separates the brute from the man, and over which, it is alleged, the army of Science can never hope to pass.

In order to present the full difficulty which is here encountered, I will allow it to be stated by the ablest of my opponents. As President of the Biological Section of the British Association in 1879, Mr. Mivart expressed his matured thought upon the subject thus :—

"The simplest element of thought seems to me to be a 'judgment,' with intuition of reality concerning some 'fact,' regarded as a fact real or ideal. Moreover, this judgment is not itself a modified imagination, because the imaginations which may give occasion to it persist unmodified in the mind side by side with the judgment they have called up. Let us take, as examples, the judgments, 'That thing is good to eat,' and 'Nothing can be and not be at the same time and in the same sense.' As to the former, we vaguely imagine 'things good to eat ;' but they must exist *beside* the judgment, not *in* it. They can be recalled, compared, and seen to co-exist. So with the other judgment, the mind is occupied with certain abstract ideas, though the imagination has certain vague

---

say that a calculating machine really calculates, or predicates the result of its calculations, as it would be to say that a musical-box composes a tune because it plays a tune, or that the love of Romeo and Juliet was an isosceles triangle, because their feelings of affection, each to each, were, like the angles at the base of that figure, equal. But, as I have said, I take it that Professor Huxley must here have been writing in some ironical sense, and therefore purposely threw his criticisms into a preposterous form.

'images' answering respectively to 'a thing being,' and 'a thing not being,' and to 'at the same time' and 'in the same sense;' but the images do not *constitute* the judgment itself, any more than human 'swimming' is made up of limbs and fluid, though without such necessary elements no such swimming could take place.*

"This distinction is also shown by the fact that one and the same idea may be suggested to, and maintained in, the mind by the help of the most incongruous images, and very different ideas by the very same image; this we may see to be the case with such ideas as 'number,' 'purpose,' 'motion,' 'identity,' &c.

"But the distinctness of 'thought' from 'imagination' may perhaps be made clearer by the drawing out fully what we really do when we make some simple judgment, as, *e.g.*, 'A negro is black.' Here, in the first place, we directly and explicitly affirm that there is a conformity between the external thing, 'a negro,' and the external quality 'blackness' —the negro possessing that quality. We affirm, secondarily and implicitly, a conformity between two external entities and two corresponding internal concepts. And thirdly, and lastly, we also implicitly affirm the existence of a conformity between the subjective judgment and the objective existence." †

I will next allow this matter to be presented in the words of another adversary, and one whom Mr. Mivart approvingly quotes.

"The question is, Can the sense say anything—make a judgment at all? Can it furnish the blank formula of a judgment—the 'is' in 'A is B'? The grass of the battlefield was green, and the sense gave both the grass and the green-

---

* The "images answering respectively to 'a thing being,' and 'a thing not being,' and to 'at the same time' and 'in the same sense,'" must indeed be "vague." How is it conceivable that "the imagination" can entertain any such "images" at all, apart from the "abstract ideas" of the "mind"? Such ideas as "a thing not being," or "being in the same sense," &c., belong to the sphere of conceptual thought, and cannot have any existence at all except as "abstract ideas of the mind."

† *Nature,* August 21, 1879.

ness ; but did it affirm that 'the grass is green'? It may be assumed that 'grass' and 'green' together form one complex object, which is an object under space and time, and therefore of sense. But against this the rejoinder at once is, that the sense may indeed take in and report (so to speak) a complex object, but that in this case the question is, not about the complex object, but about the *complexity* of the object. It is one thing to see green grass, and evidently quite another to affirm the *greenness* of the grass. The difference is all the difference between seeing two things united, and seeing them *as united*. . . . If a brute could think 'is,' brute and man would be brothers. 'Is,' as the copula of a judgment, implies the mental separation, and recombination of two terms that only exist united in nature, and can therefore never have impressed the sense except as one thing.\* And 'is,' considered as a substantive verb, as in the example 'This man is,' contains in itself the application of the copula of judgment to the most elementary of all abstractions—'thing' or 'something.' Yet if a being has the power of thinking—'thing,' it has the power of transcending space and time by dividing or decomposing the phenomenally one. Here is the point where instinct ends and reason begins." †

It would be easy to add quotations from other writers to the same effect as the above ; ‡ but these may be held sufficient to give material for the first stage of my criticism, which is of a purely technical character. I affirm that all writers who thus take their stand upon the distinctively human faculty of predication are taking their stand at the wrong place. In other words, without at present disputing whether we have to do with a distinction of kind or of degree, I say, and say con-

---

\* The statement conveyed in this sentence I am not able to understand, and therefore will not hereafter endeavour to criticize. If it be taken literally—and I know not in what other sense to take it—we must suppose the writer to mean that "greenness" only occurs in "grass," or, which is the same thing, that only grass is green.

† *Lessons from Nature*, pp. 226, 227.

‡ For instance, Professor Francis Bowen, of Harvard College, in an essay on *The Human and Brute Mind, Princeton Review*, 1880.

12

fidently, that the distinction in question—*i.e.* between animal and human intelligence—may be easily proved to occur further back than at the faculty of predication, or the forming of a proposition. The distinction occurs at the faculty of denomination, or the bestowing of a name, known as such. " The simplest element of thought " is *not* a "*judgment:*" the simplest element of thought is a *concept.* That this is the case admits of being easily demonstrated in several different ways.

In the first place, it is evident that there could be no judgments without concepts, just as there could be no propositions without terms. A judgment is the result of a comparison of concepts, and this is the reason why it can only find expression in a proposition, which sets forth the relation between the concepts by bringing into apposition their corresponding terms. Judgments, therefore, are *compounds* of thought : the *elements* are concepts.

In the second place, given the power of conceiving, and the germ of judgment is implied, though not expanded into the blossom of formal predication. For whenever we bestow a name we are implicitly judging that the thing to which we apply the name presents the attributes connoted by that name, and thus we are virtually predicating the fact. For example, when I call a man a " Negro," the very term itself affirms blackness as the distinctive quality of that individual —just as does the equivalent nursery term, " Black-man." To utter the name Negro, therefore, or the name Black-man, is to form and pronounce at least two judgments touching an individual object of sensuous perception—to wit, that it is a man, and that he is black. The judgments so formed and pronounced are doubtless not so explicit as is the case when both subject and predicate are associated in the full proposition— " A negro is black ; " but in the single term Negro, or Black-man, both these elements were already present, and *must* have been so if the name were in any degree at all conceptual—*i.e. denominative* as distinguished from *denotative.* In the illustration "Negro," or " Black-man," it so happens that the connotation of the name is directly given by the etymology of the name ; but this circumstance is immaterial. Whether or not the etymology of a connotative name happens to fit the particular subject to which it is applied, the same kind of classificatory judgment is required for any appropriate application of the same. If, with Blumenbach, I am accustomed to call a negro an Ethiopian, when I apply this name to any representative of that race, I am performing the same mental act as my neighbour who calls him a Negro, or my child who calls him a Black-man. If it should be said that in all such cases the act of naming is so immediately due to association that no demand is made upon the powers of judgment, the admission would be a dangerous one for my opponents to make, since the same remark would apply to the full proposition, "That man is black." Moreover, the objection admits of being easily disposed of by choosing instances of naming where associations have not yet been definitively fixed. If I am travelling in a strange continent, and amid all the unfamiliar flora there encountered I suddenly perceive a plant which I think I know, before I name it to my friend as that plant, I would submit it to close scrutiny—*i.e.* carefully *judge* its resemblances to the known or familiar species. In short, all connotative names, when denominatively applied, betoken acts of judgment, which differ from those concerned in full predication only as regards the form of their expression. Or, as Mill very tersely remarks, "whenever the names given to objects convey any information, that is, whenever they have properly any meaning, the meaning resides not in what they denote, but in what they connote." And although in his elaborate treatment of Names and Propositions he omits expressly to notice the point now before us, it is clearly implied in the above quotation. The point is that connotative names (or denominative terms)* are often in themselves of predicative value ; and this point is clearly implied in the above quotation,

---

* Mill, following the schoolmen, uses the terms connotation and denomination as synonymous. For the distinction which I have drawn between them see above, p. 162.

because, whenever "names given to objects convey any information," the information thus conveyed is virtually predicated :
the "meaning" connoted by the name is affirmed in the mere
act of bestowing the name, which thus in itself becomes a condensed proposition. "It is a truism of psychology that the
terms of a proposition, when closely interrogated, turn out to
be nothing but abbreviated judgments." *

This view of the matter, then, is the only one that can be
countenanced by psychology. It is likewise the only one
that can be countenanced by philology, or the study of
language in the making. Of this fact I will adduce abundant
evidence in a subsequent chapter, where it will be shown, as
Professor Max Müller says, that "every name was originally
a proposition." But at present I am only concerned with one
of the most elementary points of purely psychological analysis,
and will therefore postpone the independent illumination of
the whole philosophy of predication which of late years has
been so splendidly furnished by the comparative study of
languages.

From whatever point of view, therefore, we look at the
matter, we are bound to conclude, either that the term "judgment" must be applied indifferently to the act of denominating
and to the act of predicating, or else, if it be restricted to the
latter, that it must not be regarded as "the simplest element
of thought." And thus we are led back to the position
previously gained while treating of the Logic of Concepts.
For we then found that names are the steps of the intellectual
ladder whereby we climb into higher and higher regions of
ideation ; and although our progress is assisted by formal
predication, or discursive thought, this is but the muscular
energy, so to speak, which would in itself be useless but for
the rungs already supplied, and on which alone that energy
can be expended. Or, to vary the metaphor, conceptual
names are the ingredients out of which is formed the structure
of propositions ; and, in order that this formation should take
place, there must already be in the ingredients that element

* Sayce, *Introduction to the Science of Language*, i., 115.

of vitality which constitutes the *vis formativa*. Now, this element of vitality is the element of conceptual ideation, already exhibited in every denominative term.

Therefore, for the sake at once of clearness and of brevity, I will hereafter speak of predication as *material* and *formal*. By material predication I will mean conceptual denomination, whereby, in the mere act of bestowing a connotative term, we are virtually predicating of the thing thus designated some fact, quality, or relation, which the name bestowed is intended to indicate. By formal predication I will mean the apposition of denominative terms, with the intention of setting forth some relation which is thus expressed as subsisting between them. But, as already observed, I regard this distinction as artificial. Psychologically speaking, there is no line of demarcation between these two kinds of predication. Whether I say " Fool," or " Thou art a fool," I am similarly assigning the subject of my remark to a certain category of men : I am similarly giving expression to my judgment with regard to the qualities presented by one particular man. The distinction, then, between what I call material and formal predication is merely a distinction in rhetoric : as a matter of psychology there is no distinction at all.

If to all this it should be objected, in accordance with the psychological doctrines set forth by Mr. Mivart, above quoted, that a judgment as embodied in a proposition differs from a concept as embodied in a name in respect of the copula, and therefore in presenting the idea of existence as existence ; I answer, in the first place, that every concept must necessarily present this idea however *implicitly;* and, in the next place, that however *explicitly* it may be stated as a judgment, it is not of more conceptual value than that of any other quality belonging to a subject. As regards the first point, when an object, a quality, an action, &c., is named, it is thereby abstracted as a distinct creation of thought, separated out from other things, and made to stand before the mind as a distinct entity (see Chapter IV.). Therefore, in the very act of naming we are virtually predicating existence of the thing named : the power to " think is " is the power concerned in the *formation* of a *concept*, not in the *apposing* of concepts *when formed.* All that is done in an act of such apposition is to bring together two ideas of two things already conceived as existing : were it not so there could be *no-things* to compare.*

And now, as regards the second point, so far is it from being true that the predication of existence is the essential or most important feature even of a full or formal proposition, that it is really the least essential or least important. For existence is the category to which everything must belong if it is to be judged about at all, and therefore merely to judge that *A is* and *B is*, is to form the most barren (or least significant) judgment that can be formed with regard to A or B ; and when we bring these two judgments (concepts) together in the proposition *A is B*, the new judgment which we make has nothing to do with the existence either of A or of B, nor has it really anything to do with existence as such. The existence both of A and of B has been already pre-supposed in the two concepts, and when these two existing things are brought into apposition, no third existence is thereby supposed to have been created. The copula therefore really stands, not as a symbol of *existence*, but as the symbol of *relation*, and might just as well be replaced by any other sign (such as $=$), or, indeed, be dispensed with altogether. " As we use the verb *is*, so the Latins use their verb *est* and the Greeks their ἐστί through all its declensions. Whether all other nations of the world have in their several languages a word that answereth to it, or not, I cannot tell ; but I am sure they have no need of it. For the placing of two names in order [*i.e.* in *apposition*] may serve to signify their consequence, if it

---

* This view of a concept as already embodying the idea of existence is not really opposed to that of Mill, where he points out that if we pronounce the word " Sun " alone we are not necessarily affirming so much as existence of the sun (*Logic*, i., p. 20) ; for, although we are not affirming existence of that particular body, we must at least have the idea of its existence *as a possibility :* the use of the term carries with it the implied idea of such a possibility, and therefore the idea of existence—whether actual or potential—as already present to the mind of the speaker.

were the custom, as well as the words *is, to be,* and the like. And if it were so, that there were a language without any verb answering to *est,* or *is,* or *be,* yet the men that used it would be not a jot the less capable of inferring, concluding, and of all kind of reasoning than were the Greeks and Latins." This shrewd analysis by Hobbes is justly said by Mill to be "the only analysis of a proposition which is rigorously true of all propositions without exception ;" and Professor Max Müller says of it, "Hobbes, though utterly ignorant of the historical antecedents of language, agrees with us in the most remarkable manner." *

Thus, then, upon the whole, and without further treatment, it may be concluded that whether we look to its simplest manifestations or to its most complex, we must alike conclude that it is the faculty of conception, not that of judgment—the faculty of denomination, not that of predication—which we have to regard as "the simplest element of thought." Of course, if it were said that these two faculties are one in kind—that in order to conceive we must judge, and in order to name we must predicate—I should have no objection to offer. All I am at present engaged upon is to make it clear that the distinction between man and brute in respect of the

---

* In order to avoid misapprehension, I may observe that the criticism which Mill passes upon this analysis of the proposition by Hobbes (*Logic,* i., p. 100) has no reference to the only matter with which I am at present concerned—namely, the function of the copula. Indeed, with regard to this matter I am in full agreement with both the Mills. For James Mill, see *Analysis of the Human Mind,* i. 126, *et seq. ;* Mr. John Stuart Mill writes as follows :—"It is important that there should be no indistinctness in our conception of the nature and office of the copula ; for confused notions respecting it are among the causes which have spread mysticism over the field of logic, and perverted its speculations into logomachies. It is apt to be supposed that the copula is something more than a mere sign of predication ; that it also signifies existence. In the proposition, Socrates is just, it may seem to be implied not only that the quality *just* can be affirmed of Socrates, but moreover that Socrates *is,* that is to say exists. This, however, only shows that there is an ambiguity in the word *is ;* a word which not only performs the function of a copula in affirmations, but has also a meaning of its own, in virtue of which it may itself be made the predicate of a proposition" (*Logic,* i., p. 86). In my chapters on Philology I shall have to recur to the analysis of predication, and then it will be seen how completely the above view has been corroborated by the progress of linguistic research.

Logos must be drawn at the place where this distinction first obtains ; and this place is where judgment is concerned with conception, or with the bestowing of names in the sense previously explained as *denominative.* The subsequent working up of names into propositions is merely a further exhibition of the self-same faculty. It is as true of judgment when displayed in denomination as it is of judgment when displayed in predication, that "it is not itself a modified imagination, because the imaginations which may give rise to it persist unmodified in the mind side by side with it." For, as we have seen, the act of denominating (as distinguished from denotating) is in and of itself an act of predicating. When a naturalist bestows a name upon a new species of plant or animal, he has *judged* a resemblance and *predicates* a fact—*i.e.* that the hitherto un-named form belongs to certain *genus* or *kind.* And so it is with all other names when conceptually bestowed, because everywhere such names are expressions of conceptual *classification*—the bringing together of like things, or the separation of unlike. In short, all names which present any conceptual meaning are in themselves condensed propositions, or "material predications ;" and only as such can they afterwards become *terms, i.e.* constitute the essential elements of any more extended proposition, or "formal predication." Therefore it is the faculty of naming wherein is first displayed —and, according to the doctrine of Nominalism, *whereby is first attained*—that great and distinctive characteristic of the human mind which Mr. Mivart and those who think with him have in view ; and, unless we espouse the doctrine of Realism— which neither these nor any other psychologists with whom I have to do are likely now-a-days to countenance,—it is plain that "the simplest element of thought" is a concept.

If I do not apologize for having occupied so much space over so obvious a point, it is only because I believe that any one who reads these pages will sympathize with my desire to avoid ambiguity, and thus to reduce the question before us to its naked reality. So far, it will be observed, this

question has not been touched. I am not disputing that an
immense and an extraordinary distinction obtains, and I do
not anticipate that either Mr. Mivart or any one else will take
exception to this preliminary clearing of the ground, which
has been necessitated only on account of my opponents
having been careless enough to represent the Proposition as
the simplest exhibition of the Logos. But now the time has
arrived when we must tackle the distinction in serious
earnest.

Wherein does this distinction truly consist? It consists,
as I believe all my opponents will allow, in the power which
the human being displays of *objectifying ideas*, or of setting
one state of mind before another state, and contemplating
the relation between them. The power to " think is "—or,
as I should prefer to state it, the power to think at all—*is the
power which is given by introspective reflection in the light of
self-consciousness.* It is because the human mind is able, so
to speak, to stand outside of itself, and thus to constitute its
own ideas the subject-matter of its own thought, that it is
capable of judgment in the technical sense above explained,
whether in the act of conception or in that of predication.
For thus it is that these ideas are enabled " to exist *beside* the
judgment, not *in* it ; " thus it is that they may themselves
become objects of thought. We have no evidence to show
that any animal is capable of thus objectifying its own ideas ;
and, therefore, we have no evidence that any animal is
capable of judgment. Indeed I will go further, and affirm
that we have the best evidence which is derivable from what
are necessarily ejective sources, to prove that no animal
*can possibly* attain to these excellencies of subjective life.
This evidence will gradually unfold itself as we proceed, so
at present it is enough to say, in general terms, that it consists
in a most cogent proof of the absence in brutes of the needful
*conditions* to the occurrence of these excellencies as they
obtain in themselves. From which it follows that the great
distinction between the brute and the man really lies behind
the faculties both of conception and predication : it resides in

the conditions to the occurrence of either. What these conditions are I will consider later on. Meanwhile, and in order
that we may be perfectly clear about the all-important distinction which is before us, I will re-state it in other terms.

What is the difference between a recept and a concept?
I cannot answer this question more clearly or concisely than
in the words of the writer in the *Dublin Review* before quoted.
"The difference is all the difference between seeing two
things united, and seeing them *as united.*" The difference
is all the difference between perceiving relations, and perceiving the relations *as related*, or between cognizing a truth,
and recognizing that truth *as true.* The diving bird, which
avoids a rock and fearlessly plunges into the sea, unquestionably displays a receptual knowledge of certain "things,"
"relations," and "truths;" but it does not know any of them
*as such:* although it knows them, it does not *know that it
knows them:* however well it knows them, it does not *think*
them, or regard the things, the relations, and the truths which
it perceives as *themselves the objects of perception.* Now, over
and above this merely receptual knowledge, man displays
conceptual, which means that he *is* able to do all these things
that the bird cannot do : in other words, he is able to set
before his mind all the recepts which he has in common with
the bird, to think about them *as* recepts, and by the mere
fact, or in the very act of so doing, to convert them into
concepts. Concepts, then, differ from recepts in that they
are recepts which have themselves become objects of knowledge, and the condition to their taking on this important
character is the presence of self-consciousness in the percipient
mind.*

I have twice stated the distinction as clearly as I am able ;
but, in order to do it the fullest justice, I will now render it
a third time in the words of Mr. Mivart—some of whose
terms I have borrowed in the above paragraph, and therefore

---

* Of course concepts may be something more than mere recepts known as
such : they may be the knowledge of other concepts. But with this higher stage
of conceptual ideation I am not here concerned.

need not now repeat. He begins by conveying the distinction
as it was stated by Buffon, thus :—

"Far from denying feelings to animals, I concede to them
everything except thought and reflection. . . . They have
sensations, but no faculty of comparing them with one
another, that is to say they have not the power which pro-
duces ideas "—*i.e.* products of reflection. Then, after alluding
to Buffon's views on the distinction between "automatic
memory" and "intellectual memory" (*i.e.* the distinction
which I have recognized in the Diagram attached to my
previous work by calling the former "memory" and the latter
"recollection"), Mr. Mivart adds :—"The distinction is one
quite easy to perceive. That we have automatic memory,
such as animals have, is obvious : but the presence of
intellectual memory may be made evident by searching
our minds (so to speak) for something which we have
fully remembered before, and thus intellectually remember
to have known, though we cannot now bring it before the
imagination. And as with memory, so with other of our
mental powers, we may, I think, distinguish between a higher
and a lower faculty of each ; between our higher, self-conscious, reflective mental acts—the acts of our intellectual
faculty—and those of our merely sensitive power. This distinction I believe to be one of the most fundamental of all the
distinctions of biology, and to be one the apprehension of
which is a necessary preliminary to a successful investigation
of animal psychology." *

Were it necessary, I could quote from his work, entitled
*Lessons from Nature,* sundry further passages expressing
the same distinction in other words ; but I have already been
careful, even to redundancy, in presenting this distinction, not
only because it is the distinction on which Mr. Mivart rests
his whole argument for the separation of man from the rest
of the animal kingdom as a being unique in kind ; but still
more because it is, as he is careful to point out, the one real
distinction which has hitherto always been drawn by philo-

* *Nature,* August 21, 1879.

sophers since the time of Aristotle. And, as I have already observed, it is a distinction which I myself fully recognize, and believe to be the most important of all distinctions in psychology. The only point of difference, therefore, between my opinions and those—I will not say of Mr. Mivart, but—of any other or possible opponent who understands the psychology of this subject, is on the question whether, in view of the light which has now been shed on psychology by the theory of evolution, this important distinction is to be regarded as one of degree or as one of kind. I shall now proceed to unfold the reasons which lead me to differ on this point from Mr. Mivart, and so from all the still extensive school of which he is, in my opinion, much the ablest spokesman.

We have seen that the distinction in question consists in the presence or absence of the faculty now fully explained, of reflective thought, and that of this faculty the simplest manifestation is, as alleged by my opponents, that which is afforded by "judgment." But we have also seen that this faculty of judgment does not first appear in predication, unless we extend the term so as to embrace all acts of denomination. In other words, we have seen that judgment first arises with conception—and necessarily so, seeing that neither of these things can occur without the other, but both arise as direct exhibitions of that faculty of self-conscious or reflective thought of which they are everywhere the immediate expression. I will, therefore, begin with a careful analysis of conceptual judgment.

We must first recur to the distinctions set forth at the close of the last chapter, where it was shown that, without any prejudice to the question touching the distinction between man and brute, there are five different stages of intentional sign-making to be recognized—namely, the indicative, the denotative, the connotative, the denominative, and the predicative. From what has now been said regarding the essentially predicative nature of all conceptual names, we may disregard the last of these distinctions, and consider the denominative phase of language as psychologically identical with the predicative. Similarly, we may now neglect the indicative phase, as one which bears no relation to the matters at present before us. Thus we have to fasten attention only upon the differences between the denotative, the connotative, and the denominative phases of language. This has already been done in general terms; but must now be done in more detail. And for the sake of being clear, even at the risk of being tedious, I will begin by repeating the important distinctions already explained.

When a parrot calls a dog *Bow-wow* (as a parrot, like a child, may easily be taught to do), the parrot may be said, in one sense of the word, to be *naming* the dog; but it is not *predicating* any characters as belonging to a dog, or performing any act of *judgment* with regard to a dog. Although the bird may never (or but rarely) utter the name save when it sees a dog, this fact is attributable to the laws of association acting only in the receptual sphere: it furnishes no shadow of a reason for supposing that the bird *thinks* about a dog *as* a dog, or sets the concept Dog before its mind as a separate object of thought. Therefore, all my opponents must allow that in one sense of the word there may be names without concepts: whether as gestures or as words (vocal gestures), there may be signs of things without these signs presenting any vestige of predicative value. Names of this kind I have called *denotative :* they are marks affixed to objects, qualities, actions, &c., by receptual association alone.

Next, when a denotative name has been formed and applied as the mark of one thing, its use may be extended to denote also another thing, which is seen to belong to the same class or kind. When denotative names are thus extended, they become what I have called *connotative.* The degree to which such classificatory extension of a denotative name may take place depends, of course, on the degree in which the mind is able to take cognizance of resemblances or analogies. Now, these degrees are as various as are the degrees of intelligence itself. Long before the differential engine of Conception has come to the assistance of Mind, both animals and human beings (as previously shown) are able to go a long way in the distinguishing of resemblances, or analogies, by means of receptual ideation alone. When such receptual discrimination is expressed by the corresponding extension of denotative names, the degree of connotation which such names may thus acquire depends upon the degree of this receptual discrimination. Even my parrot was able to extend its denotative name for a particular dog to any other dog which it happened to see—thus precisely resembling my child, who extended its first denotative word *Star* to a candle. Connotation, then, begins in the purely receptual sphere of ideation; and although in man it is afterwards carried up into the conceptual sphere, it is obviously most imperative for the purposes of this analysis to draw a distinction between connotation as receptual and as conceptual.

This distinction I have drawn by assigning the word *denomination* to all connotation which is of a truly conceptual nature—or to the bestowing of names *consciously recognized as such.* And I have just shown that when connotation is thus denominative or conceptual, it is psychologically the same as predication. Therefore it is only in this denominative sense of the word, or in cases where conceptual ideation is concerned, that an act of naming involves an act of judgment, strictly so called.

Such being the psychological standing of the matter, it is evident that the whole question before us is narrowed down to a clearing up of the relations that obtain between connotation as receptual and conceptual—or between connotation, that is, and connotation that is not, denominative. To do this I will begin by quoting an instance of un-denominative or receptual connotation in the case of a young child.

"There is this peculiar to man—the sound which has been associated in his case with the perception of some particular individual is called up again, not only at the sight of absolutely similar individuals, but also by the presence of individuals strikingly different, though in some respects comprised in the same class. In other words, analogies which do not strike animals strike men. The child says *Bow-wow*, first to the house-dog, then, after a little, he says *Bow-wow* to the terriers, mastiffs, and Newfoundlands he sees in the street. A little later he does what an animal never does, he says *Bow-wow* to a paste-board dog which barks when squeezed, then to a paste-board dog which does not bark, but runs on wheels, then to the silent motionless bronze dog which ornaments the drawing-room, then to his little cousin who runs about the room on all fours, then, at last, to a picture representing a dog."*

Now, in this small but typical history we have a clear exhibition, in a simple form, of the development of a connotative name within the purely receptual sphere. At first the word *Bow-wow* was merely a denotative name—or a mark affixed to a particular object of perception. But when the child's mind took cognizance of the resemblances between the house-dog, terriers, mastiffs, and Newfoundlands, it expressed the fact by extending the name *Bow-wow* to all these dogs. The name, from being particular, thus became generic, or indicative of *resemblances ;* and, therefore, from being merely denotative, became truly connotative : it now served to express *common attributes.* Next, this receptual connotation of the name was still further widened, so as to include—or to signify—the resemblances between dogs and their images, pictures, &c. Now, in these several and successive acts of connotative naming, the child was obviously advancing to higher and higher levels of receptual classification ; but, no less obviously, it would be absurd to suppose that the child was thus raising the name *Bow-wow* to any *conceptual* value. All that any child in such a case is doing is to extend its receptual appreciation of resemblance through widening circles of generic grouping, and correspondingly to extend the receptual connotation of a denotative name. In order to

* Taine, *Intelligence,* pp. 399, 400.

do this (within the limits that we are now considering), there is no need for any introspective regarding of the name as a name: there is no need to contemplate the widening connotation of the name : there is no need to *judge*, to *define*, to *denominate.* Such classification as is here effected can be effected within the region of receptual consciousness alone (as we well know from the analogous case of the parrot, and the " practical inferences " of the lower animals generally) ; therefore, if the denotative name originally assigned to a particular dog admitted of being so assigned as merely the mark of that particular recept, there is no reason to suppose that its subsequent extension to the more generic recepts afterwards experienced involves any demand upon the conceptual faculty, or implies that the child could only extend this name from a house-dog to a terrier by first performing an act of introspective thought—which, indeed, as we shall see later on, it is demonstrably impossible that a child of this age can be able to do.

Nevertheless, it is evident that already the child has done more than the parrot. For a parrot will never extend its denotative name of a particular dog to the picture, or even to the image of a dog. The utmost that a parrot will do is to extend the denotative name from one particular dog to another particular dog, which, however, may differ considerably from the former as to size, colour, and general appearance. Still, I presume, no one will maintain that thus far there is the faintest evidence of a difference of kind between the connotative faculty of the bird and that of the child. All that these facts can be held to show is that—in the words already quoted from M. Taine while narrating these facts—" analogies which do not strike animals strike men." Or, in my own phraseology, the receptual faculties of a parrot do not go further than the receptual faculties of a very young child : consequently, the denotative name in the case of the parrot only undergoes the first step in the process of receptual extension—namely, from a house-dog to a terrier, a setter, a mastiff, a Newfoundland, &c. But in the case of the child, *after having reached this stage*, the process of extension continues, so as to embrace images, and eventually pictures of dogs. This difference, however, only shows an advance in the merely receptual faculties : does not suggest that in order to carry the extension of the name through these second and third stages, demand has yet been made on the distinctively human powers of conceptual thought—any more than such powers were required to carry it through the first stage in the case of the parrot.

Hence we see again that the distinction already drawn between denotative and connotative names is not co-extensive with the distinction between ideas as receptual and conceptual. Or, in other words, names may be in some measure connotative even in the absence of self-consciousness. For if we say that a child is connoting resemblances when it extends the name *Bow-wow* from a particular dog to dogs in general, clearly we must say the same thing of a parrot when we find that thus far it goes with the child. Therefore it is that I have distinguished between connotation as receptual and conceptual—*i.e.* by calling the latter *denomination*. Receptual connotation represents a higher level of ideational faculty than mere denotation ; but a lower level than conceptual connotation, or denomination. Moreover, receptual connotation admits of many degrees before we can discern the smallest reason for supposing that it is even in the lowest degree conceptual. Connotation of all degrees depending on perceptions of resemblances or analogies, the higher the receptual life, and therefore the greater the aptitude of receptual classification, the more will such classification become reflected in connotative expression. Therefore it is that the child will not only surpass the parrot in its receptual connotation from dogs to pictures of dogs ; but, as we shall afterwards see, will go much further even than this before it gives any signs at all of conceptual connotation, or true denomination. Thus we see that between the most rudimentary receptual connotation which a very young child shares with a parrot, and the fully conceptual connotation which it

13

subsequently attains, there is a large intervening province due to the acquisition of a higher receptual life. Or, to put the same thing in other words, there is a large tract of ideation lying between the highest receptual life of a brute and the lowest conceptual life of a man : this tract is occupied by the growing child from the time at which its ideation surpasses that of the brute, until it begins to attain the faculty of self-conscious reflection. This intervening tract of ideation, therefore, may be termed "higher receptual," in contradistinction to the lower receptual ideation which a younger child shares with the lower animals.

At this point I must ask the reader carefully to fasten in his mind these various distinctions. Nor will it be difficult to do so after a small amount of attention. It will be remembered that in Chapter IV. I instituted a distinction between concepts as higher and lower, which was methodically similar to that which I have now to institute between recepts. A "lower concept" was defined to be nothing more than a "named recept," * while a "higher concept" was understood to be one that is "compounded of other concepts"—*i.e.* the named result of a grouping of concepts, as when we speak of the "mechanical equivalent of heat." So that altogether we have four stages of ideation to recognize, each of which occupies an immensely large territory of mind. These four stages I will present in serial order.

(1) *Lower Recepts*, comprising the mental life of all the lower animals, and so including such powers of receptual connotation as a child when first emerging from infancy shares with a parrot.

(2) *Higher Recepts*, comprising all the extensive tract of ideation that belongs to a child between the time when its powers of receptual connotation first surpass those of a parrot,

---

* Or, as we may now more closely define it, a denominated recept. A merely denotated recept (such as a parrot's name for its recept of dog) is not conceptual, even in the lowest degree. In other words, named recepts, merely as such, are not necessarily concepts. Whether or not they are concepts depends on whether the naming has been an act of denotation or of denomination—conscious only, or likewise *self*-conscious.

up to the age at which connotation as merely denotative begins to become also denominative.

(3) *Lower Concepts*, comprising the province of conceptual ideation where this first emerges from the higher receptual, up to the point where denominative connotation has to do, not merely with the naming of recepts, but also with that of associated concepts.

(4) *Higher Concepts*, comprising all the further excellencies of human thought.

Higher Recepts, then, are what may be conveniently termed Pre-concepts : * they occupy the interval between the receptual life of brute and the earliest dawn of the conceptual life of man. A pre-concept, therefore, is that kind of higher recept which is not to be met with in any brute ; but which occurs in the human being after surpassing the brute and before attaining self-consciousness. Be it observed that in thus coining the words higher recepts or pre-concepts, I am not in any way prejudicing the case of my opponents ; I am merely marking off a certain territory of ideation which has now for the first time been indicated. Of course my object eventually is to show that in the history of a growing child, just as sensations give rise to percepts, and percepts to recepts (as they do among animals), so do recepts give rise to pre-concepts, pre-concepts to concepts, concepts to propositions, and propositions to syllogisms. But in now supplying this intermediate link of pre-concepts I am not in any way pre-judging the issue : I am merely marking out the ground for discussion. No one of my opponents can dispute my facts, which are too obvious to admit of question. Therefore, if they object to my classification of them so far as the novel division of pre-concepts is concerned, it must be because they think that by instituting this division I am surreptitiously bringing the mind of a child nearer to that of an animal than they deem altogether safe. What, then, I ask, would they have me do ? If I fail to

* I coin this word on the pattern already furnished by " pre-perception," which was first introduced by Lewes, and is now in general use among psychologists.

institute this division, I should have to prejudice the question indeed. Either there is some distinction between the naming powers of a parrot and those of a young child, or else there is not. If there is no distinction, so much the better for the purposes of my argument. But I allow that there is a distinction, and I draw it at the first place where it can possibly be said that the intelligence of a child differs in any way at all from that of a parrot—*i.e.* where the naming powers of a child demonstrably excel those of a parrot, or any other brute. If this place happens to be before the rise of conceptual powers, I am not responsible for the fact ; nor in stating it am I at all disparaging the position of any opponent who takes his stand upon these powers as distinctive of man. If his position were worth anything before, it cannot be affected by my drawing attention to the fact that, while a parrot will extend its denotative name of a dog from a terrier to a setter, it will not follow a child any further in the process of receptual connotation.

Or, to put it in another way, when the child says *Bow-wow* to a setter, after having learnt this name for a terrier, it is either judging a resemblance and predicating a fact, or else it is doing neither of these things. If my opponents elect to say that the child is doing both these things, there is an end of the only issue between us ; for in that case a parrot also is able both to judge and to predicate. On the other hand, if my opponents adopt the wiser course, and accept my distinction between names as receptual and conceptual, they must also follow me in recognizing the border-land of pre-concepts as lying between the recepts of a bird and the concepts of a man—*i.e.* the territory which is first occupied by the higher receptual life of a child before this passes into the conceptual life of a man,—for that such a border-land does exist I will prove still more incontestably later on. There is, then, as a matter of observable fact, a territory of ideation which separates the highest recepts of a brute from the lowest concepts of a human being ; and all that my term pre-conception is designed to do is to name this intervening territory.

Now, if this is the case with regard to naming, clearly it must also be the case with regard to judging : if there is a stage of pre-conception, there must also be a stage of pre-judgment. For we have seen that it is of the essence of a judgment that it should be concerned with concepts : if the mind be concerned merely with recepts, no act of true judgment can be said to have been performed. When a child says *Bow-wow* to the picture of a dog, no one can maintain that he is actually judging the resemblance of the picture to a dog, unless it be supposed that for this act of receptual classification distinctively human powers of conceptual thought are required. But, as just shown, no opponent of mine can afford to adopt this supposition, because behind the case of the child there stands that of the parrot. True, the parrot does not proceed in its receptual classification further than to extend its name for a particular dog to other living dogs ; but if any one were foolish enough to stake his whole argument on so slender a distinction as this—to maintain that at the place where the connotation of a child first surpasses that of a parrot we have evidence of a psychological distinction of kind, *on the sole ground that the child has begun to surpass the parrot*—it would be enough for me to remark that not *every* parrot will thus extend its denotative sign from one dog to another of greatly unlike appearance. Different birds display different degrees of intelligence in this respect. Most of them will say *Bow-wow*, will bark, or utter any other denotative sign which they may have learnt or invented, when they see dogs more or less resembling the one to which the denotative sign was originally applied ; but it is not every parrot which will thus extend the sign from a terrier to a mastiff or a Newfoundland. Therefore, if any one were to maintain that the difference between the intelligence which can discern, and one which cannot discern, the likeness of a dog in the image or the picture of a dog, is a difference of kind, consistency should lead him to draw a similar distinction between the intelligence which can discern, and one which cannot discern, the likeness of a terrier to a mastiff. But, if so, the intelligence of one

parrot would be different in kind from that of another parrot ;
and the child's intelligence at one age would differ in kind
from the intelligence of that same child when a week or two
older—both of which statements would be manifestly absurd.
The truth can only be that up to the point where the intelligence of the child surpasses that of the bird they are both in
the receptual stage of sign-making ; and that the only reason
why the child does surpass the bird is not, in the first
instance, because the child there suddenly attains the power
of conceptual ideation, but because it gradually attains a
higher level of receptual ideation. This admits of direct
proof from the fact that animals more intelligent than parrots
are unquestionably able to recognize sculptured and even
pictorial representations : hence there can be no doubt that
if talking birds had attained a similar level of intelligence—
or if the other and more intelligent animals had been able,
like the talking birds, to use denotative signs,—the child
would not have parted company with the brute at quite so
early a stage of receptual nomenclature.*

---

* Touching the power of recognizing pictorial representations among animals,
this unquestionably occurs in dogs (see *Animal Intelligence*, pp. 455, 456), and there
is some evidence to show that it is likewise displayed by monkeys.  For Isidore
Geoffroy St. Hilaire relates of a species of Midas (*Corinus*) that it distinguished
between different objects depicted on an engraving ; and Audouin "showed it the
portraits of a cat and a wasp, at which it became much terrified : whereas, at
the sight of a figure of a grasshopper or a beetle, it precipitated itself on the
picture, as if to seize the objects there represented" (Bates, *Nat. on Amaz.*, p. 60).
The age at which a young child first learns to recognize pictorial resemblances no
doubt varies in individual cases.  I have not met with any evidence on this
subject in the writings of other observers of infant psychology.  The earliest age at
which I observed any display of this faculty in my own children was at eight months,
when my son stared long and fixedly at my own portrait in a manner which left no
doubt on my mind that he recognized it as resembling the face of a man.  Moreover, always after that day when asked in that room, " Where's papa ? " he used at
once to look up and point at the portrait.  Another child of my own, which had not
seen this portrait till she was sixteen months old, immediately recognized it at first
sight, as was proved by her pointing to it and calling it " Papa."  Two months
later I observed that she also recognized pictorial resemblances of animals, and
for many months afterwards her chief amusement consisted in looking through
picture-books for the purpose of pointing out the animals or persons depicted—
calling " Ba-a-a " to the sheep, " Moo " to the cows, grunting for the pigs, &c.,
these sundry sounds having been taught her as names by the nurse.  She never

What, then, are we to say about the faculty of judgment in relation to these three stages of ideation—namely, the receptual, pre-conceptual, and conceptual? We can only institute the parallel and consequent distinction between judgment as receptual, pre-conceptual, and conceptual.* As now so often stated, the distinguishing features of a judgment as fully displayed in any act of formal predication, are the bringing together in self-conscious thought of two concepts, and the distinguishing of some relation between them as such. Therefore we do not say that a brute judges when, without any self-conscious thought, it brings together certain reminiscences of its past experience in the form of recepts, and translates for us the results of its ideation by the performance of what Mr. Mivart calls " practical inferences." Therefore, also, if a brute which is able to name each of two recepts separately (as is done by a talking bird), were to name the two recepts simultaneously when thus combined in an act of " practical inference," although there would then be the outward semblance of a proposition, we should not be strictly right in calling it a proposition. It would, indeed, be the statement of a truth *perceived;* but not the statement of a truth perceived *as true.*†

made a mistake in this kind of nomenclature, and spontaneously called all pictorial representations of men " Papa," of women " Mama," and of children " Ilda " —the latter being the name which she had given to her younger brother. Moreover, if a picture-book were given into her hands upside-down, she would immediately perceive and rectify the mistake ; and whenever she happened to see a pictorial representation of an animal—as, for instance, on a screen or wall-paper—she would touch it and utter the sound that was her name for that animal. With a third child, who was still wholly speechless at eighteen months, I tried the experiment of spreading out a number of photographic portraits, and asking him " Which is mamma? Which is papa?" &c. Without any hesitation he indicated them all correctly.

* By using the word " judgment " in all these cases I am in no way prejudicing the argument of my opponents. The explanation which immediately follows in the text is sufficient to show that the qualifying terms " receptual " and " pre-conceptual " effectually guard against any abuse of the term—quite as much, for instance, as when psychologists speak of " perceptual judgments," or " unconscious judgments," or " intuitive judgments," in connection with still lower levels of mental operation. And it seems to me better thus to qualify an existing term than to add to the already large number of words I have found it necessary to coin.

† I may here remark that this possibility of receptual predication on the part

Now, if all this be admitted in the case of a brute—as it must be by any one who takes his stand on the faculty of true or conceptual judgment,—obviously it must also be admitted in the case of the growing child.   In other words, if it can be proved that a child is able to state a truth before it can state a truth as true, it is thereby proved that in the psychological history of every human being there is first the incompleted kind of judgment required for dealing with receptual knowledge, and so for stating truths perceived, and next the completed judgment, which deals with conceptual knowledge, and so is enabled to state truths perceived as true. Of course the condition to the raising of this lower kind of judgment (if for convenience we agree so to term it) into the higher, is given by the advent of self-consciousness; and therefore the place where *statement* of truth passes into *predication* of truth must be determined by the place at which this kind of consciousness first supervenes.   Where it does first supervene we shall presently have to consider.   Meanwhile I am but endeavouring to make clear the fact that, unless my opponents abandon their position altogether, they must allow that there is *some* difference to be recognized between the connotative powers of a parrot and the connotative powers of a man.   But if they do allow this, they must further allow that between the place where the connotative powers of a child first surpass those of a parrot, and the place where those powers first become truly conceptual, there is a large tract of ideation which it is impossible to ignore.   In order, therefore, not to prejudice the question before us, I have

of talking birds is not entirely hypothetical : I have some evidence that it may be actually realized.   For instance, a correspondent writes of a cockatoo which had been ill:—"A friend came the same afternoon, and asked him how he was.   With his head on one side and one of his cunning looks, he told her that he was 'a little better;' and when she asked him if he had not been very ill, he said, 'Cockie better; Cockie ever so much better.' . . . When I came back (after a prolonged absence) he said, 'Mother come back to little Cockie: Mother come back to little Cockie.   Come and love me and give me pretty kiss.   Nobody pity poor Cockie.   The boy beat poor Cockie.'   He always told me if Jes scolded or beat him.   He always told me as soon as he saw me, and in such a pitiful tone. . . . The remarkable thing about this bird is that he does not merely 'talk' like parrots in general, but so habitually *talks to the purpose.*"

thus far confined myself to a mere designation of these great and obvious distinctions. But seeing that even this preliminary step has necessitated a great deal of explanation, I feel it may conduce to clearness if I end the present chapter with a tabular statement of the sundry distinctions in question.

By *receptual judgments* I will understand the same order of ideation as Mr. Mivart expresses by his term "practical inferences of brutes," instances of which have already been given in Chapter III.

By *pre-conceptual judgments* I will understand those acts of virtual or rudimentary judgment which are performed by children subsequent to the "practical inferences" which they share with brutes, but prior to the advent of self-conscious reflection. These pre-conceptual judgments may be expressed either by gestures, connotative classifications, or by both combined. Some instances of them have already been given in the present chapter : further and better instances will be given in the chapters which are to follow.

By *conceptual judgments* I will understand full and complete judgments in the ordinary acceptation of this term.

Receptual judgment, then, has to do with recepts ; pre-conceptual judgment with pre-concepts ; and true judgments with true concepts. Or, conversely stated, receptual knowledge leads to receptual judgment (*e.g.* when a sea-bird dives into water but alights upon land) : pre-conceptual knowledge leads to pre-conceptual judgment in the statement of such knowledge (*e.g.* when a child, by extending the name of a dog to the picture of a dog, virtually affirms, though it does not conceive, the resemblance which it perceives) : and, lastly, conceptual knowledge leads to conceptual or veritable judgment, in the statement of such knowledge known as knowledge (*e.g.* when, in virtue of his powers of reflective thought, a man not only states a truth, but states that truth as true).

Thus far I doubt whether my opponents will find it easy to meet me. They may, of course, cavil at some or all of the above distinctions ; but, if so, it is for them to show cause for complaint. They have raised objections to the theory of evolution on purely psychological grounds. I meet their objections upon these their own grounds, and therefore the only way in which they can answer me is by showing that there is something wrong in my psychological analysis. This I fearlessly invite them to do. For all the distinctions which I have made I have made out of consideration to the exigencies of their argument. Although these distinctions may appear somewhat bewilderingly numerous, I do not anticipate that any competent psychologist will complain of them on account of their having been over-finely drawn. For each of them marks off an important territory of ideation, and all the territories so marked off must be separately noted, if the alleged distinction of kind between one and another is to be seriously investigated. In his essays upon the theory of evolution, Mr. Mivart not unfrequently complains of the disregard of psychological analysis which is betokened by any expression of opinion to the effect, that as between one great territory of ideation and another there is only a difference of degree. But surely this complaint comes with an ill grace from a writer who bases an opposite opinion upon a precisely similar neglect—or upon a bare statement of the greatest and most obvious of all the distinctions in psychology, without so much as any attempt to analyze it. Therefore, if my own attempt to do this has erred on the side of over-elaboration, it has done so only on account of my desire to do full justice to the opposite side. In the result, I claim to have shown that if it is possible to suggest a difference of kind between any of the levels of ideation which have now been defined, this can only be done at the last of them—or where the advent of self-consciousness enables a mind, not only to *know*, but to *know that it knows;* not only to *receive* knowledge, but also to *conceive* it ; not only to *connotate*, but also to *denominate ;* not only to *state a truth*, but also to state that truth *as true.* The question, therefore, which now lies before us is that as to the nature of this self-consciousness— or, more accurately, whether the great and peculiar distinction which this attribute confers upon the human intellect is to be regarded as a distinction of degree only, or as a distinction of kind. To answer this question we must first investigate the rise of self-consciousness in the only place where its rise can be observed, namely, in the psychogenesis of a child.*

* Lest there should still be any ambiguity about the numerous terms which I have found it necessary to coin, I will here supply a table of definitions.

Lower recept  = an automatic grouping of percepts.
Higher recept = pre-concept ; or a degree of receptual ideation which does not occur in any brute.
Lower concept = named recept, provided that the naming be due to reflective thought.
Higher concept = a named compound of concepts.

The analogues of these terms are, in the matter of naming :—

Receptual naming  = denotation, which includes pre-conceptual naming.
Conceptual naming = denomination.

And, in the matter of judging, the analogues are :—

Receptual judgment      = automatic, " practical," or unthinking inference.
Pre-conceptual judgment = the higher, though still unthinking, inferences of a child prior to the rise of self-consciousness.
Conceptual judgment      = true judgment, whether exhibited in denomination, predication, or any act of inference for which self-conscious thought may be required.

# CHAPTER X.

## SELF-CONSCIOUSNESS.

MY contention in this chapter will be that, given the proto-plasm of the sign-making faculty so far organized as to have reached the denotative stage ; and given also the protoplasm of judgment so far organized as to have reached the stage of stating a truth, without the mind being yet sufficiently developed to be conscious of itself as an object of thought, and therefore not yet able to state to itself a truth as true ; by a confluence of these two protoplasmic elements an act of fertilization is performed, such that the subsequent processes of mental organization proceed apace, and soon reach the stage of differentiation between subject and object.

And here, to avoid misapprehension, I may as well make it clear at the outset that in all which is to follow I am in no way concerned with the philosophy of this change, but only with its history.  On the side of its philosophy no one can have a deeper respect for the problem of self-consciousness than I have ; for no one can be more profoundly convinced than I am that the problem on this side does not admit of solution.  In other words, so far as this aspect of the matter is concerned, I am in complete agreement with the most advanced idealist ; and hold that in the datum of self-consciousness we each of us possess, not merely our only ultimate knowledge, or that which only is " real in its own right," but likewise the mode of existence which alone the human mind is capable of conceiving as existence, and there-fore the *conditio sine quâ non* to the possibility of an external world. With this aspect of the question, however, I am in no way concerned. Just as the functions of an embryologist are confined to tracing the mere history of developmental changes of living structure, and just as he is thus as far as ever from throwing any light upon the deeper questions of the how and the why of life ; so in seeking to indicate the steps whereby self-consciousness has arisen from the lower stages of mental structure, I am as far as any one can be from throwing light upon the intrinsic nature of that the probable genesis of which I am endeavouring to trace. It is no less true to-day than it was in the time of Soloman, that "as thou knowest not how the bones do grow in the womb of her that is with child, thou knowest not what is the way of the spirit."

If we are agreed that it is only in man that self-consciousness is to be found at all, it follows that only to man can we look for any facts bearing upon the question of its development. And inasmuch as it is only during the first years of infancy that a normal human being is destitute of self-consciousness, the statement just made implies that only in infant psychology need we seek for the facts of which we are in search. Further, as I maintain that self-consciousness arises out of an admixture of the protoplasm of judgment with the protoplasm of sign-making (according to the signification of these terms as already explained), I have now to make good this opinion upon the basis of facts drawn from the study of infant psychology.

Nevertheless, before I proceed to the heart of the subject, I think it will be convenient to consider those faculties of mind which, occurring both in the infant and in the animal, in the former case precede the advent of self-consciousness, and, according to my view, prepare the way for it.

It will, I suppose, on all hands be admitted that self-consciousness consists in paying the same kind of attention to internal or psychical processes as is habitually paid to external or physical processes—a bringing to bear upon subjective phenomena the same powers of perception as are brought to bear upon the objective. The degrees in which such attention may be yielded are, of course, as various in the one case as in the other; but this does not affect my psychological definition of self-consciousness.

Again, I suppose it will be further admitted that in the mind of animals and in the mind of infants there is a world of images standing as signs of outward objects; and that the only reason why these images are not attended to unless called up by the sensuous associations supplied by their corresponding objects, is because the mind is not yet able to leave the ground of such association, so as to move through the higher and more tenuous medium of introspective thought.* Nevertheless, this image-world assuredly displays an internal activity which is not wholly dependent on sensuous associations supplied from without. That is to say, one image suggests another, this another, and so on—although, as I have just conceded, this cannot be due to successive acts of inward attention, or of the self-conscious contemplation of images known as such. Nevertheless, that an internal—though unintentional—play of ideation takes place in the minds of brutes, without the necessity of immediate associations supplied from present objects of sense, admits of being amply proved from the phenomena of dreaming, hallucination, home-sickness, pining for absent friends, &c., which, as I have fully shown in my previous work, can only be explained by recognizing such a play of inward ideation.† Now, I hold it of importance to note that such an internal play of ideation is thus possible even in the absence of self-consciousness, because many writers have assumed, without any justification, that unless ideas are intentionally contemplated as such, they must be wholly dependent for their occurrence upon associations supplied by present objects of sense. Of course I do not doubt that an agent who is capable of intentionally making one idea stand as the object of another, is likewise capable of

---

* See above, Chapters II. and IV.

† See *Mental Evolution in Animals*, chapter on " Imagination."

going very much further than a brute in the way of causing one idea to start from another irrespective of immediate stimulation from without. My point here is merely to remark that the ideation of brutes is not wholly dependent on such stimulation; but is capable, in a certain humble degree, of forming independent chains of its own.

The next thing which I desire to be remembered in connection with the ideation of brutes is, that it is not restricted to the mere reproduction in memory of particular objects of sensuous impressions; but, as we have so fully seen in Chapter III., admits of undergoing that amount of mental elaboration which belongs to what I have termed recepts.

Furthermore, the foundations of self-consciousness are largely laid in the fact that an organism is one connected whole; all the parts are mutually related in the unity of individual sensibility. Every stimulus supplied from without, every movement originating from within, carries with it the character of belonging to that which feels and moves. Hence a brute, like a young child, has learnt to distinguish its own members, and likewise its whole body, from all other objects; it knows how to avoid sources of pain, how to seek those of pleasure; and it also knows that particular movements follow from particular volitions, while in connection with such movements it constantly experiences the same muscular sensations. Of course such knowledge and such experience all belong to the receptual order; but this does not hinder that they play a most important part in laying the foundations of a consciousness of individuality.*

Lastly, and I believe of still more importance in the present connection than any of the above-named antecedents, a large proportional number of the recepts of a brute have reference, not to objects of sense, or even to muscular sensations, but to the *mental states of other animals.* That is

* In the opinion of Wundt, the most important of all conditions to the genesis of self-consciousness is given by the muscular sense in acts of voluntary movement (*Vorlesungen über die Menschen und Thierseele*, 18 vorl.). While agreeing with him that this is a highly important condition, I think the others above mentioned are quite as much, or even more so.

to say, the logic of recepts, even in brutes, is sufficient to enable the mind to establish true analogies between its own states (although these are not yet the objects of separate attention, or of what may be termed subjective knowledge), and the corresponding states of other minds. I need not dwell upon this point, because I take it to be a matter of general observation that animals habitually and accurately interpret the mental states of other animals, while they also well know that other animals are able similarly to interpret *theirs*—as is best proved by their practising the arts of cunning, concealment, hypocrisy, &c.* From which considerations we reach the general conclusion, that intelligent animals recognize a world of ejects as well as a world of objects : mental existence is known to them ejectively, though, as may be allowed, never *thought upon* subjectively.†

It is of importance further to observe that at this stage of mental evolution the individual—whether an animal or an infant—so far realizes its own individuality as to be informed by the logic of recepts that it is *one of a kind*. I do not mean that at this stage the individual realizes its own or any other individuality as such ; but merely that it recognizes the fact of its being one among a number of similar though distinct forms of life. Alike in conflict, rivalry, sense of

---

* See for cases of this, *Animal Intelligence*, pp. 410, 443, 444, 450–452, 458, 494.

† The following is a good example of ejective ideation in a brute—all the better, perhaps, on account of being so familiar. I quote it from Quatrefage's *Human Species,* pp. 20, 21:—"I must here beg permission to relate the remembrance of my struggles with a mastiff of pure breed and which had attained its full size, remaining, however, very young in character. We were very good friends and often played together. As soon as ever I assumed an attitude of defence before him, he would leap upon me with every appearance of fury, seizing in his mouth the arm which I had used as a shield. He might have marked my arm deeply at the first onset, but he never pressed it in a manner that could inflict the slightest pain. I often seized his lower jaw with my hand, but he never used his teeth so as to bite me. And yet the next moment the same teeth would indent a piece of wood I tried to tear away from them. This animal evidently knew what it was doing when it feigned the passion precisely opposite to that which it really felt ; when, even in the excitement of play, it retained sufficient mastery over its movements to avoid hurting me. In reality it played a part in a comedy, and we cannot act without being conscious of it."

liability to punishment or vengeance, &c., the truth is continually being borne in upon the mind of an animal that it is a separate individuality ; and this though it be conceded that the animal is never able, even in the most shadowy manner, to think about itself as such. In this way there arises a sort of "outward self-consciousness," which differs from true or inward self-consciousness only in the absence of any attention being directed upon the inward mental states as such. This outward self-consciousness is known to us all, even in adult life—it being but comparatively seldom that we pause in our daily activities to contemplate the mental processes of which these activities are the expression.

Now, if these things are so, we encounter the necessity of drawing the same distinction in our analysis of self-conscious-ness, as we have had to draw in our previous analyses of all the other faculties of mind : there is a self-consciousness that is receptual, and a self-consciousness that is conceptual. No doubt it is to the latter kind of self-consciousness alone that the term is strictly applicable, just as it is to conceptual naming or to conceptual predicating alone that the word "judgment" is strictly applicable. Nevertheless, here, as before, we must not ignore an important territory of mind only because it has hitherto remained uncharted.* Receptual or outward self-consciousness, then, is the practical recognition of self as an active and a feeling agent ; while conceptual or inward self-consciousness is the introspective recognition of

---

* Not, however, wholly so. Mr. Chauncey Wright has clearly recognized the existence of what I term receptual self-consciousness, and assigned to it the name above adopted—*i.e.* "outward self-consciousness." See his *Evolution of Self-consciousness.* Mr. Darwin, also, appears to have recognized this distinction, in the following passage :—"It may be freely admitted that no animal is self-conscious, if by this term is implied that he reflects on such points as whence he comes or whither he will go, or what is life and death, and so forth. But how can we feel sure that an old dog with an excellent memory and some power of imagination, as shown by his dreams, never reflects on his past pleasures or pains in the chase? And this would be a form of self-consciousness " (*Descent of Man,* p. 83). Of course a psychologist may take technical exception to the word "reflects" in this passage ; but that this kind of receptual reflection does take place in dogs appears to me to be definitely proved by the facts of home-sickness and pining for absent friends, above alluded to.

14

self as an object of knowledge, and, therefore, as a subject. Hence, the one form of self-consciousness differs from the other in that it is only objective and never subjective.*

I take it, then, as established that true or conceptual self-consciousness consists in paying the same kind of attention to inward psychical processes as is habitually paid to outward physical processes ; that in the mind of animals and infants there is a world of images standing as signs of outward objects, although we may concede that for the most part they only admit of being revived by sensuous association ; that at this stage of mental evolution the logic of recepts comprises an ejective as well as an objective world ; and that here we also have the recognition of individuality, so far as this is dependent on what has been termed an outward self-consciousness, or the consciousness of self as a feeling and an active agent, without the consciousness of self as an object of thought, and, therefore, as a *subject.*

Such being the mental conditions precedent to the rise of true self-consciousness, we may next turn to the growing child for evidence of subsequent stages in the gradual evolution of this faculty. All observers are agreed that for a considerable time after a child is able to use words as expressive of ideas, there is no vestige of true self-consciousness. But, to begin our survey before this period, at a year old even its own organism is not known to the child as part of the self, or, more correctly, as anything specially related to feelings. Professor Preyer observed that his boy, when more than a year old, bit his own arm just as though it had been a foreign object ; and thus may be said to have shown even

---

* In the present connection the following very pregnant sentence may be appropriately quoted from Wundt :—" Wenn wir überall auf die Empfindung als Ausgangspunkt der ganzen Entwicklungsreihe hingewiesen werden, so *müssen* auch die Anfänge jener Unterscheidung des Ichs von den Gegenständen schon in den Empfindungen gelegen sein " (*Vorlesungen über die Menschen und Thierseele,* i. 287). And to the objection that there can be no thought without knowledge of thought, he replies that before there is any knowledge of thought there must be the same order of thinking as there is of perceiving prior to the advent of self-consciousness—*e.g.* receptual ideas about space before there is any conceptual knowledge of these ideas as such.

less consciousness of a limb as belonging to "self," than did Buffon's parrot, which would first ask itself for its own claw, and then comply with the request by placing the claw in its own beak—in the same way as it would give the claw to any one else who asked for it in the same words.

Later on, when the outward self-consciousness already explained has begun to be developed, we find that the child, like the animal, has learnt to associate its own organism with its own mental states, in such wise that it recognizes its body as belonging in a peculiar manner to the self, so far as the self is recognizable by the logic of recepts. This is the stage that we meet with in animals. Next the child begins to talk, and, as we might expect, this first translation of the logic of recepts reveals the fact that as yet there is no *inward* self-consciousness, but only outward : as yet the child has paid no *attention* to his own mental states, further than to feel that he feels them ; and in the result we find that the child speaks to himself as an object, *i.e.* by his proper name or in the third person. That is to say, "the child does not as yet set himself in opposition to all outer objects, including all other persons, but regards himself as one among many objects." * The change of a child's phraseology from speaking of self as an object to speaking of self as a subject does not take place—or but rarely so—till the third year. When it has taken place we have definite evidence of true self-consciousness, though still in a rudimentary stage. And it is doubtful whether this change would take place even at so early an age as the third year, were it not promoted by the "social environment." For, as Mr. Sully observes, "the relation of self and not self, in-

---

* Sully, *loc. cit.*, p. 376. See also Wundt, *loc. cit.*, i. 289. He shows that this speaking of self in the third person is not due to "imitation," but, on the contrary, opposed to it. For "a thousand times the child hears that its elders do not thus speak of themselves." The child hears that its elders call it in the third person, and in this it follows them. But such imitation as we here find is expressive only of the fact that hitherto the child has not distinguished between self as an object and self as a subject. Only later on, when this distinction has begun to dawn, does imitation proceed to apply to the self the first person, after the manner in which other selves (now recognized by the child as such) are heard to do.

cluding that between the I and the You, is continually being pressed on the child's attention by the language of others." *
But, taking this great change during the time of life when it is actually observed to be in progress, let us endeavour to trace the phases of its development.

It will no doubt be on all hands freely conceded, that at least up to the time when a child begins to speak it has no beginning of any true or introspective consciousness of self ; and it will further be conceded that when this consciousness begins to dawn, the use of language by a child may be taken as a fair exponent of all its subsequent progress. Now we have already seen that, long before any words are used indicative of even a dawning consciousness of self as self, the child has already advanced so far in its use of language as to frame implicit propositions. But lest it should be thought that my judgment in this matter is biased by the exigencies of my argument, I may again quote Mr. Sully as at once an impartial witness and a highly competent authority on matters of purely psychological doctrine.

"When a child of eighteen months on seeing a dog exclaims ' Bow-wow,' or on taking his food exclaims ' Ot ' (Hot), or on letting fall his toy says ' Dow ' (Down), he may be said to be implicitly framing a judgment : ' That is a dog,' ' This milk is hot,' ' My plaything is down.' The first explicit judgments are concerned with individual objects. The child notes something unexpected or surprising in an object, and expresses the result of his observation in a judgment. Thus, for example, the boy more than once referred to, whom we will call C., was first observed to form a distinct judgment when nineteen months old, by saying ' Dit ki ' (Sister is crying). These first judgments have to do mainly with the child's food, or other things of prime importance to him. Thus, among the earliest attempts at combining words in propositions made by C. already referred to, were the following : ' Ka in milk,' (Something nasty in milk ) ; ' Milk dare now ' (There is still some more milk in the cup). Towards the end of the second

* *Loc. cit.*, p. 377.

year quite a number of judgments is given out having to do with the peculiarities of objects which surprise or impress the mind, their altered position in space, &c. Among these may be instanced the following : ' Dat a big bow-wow' (That is a large dog) ; ' Dit naughty' (Sister is naughty) ; 'Dit dow ga' (sister is down on the grass). As the observing powers grow, and the child's interest in things widens, the number of his judgments increases. And as his powers of detaching relations and of uttering and combining words develop, he ventures on more elaborate statements, *e.g.* 'Mama naughty say dat.' " *

Were it necessary, I could confirm all these statements from my own notes on the development of children's intelligence ; but I prefer, for the reason already given, to quote such facts from an impartial witness. For I conceive that they are facts of the highest importance in relation to our present subject, as I shall immediately proceed to show.

We have now before us unquestionable evidence that in the growing child there is a power, not only of forming, but of expressing a pre-conceptual judgment, long before there is any evidence of the child presenting the faintest rudiment of internal, conceptual, or true self-consciousness. In other words, it must be admitted that long before a human mind is sufficiently developed to perceive relations as related, or to state a truth as true, it is able to perceive relations and to state a truth : the logic of recepts is here concerned with those higher receptual judgments which I have called pre-conceptual, and is able to express such judgments in verbal signs without the intervention of true (*i.e.* introspective) self-consciousness. It will be remembered that I have coined these various terms in order to acknowledge the possible objection that there can be no true judgments without true self-consciousness. But I do not care what terms are employed whereby to designate the different and successive phases of development which I am now endeavouring to display. All that I desire to make clear is that here we unquestionably have to do with a *growth*, or

* *Loc. cit.,* pp. 435, 436.

with a continuous advance in degree as distinguished from a difference of kind.

First, then, let it be observed that in these rudimentary judgments we already have a considerable advance upon those which we have considered as occurring in animals. For in a child between the second and third years we have these rudimentary judgments, not only formed by the logic of recepts, but expressed by a logic of pre-concepts in a manner which is indistinguishable from predication, except by the absence of self-consciousness. " Dit dow ga " is a proposition in every respect, save in the absence of the copula ; which, as I have previously shown, is a matter of no psychological moment. The child here perceives a certain fact, and states the perception in words, *in order to communicate information of the fact to other minds*—just as an animal, under similar circumstances, will use a gesture or a vocal sign ; but the child is no more able than the animal designedly to make to its own mind the statement which it makes to another. Nevertheless, as the child has now at its disposal a much more efficient system of sign-making than has the animal, and moreover enjoys the double advantage of inheriting a strong propensity to communicate perceptions by signs, and of being surrounded by the medium of speech ; we can scarcely wonder that its practical judgments (although still unattended by self-consciousness) should be more habitually expressed by signs than are the practical judgments of animals. Nor need we wonder, in view of the same considerations, that the predicative phrases as used by a child at this age show the great advance upon similar phrases as used by a parrot, in that subjects and predicates are no longer bound together in particular phrases—or, to revert to a previous simile, are no longer stereotyped in such particular phrases, but admit of being used as movable types, in order to construct, by different combinations, a variety of different phrases. To a talking bird a phrase, as we have seen, is no more in point of signification than a single word ; while to the child, at the stage which we are considering, it is very much more than this : it is the separately constructed vehicle for the conveyance of a particular meaning, which may never have been conveyed by that or by any other phrase before. But while we thus attach due importance to so great an advance towards the faculty of true predication, we must notice, on the one hand, that as yet it is *not* true predication in the sense of being the expression of a true or conceptual judgment ; and, on the other hand, we must notice that the power of thus using words as movable types does not deserve to be regarded as any wonderful or unaccountable advance in the faculty of sign-making, when we pay due regard to the several considerations above stated. The really important point to notice is that, notwithstanding this great *advance* towards the faculty of predication, this faculty *has not yet been reached :* the propositions which are made are still unattended by self-consciousness : they are not conceptual, but pre-conceptual.

Given, then, this stage of mental evolution, and what follows ? Be it remembered I am not endeavouring to solve the impossible problem as to the intrinsic nature of self-consciousness, or how it is that such a thing is possible. I am merely accepting its existence (and therefore its possibility) as a fact ; and upon the basis of this fact I shall now endeavour to show how, in my opinion, self-consciousness may be seen to follow upon the stage of mental evolution which we have here reached.

The child, like the animal, is supplied by its logic of recepts with a world of images, standing as signs of outward objects ; with an ejective knowledge of other minds ; and with that kind of recognition of self as an active, suffering and accountable agent which, following Mr. Chauncey Wright, I have called " outward self-consciousness." But, over and above the animal, the child has at its command, as we have just seen, the more improved machinery of sign-making which enables it to signify to other minds (ejectively known) the contents of its receptual knowledge. Now, among these contents is the child's perception of the mental states of others as expressed in their gestures, tones, and words. These severally receive their appropriate names, and so gain clearness and precision as ejective images of the corresponding states experienced by the child itself. " Mama pleased to Dodo" would have no meaning as spoken by a child, unless the child knew from his own feelings what is the state of mind which he thus ejectively attributes to another. Therefore we cannot be surprised to find that at the same stage of mental evolution the child will say, "Dodo pleased to mama." Yet it is evident that we here approach the very borders of true self-consciousness. "Dodo" is no doubt still speaking of himself in objective terminology; but he has advanced so far in the interpretation of his own states of mind as to name them no less clearly than he names any external objects of sense perception. Thus he is enabled to fix these states before his mental vision as things which admit of being *denoted* by verbal signs, albeit he is not yet able to *denominate*.

The step from this to recognizing "Dodo" as not only the object, but also the subject of mental changes, is not a large step. The mere act of attaching verbal signs to inward mental states has the effect of focussing attention upon those states; and, when attention is thus focussed habitually, there is supplied the only further condition required to enable the mind, through its memory of previous states, to compare its past with its present, and so to reach that apprehension of continuity among its own states wherein the full introspective consciousness of self consists.

Again, as Mr. Chauncey Wright observes, "voluntary memory, or reminiscence, is especially aided by command of language. This is a tentative process, essentially similar to that of a search for a lost or missing external object. Trials are made in it to revive a missing mental image, or train of images, by means of words; and, on the other hand, to revive a missing name by means of mental images, or even by other words. It is. not certain. that this power is an exclusively human one, as is generally believed, except in respect to the high degree of proficiency attained by men in its use. It does not appear impossible that an intelligent dog may be aided by its attention, purposely directed to spontaneous necessaries, in recalling a missing fact, such as the locality of a buried bone." *

But whether or not animals possess any power of recollection as distinguished from memory, there can be no doubt that the use of words as signs necessarily leads to the cultivation of this faculty, and so to the clear perception of a continuance of internal or mental states in which consists the consciousness of an abiding self.

Further, the acquisition of language greatly advances the conception of self, both as a suffering or feeling agent, and as an active cause ; seeing that both the feelings and the actions of the self are placed clearly before the mind by means of denotative names, and even, as we have just seen, by pre-conceptual propositions. Doubtless, also, the recognition of self in each of these capacities is largely assisted by the emotions. The expressions of affection, sympathy, praise, blame, &c., on the part of others, and the feelings of emulation, pride, triumph, disappointment, &c., on the part of the self, must all tend forcibly to impress upon the growing child a sense of personality. "It is when the child's attention is driven inwards in an act of reflection on his own actions, as springing from good or bad motives, that he wakes up to a fuller consciousness of himself." †

The conspiring together of all these factors leads to the gradual attainment of self-consciousness. I say "gradual," because the process is throughout of the nature of a growth.

---

* *Philosophical Discussions*, p. 256. See also *Animal Intelligence*, pp. 269, 270, for the case of a parrot apparently endeavouring to recover the memory of a particular word in a phrase. In the course of an interesting research on the intelligence of spiders (*Journ. Morphol.*, i., p. 383–419), Mr. and Mrs. Peckham have recently found that the memory of eggs which have been withdrawn from the mother is retained by her for a period varying in different species from less than one to more than two days.

† Sully, *loc. cit.*, p. 377.

Nevertheless, there is some reason to think that when this growth has attained a certain point, it makes, so to speak, a sudden leap of progress, which may be taken to bear the same relation to the development of the mind as the act of birth does to that of the body. In neither case is the development anything like completed. Midway between the slowly evolving phases *in utero* and the slowly evolving phases of after-growth, there is in the case of the human body a great and sudden change at the moment when it first becomes separated from that of its parent. And so, there is some reason to believe, it is in the case of the human mind. Midway between the gradual evolution of receptual ideation and the no less gradual evolution of conceptual, there appears to be a critical moment when the soul first becomes detached from the nutrient body of its parent perceptions, and wakes up in the new world of a consciously individual existence. " Die Schlussprozesse, durch welche jene Trennung des Ich von der Aussenwelt vor sich geht, geschehen allmälig. Es ist eine langsame Arbeit, durch die sich die Scheidung bewerkstelligt. Doch diese Scheidung selber ist stets eine plötzliche That : es ist ein bestimmter Moment, in welchem das Ich mit einem Mal mit voller Klarheit in der Seele aufblitzt, und es ist derselbe Moment, in welchem das bewusste Gedächtniss beginnt, Sehr häufig ist es daher, dass gerade diesses erste blitzähnliche Aufleuchten des Selbstbewusstseins bis in späte Jahre noch als deutliche Erinnerung zurückbleibt." *

Of course the evidence upon this point must always be more or less unsatisfactory—first, because the powers of introspective analysis at the particular time when they first become nascent must be most incompetent to report upon the circumstances of their own birth ; and next, because we know how precarious it is to rely on adult reminiscences

---

* Wundt, *loc. cit.*, ii. 289, 290. He gives cases where such a definite memory of the moment has persisted, and elsewhere states that such is the case in his own experience. The circumstance which here was connected with the sudden birth of self-consciousness consisted in rolling down stairs into a cellar—an event which no doubt was well calculated forcibly to impress upon infant consciousness that it was itself, and nobody else.

of childhood's experience. Therefore, I have only mentioned this evidence for what it is worth, in order to remark that it has no important bearing upon our present subject. Whether or not there is in the life of every human being some particular moment between the ages of two and three when the fact of its own personality is revealed to the growing mind, the results of the present analysis are in no way affected. For, even if such were supposed to be invariably the case, it could not be supposed that the revelation were other than low and feeble to a degree commensurate with the still almost infantile condition of all the other mental powers. Nor could it be doubted that this revelation needed to be led up to by that gradual process of receptual evolution with which my analysis has been concerned, and which in the terms of our previous analogy we may liken to the pre-natal life of an embryo. While, on the other hand, as little can it be doubted that such consciousness of self as is then revealed, requires to be afterwards supplemented by another prolonged course of mental evolution in the conceptual sphere, before those completed faculties of introspective thought are attained, which serve to difference the mind of a full-grown man from that of a babbling child almost as widely as the same interval of time is found to difference the body of an adult from that of a new-born babe,

In this brief analysis of the principles which are probably concerned in the evolution of self-consciousness, I should like to lay particular stress upon the point in it which I do not think has been sufficiently noticed by previous writers— namely, the ejective origin of subjective knowledge. The logic of recepts furnishes both the infant and the animal with a marvellously efficient store of ejective information. Indeed, we can scarcely doubt that to a very considerable extent this information is hereditary : witness the smile of an infant in answer to a caressing tone, and its cry in answer to a scolding one ; not to mention the still more remarkable cases which we meet with in animals, such as newly-hatched chickens understanding the different sounds made to them by the hen, being terror-stricken at the voice of a hawk, newly-born mammals knowing the voice of their mother, &c.*   Moreover, we find that the child, even for a considerable time after it has begun to use words, manifests a strong tendency to regard all objects, whether animate or inanimate, as ejects. This fact is a matter of such general observation that I need not wait to give special instances.   I will, therefore, merely observe that the tendency is not wholly obliterated even when the faculty of speech has been fully acquired, and with it a general knowledge of the distinction between objects as animate and inanimate.   Mr. Sully, for instance, gives a case of this when he records the saying of a little girl of five—" Ma, I do think this hoop must be alive ; it is so sensible ; it goes wherever I want it to."†   Again, we meet with the same tendency in the psychology of uncultured man.   Pages might be filled with illustrations showing that savages all over the world both mentally and expressly personify, or endow with psychical attributes, the inanimate objects and forces of nature; while language, even in its most highly developed forms, still retains the impress of an originally ejective terminology. And, if Professor Max Müller is right in his generalization that the personal pronoun " I " is in all languages traceable to roots equivalent to " This one " (indicative of an accompanying gesture-sign), we have additional and more particular evidence of the originally ejective character of the idea of self.   Nor is it too much to say that even civilized man is still under the sway of this innate propensity to attribute to external things the faculties of feeling and willing of which he is conscious in himself.   On the one side we have proof of this in the universal prevalence of the hypothesis of psychism in Nature, while on the other side we meet with further proof in the fact of psychological analysis revealing that our idea of cause is derived from our idea of muscular effort.

* See *Mental Evolution in Animals*, pp. 161–165.   Perez records analogous facts with regard to the infant as unmistakably displayed in the fourteenth week (*First Three Years of Childhood*, English trans., p. 29).

† *Outlines of Psychology*, p. 378.

Now it is evident that in all these cases the tendency which is shown by the human mind, in every stage of its development, to regard external phenomena ejectively, arises from man's intuitive knowledge—or the knowledge which is given in the logic of recepts—of his own existence as two-fold, bodily and mental. This in his early days leads him to regard the Ego as an eject, resembling the others of his kind by whom he is surrounded. But as soon as the power of pre-conceptual predication has been attained, the child is in possession of a psychological instrument wherewith to observe his own mental states; and as soon as attention is thus directed upon them, there arises that which is implied in every act of such attention—namely, the consciousness of a self as at once the subject and object of knowledge.

I may remark that this analysis is not opposed, as at first sight it may appear to be, to the conclusion with regard to the same subject which is thus given by Wundt :—" It is only after the child has distinguished by definite charac-teristics its own being from that of other people, that it makes the further advance of perceiving that these other people are also beings in or for themselves." * In other words, the attribution of personality to self is prior to the attribution of personality to others. Now this I do not question, although I do not think there can be much before or after in these two concepts. But the point which I have been endeavouring to bring out is that, prior to either of these concepts, there are two corresponding recepts—namely, first the receptual apprehension of self as an agent, and, second, the eject of this receptual apprehension, whereby "other people" are recognized as agents. Out of these two recepts there subsequently develop the corresponding concepts of personality. The order of development, therefore, is :—

(A) Receptual Subject.     (a) Receptual Eject.
(B) Conceptual Subject.     (b) Conceptual Eject.

Upon the whole, then, it appears to me perfectly evident

* *Vorlesungen, &c.,* i. 289.

that language is quite as much the antecedent as it is the consequent of self-consciousness. We have seen that in its first beginnings, or before the child is able to state a truth as true, what I have called rudimentary or pre-conceptual predication is concerned only with existence as objective or ejective : all these propositions, which are made by children during the first two years of their life, have reference to objects of sense, states of feeling, &c. ; but never to self as self, and therefore never to truths as true. But as soon as the protoplasm of predication, or sign-making at this stage of elaboration, begins to mix freely with the protoplasm of judgment, or the logic of recepts at that stage of elaboration, an intimate movement of action and reaction ensues : the judgments are rendered clearer and more comprehensive by being thrown into the formal shape of even rudimentary propositions, while the latter are promoted in their development by the growing powers of judgment. And when this advancing organization of faculties has proceeded to the extent of enabling the mind incipiently to predicate its own states, the mental organism may be said for the first time to be quickening into the life of true self-consciousness.*

* In the above sketch of the principles which are concerned in the development of self-consciousness, I have only been concerned with the matter on the side of its psychology, and even on this side only so far as my own purposes are in view. Those who wish for further information on the psychology of the subject may consult Wundt, *loc. cit. ;* Sully, *loc. cit.*, and *Illusions*, ch. x. ; Taine, *On Intelligence*, pt. ii., bk. iii. ; Chauncey ,Wright, *Evolution of Self-consciousness ;* and Waitz, *Lehrbuch der Psychologie*, 58. On the side of its physiology and pathology Taine, Maudsley, and Ribot may be referred to (*On Intelligence, Pathology of Mind, Diseases of Memory*), as also a paper by Herzen, entitled, *Les Modifications de la Conscience du moi* (*Bull. Soc. Hand. Sc. Nat.*, xx. 90). *An Essay on the Philosophy of Self-consciousness*, by P. F. Fitzgerald, is written from the side of metaphysics. On this side, also, we are met by the school of Hegel and the Neo-Kantians with a virtual denial of the origin and development of self-consciousness in time. Thus, for instance, Green expressly says : —"Should the question be asked, If this self-consciousness is not derived from nature, what then is its origin ? the answer is, that it has no origin. It never began because it never was not. It is the condition of there being such a thing as beginning or end. Whatever begins or ends does so for it, or in relation to it " (*Prolegomena to Ethics,* p. 119). To this I can only answer that for my own part I feel as convinced as I am of the fact of my self-consciousness itself that it had a beginning in time, and was afterwards the subject of a gradual development. " Das Ich ist ein Ent- wicklungsprodukt, wie der ganze Mensch ein Entwicklungsprodukt ist " (Wundt).

# CHAPTER XI.

## THE TRANSITION IN THE INDIVIDUAL.

WE are now, I think, in possession of sufficient material to begin our answer to the question with which we set out—namely, Is it conceivable that the human mind can have arisen by way of a natural genesis from the minds of the higher quadrumana? I maintain that the material now before us is sufficient to show, not only that this is conceivable, but inevitable.

First of all we must remember that we share in common with the lower animals not only perceptual, but also what I have termed receptual life. Thus far, no difference of kind can be even so much as suggested. The difference then, be it one of kind or of degree, concerns only those superadded elements of psychology which are peculiar to man, and which, following other psychologists, I have termed conceptual. I say advisedly the *elements*, because it is by no one disputed that all differences of conceptual life are differences of degree, or that from the ideation of a savage to that of a Shakespeare there is unquestionably a continuous ascent. The only question, then, that obtains is as to the relation between the highest recept of a brute and the lowest concept of a man.

Now, in considering this question we must first remember to what an extraordinarily high level of adaptive ideation the purely receptual life of brutes is able to carry them. If we contrast the ideation of my cebus, which honestly investigated the mechanical principle of a screw, and then applied his specially acquired knowledge to screws in general—if we contrast this ideation with that of palæolithic man, who for untold thousands of years made no advance upon the chipping of flints, we cannot say that, when gauged by the practical test of efficiency or adaptation, the one appears to be very much in advance of the other. Or, if we remember that these same men never hit upon the simple expedient of attaching a chipped flint to a handle, so as to make a hatchet out of a chisel,* it cannot be said that in the matter of mechanical discovery early conceptual life displayed any great advance upon the high receptual life of my cebus. Nevertheless, I have allowed—nay insisted—that no matter how elaborate the structure of receptual knowledge may be, or how wonderful the adaptive action it may prompt, a " practical inference " or " receptual judgment " is always separated from a conceptual inference or true judgment by the immense distinction that it is not itself an object of knowledge. No doubt it is a marvellous fact that by means of receptual knowledge alone a monkey should be able to divine the mechanical principle of *a screw*, and afterwards apply his discovery to all cases of *screws*. But even here there is nothing to show that the monkey ever *thought* about the principle *as* a principle ; indeed, we may rest well assured that he cannot possibly have done so, seeing that he was not in possession of the intellectual instruments—and, therefore, of the *antecedent conditions*—requisite for the purpose. All that the monkey did was to perceive receptually certain analogies : but he did not *conceive* them, or constitute them objects of thought *as* analogies. He was, therefore, unable to *predicate* the discovery he had made, or to set before his own mind as knowledge the knowledge which he had gained.

Or, to take another illustration, the bird which saw three men go into a building, and inferred that one must still have remained when only two came out, conducted the inference receptually : the only data she had were those supplied by differential sense-perceptions. But although these data were

---

* "Of all the neolithic implements the axe was by far the most important. It was by the axe that man achieved his greatest victory over nature " (Boyd Dawkins, *Early Man in Britain*, p. 274).

sufficient for the purpose of conducting what Mr. Mivart calls a "practical inference," and so of enabling her to know that a man still remained behind, they were clearly not enough to enable her to know the numerical relations *as* relations, or in any way to predicate to herself, 3—2 = 1. In order to do this, the bird would have required to quit the region of receptual knowledge, and rise to that of conceptual: she would have required in some form or another to have substituted symbols for ideas. It makes no difference, so far as this distinction is concerned, when we learn that in dealing with certain savages "each sheep must be paid for separately : thus, suppose two sticks of tobacco to be the rate of exchange for one sheep, it would sorely puzzle a Dammara to take two sheep and give him two sticks." * All that such facts show is that in some respects the higher receptual life of brutes attains almost as high a level of ideation as the lower conceptual life of man ; and although this fact no doubt greatly lessens the difficulty which my opponents allege as attaching to the supposition that the two were genetically continuous, it does not in itself dispose of the psychological distinction between a recept and a concept.

This distinction, as we have now so often seen, consists in a recept being an idea which is not itself an object of knowledge, whereas a concept, in virtue of having been named by a self-conscious agent, is an idea which stands before the mind of that agent *as* an idea, or as a state of mind which admits of being introspectively contemplated as

---

* Galton, *Tropical South Africa*, p. 213. The author adds, "Once, while I watched a Dammara floundering hopelessly in a calculation on one side of me, I observed Dinah, my spaniel, equally embarrassed on the other. She was over-, looking half a dozen of her new-born puppies, which had been removed two or three times from her, and her anxiety was excessive, as she tried to find out if they were all present, or if any were still missing. She kept puzzling and running her eyes over them, backwards and forwards, but could not satisfy herself. She evidently had a vague notion of counting, but the figure was too large for her brain. Taking the two as they stood, dog and Dammara, the comparison reflected no great honour on the man." As previously stated, I taught the chimpanzee "Sally" to give one, two, three, four, or five straws at word of command.

15

such.  But although we have in this distinction what I agree with my opponents in regarding as the greatest single distinction that is to be met with in psychology, I altogether object to their mode of analyzing it.  For what they do is to take the concept in its most highly developed form, and then contrast this with the recept of an animal.  Nay, as we have seen, they even go beyond a concept, and allege that "the simplest element of thought" is a judgment as bodied forth in a proposition—*i.e.* *two* concepts *plus* the predication of a relationship between them!  Truly, we might as well allege that the simplest element of matter is $H_2 S O_4$, or the simplest element of sound a bar of the C Minor Symphony. Obviously, therefore, or as a mere matter of the most rudimentary psychological analysis, if we say that the simplest element of thought is a judgment, we must extend the meaning of this word from the mental act concerned in full predication, to the mental act concerned in the simplest conception.

And not only so.  Not only have my opponents committed the slovenly error of regarding a predicative judgment as "the simplest element of thought;" they have also omitted to consider that even a concept requires to be analyzed with respect to its antecedents, before this the really simplest element of thought can be pointed to as proving a psychological distinction of kind in the only known intelligence which presents it.  Now, the result of my analysis of the concept has been to show that it is preceded by what I have termed pre-concepts, which admit of being combined into what I have termed nascent, rudimentary, or pre-conceptual judgments.  In other words, we have seen that the receptual life of man reaches a higher level of development than the receptual life of brutes, even before it passes into that truly conceptual phase which is distinguished by the presence of self-conscious reflection.  In order, therefore, to mark off this higher receptual life of a human being from the lower receptual life of a brute, I have used the terms just mentioned.

So much, then, for these several stages of ideation, which

I have now reiterated *ad nauseam.* Turning next to my analysis of their several modes of expression, or of their translation into their severally equivalent systems of signs, we have
seen that many of the lower animals are able to communicate
their recepts by means of gestures significant of objects,
qualities, actions, desires, &c. ; and that in the only case
where they are able to articulate, they so communicate their
recepts by means of words. Therefore, in a sense, these
animals may be said to be using names ; but, in order not to
confuse this kind of naming with that which is distinctive of
conceptual thought, I have adopted the scholastic terminology,
and called the former kind of naming an act of denotating, as
distinguished from an act of denominating. Furthermore,
seeing that denotative language is able, as above observed, to
signify qualities and actions as well as objects, it follows
that in the higher receptual (*i.e.* pre-conceptual) stages of
ideation, denotative language is able to construct what I have
termed pre-conceptual propositions. These differ from true
or conceptual propositions in the absence of true self-consciousness on the part of the speaker, who therefore, while
communicating receptual knowledge, or stating truths, cannot
yet know his own knowledge, or state the truths as true. But
it does not appear that a pre-conceptual proposition differs
from a conceptual one in any other respect, while it does
appear that the one passes gradually into the other with
the rise of self-consciousness in every growing child. Now, if
all these things are so, we are entitled to affirm that analysis
has displayed an uninterrupted transition between the denotation of a brute and the predication of a man. For the mere
fact that it is the former phase alone which occurs in the
brute, while in the man, *after having run a parallel course of
development*, this phase passes into the other—the mere fact
that this is so cannot be quoted as evidence that a similar
transition never took place in the psychological history of our
species, unless it could be shown that when the transition
takes place in the psychological history of the individual, it
does so in such a sudden and remarkable manner as of itself

to indicate that the intellect of the individual has there and then undergone a change of kind.

Such being an outline sketch of my argument, I will now proceed to fill in the details, taking in historical order the various stages of ideation which I have named—*i.e.* the receptual, the pre-conceptual, and the conceptual.

Seeing that this is, as I apprehend, the central core of the question, I will here furnish some additional instances of receptual and pre-conceptual ideation as expressed by denotative and connotative signs on the part of a child which I carefully observed for the purpose.

At eighteen months old my daughter, who was late in beginning to speak, was fond of looking at picture-books, and as already stated in a previous chapter, derived much pleasure from naming animals therein represented,—saying *Ba* for a sheep, *Moo* for a cow, uttering a grunt for a pig, and throwing her head up and down with a bray for a horse or an ass. These several sounds and gestures she had been taught by the nurse as noun-substantives, and she correctly applied them in every case, whether the picture-book happened to be one with which she was familiar or one which she had never seen before ; and she would similarly name all kinds of animals depicted on the wall-paper, chair-covers, &c., in strange houses, or, in short, whenever she met with representations of objects the nursery names of which she knew. Thus there is no doubt that, long before she could form a sentence, or in any proper sense be said to speak, this child was able to denote objects by voice and gesture. At this time, also, she correctly used a limited number of denotative words significant of actions—*i.e.* active verbs.

Somewhat later by a few weeks she showed spontaneously the faculty of expressing an adjective. Her younger brother she had called "Ilda," and soon afterwards she extended the name to all young children.* Later still, while looking

---

* The boy's name was Ernest, and was thus called by all other members of the household. As I could not find any imitative source of the dissimilar name used

over her picture-books, whenever she came upon a representation of a sheep with lambs, she would point to the sheep and say *Mama-Ba*, while to the lambs she would say *Ilda-Ba*. Similarly with ducks and ducklings, hens and chickens, and indeed with all the animals to which she had given names. Here it is evident that *Ilda* served to convey the generic idea of *Young*, and so, from having been originally used as a proper or denotative name, was now employed as an adjective or connotative name. But although it expressed a quality, the quality was one of so sensible a kind that the adjective amounted to virtually the same thing as substantive, so far as any faculty of abstraction was concerned : it was equivalent to the word *Baby*, when by connotative extension this comes to be used as an adjective in the apposition *Baby-Ba* for a lamb, &c.

Almost contemporaneously with the acquisition of adjectives, this child began to learn the use of a few passive verbs, and words significant of certain states of feeling ; she also added to her vocabulary a few prepositions indicating space relations, such as *Up, Down,* &c.*

While these advances were being made, a general progress of the sign-making faculty was also, and even more conspicuously, shown in another direction. For speech, in the sense of formal predication, not having yet begun, the development in question took place in the region of gesture. She was then (two years) able to express a great many simple ideas by the combined use of gesture-signs, vocal-tones, and a

by his sister, this is probably an instance of the spontaneous invention of names by young children, which has already been considered at the close of my chapter on "Articulation." Touching the use of adjectives by young children, I may quote the following remark from Professor Preyer :—"A very general error must be removed, which consists in the supposition that all children on first beginning to speak use substantives only, and later pass on to the use of adjectives. This is certainly not the case." And he proceeds to give instances drawn from the daily observations of his own child, such as the use of the word "heiss" in the twenty-third month.

* We shall subsequently see that at this stage of mental evolution there is no well-defined distinction between the different parts of speech. Therefore here, and elsewhere throughout this chapter, I use the terms "noun," "adjective," "verb," &c., in a loose and general sense.

large connotative extension of her words.   The gesture-signs, however, were still of the simplest or most receptual order, such as pulling one by the dress to open a door, pointing to a tumbler to signify her desire for a drink, &c.   That is to say, the indicative stage of language largely coincided with, or over-lapped, the earliest phases of the denotative and receptually connotative.   I have already said that this indicative stage of language constituted the earliest appearance of the sign-making faculty which I observed in my own children, at a time when the only desire expressed seemed to be that of being taken to the object indicated ; and, so far as I can ascertain, this is universally true of all children.   But the point now is, that when the logic recepts had become more full, the desires expressed by pointing became of a more and more varied kind, until, at the age of two and a half (*i.e.* after significant articulation or true word-making had well set in), the indicative phase of language developed into regular pantomime, as the following instance will show.   Coming into the house after having bathed in the sea for the first time, she ran to me to narrate her novel experience.   This she did by first pointing to the shore, then pretending to take off her clothes, to walk into the sea, and to dip : next, passing her hands up the body to her head, she signified that the water had reached as high as her hair, which she showed me was still wet.   The whole story was told without the use of a single articulate sound.

Now, in the case of these illustrations (and many more of the same kind might be added if needful), we find the same general fact exemplified—namely, that the earliest phase of language in the young child is that which I have called the indicative,—*i.e.* tones and gestures significant of feelings, objects, qualities, and actions.   This indicative phase of language, or sign-making, lasts much longer in some children than in others (particularly in those who are late in beginning to speak) ; and the longer it lasts the more expressive does it become of advancing ideation.   But in all cases two things have to be observed in connection with it.   The first is that, in its earliest stages, and onwards through a considerable part of its history, it is precisely identical with the corresponding phases of indicative sign-making in the lower animals. Thus, for instance, Professor Preyer observed that at sixteen months his own child—who at that age could not speak a word—used to make a gesture significant of petitioning with its hands ("Bittbewegung"), as indicative of desire for something to be done. This, of course, I choose as an instance of indicative sign-making at a comparatively high level of development; but it is precisely paralleled by an intelligent dog which "begs" before a water-jug to signify his desire for a drink, or before any other object in connection with which he desires something to be done.* And so it is with children who pull one's dress towards a closed door through which they wish to pass, significantly cry for what they want to possess, or to have done for them, &c. : children are here doing exactly what cats and dogs will do under similar circumstances.† And although many of the gesture-signs of children at this age (*i.e.* up to about eighteen months) are not precisely paralleled by those of the lower animals, it is easy to see that where there is any difference it is due to different circumstances of bodily shape, social conditions, &c. : it is not due to any difference of ideation. That the kind of ideation which is expressed by the indicative gestures of young children is the same as that which prompts the analogous gestures of brutes, is further shown by the fact that, even before any articulate words are uttered, the infant (like the animal) will display an understanding of many articulate words when uttered in its presence, and (also like the animal) will respond to such words by appropriate gestures. For instance, again to quote Preyer, he found that his hitherto speechless infant was able correctly to point to certain colours which he named ; and

* I have seen a terrier of my own (who habitually employed this gesture-sign in the same way as Preyer's child, namely, as expressive of desire), assiduously though fruitlessly "beg" before a refractory bitch.

† Many dogs will significantly bark, and cats significantly mew, for things which they desire to possess or to be done. For significant crying by children, see above, p. 158.

although, as far as I am aware, no one has ever tried to teach an animal to do this, we know that trained dogs will display an even better understanding of words by means of appropriate gestures.*

The other point which has to be noticed in connection with these early stages of indicative sign-making in the young child is that, sooner or later, they begin to overlap the earliest stage of articulate sign-making, or verbal denotation. In other words, denotative sign-making never begins to occur until indicative sign-making has advanced considerably ; and when denotative sign-making does begin, it advances parallel with indicative : that is to say, both kinds of sign-making then proceed to develop simultaneously. But when the vocabulary of denotation has been sufficiently enriched to enable the child to dispense with the less efficient material furnished by indication, indicative signs gradually become starved out by denotative, and words replace gestures.

So far, then, as the earliest or indicative phase of language is concerned, no difference even of degree can be alleged between the infant and the animal. Neither can any such difference be alleged with respect to the earliest exhibitions of the next phases of language, namely, the denotative and receptually connotative. For we have seen that the only animals which happen to be capable of imitating articulate sounds will use these sounds with a truly denotative significance. Moreover, as we have also seen, within moderate limits they will even extend such denotative significance to other objects seen to belong to the same class or kind—thus raising the originally denotative sign to an incipiently connotative value. And although these receptually connotative powers of a parrot are soon surpassed by those of a young child, we have

---

* For the case of the ape in this connection see above, p. 126. I took my daughter when she was seven years of age to witness the understanding of the ape "Sally." On coming away, I remarked to her that the animal seemed to be "quite as sensible as Jack "—*i.e.* her infant brother of eighteen months. She considered for a while, and then replied, "Well, I think she is sensibler." And I believe the child was right.

further seen that this is merely owing to the rapid advance in the *degree* of receptual life which takes place in the latter—or, in other words, that if a parrot resembled a dog in being able to see the resemblance between objects and their pictures, and also in being so much more able to understand the meanings of words, then, without doubt, their connotative extension of names would proceed further than it does ; and hence in this matter the parallel between a parrot and child would proceed further than it does. The only reason, there-fore, why a child thus gradually surpasses a parrot in the matter of connotation, is because the receptual life of a child gradually rises to that of a dog—as I have already proved by showing that the indicative or gesture-signs used by a child after it has thus surpassed the parrot, are psychologically identical with those which are used by a dog. Moreover, where denotation is late in beginning and slow in developing —as in the case of my own daughter—these indicative signs admit, as we have seen, of becoming much more highly perfected, so that under these circumstances a child of two years will perform a little pantomime for the pur-pose of relating its experiences. Now, this fact enables me to dispense with the imaginary comparison of a dog that is able to talk, or of a parrot as intelligent as a dog ; for the fact furnishes me with the converse case of a child *not* able to talk at the usual age. No one can suggest that the intelli-gence of such a child at two years old differs in kind from that of another child of. the same age, who, on account of having been earlier in acquiring the use of words, can afford to become less proficient in the use of gestures.* The case of a child late in talking may therefore be taken as a psycho-

---

* Or, if any opponent were to suggest this, he would be committing argumentative surrender. For the citadel of his argument is, as we know, the faculty of conception, or the distinctively human power of objectifying ideas. Now, it is on all hands admitted that this power is impossible in the absence of self-consciousness. Will it, then, be suggested that my daughter had attained to self-consciousness and the introspective contemplation of her own ideas before she had attained to the faculty of speech, and therefore to the very *condition* to the naming of her ideas ? If so, it would follow that there may be concepts without names, and thus the whole fortress of my opponents would crumble away.

logical index of the development of human ideation of the receptual order, which by accident admits of closer comparison with that of the higher mammalia than is possible in the case of a child who begins to talk at the usual age. But, as regards the former case, we have already seen that the gestures begin by being much less expressive than those of a dog, then gradually improve until they become psychologically identical, and, lastly, continue in the same gradual manner along the same line of advance. Therefore, if in this case no difference of kind can be alleged *until* the speaking age is reached, neither can it be alleged *after* the speaking age is reached in the case where this happens to be earlier. Or, in the words previously used, if a dog like a parrot were able to use verbal signs, or if a parrot were equal in intelligence to a dog, the connotative powers of a child would continue parallel with those of a brute through a somewhat longer reach of psychological development than we now find to be the case.

Remembering, then, that brutes so low in the psychological scale as talking birds reach the level of denotating objects, qualities, &c. ; remembering that some of these birds will extend their denotative names to objects and qualities conspicuously belonging to the same class ; remembering, further, that all children before they begin to speak have greatly distanced the talking birds in respect of indicative language or gesture-signs, while some children (or those late in beginning to speak) will raise this form of language to the level of pantomime, thus proving that the receptual ideation of infants just before they begin to speak is invariably above that of talking birds, and often far above that of any other animal ;—remembering all these things, I say it would indeed be a most unaccountable fact if children, soon after they do begin to speak, did *not* display a great advance upon the talking birds in their use of denotative signs, and also in their extension of such signs into connotative words. As we have seen, it must be conceded by all prudent adversaries that, before he is able to use any of these signs, an infant is moving in the receptual sphere of ideation, and that this sphere is already (between one and two years) far above that of the parrot. Yet, like the parrot, one of the first uses that he makes of these signs is in the denotation of individual objects, &c. Next, like the more intelligent parrots, he extends the meaning of his denotative names to objects most obviously resembling those which were first designated. And from that point onwards he rapidly advances in his powers of connotative classification. But can it be seriously maintained, in view of all the above considerations, that this rapid advance in the powers of connotative classification betokens any difference of kind between the ideation of the child and that of the bird? If it is conceded (as it must be unless my opponents commit argumentative suicide), that before he could speak at all the infant was confined to the receptual sphere of ideation, and that within this sphere his ideation was already superior to the ideation of a bird,—this is merely to concede that analogies *must* strike the child which are somewhat too remote to strike the bird. Therefore, while the bird will only extend its denotative name from one kind of dog to another, the child, after having done this, will go on to apply the name to an image, and, lastly, to the picture of a dog. Surely no one will be fatuous enough to maintain that here, at the commencement of articulate sign-making, there is any evidence of generic distinction between the human mind and the mind of even so poor a representative of animal psychology as we meet with in a parrot. But, if no such distinction is to be asserted here, neither can it be asserted anywhere else, until we arrive at the stage of human ideation where the mind is able to contemplate that ideation as such. So far, therefore, as the stages which we are now considering are concerned (*i.e.* the denotative and receptually connotative), I submit that my case is made out. And yet these are really the most important stages to be clear about ; for, on account of their having been ignored by nearly all writers who argue that there is a difference of kind between man and brute, the most important— because the initial—stages of transition have been lost sight of, and the fully developed powers of human thought contrasted with their low beginnings in the brute creation, without any attention having been paid to the probable history of their development. Hitherto, so far as I can find, no psychologist has presented clearly the simple question whether the faculty of naming is always and necessarily co-extensive with that of *thinking the names;* and, therefore, the two faculties have been assumed to be one and the same. Yet, as I have shown in an earlier chapter, even in the highest forms of human ideation we habitually use names without waiting to think of them as names—which proves that even in the highest regions of ideation the two faculties are not *necessarily* coincident.* And here I have further shown that, whether we look to the brute or to the human being, we alike find that the one faculty is in its inception *wholly independent* of the other—that there are connotative names before there are any denominative thoughts, and that these connotative names, when they first occur in brute or child, betoken no further aptitude of ideation than is betokened by those stages in the language of gesture which they everywhere overlap. The named recepts of a parrot cannot be held by my opponents to be true concepts, any more than the indicative gestures of an infant can be held by them to differ in kind from those of a dog.

I submit, then, that neither as regards the indicative, the denotative, nor the connotative stages of sign-making is it argumentatively possible to allege any difference of kind between animal and human intelligence—apart, I mean, from any evidence of self-consciousness in the latter, or so long as the intelligence of either is moving in what I have called the receptual sphere. Let us, then, next consider what I have called the pre-conceptual stage of ideation, or that higher

---

* See pp. 81–83, where it is shown that even in cases where conceptual thought is necessary for the original formation of a name, the name may afterwards be used without the agency of such thought—just in the same way as actions originally due to intelligence may, by frequent repetition, become automatic. At the close of the present chapter it will be shown that the same is true even of full or formal predication.

receptual life of a child which, while surpassing the receptual life of any brute, has not yet attained to the conceptual
life of a man.

From what I have already said it must, I should suppose,
be now conceded that, at the place where the receptual life of
a child first begins to surpass the receptual life of any other
mammal, no psychological difference of kind can be affirmed.
Let us, therefore, consent to tap this pre-conceptual life at
a considerably higher level, and analyze the quality of
ideation which flows therefrom : let us consider the case of
a child about two years old, who is able to frame such a
rudimentary, communicative, or pre-conceptual proposition as
*Dit ki* (Sister is crying). At this age, as already shown, there
is no consciousness of self as a thinking agent, and, therefore,
no power of stating a truth as true. *Dit* is the denotative
name of one recept, *ki* the denotative name of another : the
object and the action which these two recepts severally
represent happen to occur together before the child's
observation : the child therefore denotes them both simultaneously—i.e. *brings them into apposition.* This it does
by merely following the associations previously established
between the recept of a familiar object with its denotative
name *dit*, and the recept of a frequent action with its
denotative name *ki*. The apposition in consciousness of
these two recepts, with their corresponding denotations, is
thus effected *for* the child by what may be termed *the logic
of events :* it is not effected *by* the child in the way of any
intentional or self-conscious grouping of its ideas, such as we
have seen to constitute the distinguishing feature of the logic
of concepts.

Such being the state of the facts, I put to my opponents
the following dilemma. Either you here have judgment, or
else you have not. If you hold that this is judgment, you
must also hold that animals judge, because I have proved
already that (according to your own doctrine as well as
mine) the only point wherein it can be alleged that the
faculty of judgment differs in animals and in man consists

in the presence or absence of self-consciousness. If, on the other hand, you answer that here you have not judgment, inasmuch as you have not self-consciousness, I will ask you at what stage in the subsequent development of the child's intelligence you would consider judgment to arise? If to this you answer that judgment first arises when self-consciousness arises, I will ask you to note that, as already proved, the growth of self-consciousness is itself a gradual process ; so that, according to your present limitation of the term judgment, it becomes impossible to say when this faculty does arise. In point of fact, it grows by stages, *pari passu* with the growth of self-consciousness. But, if so, where the faculty of stating a truth perceived passes into the higher faculty of perceiving the truth as true, there must be a continuous series of gradations connecting the one faculty with the other. Up to the point where this series of gradations begins, we have seen that the mind of an animal and the mind of a man are parallel, or not distinguishable from each other by any one principle of psychology. Will you, then, maintain that up to this time the two orders of psychical existence are identical in kind, but that during its ascent through this final series of gradations the human mind in some way becomes distinct in kind, not merely from the mind of animals, *but also from its own previous self?* If so, I must at this point part company with you in argument, because at this point your argument ends in a contradiction. If A and B are affirmed to be similar in origin or kind, and if B is affirmed to grow into C —or to differ from both A and B only in degree,—it becomes a contradiction further to affirm that C differs from A in kind. Therefore I submit that, so far as the pre-conceptual stage of ideation is concerned, it is still argumentatively impossible for my opponents to show that there is any psychological difference of kind between man and brute.

As regards this stage of ideation, then, I claim to have shown that, just as there is a pre-conceptual kind of naming, wherein originally denotative words are progressively extended through considerable degrees of connotative meaning ; so there is a pre-conceptual kind of predication, wherein denotative and connotative terms are brought together without any conceptual cognizance of the relation thus virtually alleged between them. For I have proved in the last chapter that it is not until its third year that a child acquires true or conceptual self-consciousness, and therefore attains the condition to true or conceptual predication. Yet long before that time, as I have also proved, the child forms what I have called rudimentary, or pre-conceptual, and, therefore, *unthinking* propositions. Such propositions, then, are statements of truth made for the practical purposes of communication ; but they are not statements of truth as true, and therefore not, strictly speaking, propositions at all. They are translations of the logic of recepts ; but not of the logic of concepts. For neither the truth so stated, nor the idea thus translated, can ever have been placed before the mind as itself an object of thought. In order to have been thus placed, the mind must have been able to dissociate this its product from the rest of its structure—or, as Mr Mivart says, to make the things affirmed " exist *beside* the judgment, not *in* it." And, in order to do this, the mind must have attained to self-consciousness. But, as just remarked, such is not yet the case with a child of the age in question ; and hence we are bound to conclude that before there is judgment or predication in the sense understood by psychologists (conceptual), there is judgment and predication of a lower order (pre-conceptual), wherein truths are stated for the sake of communicating simple ideas, while the propositions which convey them are not themselves objects of thought. And, be it carefully observed, predication of this rudimentary or pre-conceptual kind is accomplished by the mere apposition of denotative signs, in accordance with the general principles of association. *A* being the denotative name of an object *a*, and *B* the denotative name of a quality or action *b*, when *a b* occur together in nature, the relation between them is pre-conceptually affirmed by the mere act of bringing into apposition the corresponding denotations

*A B*—an act which is rendered inevitable by the elementary laws of psychological association.*

The matter, then, has been reduced to the last of the three stages of ideation which have been marked out for discussion —namely, the conceptual. Now, whether or not there is any difference of kind between the ideation which is capable and the ideation which is not capable of itself becoming an object of thought, is a question which can only be answered by studying the relations that obtain between the two in the case of the growing child. But, as we have seen, when we do study these relations, we find that they are clearly those of a gradual or continuous passage of the one ideation into the other—a passage, indeed, so gradual and continuous that it is impossible, even by means of the closest scrutiny, to decide within wide limits where the one begins and the other ends. Therefore I need not here recur to this point. Having already shown that the very condition to the occurrence of conceptual ideation (namely, self-consciousness) is of gradual development in the growing child, it is needless to show at any greater length that the development of conceptual out of pre-conceptual ideation is of a similarly gradual occurrence. This fact, indeed, is in itself sufficient to dispose of the allegation of my opponents—namely, that there is evidence of receptual ideation differing from conceptual in origin or kind.

In this connection it is interesting to observe the absence of the copula. Notwithstanding the strongly imitative tendencies of a child's mind, and notwithstanding that our English children hear the copula expressed in almost every statement that is made to them, their own propositions, while still in the pre-conceptual phase, dispense with it (see above, p. 204). In thus trusting to apposition alone, without expressing any sign of relation, the young child is conveying in spoken language an immediate translation of the mental acts concerned in predication. As previously noticed, we meet with precisely the same fact in the natural language of gesture, even after this has been wrought up into the elaborate conceptual systems of the Indians and deaf-mutes. Lastly, in a subsequent chapter we shall see that the same has to be said of all the more primitive forms of spoken language which are still extant among savages. So that here again we meet with additional proof, were any required, of the folly of regarding the copula as an essential ingredient of a proposition.

Only if it could be shown—either that the receptual ideation of an infant differs in kind from that of an animal, or that the pre-conceptual ideation of a child so differs from the preceding receptual ideation of the same child, or lastly, that this pre-conceptual ideation so differs from the succeeding conceptual ideation—only if one or other of the alternatives could be proved would my opponents be able to justify their allegation. And, as a mere matter of logic, to prove either of the last two alternatives would involve a complete reconstruction of their argument. For at present their argument goes upon the assumption that throughout all the phases of its development a human mind is one in kind—that it is nowhere fundamentally changed from one order of existence to another. But in case any subtle opponent should suggest that, although I have proved the first of the above three alternatives untenable—and, therefore, that there is no difference even of degree between the mind of an infant and that of an animal,—I have nevertheless ignored the possibility that in the subsequent development of every human being a special miracle may be wrought, which regenerates that mind, gives it a new origin, and so changes it as to kind—in case any one should suggest this, I here entertain the two last alternatives as logically possible. But, even so, as we have now so fully seen, study of the child's intelligence while passing through its several phases of development yields no shadow of evidence in favour of any of these alternatives ; while, on the contrary, it most clearly reveals the fact that transition from each of the levels of ideation to the next above it is of so gradual and continuous a character that it is practically impossible to draw any real lines of demarcation between them. This, then, I say is in itself enough to dispose of the allegation of my opponents, seeing that it shows the allegation to be, not only gratuitous, but opposed to the whole body of evidence which is furnished by a study of the facts. Nevertheless, still restricting ourselves to grounds of psychology alone, there remains two general and important considerations of an independent or supplementary kind, which tend strongly

16

to support my side of the argument. These two considerations, therefore, I will next adduce.

The first consideration is, that although the advance to self-consciousness from lower grades of mental development is no doubt a very great and important matter, it is not so great and important in comparison with what this development is afterwards destined to become, as to make us feel that it constitutes any distinction *sui generis*—or even, perhaps, the principal distinction—between the man and the brute. For while, on the one hand, we have now fully seen that, given the protoplasm of judgment and of predication as these occur in the young child (or as they may be supposed to have occurred in our semi-human ancestors), and self-consciousness must needs arise; on the other hand, there is evidence to show that when self-consciousness does arise, and even when it is fairly well developed, the powers of the human mind are still in an almost infantile condition. Thus, for instance, I have observed in my own children that, while before their third birthday they employed appropriately and always correctly the terms " I," " my," " self," " myself," at that age their powers of reasoning were so poorly developed as scarcely to be in advance of those which are exhibited by an intelligent animal. To give only one instance of this. My little girl when four and a half years old—or nearly two years after she had correctly used the terms indicative of true self-consciousness—wished to know what room was beneath the drawing-room of a house in which she had lived from the time of her birth. When she asked me to inform her, I told her to try to think out the problem for herself. She first suggested the bath-room, which was not only above the drawing-room, but also at the opposite side of the house; next she suggested the dining-room, which, although below the drawing-room, was also at the other side of the house; and so on, the child clearly having no power to think out so simple a problem as the one which she had spontaneously desired to solve. From which (as from many other instances on my notes in this connection) I conclude that the genesis of self-consciousness marks a comparatively low level in the evolution of the human mind—as we might expect that it should, if its genesis depends on the not unintelligible conditions which I have endeavoured to explain in the last chapters. But, if so, does it not follow that great as the importance of self-consciousness afterwards proves to be as a condition to the higher development of ideation, in itself, or in its first beginning, it does not betoken any very perceptible improvement upon those powers of pre-conceptual ideation which it immediately follows? In other words, there is thus shown to be even less reason to regard the advent of self-consciousness as marking a psychological difference of kind, than there would be so to regard the advent of those higher powers of conceptual ideation which subsequently— though as gradually—supervene between early childhood and youth. Yet no one has hitherto ventured to suggest that the intelligence of a child and the intelligence of a youth display a difference of kind.

Or, otherwise stated, the psychological interval between my cebus and my child (when the former successfully investigated the mechanical principle of the screw by means of his highly developed receptual faculties, while the latter unsuccessfully attempted to solve a most simple topographical problem by means of her lowly developed conceptual faculties), was assuredly much less than that which afterwards separated the intelligence of my child from this level of its own previous self. Therefore, on merely psychological grounds, I conclude that there would be better—or *less bad*— reasons for alleging that there is an observable difference of kind between the lowest and the highest levels of conceptual ideation, than there is to allege that any such difference obtains between the lowest level of conceptual ideation and the highest level of receptual.

"The greatest of all distinctions in biology," when it first arises, is thus seen to lie in its *potentiality* rather than in its *origin*. Self-consciousness is, indeed, the condition to an immeasurable change in the mind which presents it; but, in order to become so, it must be itself conditioned : it must itself undergo a long and gradual development under the guiding principles of a natural evolution.

And, now, lastly, the second supplementary consideration which I have to adduce is, that even in the case of a fully developed self-conscious intelligence, both receptual and pre-conceptual ideation continue to play an important part. That is to say, even in the full-summed powers of the human intellect, the three descriptions of ideation which I have distinguished are so constantly and so intimately blended together, that analysis of the adult mind corroborates the fact already yielded by analysis of the infantile mind, namely, that the distinctions (which I have been obliged to draw in order to examine the allegations of my opponents) are all essentially or intrinsically artificial. My position is that Mind is everywhere continuous, and if for purposes of analysis or classification we require to draw lines of demarcation between the lower and the higher faculties thereof, I contend that we should only do so as an evolutionist classifies his animal or vegetable species : higher or lower do not betoken differences of *origin*, but differences of *development*. And just as the naturalist finds a general corroboration of this view in the fact that structural and functional characters are carried upwards from lower to higher forms of life, thus knitting them all together in the bonds of organic evolution ; so may the psychologist find that even the highest forms of human intelligence unmistakably share the more essential characters met with in the lower, thus bearing testimony to their own lineage in a continuous system of mental evolution.

Let us, then, briefly contemplate the relations that obtain in the adult human mind between the boasted faculties of conceptual judgment, and the lower faculties of non-conceptual. Although I agree with my opponents in holding that predication (in the strict sense of the term) is dependent on introspection, I further hold that not every statement made by adult man is a predication in this sense : the vast majority of our verbal propositions are made for the practical purposes of communication, or without the mind pausing to contemplate the propositions as such in the light of self-consciousness. When I say "A negro is black," I do not require to think all the formidable array of things that Mr. Mivart says I affirm * ; and, on the other hand, when I perform an act of conscious introspection, I do not always require to perform an act of mental predication. No doubt in many cases, or in those where highly abstract ideation is concerned, this independence of the two faculties arises from each having undergone so much elaboration by the assistance which it has derived from the other, that both are now, so to speak, in possession of a large body of organized material on which to operate, without requiring, whensoever they are exercised, to build up the structure of this material *ab initio*. Thus, to take an example, when I say " Heat is a mode of motion," I am using what is now to me a merely verbal sign which expresses an external fact : I do not require to examine my own ideas upon the abstract terms in the abstract relation which the proposition sets forth. But for the *original attainment* of these ideas I had to exercise many and complex efforts of conceptual thought, without the previous occurrence of which I should not now have been able to use, with full understanding of its import, this verbal sign. Thus all such predications, however habitual and mechanical they may become, must at some time have required the mind to examine the ideas which they announce. And, similarly, all acts of such mental examination—*i.e.* all acts of introspection,—however superfluous they may now appear when their known product is used for further acts of mental examination, must originally have required the mind to pause before them and make to itself a definite statement or predication of their meaning. †

* See p. 166.

† Thus far, it will be observed, the case of predication is precisely analogous to that of denomination, alluded to in the foot-note on page 226. Just as instincts may arise by way of " lapsed intelligence," so may originally conceptual names, and even originally conceptual propositions, become worn down by frequent use,

But although I hold this to be the true explanation of the *apparent* independence of predication and introspection in all cases of highly abstract thought, I am firmly convinced that in all cases where those lower orders of ideation to which I have so often referred as receptual and pre-conceptual are concerned, the independence is not only *apparent*, but *real*. This, indeed, I have already proved *must* be the case with the pre-conceptual propositions of a young child, inasmuch as such propositions are then made in the absence of self-consciousness, or of the necessary condition to their being *in any degree* introspective. But the point now is, that even in the adult human mind non-conceptual predication is habitual, and that, in cases where only receptual ideation is concerned, predication of this kind need *never have been* conceptual. For, as Mill very truly says, " it will be admitted that, by asserting the proposition, we wish to communicate information of that physical fact (namely, that the summit of Chimborazo is white), and are not thinking of the names, except as the necessary means of making that communication. The meaning of the proposition, therefore, is that the individual thing denoted by the subject has the attributes connoted by the predicate." *

Now, if it is thus true that even in ordinary predication we may not require to take conceptual cognizance of the matter predicated—having to do only with the apposition of names immediately suggested by association,—the ideation concerned becomes so closely affiliated with that which is expressed in the lower levels of sign-making, that even if the connecting links were not supplied by the growing child, no one would be justified, on psychological grounds alone, in alleging any difference of kind between one level and another. The object of all sign-making is primarily that of communication, and from our study of the lower animals we know that communication first has to do exclusively with recepts, while

until they are, as it were, degraded into the pre-conceptual order of ideation. Be it observed, however, that the paragraphs which *follow* in the text have reference to a totally different principle—namely, that there may be propositions strictly conceptual as to form, which, nevertheless, need never at any time have been conceptual as to thought.

* *Logic*, vol. i., p. 108.

from our study of the growing child we know that it is the signs used in the communication of recepts which first lead to the formation of concepts. For concepts are first of all named recepts, known as such; and we have seen in previous chapters that this kind of knowledge (*i.e.* of names as names) is rendered possible by introspection, which, in turn is reached by the naming of self as an agent. But even after the power of conceptual introspection has been fully reached, demand is not always made upon it for the communication of merely receptual knowledge; and therefore it is that not every proposition requires to be introspectively contemplated as such before it can be made. Given the power of denotative nomination on the one hand, and the power of even the lowest degree of connotative nomination on the other, and all the conditions are furnished to the formation of non-conceptual statements, which differ from true propositions only in that they do not themselves become objects of thought. And the only difference between such a statement when made by a young child, and the same statement when similarly made by a grown man, is that in the former case it is not even *potentially* capable of itself becoming an object of thought.

Here, then, the psychological examination of my opponents' position comes to an end. And, in the result, I claim to have shown that in whatever way we regard the distinctively human faculty of conceptual predication, it is proved to be but a higher development of that faculty of receptual communication, the ascending degrees of which admit of being traced through the brute creation up to the level which they attain in a child during the first part of its second year,—after which they continue to advance uninterruptedly through the still higher receptual life of the child, until by further though not less imperceptible growth they pass into the incipiently conceptual life of a human mind—which, nevertheless, is not even then nearly so far removed from the intelligence of the lower animals, as it is from that which in the course of its own subsequent evolution it is eventually destined to become.

# CHAPTER XII.

## COMPARATIVE PHILOLOGY.

WE have now repeatedly seen that there is only one argument in favour of the view that the elsewhere continuous and universal process of evolution—mental as well as organic—was interrupted at its terminal phase, and that this argument stands on the ground of psychology. But we have also seen that even upon this its own ground the argument admits of abundant refutation. In order the more clearly to show that such is the case, I have hitherto designedly kept my discussion within the limits of psychological science. The time, however, has now come when I can afford to take a new point of departure. It is to Language that my opponents appeal : to Language they shall go.

In previous chapters I have more than once remarked that the science of historical psychology is destitute of fossils : unlike pre-historic structures, pre-historic ideas leave behind them no record of their existence. But now a partial exception must be taken to this general statement. For the new science of Comparative Philology has revealed the important fact that, if on the one hand speech gives *ex*pression *to* ideas, on the other hand it receives *im*pression *from* them, and that the impressions thus stamped are surprisingly persistent. The consequence is that in philology we possess the same kind of unconscious record of the growth and decay of ideas, as is furnished by palæontology of the growth and decay of species. Thus viewed, language may be regarded as the stratified deposit of thoughts, wherein they lie embedded ready to be unearthed by the labours of the man of science.

In now turning to this important branch of my subject, I may remark *in limine* that, like all the sciences, philology can be cultivated only by those who devote themselves specially to the purpose. My function, therefore, will here be that of merely putting together the main results of philological research, so far as this has hitherto proceeded, and so far as these results appear to me to have any bearing upon the "origin of human faculty." Being thus myself obliged to rely upon authority, where I find that authorities are in conflict—which, I need hardly say, is often the case—I will either avoid the points of disagreement, or else state what has to be said on both sides of the question. But where I find that all competent authorities are in substantial agreement, I will not burden my exposition by tautological quotations.

Among the earlier students of language it was a moot question whether the faculty had its origin in Divine inspiration or in human invention. So long as the question touching the origin of language was supposed to be restricted to one or other of these alternatives, the special creationists in this department of thought may be regarded as having had the best of the argument. And this for the following reasons. Their opponents, for the most part, were unfairly handicapped by a general assumption of special creation as regards the origin of man, and also by a general belief in the confusion of tongues at the Tower of Babel. The theory of evolution having been as yet unformulated, there was an antecedent presumption in favour of the Divine origin of speech, since it appeared in the last degree improbable that Adam and Eve should have been created "with full-summed powers" of intellect, without the means of communicating their ideas to one another. And even where scientific investigators were not expressly dominated by acceptance of the biblical cosmology, many of them were nevertheless implicitly influenced by it, to the extent of supposing that if language were not the result of direct inspiration, it can only have been the result of deliberate invention. But against this supposition of language having been deliberately invented, it was easy for orthodox opponents to answer—" Daily experience informs us, that men who have not learned to articulate in their childhood, never afterwards acquire the faculty of speech but by such helps as savages cannot obtain ; and therefore, if speech were invented at all, it must have been either by children who were incapable of invention, or by men who were incapable of speech. A thousand, nay, a million, of children could not think of inventing a language. While the organs are pliable, there is not understanding enough to frame the conception of a language ; and by the time that there is understanding, the organs are become too stiff for the task, and therefore, say the advocates for the Divine origin of language, reason as well as history intimates that mankind in all ages must have been speaking animals—the young having constantly acquired this art by imitating those who are older ; and we may warrantably conclude that our first parents received it by immediate inspiration." *

There remained, however, the alternative that language might have been the result neither of Divine inspiration nor of human invention ; but of natural growth. And although this alternative was clearly perceived by some of the earlier philologists, its full significance could not be appreciated before the advent of the general theory of evolution.† Nevertheless, it is here of interest to observe that the theory of evolution

---

* *Encyclopædia Britannica*, eighth edition, 1857, Art. " Language."

† Of course in classical times, when there was no theological presumption against the theory of development, this alternative met with a fuller recognition ; as, for example, by the Latin authors, Horace, Lucretius, and Cicero. Before that time Greek philosophers had been much exercised by the question whether speech was an intuitive endowment (analogists), or a product of human invention (anomalists) ; and, earlier still, astonishing progress had been made by the grammarians of India in a truly scientific analysis of language-growth. But in the text I am speaking of modern times ; and here I think there can be no doubt that till the middle of the present century the possibility of language having been the result of a natural growth was not sufficiently recognized. Among those who did recognize it, Herder, Monboddo, Sir W. Jones, Schlegel, Bopp, Humboldt, Grimm, and Pott, are most deserving of mention. The same year that witnessed the publication of the *Origin of Species* (1859), gave to science the first issue of Steinthal's *Zeitschrift für Völkerpsychologie und Sprachwissenschaft*. From that date onwards the theory of evolution in its application to philology has held undivided sway.

was clearly educed from, and applied to, the study of languages by some of the more scientific philologists, before it had been clearly enunciated by naturalists. Thus, for instance, Dr. Latham, while criticizing the passage above quoted, wrote in 1857 :—" In the actual field of language, the lines of demarcation are less definitely marked than in the preceding sketch. The phenomena of growth, however, are, upon the whole, what it suggests. . . . In order to account for the existing lines of demarcation, which are broad and definite, we must bear in mind a fresh phenomenon, viz. the spread of one dialect at the expense of others, a fact which obliterates intermediate forms, and brings extreme ones into geographical juxtaposition." *

Now, at the present day—owing partly to the establishment of the doctrine of evolution in the science of biology, but much more to direct evidence furnished by the science of philology itself—students of language are unanimous in their adoption of the developmental theory. Even Professor Max Müller insists that " no student of the science of language can be anything but an evolutionist, for, wherever he looks, he sees nothing but evolution going on all around him ; " † while Schleicher goes so far as to say that " the development of new forms from preceding forms can be much more easily traced, and this on even a larger scale, in the province of words, than in that of plants and animals." ‡

Here, however, it is needful to distinguish between language and languages. A philologist may be firmly convinced that all languages have developed by way of natural growth from those simplest elements, or " roots," which we shall presently have to consider. But he may nevertheless hesitate to conclude, with anything like equal certainty, that these simplest elements were themselves developed from still

---

* *Encycl. Brit., loc. cit.* Remembering that the above was published two years before the *Origin of Species by means of Natural Selection*, this clear enunciation of the struggle for existence in the field of philology appears to me deserving of notice.

† *Science of Thought*, preface, p. xi.

‡ *Darwinism tested by the Science of Language*, p. 41.

lower ingredients of the sign-making faculty; and hence that not only all languages in particular, but the faculty of language in general, has been the result of a natural evolution.

Here then, let it be noted, we are in the presence of exactly the same distinction with regard to the origin of language, as we were at the beginning of this treatise with regard to the origin of man. For we there saw that while we have the most cogent historical evidence in proof of the principles of evolution having governed the progress of civilization, we have no such direct evidence of the descent of man from a brutal ancestry. And here also we find that, so long as the light of history is able to guide us, there can be no doubt that the principles of evolution have determined the gradual development of languages, in a manner strictly analogous to that in which they have determined the ever-increasing refinement and complexity of social organization. Now, in the latter case we saw that such direct evidence of evolution from lower to higher levels of culture renders it well-nigh certain that the method must have extended backwards beyond the historical period; and hence, that such direct evidence of evolution uniformly pervading the historical period, in itself furnishes a strong *prima facie* presumption that this period was itself reached by means of a similarly gradual development of human faculty. And thus, also, it is in the case of language. If philology is able to prove the fact of evolution in all known languages as far back as the primitive roots out of which they have severally grown, the presumption becomes exceedingly strong that these earliest and simplest elements, like their later and more complex products, were the result of a natural growth.

Nevertheless, as I have said, it is important to distinguish between demonstrated fact and speculative inference, however strong; and, therefore, I will begin by briefly stating the stages of evolution through which languages are now generally recognized by philologists to have passed, without at present considering the more difficult question as to the origin of roots.

Supposing we take such a word as "uncostliness." Obviously here the "un" the "li" and the "ness" are derivative appendages, demonstrative elements, suffixes and affixes, or whatever else we care to call *modifying constants* which the speakers of a language are in the habit of adding to their root-words, for the sake of ringing upon those words whatever changes of meaning occasion may require. These modifying constants, of course, have all had a history, which often admits of being traced. Thus, for instance, in the above illustration, we know that the "li" is an abbreviation of what used to be pronounced as "like;" the "ness," however, being older than the English language; while the "un" dates back still further. The word "cost," then, is here the root, as far as English is concerned—though it can be followed (through the Latin *con-sta*) to an Aryan root, signifying "stand."

These modifying constants, moreover, are not restricted to suffixes, infixes, and affixes attached to roots, so as to constitute single (or compound) words : they also occur as themselves separate words, which admit of being built into the structure of sentences as pronouns, adverbs, prepositions, &c. And they may occur likewise as so-called "auxiliary verbs," in the case of some languages, while in the case of others their functions are served by grammatical "inflection" of the words themselves. Thus, according to the "genius" of a language, its roots are made to lend themselves to significant treatment in different ways, or according to different methods. But in all cases the roots are present, and serve as what may be termed the back-bone of a language : the demonstrative elements, in whatever form they appear, are merely what I have termed modifying constants.

From this general fact we may be prepared to expect, on the theory of evolution, that in all languages the roots should be the oldest elements ; those elements which serve only the function of "demonstrating" the particular meaning which is to be assigned to the roots on particular occasions, we should

expect to have been of later growth.  For they serve only
the function of giving specific meanings to the general
meanings already present in the roots ; and, therefore, in the
absence of the roots would themselves present no meaning at
all.  Consequently, as I have said, we should antecedently
expect to find that the roots are the earliest discoverable
(though not on this account necessarily the most primitive)
elements of all languages.  And this, as a general rule, is
what we do find.  In tracing back the family tree of any
group of languages, different demonstrative elements are
found on different branches, though all these branches proceed
from (*i.e.* are found to contain) the same roots.  Of course
these roots may be variously modified, both as to sound and
the groups of words to which in the different branches they
have given origin ; but such divergent evolution merely
tends to corroborate the proof of a common descent among
all the branches concerned.*

I have said that all philologists now agree in accepting the
doctrine of evolution as applied to languages in general ; while
there is no such universal agreement touching the precise
method or history of evolution in the case of particular
languages.  I will, therefore, first give a brief statement of the
main facts of language-structure, and afterwards render an
equally short account of the different views which are enter-

---

* There is a difference of opinion among philologists as to the extent in which
modifying constants were themselves originally roots.  The school of Ludwig
regards demonstrative elements as never having enjoyed existence as independent
words ; but, even so, they must have had an independent existence of some kind,
else it is impossible to explain how they ever came to be employed as constantly
modifying different roots in the same way.  Moreover, as Max Müller well
observes, "to suppose that Khana, Khain, Khanana, Khaintra, Khatra, &c.,
all tumbled out ready-made, without any synthetical purpose, and that their
differences were due to nothing but an uncontrolled play of the organs of speech,
seems to me an unmeaning assertion. . . . What must be admitted, however, is
that many suffixes and terminations had been wrongly analyzed by Bopp and his
school, and that we must be satisfied with looking upon most of them as in the
beginning simply demonstrative and modificatory " (*loc. cit.*, pp. 224 and 225).
See also Farrar, *Origin of Language*, pp. 100, *et seq.;* Donaldson, *Greek Grammar*,
pp. 67–79 ; and Hovelacque, *Science of Language*, p. 37.  It will be remarked
that this question does not affect the exposition in the text.

tained upon the question of language-development. Or, to borrow terms from another science, I will first deal with the morphology of the main divisions of the language-kingdom, and then proceed to consider the question of their phylogeny.

More than a thousand languages exist as "living" languages, no one of which is intelligible to the speakers of another. These separate languages, however, are obviously divisible into families—all the members of each family being more or less closely allied, while members of different families do not present any such evidence of genetic affinity. The test of genetic affinity is resemblance in structure, grammar, and roots. Judged by this test, the thousand or more living languages are classified by Professor Friedrich Müller under "about one hundred families." * Therefore, again to borrow biological terms, we may say that there are about one thousand existing "species" of language, which fall into about one hundred "genera"—all the species in each genus being undoubtedly connected by the ties of genetic affinity.

But besides these species and genera of language, there are what may be termed "orders"—or much larger divisions, each comprising many of the genera. By philologists these orders are usually called "groups," and whether or not there is any genetic relation among them is still an unsettled question. From the very earliest days of true linguistic research, three of these groups have been recognized, and called respectively, (1) the Isolating, (2) the Agglutinative, and (3) the Inflectional. I will first explain the meaning which these names are intended to bear, and then proceed to consider the results of more recent research upon the question of their phylogeny.

In the *Isolating* forms of language every word stands by itself, without being capable of inflectional change for purposes of grammatical construction, and without admitting

---

* *Grundriss der Sprachwissenschaft*, I. i. 77. This estimate is accepted by Professor Sayce, *Introduction to the Science of Language*, vol. ii., p. 32.

of much assistance for such purposes from demonstrative elements, or modifying constants. Languages of this kind are often called *Monosyllabic*, from the fact that the isolated words usually occur in the form of single syllables. They have also been called *Radical*, from the resemblance which their monosyllabic and isolated words present to the primitive roots of languages of other types—roots which, as already indicated, have been unearthed by the labours of the comparative philologist. Thus, upon the whole, the best idea of an isolating language may be gained by comparing it with the "nursery-language" of our own children, who naturally express themselves, when first beginning to speak, by using monosyllabic and isolated words, which further resemble the languages in question by not clearly distinguishing between what we understand as "parts of speech." For in isolating tongues such variations of grammatical meaning as the words are capable of conveying are mainly produced, either by differences of intonation, or by changing the positions which words occupy in a sentence. Of course these expedients obtain more or less in languages of both the other types; but in the isolating group they have been wrought up into a much greater variety and nicety of usage, so as to become fairly good substitutes for modifying constants on the one hand, and inflectional change on the other. Nevertheless, although inflectional change is wholly absent, modifying constants in the form of auxiliary words are not so. In Chinese, for example, there are what the native grammarians call "full words," and "empty words." The full words are the monosyllabic terms, which, when standing by themselves, present meanings of such vague generality as to include, for instance, *a ball, round, to make round, in a circle:* that is to say, the full words when standing alone do not belong to any one part of speech more than to another. Moreover, one such word may present many totally different meanings, such as *to be, truly, he, the letter, thus.* In order, therefore, to notify the particular meaning which a full word is intended to convey, the empty words are used as aids supplementary to the devices of intonation and syntax. It is probable that all these empty words were once themselves full words, the meanings of which gradually became obscured, until they acquired a purely arbitrary use for the purpose of defining the sense in which other words were to be understood—just as our word " like," in its degenerated form of " ly," is now employed to give adjectives the force of adverbs ; although, of course, there is the difference that in isolating tongues the empty or defining words are not fused into the full ones, but themselves remain isolated. In the opinion of many philologists, however, " the use of accessory words, in order to impart the required precision to the principal terms, is the path that leads from monosyllabic to the agglutinative state." *

This *Agglutinative*, or, as it is sometimes called, *Agglomerative* state belongs to languages of the second order. Here the words which serve the purpose of modifying constants, or marks of relationship, become fusible with the words which they serve to modify or define, so as to constitute single though polysyllabic compounds, as in the above example, " *un-cost-li-ness.*" I have already remarked that by long usage many of these modifying constants have had their own original meanings as independent words so completely obscured as to baffle the researches of philologists.

If all our words had been formed on the type of this example *un-cost-li-ness*, English would have been an agglutinative language. But, as a matter of fact, English, like the rest of the group to which it mainly belongs, has adopted the device of inflecting many of its words (or, rather, has inherited this device from some of its progenitors), and thus belongs to the third order of languages which I have mentioned, namely, the *Inflective*. Languages of this type are also often termed *Transpositive*, because the words now admit of being shifted about as to their relative positions in a sentence, without the meaning being thereby affected. That is to say, relations between words are now marked much less by syntax, and

---

* Hovelacque, *Science of Language*, English trans., p. 37.

17

much more by individual change. In languages of this kind the principle of agglutination has been so perfected that the original composition is more or less obscured, and the resulting words therefore admit of being themselves twisted into a variety of shapes significant of finer grades of meaning, in the way of declension, conjugation, &c. Or, to state the case as it has been stated by some philologists, in agglutinative tongues the welded elements are not sufficiently welded to admit of flexion : they are too loosely joined together, or still too independent one of another. But when the union has grown more intimate, the structure allows of more artistic treatment at the hands of language-makers : the "amalgamation" of elements having become complete, the resulting alloy can be manipulated in a variety of ways without involving its disintegration. Moreover, this principle of inflection may extend from the component parts to the root itself ; not only suffixes and prefixes, but even the word which these modify, may undergo inflectional change. So that, upon the whole, the best general idea of these various types of language-structure may perhaps be given by the following formulæ, which I take from Hovelacque.*

In the isolating type the formula of a word is simply R, and that of a sentence $R + R + R$, &c., where R stands for "root." If we represent by r those roots whose sense has become obscured so as to pass into the state of prefixes and suffixes significant only of relationship between other words, we shall have a formula of agglutination, Rr, Rrr, rR, rRr, &c. Lastly, the essence of an inflecting language consists in the power of a root to express, by modification of its own form, its various relations to other roots. Not that the roots of all words are necessarily modified ; for they often remain as they do in agglutinating tongues. But they *may* be modified, and "languages in which relations may be thus expressed, not only by suffixes and prefixes, but also by a

---

* This method of representation was devised by Schleicher, who carries it further than I have occasion to do in the text. See *Memoirs of Academy of St. Petersburg,* vol. i., No. 7, 1859.

modification of the form of the roots, are inflectional languages." Therefore, if we represent this power of inflectional change on the part of the root itself by the symbol $^x$, the agglutinating formula Rr may become R$^x$r. Moreover, the modifying elements may also be inflected, words thus yielding such formulæ as Rr$^x$, Rrr$^x$, &c.

Such, then, are the three main groups or orders of language. But in addition to them we must notice three others, which have been shown to be clearly separable. These three additional groups are the Polysynthetic, the Incorporating, and the Analytic.

The *Polysynthetic* ( = *Incapsulating*) order is found among certain savages, especially on the continent of America, where, according to Duponceau, more or less distinctive adherence to this type is to be met with from Greenland to Chili. The peculiarity of such languages consists in the indefinite composition of words by syncope and ellipsis. That is to say, sentences are formed by the running together of compound words of inordinate length, and in the process of fusion the constituent words are so much abbreviated as often to be represented by no more than a single intercalated letter. For example, the Greenland *aulisariartorasuarpok,* " he-hastened-to-go-afishing," is made up of *aulisar,* "to fish," *peartor,* "to be engaged in anything," *pinnesuarpok,* "he hastens : " and the Chippeway *totoccabo,* "wine," is formed of *toto,* "milk," with *chominabo,* "a bunch of grapes." Thus, polysynthesis consists of fusion with contraction, some of the component words losing their first, and others their last syllables. Moreover, composition of this kind further differs from that which occurs in many other types of language (*e.g.* our adjectival *never-to-be-forgotten*), in that the constituent parts may never have attained the rank of independent words, which can be set apart and employed by themselves.

The *Incorporating* order is merely a subdivision of the agglutinative, and represents an earlier stage of it, wherein the speakers had not yet begun to analyze their sentences, and so still retain in their sentences subordinate words in cumbersome variety, as, for example, " House-I-it-built ; " " They-have-them-their-books."

Again, the *Analytic* order is merely a subdivision of the inflectional, and represents a later stage of it. " One by one the grammatical relations implied in an inflectional compound are brought out into full relief, and provided with special forms in which to be expressed." Thus, in English, for example, inflections have largely given place to the use of " auxiliary " words, whereby most of the advantages of refined distinction are retained, while the machinery of expression is considerably simplified.

So that, on the whole, we may classify the Language-kingdom thus :—

Order I.    Isolating.

Order II.   Agglutinative : (Sub-orders, Polysynthetic and Incorporating).

Order III.  Inflectional : (Sub-order, Analytic).

In the opinion of some philologists, however, the Polysynthetic type deserves to be regarded, not as a sub-order of the Agglutinative, but as itself independent of all the other three, and therefore constituting a fourth order. Thus, on the one hand, we have it said that polysynthetic languages must " simply be placed last in the ascending order of the agglutinating series ; " * while, on the other hand, it is said, " the conception of the sentence that underlies the polysynthetic dialects is the precise converse of that which underlies the isolating or the agglutinative types ; the several ideas into which the sentence may be analyzed, instead of being made equal or independent, are combined, like a piece of mosaic, into a single whole." †

These two representative quotations may serve to show how accentuated is the difference of teaching with regard to this particular group of languages. As a mere matter of classification, of course, the question would not be of any importance for us ; but as the question of classification

---

* Hovelacque, *loc. cit.*, p. 130.
† Sayce, *Introduction, &c.*, i. 126.

involves one of phylogeny, the matter does acquire considerable interest in relation to our subject.

Turning, then, from the classification of language-types to their phylogeny, no one disputes that what I have called the sub-order Incorporating is genetically connected with the order Agglutinative; or that the sub-order Analytic is similarly connected with the order Inflectional. Indeed, these sub-orders are merely branches of these two respective trunks. The question before us, therefore, reduces itself to the relations between the three orders *inter se*, and also between the polysynthetic type and Order II. I will deal with these two cases separately.

On the one hand it is argued that the isolating, monosyllabic, or "nursery" type of speech must be regarded as the most primitive—in fact, that it presents to actual observation the continued "survival" of that embryonic or "radical" stage of development out of which all the subsequent growths of language have arisen. Again, the proved fact of agglutination is seen to represent a long course of development, wherein words previously isolated were run together into compounds for the purpose of securing that higher differentiation of language-growth which we know as parts of speech. Similarly, the inflectional stage is taken to have been a further elaboration of the agglutinative, in the manner already explained; while, lastly, the use of auxiliary words in analytic tongues is regarded as the final consummation of language-growth.

The theory thus briefly sketched is still maintained by many philologists; and, indeed, in some of its parts is not a theory at all, but a matter of demonstrable fact. Thus, it is manifestly impossible that the phenomena of agglutination can be presented before there are elements to agglutinate: these elements, therefore, must have preceded that process of fusion wherein the "genius" of agglutinated speech consists. Similarly, of course, agglutination must have preceded the inflection of already agglutinated words; while the use of auxiliaries can be proved to have been historically subsequent to inflection. Nevertheless, other philologists have shown good ground for questioning our right to regard these facts as justifying so universal a theory as that the law of language-growth is always to be found in these particular lines, or that all languages of one type must have passed through the lower phase, or phases, before reaching that in which they now appear. The most recent argument on this side of the question is by Professor Sayce, whom, therefore, I will quote.

"We are apt to assume that inflectional languages are more highly advanced than agglutinative ones, and agglutinative languages than isolating ones, and hence that isolation is the lowest stage of the three, at the top of which stands flection. But what we really mean when we say that one language is more advanced than another, is that it is better adapted to express thought, and that the thought to be expressed is itself better. Now, it is a grave question whether from this point of view the three classes of language can really be set the one against the other." *

He then proceeds to argue that isolating languages have an advantage over all other forms in "the attainment of terseness and vividness;" that "the agglutinative languages are in advance of the inflectional in one important point, that, namely, of analyzing the sentence into its component parts, and distinguishing the relations of grammar one from another. . . . In fact, when we examine closely the principle upon which flection rests, we shall find that it implies an inferior logical faculty to that implied by agglutination." †

Elsewhere he says, "As for the primeval root-language, we have no proof that it ever existed, and to confound it with a modern isolating language is simply erroneous. Equally unproved is the belief that isolating languages develop into agglutinative, and agglutinative into inflectional. At all events, the continued existence of isolating tongues like the

---

* *Introduction, &c.*, vol. i., p. 374.
† *Ibid.*, vol. i., pp. 375, 376.

Chinese, or of agglutinative like the Magyar and Turkish, shows that the development is not a necessary one." *

I could quote other passages to the same effect; but the above are sufficient to show that we must not unreservedly accept the earlier doctrines previously sketched. There is, indeed, no question about the fact of language-growth as regards particular languages; the question here is as to the evolution of language-types one from another. And I have given prominence to this question in order to make the following remarks upon it.

When we are told that "the continued existence of isolating tongues like the Chinese, or of agglutinative tongues like the Magyar and Turkish, shows that the development is not a necessary one," we of course at once perceive the unquestionable truth of the statement. But the fact is without relevance to the only question in debate. The continued existence of the Protozoa unquestionably proves that their development into the Metazoa is not necessary; but this fact raises no presumption at all against the doctrine that all the Metazoa have been evolved from the Protozoa.

Similarly, when we are told that "what we really mean when we say that one language is more advanced than another, is that it is better adapted to express thought," we are again being shunted from the question. The question is whether one type of language-structure *develops* into another: not whether, when developed, it is "*more advanced*" than another in the sense of being "better adapted to express thought." This it may or may not be; but in either case the question of its efficiency as a language has no necessary connection with the question of its development as a language For it may very well be that from the same origin two or more lines of development may occur in different directions. It is doubtless perfectly true, as Professor Sayce says, that modern Chinese is a higher product of evolution than ancient Chinese along the line of isolating condensation; but this is

* *Ibid.*, p. 120.   See also his *Principles of Comparative Philology*, 2nd ed., p. ix.

no proof that the agglutinative languages did not start from an isolating type, and thereafter proceed on a different line of development in accordance with their different "genius," or method of growth. Naturalists entertain no doubt that two different types of morphological structure, *b* and $\beta$, are both descended from a common parent form B, even though *b* has "advanced" in one line of change and $\beta$ in another, so that both are now equally efficient from a morphological point of view. Why, then, should a philologist dispute genetic relationship in what appears to be a precisely analogous case, on the sole ground that *b* is, to his thinking, no less psychologically efficient a language than $\beta$?

Lastly, as I have before indicated, it appears to me impossible to dispute that every agglutinative language, in whatever measure it can be proved to be agglutinative, in that measure is thereby proved to have been derived from a language less agglutinative, and therefore more isolating. And, similarly, in whatever measure an inflective language can be proved to inflect its agglutinated words, in that measure is it thereby proved to have been derived from a language less inflective, or a language whose agglutinations had not yet undergone so much of the inflective modification.

On the other hand, as there is no necessary reason why an isolating language should develop into an agglutinative, or an agglutinative into an inflectional, it may very well be that the higher evolution of isolating tongues has proceeded collaterally with that of agglutinative, while the higher evolution of agglutinative has proceeded collaterally with that of inflectional. If this were so, both the schools of philology which we are considering would be equally right, and equally wrong: each would represent a different side of the same truth.

Thus it appears to me that, so far as the purposes of the present treatise, are concerned, we may neglect the question of phylogenesis as between these three orders of languages. For, so long as it is on all hands agreed that the principles of evolution are universally concerned in the genesis of every language, it will make no difference to my future argument whether these principles have obtained in one or in more lines of development. There can be no reasonable doubt that in some greater or less degree the three orders are connected : in what precise degree this connection obtains is doubtless a question of high importance to the science of philology : it is of scarcely any importance to the problems which we shall presently have to consider.

But the issue touching the relation between the poly-synthetic and other types of language is of more importance for us, inasmuch as it involves the question whether or not we have here to do with the most primitive type of language. In the opinion of some philologists, "these polysynthetic languages are an interesting survival of the early condition of language everywhere, and are but a fresh proof that America is in truth 'the new world :' primitive forms of speech that have elsewhere perished long ago still survive there, like the armadillo, to bear record of a bygone past." [*] On the other hand, it is with equal certainty affirmed that "polysynthesis is not a primitive feature, but an expansion, or, if you will, a second phase of agglutination." [†]

Of course in dealing with this issue I can only do so as an amateur, quite destitute of authority in matters pertaining to philology ; but the points on which I am about to speak have reference to principles so general, that in trying them the lay mind may not be without its uses in the jury-box. Moreover, philologists themselves are at present so ill-informed touching the facts of polysynthetic language, that there is less presumption here than elsewhere in any outsider offering his opinion upon the matters in dispute.[‡] It is

[*] Sayce, *Introduction, &c.,* i., 125, 126.

[†] Hovelacque, *Science of Language,* p. 130.

[‡] " What we most need to note is the very narrow limitation of our present knowledge. Even among the neighbouring families like the Algonquin, Troquois, and Dakota, whose agreement in style of structure (polysynthetic), taken in con-nection with the accordant race-type of their speakers, forbids us to regard them as ultimately different, no material correspondence, agreements in words and meanings, is to be traced ; and there are in America all degrees of polysynthetism, down to the lowest, and even to its entire absence. Such being the case, it ought to be evident that all attempts to connect American languages as a body with

however, undesirable to occupy space with any tedious rehearsal of the facts on which, after reading the more important literature of the subject, my judgment is based. For what it is worth, this judgment is as follows.

In the first place, it appears to me that those experts have an overwhelmingly strong case who argue in favour of the polysynthetic languages as presenting a highly primitive form of speech. Indeed, so undifferentiated do I think they prove this type of language-structure to be, that I agree with them in concluding that it probably brings us nearer "the origin of speech" than any other type now extant. Furthermore, looking to the wide contrast between this type and that which is presented by the isolating tongues, it appears to me impossible that the one can be genetically connected with the other. For it appears to me that the experts on the opposite side have no less completely proved, that the isolating tongues also present evidence of a highly primitive origin; and, therefore, that whatever amount of evolution and subsequent degeneration ("phonetic decay") the Chinese language, for instance, may be proved to have undergone, this only goes to show that it has throughout remained true to the isolating principle—just as the Protozoa, through all their long history of evolution, have remained true to *their* "isolating" type, notwithstanding that some of their branches must long ago have given origin to the "agglutinated" Metazoa. In other words, it appears to me that the experts on this side of the question have been able to place the isolating type of speech on as low a level of development— and, therefore, presumably on as high a level of antiquity—as experts on the other side have been able to claim for the polysynthetic.

If I am right in this opinion, it follows that there must have been at least two points of origin from which all existing languages arose—or rather, let me say, at least two

languages of the Old World are, and must be, fruitless : in fact, all discussions of the matter are at present unscientific " (Professor Whitney in *Encyc. Brit.*, art. " Philology," 1885).

types of language-formation upon which the earliest materials of speech were moulded. For even the strongest advocates of the polysynthetic origin of speech do not venture to question the highly primitive nature of the monosyllabic type. Thus, for instance, Professor Sayce is the principal upholder of the polysynthetic view, and yet he quotes the isolating forms of Chinese and Taic as furnishing "excellent illustrations of the early days of speech ; " * and he adduces them as " examples from the far East to show us the way in which our words first came into existence." † But if this is allowed to be so even by the leading advocate of the poly-synthetic view, I cannot conceive the possibility of the one type having become so completely transformed into the other as to have left no trace in the isolating type of its poly-synthetic origin. For, in view of the above admissions, we are left to conclude that the transformation must have taken place soon after the birth of language in any form—notwith-standing that, as Professor Sayce elsewhere insists (in the passage already quoted), " the conception of the sentence which underlies the polysynthetic dialects is the precise converse of that which underlies the isolating or the agglutinative type."

In view of these statements, therefore, by Professor Sayce himself, I do not think it is necessary for me to go further in justification of the opinion already expressed—namely, that we must recognize at least two types of language-formation upon which the earliest materials of speech were moulded. It is probable enough that both these types of language-formation were independently originated in many parts of the earth's surface at different times ; and it is possible that yet other types may have arisen, which are now either extinct, or fused with some of the later developments of the two which have survived. But, be these things as they may, I believe that both the schools of philology which we are considering have made out their respective cases ; and, there-

* *Introduction, &c.,* i. 120.
† *Ibid.,* i. 116.

fore, that they both err in so often assuming that these cases are mutually exclusive.

It will thus be apparent that I am altogether in favour of the polyphylectic theory of language-development. Even if it were not for the specially philological considerations just adduced, on grounds of merely general reasoning it would appear to me much more probable that so useful a sociological instrument as that of articulate sign-making should have been evolved from the sign-making of tone and gesture, wherever the psychological powers of mankind were far enough advanced to admit of the evolution. And, if this is so, it clearly becomes probable that any aboriginal races which were geographically separated would have slowly and independently elaborated their primitive forms of utterance—supposing, of course, that mankind had become segregated while still in the speechless state, which, as I will subsequently explain, seems to me the most probable supposition. And, if this were the case, it appears to me highly improbable that languages which originated and developed independently of one another should all have been under the necessity of starting either on the monosyllabic, the polysynthetic, or any other type exclusively. That the existing languages of the earth did originate in more than one centre is now the almost universal belief of competent authorities.* But too many of these authorities are still bound by what appears to me the wholly gratuitous and highly improbable assumption, that although various languages thus originated in different centres, they must all have been born with an exact family resemblance to one another, so far as type or "genius" is

* "The number of separate families of speech now existing in the world, which cannot be connected with one another, is at least seventy-five ; and the number will doubtless be increased when we have grammars and dictionaries of the numerous languages and dialects which are still unknown, and better information as regards those with which we are partially acquainted. If we add to these the innumerable groups of speech which have passed away without leaving behind even such waifs as the Basque of the Pyrenees, or the Etruscan of ancient Italy, some idea will be formed of the infinite number of primæval centres or communities in which language took its rise" (Sayce, *Introduction, &c.*, ii. 323).

concerned. But there is no basis for such an assumption, either in the physiology or the psychology of mankind. On the contrary, if we look to the nearest analogue of the case, namely, the growing child, we may find abundant evidence of the fact that the earliest attempts at articulate utterance may occur on different types, as we saw so strikingly proved by quotations from Dr. Hale in a previous chapter.

In this connection I would like to conclude the present chapter by giving prominence to an interesting and ingenious hypothesis, which has been suggested by Dr. Hale on the basis of the facts just alluded to.

In order that the merits of this suggestion may be appreciated, it is desirable to remind the reader that the languages now spoken by the native tribes of the American continent present so many and such radical differences among themselves, that, with regard to a large proportion of them, philologists are unable so much as to suggest any philological classification. Thus, to quote Professor Whitney, "as regards the material of expression, it is fully confessed that there is irreconcilable diversity among them. There are a very considerable number of groups, between whose significant signs exist no more apparent correspondencies than between those of English, Hungarian, and Malay ; none, namely, which may not be merely fortuitous."[*] And, what is most curious, these immense differences may obtain between neighbouring tribes who are to all appearance ethnologically identical—as, for instance, the Algonkin, Iroquois, and Dakota groups. Moreover, this diversity of language-structure in some cases goes so far as to reach the very roots of language-growth ; "the polysynthetic structure does not belong in the same degree to all American languages : on the contrary, it seems to be altogether effaced, or originally wanting, in some."[†] Nay, even the isolating type of language has gained a footing, and this in its properly monosyllabic and uninflective form.

[*] *Life and Growth of Language,* p. 259.   [†] *Ibid.,* p. 262.

Such being the state of matters on the American continent (and also, though to a lesser extent, in the Southern parts of the African), Dr. Hale suggests the following hypothesis by way of explanation. To me it certainly appears a plausible one, and if it should eventually be found to furnish a key for unlocking the mysteries of language-growth in the New World, it would obviously become available as a sufficient explanation of radical diversities of language elsewhere.

Starting from the facts which I have already quoted from his paper at the close of my chapter on Articulation, he argues that if children will thus spontaneously devise a language of their own in a wholly arbitrary manner, even when surrounded by the spoken language of a civilized community, much more would children be likely to do this if they should be accidentally separated from human society, and thus thrown upon their own resources in an isolated condition. Now, "if, under such circumstances, disease or the casualties of a hunter's life should carry off the parents, the survival of the children would, it is evident, depend mainly upon the nature of the climate and the ease with which food could be procured at all seasons of the year. In ancient Europe, after the present climatical conditions were established, it is doubtful if a family of children under ten years of age could have lived through a single winter. We are not, therefore, surprised to find that no more than four or five linguistic stocks are represented in Europe, and that all of them, except the Basque, are believed, on good evidence, to have been of comparatively late introduction. Even the Basque is traced by some, with much probability, to a source in North Africa. Of Northern America, east of the Rocky Mountains and north of the tropics, the same may be said. The climate and the scarcity of food in winter forbid us to suppose that a brood of orphan children could have survived, except possibly, by a fortunate chance, in some favoured spot on the shore of the Mexican Gulf, where shell-fish, berries, and edible roots are abundant and easy of access.

"But there is one region where Nature seems to offer herself as the willing nurse and bountiful step-mother of the feeble and unprotected. Of all countries on the globe, there is probably not one in which a little flock of very young children would find the means of sustaining existence more readily than in California. Its wonderful climate, mild and equable beyond example, is well known. Mr. Cronise, in his volume on the 'Natural Wealth of California,' tells us, that 'the monthly mean of the thermometer at San Francisco in December, the coldest month, is 50°; in September, the warmest month, 61°.' And he adds:—'Although the State reaches to the latitude of Plymouth Bay on the north, the climate, for its whole length, is as mild as that of the regions near the topics. Half the months are rainless. Snow and ice are almost strangers, except in the high altitudes. There are fully two hundred cloudless days in every year. Roses bloom in the open air through all seasons.' Not less remarkable than this exquisite climate is the astonishing variety of food, of kinds which seem to offer themselves to the tender hands of children. Berries of many sorts—strawberries, blackberries, currants, raspberries, and salmon-berries—are indigenous and abundant. Large fruits and edible nuts on low and pendent boughs may be said, in Milton's phrase, to 'hang amiable.' Mr. Cronise enumerates, among others, the wild cherry and plum, which 'grow on bushes;' the barberry, or false grape (*Berberis herbosa*), a 'low shrub,' which bears edible fruit; and the Californian horse-chestnut (*Æsculus Californcia*), 'a low, spreading tree or shrub, seldom exceeding fifteen feet high,' which 'bears abundant fruit much used by the Indians.' Then there are nutritious roots of various kinds, maturing at different seasons. Fish swarm in the rivers, and are taken by the simplest means. In the spring, Mr. Powers informs us, the whitefish 'crowd the creeks in such vast numbers that the Indians, by simply throwing in a little brushwood to impede their motion, can literally scoop them out.' Shell-fish and grubs abound, and are greedily eaten by the natives. Earthworms, which are found everywhere and at all seasons, are a favourite article of diet.   As to clothing, we are told by the authority just cited that ' on the plains all adult males and all children up to ten or twelve went perfectly naked, while the women wore only a narrow strip of deer-skin around the waist.'   Need we wonder that, in such a mild and fruitful region, a great number of separate tribes were found, speaking languages which a careful investigation has classed in nineteen distinct linguistic stocks ?

" The climate of the Oregon coast region, though colder than that of California, is still far milder and more equable than that of the same latitude in the east ; and the abundance of edible fruits, roots, river-fish, and other food of easy attainment, is very great.   A family of young children, if one of them were old enough to take care of the rest, could easily be reared to maturity in a sheltered nook of this genial and fruitful land.   We are not, therefore, surprised to find that the number of linguistic stocks in this narrow district, though less than in California, is more than twice as large as in the whole of Europe, and that the greater portion of these stocks are clustered near the Californian boundary. . . .

"Some reminiscences of the parental speech would probably remain with the older children, and be revived and strengthened as their faculties gained force.   Thus we may account for the fact, which has perplexed all inquirers, that certain unexpected and sporadic resemblances, both in grammar and in vocabulary, which can hardly be deemed purely accidental, sometimes crop up between the most dissimilar languages. . . .

"A glance at other linguistic provinces will show how aptly this explanation of the origin of language-stocks everywhere applies.   Tropical Brazil is a region which combines perpetual summer with a profusion of edible fruits and other varieties of food, not less abundant than in California.   Here, if anywhere, there should be a great number of totally distinct languages.   We learn on the best authority, that of Baron J. J. von Tschudi, in the Introduction to his recent work on the Khetshua Language, that this is the fact.   He says :—' I possess a collection made by the well-known naturalist, J. Natterer, during his residence of many years in Brazil, of more than a hundred languages, lexically completely distinct, from the interior of Brazil.' And he adds : —' The number of so-called isolated languages — that is, of such as, according to our present information, show no relationship to any other, and which therefore form distinct stocks of greater or less extent—is in South America very large, and must, on an approximate estimate, amount to many hundreds. It will perhaps be possible hereafter to include many of them in larger families, but there must still remain a considerable number for which this will not be possible.' "

I have quoted this hypothesis, as previously remarked, because it appears to me philologically interesting ; but whatever may be thought of it by professional authorities, the evidence which the American continent furnishes of a polygenetic and polytypic origin of the native languages remains the same. And if there is good reason for concluding in favour of polygenetic origins of different types as regards the languages on that continent, of course the probability arises that radical differences of structure among languages of the Old World admit of being explained by their having been derived from similarly independent sources.*

* I may add that the hypothesis admits of corroboration from sources not mentioned by its author. For Archdeacon Farrar wrote in 1865 :—" The neglected children in some of the Canadian and Indian villages, who are left alone for days, can and do invent for themselves a sort of *lingua franca,* partially or wholly unintelligible to all except themselves ; " and he quotes Mr. R. Moffat as " testifying to a similar phenomenon in the villages of South Africa (*Mission Travels*)." He also alludes to the fact that " deaf-mutes have an instinctive power to develop for themselves a language of signs," which, as we have seen in an earlier chapter, embraces the use of arbitrary articulations, even though in this case the speakers cannot themselves hear the sounds which they make.

While this work is passing through the press an additional paper has been published by Dr. Hale, entitled, *The Development of Language.* It supplies further evidence in support of this hypothesis.

18

# CHAPTER XIII.

## ROOTS OF LANGUAGE.

IN the last chapter my treatment of the classification and phylogeny of languages may have led the general reader to feel that philologists display extraordinary differences of opinion with regard to certain first principles of their science. I may, therefore, begin the present chapter by reminding such a reader that I have hitherto been concerned more with the differences of opinion than with the agreements. If one takes a general view of the progress of philological science since philology—almost in our own generation—first became a science, I think he must feel much more impressed by the amount of certainty which has been attained than by the amount of uncertainty which still remains. And the uncertainty which does remain is due rather to a backwardness of study than to differences of interpretation. When more is known about the structure and mutual relations of the polysynthetic tongues, it is probable that a better agreement will be arrived at touching the relation of their common type to that of isolating tongues on the one hand, and agglutinating on the other. But, be this as it may, even as matters stand at present, I think we have more reason to be surprised at the certainty which already attaches to the principles of philology, than at the uncertainty which occasionally arises in their applications to the comparatively unstudied branches of linguistic growth.

Furthermore, important as these still unsettled questions are from a purely philological point of view, they are not of any great moment from that of the evolutionist, as I have already observed. For, so long as it is universally agreed that all the language-groups have been products of a gradual development, it is, comparatively speaking, immaterial whether the groups all stand to one another in a relation of serial descent, or whether some of them stand to others in a relation of collateral descent. That is to say, the evolutionist is under no obligation to espouse either the monotypic or the polytypic theory of the origin of language. Therefore, it will make no material difference to the following discussion whether the reader feels disposed to follow the doctrine, that all languages must have originated in such monosyllabic isolations as we now meet with in a radical form of speech like the Chinese ; that they all originated in such polysynthetic incapsulations as we now find in the numberless dialects of the American Indians ; or, lastly, and as I myself think much more probably, that both these, and possibly other types of language-structure, are all equally primitive. Be these things as they may, my discussion will not be overshadowed by their uncertainty. For this uncertainty has reference only to the *origin* of the existing language-types as independent or genetically allied : it in no way affects the certainty of their subsequent *evolution.* Much as philologists may still differ upon the mutual relations of these several language-types, they all agree that "von der ersten Entstehung der Sprachwurzeln an bis zur Bildung der volkommenen Flexionssprachen, wie des Sanskrit, Griechischen, oder Deutschen, ist Alles in der Entwicklung der Sprache verständlich . . . Sobald nur die Wurzeln als die fertigen Bausteine der Sprache einmal da sind, lässt sich Schritt für Schritt das Wachsthum des Sprachgebäudes verfolgen." *

Therefore, having now said all that seems necessary to say on the question of language-types, I will pass on to consider the information that we possess on the subject of language-roots.

* Wundt, *Vorlesungen, &c.*, ii., 380, 381.

First, let us consider the number of roots out of which languages are developed—or, rather, let me say, the number of elementary constituents into which the researches of philologists have been able to reduce those languages which have been most closely studied. Of course the probability —nay, the certainty—is that the actual number of roots must in all cases be considerably less than philologists are now able to prove.

Chinese is composed of about five hundred separate words, each being a monosyllable. In actual use, these five hundred root-words are multiplied to over fifteen hundred by significant variety of intonation ; but the entire structure of this still living language is made up of five hundred mono-syllabic words. In the opinion of most philologists we have here a survival of the root stage of language ; but in the opinion of some we have the remnants of erosion, or " pho-netic decay." * This difference of opinion, however, is not a matter of importance to us ; and therefore I will not discuss it, further than to say that on account of it I will not here-after draw upon the Chinese language for illustrations of " radical " utterance, except in so far as philologists of all schools would allow as legitimate.†

Hebrew has been reduced to about the same number of roots as Chinese—Renan stating it in round numbers at five hundred. ‡ But without doubt this number would admit of being consideraly reduced, if inquiries were sufficiently extended to the whole Semitic family.

According to Professor Skeat, English is entirely made up of 461 Aryan roots, in combination with about twenty modifying constants. § The remote progenitor, Sanskrit, has

---

* Sayce, *Introduction to Science of Language*, ii. 13.

† The difference of opinion in question seems to arise from individual prepossessions with regard to the ulterior question whether or not the aboriginal roots of all languages must have been polysyllabic. For my own part, and for the reasons already given, I can see no presumption in favour of the view that primitive languages must all have presented the "polysenthetic genius."

‡ *Histoire des Langues Semitique*, p. 138.

§ *Etymological Dictionary*, p. 746.

been estimated to present as many as 850 roots, or, according to Benfey, just about twice that number.* On the other hand, Max Müller, as a result of more recent researches, professes to have reduced the total number of Sanskrit roots to 121.†

It is needless to give further instances. For these are enough to show that, even if we were to regard the analytic powers of comparative philology as adequate to resolve all the compounds of a language into its primitive elements the estimate of Pott would probably be high above the mark, when he states that on an average the roots of a language may be taken at a thousand.‡ Seeing that Chinese only contains in its whole vocabulary half that number of words, and that both Hebrew and English have similarly yielded each about five hundred radicals in the crucible of more modern research, I think we may safely reduce the general estimate of Pott by one-half, and probably would be nearer the truth if we were to do so by three-quarters, or more. At all events, we may be satisfied that the total number of radicals sufficient to feed the most luxuriant of languages is expressible in three figures ; and this, as we shall presently see, is enough for all the purposes of my subsequent discussion.

Passing on now from the question of number to that of character, we have first to meet the question—What *are* these roots ? Are they the actually primitive words of pre-historic languages, or are they what Max Müller has aptly termed "phonetic types"? Here again we encounter a difference of opinion among philologists. Thus, for instance, Professor Whitney tells us that the Indo-European languages are all descended from an original monosyllabic tongue, and, therefore, that " our ancestors talked with one another in simple syllables, indicative of ideas of prime importance, but wanting all designation of their relations." § On the other hand, it is

---

* See Max Müller, *Science of Thought*, p. 332.

† *Ibid.*, p. 404.

‡ *Ethnologische Forschungen*, ii., s. 73, *et seq.* He here quotes Varro to the effect that the roots of Latin amount to about a thousand.

§ *Language and the Study of Language*, p. 256.

objected to this view that "such a language is a sheer impossibility;" [*] that "there could be no hope of any mutual understanding" with a language restricted to such isolated and general terms, &c. [†]  On this side of the question it is represented that "roots are the phonetic and significant types discovered by the analysis of the comparative philologist as common to a group of allied words;" [‡] that "a root is the *core* of a group of allied words," [§] "the naked kernel of a family of words." [||]  Or, to adopt a simile previously used in another connection, we may say that a root as now presented by the philologist is a composite photograph (or *phonogram*) of a number of words, all belonging to the same pre-historic language, and all closely allied in meaning.

The difference of authoritative teaching thus exhibited is not a matter of much importance for us.  Nor, indeed, as we shall subsequently see, is it a difference so great as may at first sight appear.  For even the phonetic-type theory does not doubt that all the aboriginal and unknown words, out of the composition of which a root is now extracted, must have been genetically allied with one another, and exhibited the closeness of their kinship by a close similarity of sound. Therefore, it does not make any practical difference whether we regard a root as itself a primitive word, which was used in some such way as the Chinese now use their monosyllabic terms; or whether we regard it as a generalized expression of a group of cognate words, all closely allied as to meaning.  In fact, even so strong an adherent of the phonetic-type theory as Professor Max Müller very clearly states this, where he says that, although "the mere root, *quâ* root, may be denied the dignity of a word, as soon as a root is used for predication it becomes a word, whether outwardly it is changed or not." [¶]

Seeing, then, that this difference of opinion among philo-

---

[*] Sayce, *Introduction to the Science of Language*, ii., p. 4.
[†] Geiger, *Ursprung der Sprache*, s. 16.
[‡] Sayce, *loc. cit.*, ii. p. 6.
[§] Wedgwood, *Entymol. Dict.*, p. iii.
[||] Farrar, *Origin of Language*, p. 53.
[¶] *Science of Thought*, p. 439.

logists is not one of great importance for us, I will henceforth disregard it. And, as it will be conducive to brevity, if not also to clearness, I will speak of roots as archaic words, although by so doing I shall not intend to assume that they are more than phonetic types, or the nearest approach we can make to the words out of which they were generated.

We may next consider the kind of meanings which roots convey. Antecedently we might form various anticipations on this head, such as that they should be imitative of natural sounds, expressive of concrete ideas, and so forth. As a matter of fact, we find that they are not expressive of natural sounds ; but, as far as we have now any means of judging, quite arbitrary. Moreover, they are not expressive of concrete or particular ideas ; but always of abstract or general. Here, then, to begin with, we have two facts of apparently great importance. And they are both facts which, at first sight, seem to countenance the view that, in its last resort, comparative philology fails to testify to the natural origin of speech. But we must look into the matter more closely, and, in order to do this most fairly, I will quote from Professor Max Müller the 121 roots into which he analyzes the Sanskrit language. This is the language which has been most carefully studied in the present connection, and of all its students Professor Max Müller is least open to any suspicion of inclining to the side of " Darwinism." The following is a list of what he calls "the 121 original concepts."

1. Dig.
2. Plat, weave, sew, bind.
3. Crush, pound, destroy, waste, rub, smooth.
4. Sharpen.
5. Smear, colour, knead, harden.
6. Scratch.
7. Bite, eat.
8. Divide, share, eat.
9. Cut.
10. Gather, observe.
11. Stretch, spread.
12. Mix.
13. Scatter, strew.
14. Sprinkle, drip, wet.
15a. Shake, tremble, quiver, flicker.
15b. Shake, mentally, be angry, abashed, fearfully, etc.
16. Throw down, fall.
17. Fall to pieces.
18. Shoot, throw at.
19. Pierce, split.
20. Join, fight, check.

21. Tear.
22. Break, smash.
23. Measure.
24. Blow.
25. Kindle.
26. Milk, yield.
27. Pour, flow, rush.
28. Separate, free, leave, lack.
29. Glean.
30. Choose.
31. Cook, roast, boil.
32. Clean.
33. Wash.
34. Bend, bow.
35. Turn, roll.
36. Press, fix.
37. Squeeze.
38. Drive, thrust.
39. Push, stir, live.
40. Burst, gush, laugh, beam.
41. Dress.
42. Adorn.
43. Strip, remove.
44. Steal.
45. Check.
46. Fill, thrive, swell, grow strong.
47. Cross.
48. Sweeten.
49. Shorten.
50. Thin, suffer.
51. Fat, stick, love.
52. Lick.
53. Suck, nourish.
54. Drink, swell.
55. Swallow, sip.
56. Vomit.
57. Chew, eat.
58. Open, extend.
59. Reach, strive, rule, have.
60. Conquer, take by violence, struggle.
61. Perform, succeed.
62. Attack, hurt.
63. Hide, drive.
64. Cover, embrace.

65. Bear, carry.
66. Can, be strong.
67. Show.
68. Touch.
69. Strike.
70. Ask.
71. Watch, observe.
72. Lead.
73. Set.
74. Hold, wield.
75. Give, yield.
76. Cough.
77. Thirsty, dry.
78. Hunger.
79. Yawn.
80. Spue.
81. Fly.
82. Sleep.
83. Bristle, dare.
84. Be angry, harsh.
85. Breathe.
86. Spea.
87. Seek.
88. Hear.
89. Smell, sniff.
90. Sweat.
91. Seethe, boil.
92. Dance.
93. Leap.
94. Creep.
95. Stumble.
96. Stick.
97. Burn.
98. Dwell.
99. Stand.
100. Sink, lie, fail.
101. Swing.
102. Hang down, lean.
103. Rise up, grow.
104. Sit.
105. Toil.
106. Weary, waste, slacken.
107. Rejoice, please.
108. Desire, love.
109. Wake.
110. Fear.

111. Cool, refresh.
112. Stink.
113. Hate,
114. Know.
115. Think.
116. Shine.

117. Run.
118. Move, go.
119a. Noise, inarticulate.
119b. Noise, musical.
120. Do.
121. Be.

"These 121 concepts constitute the stock-in-trade with which I maintain that every thought that has ever passed through the mind of India, so far as it is known to us in its literature, has been expressed. It would have been easy to reduce that number still further, for there are several among them which could be ranged together under more general concepts. But I leave this further reduction to others, being satisfied as a first attempt with having shown how small a number of seeds may produce, and has produced, the enormous intellectual vegetation that has covered the soil of India from the most distant antiquity to the present day." *

Now, the first thing which strikes one on reading this list is, that it unquestionably justifies the inference of its compiler, namely, "if the Science of Language has proved anything, it has proved that every term which is applied to a particular idea or object (unless it be a proper name) is already a general term." But the next thing which immediately strikes one is that the list, surprisingly short as it is, nevertheless is much too long to admit of being interpreted as, in any intelligible sense of the words, an inventory of "original concepts"—unless by "original" we are to understand the ultimate results of philological analysis. That all these concepts are not "original" in the sense of representing the ideation of really primitive man, is abundantly proved by two facts.

The first is that fully a third of the whole number might be dispensed with, and yet leave no important blank in the already limited resources of the list for the purposes either of communication or reflection. To yawn, to spew, to vomit, to sweat, and so on, are not forms of activity of any such

* *Science of Thought*, p. 549.

vital importance to the needs of a primitive community, as to demand priority of naming by any aboriginal framers of language. Moreover, as Professor Max Müller himself elsewhere observes, " even these 121 concepts might be reduced to a much smaller number, if we cared to do so. Any one who examines them carefully, will see how easy it would have been to express to dig by to cut or to strike ; to bite by to cut or to crush ; to milk by to squeeze ; to glean by to gather ; to steal by to lift. . . . If we see how many special purposes can be served by one root, as *I*, to go, or *Pas*, to fasten, the idea that a dozen of roots might have been made to supply the whole wealth of our dictionary, appears in itself by no means so ridiculous as is often supposed." *

Again, in the second place, a large proportional number of the words have reference to a grade of culture already far in advance of that which has been attained by most existing savages. " Many concepts, such as to cook, to roast, to measure, to dress, to adorn, belong clearly to a later phase of civilized life." †   It might have been suitably added that such " concepts " as to dig, to plat, to milk, &c., betoken a condition of *pastoral* life, which, as we know from abundant evidence, is representative of a comparatively high level of social evolution. ‡   But if " many " of these concepts are thus

---

* *Science of Thought*, pp. 551, 552.

† *Ibid.*, pp. 551, 552.

‡ " The Aryan languages are the languages of a civilized race ; the parent speech to which we may inductively trace them was spoken by men who stood on a relatively high level of culture " (Sayce, *Introduction, &c.,* i. 56). " The primitive tribe which spoke the mother-tongue of the Indo-European family was not nomadic alone, but had settled habitations, even towns and fortified places, and addicted itself in part to the rearing of cattle, in part to the cultivation of the earth. It possessed our chief domesticated animals—the horse, the ox, the goat, and the swine, besides the dog : the bear and the wolf were foes that ravaged its flocks ; the mouse and the fly were already domestic pests. . . . Barley, and perhaps also wheat, was raised for food, and converted into meal. Mead was prepared from honey, as a cheering and inebriating drink. The use of certain metals was known ; whether iron was one of them admits of question. The art of weaving was practised ; wool and hemp, and possibly flax, being the materials employed. . . . The weapons of offence and defence were those which are usual among primitive peoples, the sword, spear, bow, and shield. Boats were manufactured and moved by oars. . . . The art of numeration was learned, at least up to a

unmistakably referable to semi-civilized as distinguished from savage life, what guarantee can we have that the remainder are "original"? Obviously we can have no such guarantee; but, on the contrary, find the very best, because *intrinsic* evidence, that they belong to a more or less high level of culture, far removed from that of primitive man. In other words, we must conclude that these 121 concepts are "original" only in the sense that they do not now admit of further analysis at the hands of comparative philologists: they are not original in the sense of bringing us within any measurable distance of the first beginnings of articulate speech.*

Nevertheless, they are of the utmost value and significance, in that they bring us down to a period of presumably restricted ideation, as compared with the enormous development since attained by various branches of this Indo-European stock—so far, at least, as the growth of language can be taken as a fair expression of such development. They are likewise of the highest importance as showing in how presumably short a period of time (comparatively speaking) so immense and divergent a growth may proceed from such a simple and germ-like condition of thought.† Lastly, they serve to show in a most striking manner that the ideas represented, although all of a general character, are nevertheless of the lowest degree of generality. Scarcely any of them present us with evidence of reflective thought, as distinguished from the naming of objects of sense-perception, or of the

hundred; there is no general Indo-European word for 'thousand.' Some of the stars were noticed and named; the moon was the chief measurer of time. The religion was polytheistic, a worship of the personified powers of nature" (Whitney, *Language and the Study of Language*, pp. 207, 208). For a more detailed account of this interesting people, see Poescher, *Die Arier.*

\* " Unsere Wurzeln sind die Urwurzeln nicht; wir haben vielleicht, von keiner einzigen die erste, ursprüngliche Laut-form mehr vor uns, ebensowenig wohl die Urbedeutung " (Geiger, *Ursprung der Sprache*, s. 65). And this opinion, so far as I know, is adopted as an axiom by all other philologists.

† "It is impossible to bring down the epoch at which the Aryan tribes still lived in the same locality, and spoke practically the same language, to a date much later than the third millennium before the Christian era " (Sayce, *Introduction, &c.*, ii., p. 320).

simplest forms of activity which are immediately cognizable as such.* In other words, few of these "original concepts" rise much higher in the scale of ideation than the level to which I have previously assigned what I have called "named recepts" or "pre-concepts." A dumb animal, or an infant, presents a full receptual appreciation of the majority of actions which the catalogue includes ; and, therefore, so that a society of human beings can speak at all (*i.e.* presents the power of naming their recepts), it is difficult to see how they could have avoided a denotation of the more important recepts which are here concerned.

Another most interesting feature of a general kind which the list presents is, that it is composed exclusively of verbs.† This peculiarity of the ultimate known roots of all languages, which shows them to have been expressive of actions and states as distinguished from objects and qualities, is a peculiarity on which Professor Max Müller lays much stress. But the inference which he draws from the fact is clearly not justifiable. This inference is that, as every root expresses "the consciousness of repeated acts, such as scraping, digging, striking," &c., the naming of actions, as distinguished from objects, "must be considered as the first step in the formation of concepts." Now, in drawing this inference—and, indeed, throughout all his works as far as I remember—Professor Max Müller has entirely overlooked two most important considerations. First, as already observed, that the roots in question are *demonstrably* very far from having been the original material of language as first coined by primitive man ; and, next, that whatever

---

* This fact alone would be sufficient to dispose of what I cannot but consider, from any and every point of view, the transparent absurdity of the doctrine that "the formation of thought is the first and natural purpose of language, while its communication is accidental only" (*Science of Thought*, p. 40). Such a "purpose" would imply "thought" as already formed ; and, therefore, the doctrine must suppose a purpose to precede the conditions of its own possibility.

† I use the term "verbs" merely for the sake of brevity and clearness. Of course there cannot have been verbs, strictly so-called, before there were parts of speech of any kind. The more accurate statement is given in the next sentence, and is the one which I desire to be understood hereafter in the short-hand expression "verbs."

this original material may have been, from the first there must have been a struggle for existence among the really primitive roots—only those surviving which were most fitted to survive as roots, *i.e.* as the parent stems of subsequent word-formations. Now, it appears to me obvious enough that archaic—though not necessarily aboriginal—words which were expressive of actions, would have stood a better chance of surviving as roots than those which may have been expressive of objects ; first because they were likely to have been more frequently employed, and next because many of them must have lent themselves more readily to metaphorical extension—*especially under a system of animistic thought.*\* And, if these things were so, there is nothing remarkable in words significant of actions having alone survived as roots.†

The consideration that it is only those words which were successful in the struggle for existence that can have become the progenitors of subsequent language—and therefore the only

---

\* " It must be borne in mind that primitive man did not distinguish between phenomena and volitions, but included everything under the head of actions, not only the involuntary actions of human beings, such as breathing, but also the movements of inanimate things, the rising and setting of the sun, the wind, the flowing of water, and even such purely inanimate phenomena as fire, electricity, &c. ; in short, all the changing attributes of things were conceived as voluntary actions " (Sweet, *Words, Logic and Grammar*, p. 486).

† As a matter of fact, and as we shall subsequently see, there is an immense body of purely philological evidence to show that verbs are really a much later product of linguistic growth than either nouns or pronouns. This is proved by their comparative paucity in many existing languages of low development (their place being taken by pronominal appositions, &c.) ; and also by tracing the origin of many of them to other parts of speech. (See especially Garnett's *Essays, Pritchard on the Celtic Languages, Quart. Rev.*, Sept. 1876 ; *The Derivation of Words from Pronominal and Prepositional Roots, Proc. Philol. Soc.* vol. ii. ; and *On the Nature and Analysis of the Verb*, ibid., vol. iii.) Later on it will be shown that in the really primitive stages of language-growth there is no assignable distinction between any of the parts of speech. Archdeacon Farrar well remarks, " The invention of a verb requires a greater effort of abstraction than that of a noun. . . . We cannot accept it as even *possible* that from roots meaning *to shine, to be bright*, names were formed for *sun, moon, stars*, &c. . . . In some places, indeed, Professor Müller appears to hold the correct view, that at first 'roots' stood for any and every part of speech, just as the monosyllabic expressions of children do" (*Chapters on Language*, pp. 196, 197 ; see, also, some good remarks on the subject by Sir Graves Haughton, *Bengali Grammar*, p. 108).

words that have been handed down to us as roots—has a still more important bearing upon another of Professor Max Müller's generalizations. From the fact that all his 121 Sanskrit roots are expressive of "general" ideas (by which term he of course includes what I call generic ideas), he concludes that from its very earliest origin speech must have been thus expressive of general ideas ; or, in other words, that human language could not have begun by the naming of particulars : from the first it must have been concerned with the naming of "notions." Now, of course, if any vestige of real evidence could be adduced to show that this "must have been" the case, most of the foregoing chapters of the present work would not have been written. For the whole object of these chapters has been to show, that on psychological grounds it is abundantly intelligible how the conceptual stage of ideation may have been gradually evolved from the receptual—the power of forming general, or truly conceptual ideas, from the power of forming particular and generic ideas. But if it could be shown—or even rendered in any degree presumable—that this distinctly human power of forming truly general ideas arose *de novo* with the first birth of articulate speech, assuredly my whole analysis would be destroyed : the human mind would be shown to present a quality different in origin—and, therefore, in kind—from all the lower orders of intelligence : the law of continuity would be interrupted at the terminal phase : an impassable gulf would be fixed between the brute and the man. As a matter of fact, however, there is not only no vestige of any such proof or even presumption ; but, as we shall see in our two following chapters, there is uniform and overwhelming proof of precisely the opposite doctrine—proof, indeed, so uniform and overwhelming that it has long ago induced all other philologists to accept this opposite doctrine as one of the axioms of their science. Leaving, however, this proof to be adduced in its proper place, I have now merely to point out the futility of the evidence on which Professor Max Müller relies.

This evidence consists merely in fact that the " 121 original concepts," which are embodied in the roots of Aryan speech, are expressive of "general ideas." Now, this argument might be worth considering if there were the smallest reason to suppose that in these roots of Aryan speech we possess the aboriginal elements of language as first spoken by man. But as we well know that this is immeasurably far from being the case, the whole argument collapses. The mere fact that many words which have survived as roots are words expressive of general ideas, is no more than we might have antecedently expected. Remembering that it is a favourable condition to a word surviving as a root that it should prove itself a prolific parent of other words, obviously it is those words which were expressive of ideas presenting some degree of generality that would have had the best chance of thus coming down to us, even from the comparatively high level of culture which, as we have seen, is testified to by "the 121 original concepts." Of course, as I have already said, the case would have been different if any one were free to suppose, even as a merely logical possibility, that this level of culture represented that of primitive man when he first began to employ articulate speech. But any such supposition is beyond the range of rational discussion. The 121 concepts themselves yield overwhelming evidence of belonging to a time *immeasurably remote* from that of any speechless progenitor of *Homo sapiens ;* and in the enormous interval (whatever it may have been) many successive generations of words must *certainly* have flourished and died.*

These remarks are directed to the comparatively few instances of general ideas which, as a matter of fact, the list of " 121 concepts " presents. As already observed, the great majority of these "concepts" exhibit no higher degree of

---

* "Standst du dabei, als sich der Brust des noch stummen Urmenschen der erste Sprachlaut entrang? und verstandst du ihn? Oder hat man dir die Urwurzeln jener ersten Menschen vor hundert tausend Jahren überliefert? Sind das, was du als Wurzeln hinstellst, und was wirklich Wurzeln sein mögen, auch Wurzeln der Urzeit, unveränderte Reflexlaute? Sind jene deine Wurzeln älter als sechstausend, als zehntausend Jahre? und wie viel mögen sie sich in den früheren Jahrzehntausenden verändert haben? wie mag sich ihre Bedeutung verändert haben?" (Steinthal, *Zeits. b. Volkerpysch. u. Sprachwiss.,* 1867, s. 76).

"generality" than belongs to what I have called a "pre-con-cept," *i.e.* a "named recept." But precisely the same con-siderations apply to both. For, even supposing that a named recept was originally a word used only to designate a "par-ticular" as distinguished from a "generic" idea, obviously it would have stood but a poor chance of surviving as a root unless it had first undergone a sufficient degree of extension to have become what I call receptually connotative. A proper name, for instance, could not, as such, become a root. Not until it had become extended to other persons or things of a like class could it have secured a chance of surviving as a root in the struggle for existence. As a matter of fact, I think it most probable—not only from general considerations, but also from a study of the spontaneous names first coined in "baby-language,"—that aboriginal speech was concerned simultaneously with the naming both of particular and of generic ideas—*i.e.* of individual percepts and of recepts. It will be remembered that in Chapter III., while treating of the Logic of Recepts, I dealt at some length with this subject. Here, therefore, it will be sufficient to quote the conclusion to which my analysis led.

"A generic idea is generic because the particular ideas of which it is composed present such obvious points of resem-blance that they spontaneously fuse together in consciousness ; but a general idea is general for precisely the opposite reason—namely, because the points of resemblance which it has seized are obscured from immediate perception, and therefore could never have fused together in consciousness but for the aid of intentional abstraction, or of the power of a mind knowingly to deal with its own ideas as ideas. In other words, the kind of classification with which recepts are concerned is that which lies nearest to the kind of classification with which all processes of so called perceptual inference depend—such as mistaking a bowl for a sphere. But the kind of classification with which concepts are concerned is that which lies furthest from this purely automatic grouping of perceptions. Classi-fication there doubtless is in both cases ; but in the one order it is due to the closeness of resemblances in an act of perception, while in the other it is due to their remoteness." [*]

Of course it goes without saying that this "closeness of resemblances in an act of perception" may be due either to similarities of sense-perceptions themselves (as when the colour of a ruby is seen to resemble that of "pigeon's blood"), or to frequency of their associations in experience (as when a sea-bird groups together in one recept the sundry sensations which go to constitute its perception of water, with its generic classification of water as a medium in which it is safe to dive). Now, if we remember these things, can we possibly wonder that the palæontology of speech should prove early roots to have been chiefly expressive of "generic" as distinguished from "general" ideas on the one hand, or "particular" ideas on the other? By failing to observe this real distinction between classification as receptual and conceptual—*i.e.* as given immediately in the act of perception itself, or as elaborated of set purpose through the agency of introspective thought, Professor Max Müller founds his whole argument on another and an unreal distinction : he everywhere regards the bestowing of a name as in itself a sufficient proof of conceptual thought, and therefore constitutes the faculty of denotation, equally with that of denomination, the distinctive criterion of a self-conscious mind. But, as we have now so repeatedly seen, such is certainly not the case. Actions and processes so habitual, or so immediately apparent to perception, as those with which the great majority of these "121 concepts" are concerned, do not betoken any order of ideation higher than the pre-conceptual, in virtue of which a young child is able to give expression to its higher receptual life prior to the advent of self-consciousness. Or, as Geiger tersely says :—"In enzelnen Fällen ist die Entstehung von Gattungsbegriffe aus Mangel an Unterscheidung gleichwohl kaum zu bezweifeln." [†]

---

[*] *Supra*, p. 68, *et seq.*

[†] *Ursprung der Sprache*, s. 74. To the same effect, and from the side of psychology, I may quote Wundt :—" Oft hat man desshalb in der Sprache einen

19

Again, if we look to the still closer analogy furnished by savages, we meet with a still further corroboration of this view. For instance, Professor Sayce remarks that in "all savage and barbarous dialects, while individual objects of sense have a super-abundance of names, general terms are correspondingly rare." And he gives a number of remarkable illustrations.*

In view of these considerations, my only wonder is that these 120 root-words do not present *better* evidence of conceptual thought. I have already given my reasons for refusing to suppose that we have here to do with the " original " framers of spoken language ; and looking to the comparatively high level of culture which the people in question must have reached, it seems remarkable that the root-words of their language should only in so few instances have risen above the level of pre-conceptual utterance.† This, however, only shows how comparatively small a part self-conscious reflection need play in the practical life of uncultured man : it does not show that the people in question were remarkably deficient in this distinctively human faculty. Archdeacon Farrar tells us that he has observed the whole conversational vocabulary of certain English labourers not to exceed a hundred words, and probably further observation would have

Übergang vom Abstrakten zum Konkreten zu finden geglaubt, weil dieselbe thatsächlich zunächst umfassendere, dann individuellere Vorstellungen bezeichnet und erst zuletzt wieder die Namen individueller Objekte zu Gemeinnamen stempelt. Aber was am Anfang dieser Reihe liegt ist etwas ganz anderes als was den Schluss derselben bildet : Gemeinnamen sind wirkliche Zeichen für Allgemeinvorstellungen und Begriffe. Jene ersten Vorstellungen, welche das Bewusstsein bildet und die Sprache ausdrückt, sind nicht *Allgemein*vorstellungen sondern *umfassende* Vorstellungen. Beides ist wesentlich aus einander zu halten " (*Vorlesungen, &c.,* ii. 382). The passage then proceeds to discuss the psychology of the subject.

* *Introduction, &c.,* ii. 5, 6.

† And even as regards this minority (such as " to be," " to think," " to do," &c.), we must remember an important consideration on which Geiger bestows a number of excellent pages. Briefly put, this consideration is that the offspring of words are everywhere proved to have progressively changed their meanings by successive steps and in divergent lines : applying this general law to the case of roots, it follows that the oldest meaning which philology is able to trace as expressed by a root, need not be anywhere near the meaning which attached to its remoter parents : the latter may have been much less conceptual.

shown that the great majority of these were employed without conceptual significance. Therefore, if these labourers had had to coin their own words, it is probable that, without exception, their language would have been destitute of any terms betokening more than a pre-conceptual order of ideation. Neverthless, these men must have been capable, in however undeveloped a degree, of truly conceptual ideation : and this proves how unsafe it would be to argue from the absence of distinctively conceptual terms to the poverty of conceptual faculty among any people whose root-words may have come down to us—although, no doubt, in such a case we appear to be getting within a comparatively short distance of the origin of this faculty.

The point, however, now is that really aboriginal, and therefore purely denotative names, must certainly have been " generic " as well as " particular ": they must have been the names of recepts as well as of percepts, of actions as well as of objects and qualities. Moreover, it is equally certain that among this aboriginal assemblage of denotative names as particular and generic, only those belonging to the latter class could have stood much chance of surviving as roots. In other words, no aboriginal name could have survived as a root until it had acquired some greater or less degree of receptual and, therefore, of connotative value. Hence the fact that the ultimate result of the philological analysis of any language is that of reducing the language to a certain small number of roots, and the fact that all these roots are expressive of general and generic ideas,—these facts in themselves yield no support whatever to the doctrine, either that these roots were themselves the aboriginal elements of language, or, *a fortiori*, that the aboriginal elements of language were expressive of general ideas. *

And this conclusion involves another of scarcely less

* Professor Max Müller says in one place, " The Science of Language, by inquiring into the origin of general terms, has established two facts of the highest importance, namely, first, that all terms were originally general ; and, secondly,

importance. A great deal of discussion has been expended over the question as to whether, or how far, aboriginal language was indebted to the principle of onomatopœia, or the imitation by articulate names of sounds obviously distinctive of the objects or actions named. Of course, on evolutionary principles we should be strongly inclined to suppose that aboriginal language must have been largely assisted in its formation by such intentional imitation of natural sounds, seeing that of all forms of vocal expression they admit of most readily conveying an idea of the object or action named. And the same applies to the so-called interjectional element in word-formation, or the utilization as names of sounds which are naturally expressive of states of human feeling. On the other hand, contempt has been poured upon this theory as an adequate explanation of the first beginnings of articulate speech, on the ground that it is not supported either by history * or by the results of philogenetic inquiry.† It is, however, forgotten by those who argue on this side that names of onomatopoetic origin

that they could not be anything but general" (*Science of Thought*, p. 456). Elsewhere, however, he says, "Although during the time when the growth of anguage becomes historical and most accessible, therefore, to our observation, the tendency certainly is from the general to the special, I cannot resist the conviction that before that time there was a prehistoric period during which language followed an opposite direction. During that period roots, beginning with special meanings, became more and more generalized, and it was only after reaching that stage that they branched off again into special channels" (*ibid.*, pp. 383, 384). Again, in his earlier work on the *Science of Language* (vol. i., pp. 425–432), he argues in favour of terms having been aboriginally general. It will thus be seen that with reference to this question he is not consistent. Touching the first of his doctrines above quoted, Geiger pertinently observes that against such a conclusion there lies the obvious absurdity, that if a language were to consist exclusively of general terms, it would be *ipso facto* unintelligible to its own speakers; "for what hope could there be of any mutual understanding with a language comprising only such words as "to bind," "to sound," &c. ? (*Ursprung der Sprache*, s. 16). Clearly, Professor Max Müller's difficulties regarding this subject are quite imaginary, and would disappear if he were to entertain the natural alternative that there is no reason to suppose aboriginal words were exclusively restricted to being either special or general—*i.e.* generic.

* Bunsen, *Philosophy of Universal History*, ii. 131.

† Professor Max Müller in all his works ; but it is observable that his opposition to what he calls the "bow-wow and pooh-pooh theory" was more strenuous in his earlier publications than it is in his later.

must always be, in the first instance, particular ; that so long as they remain particular (as, for example, is the case with our word " cuckoo "), they cannot have much chance of surviving as roots ; that in proportion as they increase their chances of survival as roots by becoming more general, they must do so by becoming more conventional ; and, therefore, that the vast majority of roots, even if aboriginally they were of onomatopoetic origin, must necessarily have had that origin obscured.

In order to illustrate each and all of these general considerations, let us turn to the example of our own " baby-language." The fact that such language presents so large an element of onomatopœia in itself furnishes a strong presumption that what is now seen to constitute so important a principle in the infancy of the individual (notwithstanding the hereditary tendency to speak), must have constituted at least as important a principle in the infancy of the race. But the point now is, that if we mark the connotative extension of any such nursery word, we may find that just in proportion as it becomes general does its onomatopoetic origin become obscure. For instance, the late Mr. Darwin gave me the following particulars with regard to a grandchild of his own, who was then living in his house. I quote the account from notes taken at the time.

" The child, who was just beginning to speak, called a duck ' quack '; and, by special association, it also called water ' quack.' By an appreciation of the resemblance of qualities, it next extended the term ' quack ' to denote all birds and insects on the one hand, and all fluid substances on the other. Lastly, by a still more delicate appreciation of resemblance, the child eventually called all coins ' quack,' because on the back of a French sou it had once seen the representation of an eagle. Hence, to the child, the sign ' quack,' from having originally had a very specialized meaning, became more and more extended in its signification, until it now serves to designate such apparently different objects as ' fly,' ' wine,' and ' coin.' "

Now, if any such process of extending or generalizing aboriginally onomatopoetic terms were to have taken place among the primitive framers of human speech, how hopeless would be the task of the philologist who should now attempt to find the onomatopoetic root! Yet, as above observed, not only may we be perfectly certain that such extensions of aboriginal onomatopoetic terms must have taken place, if any such terms were ever in existence at all (and this cannot be doubted), but also that it must have been almost a necessary condition to the survival of an onomatopoetic term as a root that such an extension of its meaning should have taken place. In other words, we can see very good reason to conclude that, as a rule, only those instances of primitive onomatopœia can have survived as roots, which must long ago have had their onomatopoetic origin hopelessly obscured. So that nowhere so much as in this case should we be prepared to entertain the general principle of philological research, that, as Goethe graphically states it, the original meanings of words become gradually worn out, like the image and superscription of a coin.*

In view of such considerations, my only wonder is that this origin admits of being traced so often as it does, even as far back as the comparatively recent times when a pastoral people coined the terms which afterwards constituted the roots of Sanskrit. *Kas*, to cough ; *kshu*, to sneeze ; *proth*, to snort ; *ma*, to bleat, and not a few others, are conceded, even by Professor Max Müller, to be of obviously imitative

---

* It is needless to say that innumerable instances might be quoted of this metaphorical change in the meanings of words, even in existing languages,—so much so, indeed, that, as Richter says, all languages are but dictionaries of forgotten metaphors. For example, there is a single Hebrew word of three letters which may bear any one of the following significations :—to mix, to exchange, to stand in place of, to pledge, to interfere, to be familiar, to disappear, to set, to do a thing in the evening, to be sweet, a fly or beetle, an Arabian, a stranger, the weft of cloth, the evening, a willow, and a raven. (See Farrar, *Chapters on Language*, p. 229. He adds, " Assuming that all these significations are ultimately deducible from one and the same root, we see at once the extent to which metaphor must have been at work." For further examples of the same principle, see *ibid.*, pp. 234, 251, 252.)

origin. In the present connection, however, it is of interest to notice how this authority deals with such cases. He says :—" Not one of them is of any importance in helping us to account for real words in Sanskrit. Most of them have had no offspring at all, others have had a few descendants, mostly sterile. Their history shows clearly how far the influence of onomatopœia may go, and if once we know its legitimate sphere, we shall be less likely to wish to extend it beyond its proper limits." *

Now, under our present point of view we can see a very good reason why this element of sterility should have attached to these roots of Sanskrit whose onomatopoetic origin still admits of being clearly traced : it is just because they failed to be extended that their imitative source continues to be apparent.† But suppose, for the sake of illustration, that any one of them had been extended, and what would have happened? If *ma*, to bleat, had been metaphorically applied to the crying of a child, and had then become more and more habitually used in this new signification, while the original meaning became more and more obsolete, it might have taken the place of any such root as *bhi*, to fear; *ish*, to love, &c. ; and in all the progeny of words which in this its conventional use it might subsequently have generated, no trace of imitative origin could now have been met with—any more than such an origin can be detected in the sound "quack," as used by the above-mentioned child to designate a shilling.

Several other considerations to the same general effect might be adduced. But, to mention only some of the more important, Steinthal points out that imitative utter-

---

* *Science of Thought*, pp. 317, 318.

† Or, as Heyse puts it, many onomatopœias are not "old fruitful roots of language, but modern inventions which remain isolated in language, and are incapable of originating any families of words, because their meaning is too limited and special to admit of a manifold application " (*System*, s. 92, quoted by Farrar, *Chapters on Language*, p. 152, who also shows that words of onomatopoetic origin are not invarial·ly sterile. When such origin is not so remote as to have become wholly obscured by a widely connotative extension, it does remain possible to trace its progeny through areas of smaller extension).

ance differs widely even among different races of existing
men, so that the onomatopoetic words of one race do not
convey any imitative suggestion to the minds of another.*
Similarly, Professor Sayce insists, " it is not necessary that
the imitation of natural sounds should be an exact one ;
indeed, that it never can be : all that is wanted is that the
imitation should be recognizable by those addressed. The
same natural sound, consequently, may strike the ear of
different persons very differently, and so be represented in
articulate speech in a strangely varying manner." †    Another
very good illustration of the same point is to be found in the
names for a grass-hopper in different languages. After giving
a number, Archdeacon Farrar remarks that obviously they are
" all imitative : yet how immensely varied by the fantasies
of imitation ! How is this to be explained ? Simply by the
fact to which it is so often necessary to recur, that words are
not mere imitations, but subjective echoes and reproduc-
tions—repercussions which are modified both organically
and ideally—which have moreover been immensely blurred
and disintegrated by the lapse of ages." ‡

But perhaps the best illustration that has been given of
this point is in the different words which obtain in different
languages as names for Thunder. Two independent treatises
have been written on the subject, one by Grimm, § and
the other by Pott. ‖ While in nearly all the languages the

---

* " Nichtsdestoweniger bleibt es eine wichtige psychologische Thatsache,
dass die Laute einen onomatopoetischen Werth haben, dass wir diesen Werth
heute noch fühlen. Nur ist dieses Gefühl nicht sicher genug, um als wissen-
schaftlicher Beweis zu gelten, wie es denn auch bei den verschiedenen Racen
verschieden ist. Die Sprachen der mongolischen Race haben zur Bezeichnung
von Naturereignissen viele Onomatopöien, welche wir nicht mitfühlen. Und das
ist weder zu verwundern, noch ist es ein Beweis gegen die geistige Einheit des
Menschengeschlechtes. Das Gefühl wird ja vielfach durch Associationen der
Vorstellungen bestimmt. Andere Associationen aber walten im Kaukasier,
andere im Mongolen " (*Zeits. b. Volkerpsych. u. Sprachwissen.*, 1867, s. 76).

† *Introduction, &c.*, i., p. 108. He points out that " *bilbit, glut-glut,* and *puls,*
are all attempts to represent the same sound."

‡ *Chapters on Language,* p. 154.

§ *Ueber Namen des Donners,* 1855.

‖ Steinthal's *Zeitschrift,* &c.

principle of imitation is more or less clearly apparent, the greatest diversities occur among the resulting sounds.* In this connection, also, I may adduce yet one further consideration. In his *Introduction to the Science of Language*, Professor Sayce argues on several grounds that, when articulation first began, the articulate sounds were probably in large part dependent for their meaning on the gestures with which they were accompanied. Consequently, aboriginal root-words, even supposing that any such had come down to us, and that their origin were imitative, inasmuch as their imitative value may thus have in large part depended on appropriately accompanying gestures, their imitative source would long ago have become obscured.

In view of all these considerations, therefore, I cannot deem the merely negative evidence against the onomatopoetic origin of articulate sounds as of any value at all. Even if we had any reason to suppose that philological analysis were in possession of the really aboriginal commencements of spoken language, we should still be unable reasonably to conclude against their imitative origin, merely on the ground that in our greatly altered circumstances of life and of mind we are not now able to trace the imitations.

As a matter of fact, however, the evidence which we have on the subject is not all negative. On the contrary, there is an overwhelming body of actual and unquestionable proof of the imitative origin of very many words in all languages— especially those which are spoken by savages, and are known from their general structure to be in a comparatively undeveloped state. The evidence being much too copious for quotation, I must content myself with referring to the

---

* Professor Max Müller has argued that in the Indo-European languages the apparently onomatopoetic words signifying "thunder" are derived from the root *tan*, to "stretch," and therefore were not of imitative origin. But Farrar has satisfactorily met this objection, even as regards this one particular case, by showing that even if not originally onomatopoetic, these words afterwards "became so from a feeling of the need that they should be" (*Origin of Language*, p. 82). See also, *Chapters on Language*, pp. 178–182 ; Heyse, *System*, s. 93 ; and Wundt, *Vorlesungen*, &c., ii. 396.

excellent and most forcible epitome which is given of it by Archdeacon Farrar in his works on the *Origin of Language* and *Chapters on Language*.* The foregoing remarks, therefore, which I have made on the negative side of the question, are merely intended to show that the element of onomatopœia must have entered into the composition of aboriginal speech much more largely than philologists are now able to prove, notwithstanding that they have been able to prove how immensely important an element it has been in this respect. The only wonder is, that when so many causes have been at work in obscuring and corroding the originally imitative significance of words, this significance should still admit of being traced in all languages—even the most highly conventionalized—to the very large extent in which it does.

The hostility which Professor Max Müller has displayed to the onomatopoetic theory of the origin of language is the more remarkable, because in his latest work he has enthusiastically embraced a special branch of this theory, which has been put forward by M. Noiré. This special branch of the onomatopoetic theory is that articulate sign-making had its origin in sounds which are made by bodies of men when engaged in some common occupation. When sailors row, soldiers march, builders co-operate in pulling or in lifting, &c., there is always a tendency to give vent to appropriate sounds, which the nature of the occupation usually breaks up into rhythmic periods. "These utterances, noises, shouts, hummings, or songs are a kind of natural reaction against the inward disturbance caused by muscular effort. They are the almost involuntary vibrations of the voice, corresponding to the more or less regular movements of our whole bodily frame." The hypothesis, therefore, is that sounds thus naturally evolved, and differing with different occupations, would sooner or later come to be conventionally used as the names of these different occupations. And, if thus used habitually, they would be virtually the same as words, inasmuch as they

* See also Nodier, *Dictionnaire des Onomatopées ;* and Wedgwood, *Dictionary of English Etymology.*

would not merely admit of immediate understanding on the part of others, but, what is even of more importance, they would, by the mere fact of such conventional usage of names, elevate what had previously been but a receptual appreciation of an act into a pre-conceptual designation of it.

Now, I say that this hypothesis, whatever may be thought as to its probability, is clearly but a special branch of the general theory of onomatopœia. So that primitive names were intentionally imitative of natural sounds, for all the purposes of onomatopoetic theory it makes no difference whether such sounds were made by natural objects or by man himself. Nor, of the natural sounds which were made by man himself, does it in any way affect this theory whether the naturally human sounds were "interjectional" only, "co-operative" only, or sometimes one and sometimes the other. If, following the example set by Professor Max Müller, I may be allowed to designate Noiré's special branch of the onomatopoetic theory as the Yeo-he-ho theory, it appears to me impossible to distinguish it in any essential particular from those other branches which are called by him the Bow-wow and Pooh-pooh theories —*i.e.* the imitative and the interjectional. Yet he has become as ardent a supporter of the one branch as he was a vehement opponent of the others.*

* Probably the explanation of this apparent inconsistency is to be found in the fact that Noiré's special version of the onomatopoetic theory comes within easy distance of a hypothesis which Max Müller had himself previously sanctioned. This hypothesis, originally propounded by Heyse in his *System der Sprachwissenschaft*, is that, just as every inorganic substance in nature gives out a particular sound when struck—metal one sound, wood another, stone another, &c.—so different animals have inherent tendencies (or "instincts") to emit distinctive sounds. In the case of primitive man this inherent tendency was in the direction of articulate speech. For my own part, I do not see that this theory explains anything ; and therefore agree with Geiger, who says of it :—"Die Annahme eines jetzt erloschenen Vermögens der Sprachschöpfung und die damit zusammenhängende von einem vollkommenen Urzustande des Menschen ist eine Zuflucht zum Unbegreiflichen, und nicht weit von dem Eingeständnisse entfernt, dass es uns der Natur der Dinge nach für immer unmöglich sei, den wahren Sinn der Urwurzeln zu erkennen und den Vorgang des Sprachursprunges zu erklären. Wir würden mit einer solchen Annahme auf einen mystischen Standpunkt zurückgeführt sein, da doch schon Herder das 'Gespenst vom Wort Fähigkeit' bekämpft und gesagt hat : 'Jch gebe den Menschen nicht gleich plötzlich neue

For my own part, I think it highly probable that there is an element of truth in the Yeo-he-ho theory, although I deem it in the last degree improbable that imitative sounds of this kind constituted the *only* source of aboriginal speech. At the most, it seems to me, this branch of onomatopœia can be accredited with supporting but a small proportional part of aboriginal language-growth. Nevertheless, as already observed, I can have no doubt at all that the principle of onomatopœia in all its branches has been the most important of all principles which were concerned in the first genesis of speech. That is to say, I fully agree with the almost unanimous voice of philological authority on this matter, which may be tersely expressed by allowing Professor Whitney to act as spokesman.

"Beyond all reasonable question, there was a positively long period of purely imitative signs, and a longer one of mixed imitative and traditional ones, the latter gradually gaining upon the former, before the present condition of things was reached, when the production of new signs by imitation is only sporadic and of the utmost rarity, and all language-signs besides are traditional, their increase in any community being solely caused by variation and combination, and by borrowing from other communities." *

But now, having thus stated as emphatically as possible my acceptance of the theory of onomatopœia, I have to express dissent from many of its more earnest advocates where they represent that it is necessarily the only theory to be entertained. In other words, I do not agree with the dogma that articulate speech cannot possibly have had any source, or sources, other than that which is supplied by vocal imitations.† For, on merely antecedent grounds, I can see

---

Kräfte, keine sprachschaffende Fähigkeit, wie eine willkürliche qualitas occulta ' " (*Ursprung der Sprache*, s. 24). Sayce, also, well remarks of this hypothesis, "It really rests upon an *a priori* conception of the origin of speech, which is neither borne out by linguistic facts nor easily intelligible. . . . Such a theory of language is plainly mystical" (*Introduction to Science of Language*, vol. i., pp. 66, 67).

   * *Encyclo. Brit.*, art. " Philology," vol. xviii., p. 769.

   † See, for instance, Farrar, *Chapters on Language*, p. 184.

no adequate reason for arbitrarily excluding the possibility of arbitrary invention. If even civilized children, who are not under the discipline of the "mother of invention," will coin a language of their own in which the element of onomatopœia is barely traceable ; * and if uneducated deaf-mutes will spontaneously devise articulate sounds which are necessarily destitute of any imitative origin ; † I do not see why it should be held antecedently impossible that primitive man can have found any other means of word-formation than that which is supplied by mimicry. Therefore, while I fully agree with Professor Wundt in holding that the question before us is one to be dealt with by psychology rather than philology (seeing that language cannot record the conditions of its own birth, and that so many causes have been at work to obliterate aboriginal onomatopœia), I cannot follow him where he argues that on grounds of psychology there is no room for any other inference than that the principle of onomatopœia in its widest sense must have constituted the sole origin of significant articulation. ‡

We have already seen that even the most imitative of vocalists, the talking birds, will invent wholly arbitrary sounds as denotative names,§ and it would be psychologically absurd to suppose that they are superior to what primitive man must have been in the matter of finding expedients for semiotic utterance. Again, the clicks of Hottentots and Bushmen, whatever we suppose their origin to have been, certainly cannot have had that origin in onomatopœia ; and no less certainly, as Professor Sayce remarks, they still survive to show how the utterances of speechless man could be made to embody and convey ideas.‖ Lastly, on the general principle that the development of the individual furnishes information touching the development of the race, it is highly significant

* See above, pp. 138-144.
† See above, pp. 121, 122.
‡ See *Vorlesungen, &c.*, ii. 394, 395.
§ See above, pp. 132-136.
‖ *Introduction to the Science of Language*, ii. 302.

that the *hitherto speechless* child will spontaneously use
arbitrary sounds (both articulate and otherwise) whereby to
denotate habitual recepts. And even after it has begun
to learn the use of actual words, arbitrary additions are
frequently made to its vocabulary which defy any explanation
at the hands of onomatopœia—not only, as in the cases above
alluded to, where they are left to themselves, but even in
cases where they are in the closest contact with language as
spoken by their elders. I could quote many instances of this
fact; but it will be enough to refer to one already given on
page 144 (foot-note). When, however, these spontaneous
efforts are not controlled by constant association with elders,
but fostered by children of about the same age being left
much together, the remarkable consequence previously alluded
to arises—namely, a newly devised language which depends
but in small part upon the principle of onomatopœia, and is
therefore wholly unintelligible to all but its inventors.*

I have now briefly stated all the main facts and considerations which appear to me worth stating, both for and against
the theory of onomatopœia. And, having done this, I wish
in conclusion to make it clear that the matter is not one
which seriously affects the theory of evolution. To the
philologist, no doubt, the question as to how far the element
of onomatopœia entered into the formation of aboriginal
speech is a really important question, so that, as Geiger says,
"Diess ist die gemeinsame Frage, und die Antwort wird auf
der einen Seite von einem inneren Zusammenhang zwischen
je einem Laut und dem entsprechenden Begriffe, auf der
andern aus Willkür und Uebereinkunft hergeleitet."† But
the question is one which the evolutionist may view with
indifference. Whether words were all originally dependent
on an inherent connection between every sound they made

---

* See above, pp. 138–143.

† *Der Ursprung der Sprache*, s. 31. His own answer to the question is as
follows :—"Sind die Wörter Produkte der Natur order der Willkür? Beides,
und beides nicht. Kein Wort hat naturnothwendig seine bestimmte Bedeutung ;
insofern sind sie alle willkürlich : aber keines ist zu seiner Bedeutung durch
menschliche Willensthätigkeit gekommen " (*ibid.*, s. 113).

and the idea thereby expressed, or whether they were all due to arbitrary invention, in either case the evolutionist may see that they can equally well have come into existence as the natural products of a natural psychogenesis. And, *a fortiori*, as an evolutionist, he need not greatly concern himself with any further question as to the relative degrees in which imitation and invention may have entered into the composition of primitive speech.

# CHAPTER XIV.

## THE WITNESS OF PHILOLOGY.

WE are now in a position to consider certain matters which are of high importance in relation to the subject of the present work. In earlier chapters I have had occasion to show that the whole stress of the psychological distinction between man and brute must be laid—and, in point of fact, has been laid by all competent writers who are against me—on the distinctively human faculty of judgment. Moreover, I have shown that, by universal consent, this faculty is identical with that of predication. Any mind that is able, in the strict psychological signification of the term, to judge, is also able to predicate, and *vice versâ*. I claim, indeed, to have conclusively shown that certain writers have been curiously mistaken in their analysis of predication. These mistakes on their part, however, do not relieve me of the burden of explaining the rise of predication; and I have sought to discharge the burden by showing how the faculty must have been given in germ so soon as the denotative stage of sign-making passed into the connotative, and thus furnished the condition to bringing into contact, or *apposition*, the names of objects and the names of qualities or actions. The discussion of this important matter, however, has so far proceeded on grounds of psychological analysis alone. The point has now arrived when we may turn upon the subject the independent light of philological analysis. Whereas we have hitherto considered, on grounds of mental science only, what *must have been* the genesis of predication—supposing predication to have had a genesis,—we have next to ascertain whether our deduction admits of corroboration by any inductive evidence supplied by the science of language, as to what this genesis *actually was.*

And here I had better say at once that the results of philological science will be found to carry us back to an even more primitive state of matters than any which I have hitherto contemplated. For, so long as I was restricted to psychological analysis, I was obliged to follow my opponents where they take language as it now exists. In order to argue with them at all upon these grounds, it was necessary for me to consider what they had said on the philosophy of predication ; and, in order to do this, it was further necessary that I should postpone for independent treatment those results of philological inquiry which they have everywhere ignored. But now we have come to the place where we can afford to abandon psychological analysis altogether, and take our stand upon the still surer ground of what I have already termed the palæontological record of mental evolution as this has actually been preserved in the stratified deposits of language. Now, when we do this, we shall find that hitherto we have not gone so far back in tracing the genesis of conceptual out of receptual ideation as in point of fact we are able to go on grounds of the most satisfactory evidence.

Up to this time, then, I have been meeting my opponents on their own assumptions, and one of these assumptions has been that language must always have existed as we now know it—at least to the extent of comprising words which admit of being built up into propositions to express the semiotic intention of the speaker. But this assumption is well known by philologists to be false. As a matter of fact, language did not begin with any of our later-day distinctions between nouns, verbs, adjectives, prepositions, and the rest : it began as the undifferentiated protoplasm of speech, out of which all these "parts of speech" had afterwards to be developed by a prolonged course of gradual evolution. "Die Sprache ist nicht stückweis oder atomistisch ; sie ist gleich

20

in allen ihren Theilen als Ganzes und demnach organisch entstanden." *

This highly general and most important fact is usually stated as it was, I believe, first stated by the anthropologist Waitz, namely, that "the unit of language is not the word, but the sentence;" † and, therefore, that historically the sentence preceded the word. Or, otherwise and less ambiguously expressed, every word was originally itself a proposition, in the sense that of and by itself it conveyed a statement. Of course the more that a single word thus assumed the functions now discharged by several words when built into a proposition, the more generalized—that is to say, the less defined—must have been its meaning. The sentence or proposition as we now have it represents what may be termed a psychological division of labour as devolving upon its component parts : subject-words, attributive-words, qualifying-words indicative of time, place, agent, instrument, and so forth, are now all so many different organs of language, which are set apart for the performance of as many different functions of language. The life of language under this its fully evolved form is, therefore, much more complex, and capable of much more refined operations, than it was while still in the wholly undifferentiated condition which we have now to contemplate.

In order to gain a clear conception of this protoplasmic condition of language, we had better first take an example of it as it is presented to our actual observation in the child which is just beginning to speak. For instance, as Professor Max Müller points out, "if a child says 'Up,' that *up* is, to his mind, noun, verb, adjective, all in one. If an English child says 'Ta,' that *ta* is both noun (thanks), and a verb (I thank you). Nay, even if a child learns to speak grammatically, it does not yet think grammatically ; it seems, in speaking, to wear the garments of its parents, though it has not yet grown into them." ‡

* Schelling, *Einl. in die Philos. d. Mythologie*, s. 51.
† *Anthropologie der Naturvölker*, i., 272. See also, F. Müller, *Grundriss der Sprachwissenshaft*, I. i. 49.
‡ *Science of Language*, ii. 91, 92.

Again, as Professor Friedrich Müller says, "the child's word *Ba-ba*, sleep, does not mean sleep only, as a particular kind of repose, but rather also all the circumstances which appertain to sleep, such as cot, bed, bolster, bed-clothes, &c.* It likewise and indifferently means, sleeping, sleepy, sleeper, &c., and may stand for any variety of propositions, such as "I am sleepy," "I want to go to sleep," "He is asleep," &c.

Of course innumerable other illustrations might be given ; but these are enough to show what is meant by a "sentence-word." The next thing we have to notice is the manner in which a young child particularizes the meanings of its sentence-words, so as to limit their highly generic significance *per se*, and thus to make them convey the special significance intended. Briefly, the one and only means which the child has of doing this is by the employment of tone and gesture. Here the suiting of the action to the word is a necessary condition to semiotic utterance ; the more primitive forms of sign-making are the needful supplements to these commencements of higher forms. And not only so ; they are likewise in large part the parents of these higher forms. It is by pointing (*i.e.* falling back on what I have called the earliest or "indicative stage" of language) that a child is able to signify the place, agent, instrument, &c., to which it requires a sentence-word to apply ; and thus we catch our first glimpse of the highly important fact that the earliest indications of grammar are given by the simultaneous use of sentence-words and gesture-signs.

It will now be my object to prove, that in the history of the race spoken language began in the form of sentence-words ; that grammar is the child of gesture ; and, consequently, that predication is but the adult form of the self-same faculty of sign-making, which in its infancy we know as indication. Being myself destitute of authority in matters philological, I will everywhere rely upon the agreement of recognized leaders of the science.

Bunsen, I believe, was the first to point out that in

---

* *Grund. d. Sprachwiss.*, i., 43.

Egyptian there is no formal distinction between noun, adjective, verb, or particle; such a word as *anh*, for instance, meaning indifferently, life, alive, to live, lively, &c.* Similarly, in Chinese "the word can still be used indifferently as a noun, a verb, an adverb, or the sign of a case, much like such English words as silver, and picture, and its place in the sentence alone determines in what sense it shall be construed. This is an excellent illustration of the early days of speech, when the sentence-words contained within themselves all the several parts of speech at once—all that was needed for a complete sentence; and it was only by bringing them into contact and contrast [i.e. *apposition*] with other sentence-words, that they came to be restricted in their meaning and use, and to be reduced to mere 'words.'" †

Later on I will give abundant evidence of a similar state of matters in the case of other existing languages presenting a low order of development—especially those of savages. But perhaps it is even of more importance to prove that the most highly developed of all languages—namely, the Indo-European group—still bears unmistakable evidence of having passed through this primitive phase. This is a statement which it would be easy to substantiate by any number of quotations; but I will only call the testimony of one witness in the person of Professor Max Müller, whose evidence on this point may be regarded as that of an opponent.

"Nothing, it is true, can exist in language except what is a sentence, *i.e.* that conveys a meaning; but for that very reason it ought to have been perceived that every word must originally have been a sentence. The mere root, *quâ* root, cannot be called a sentence, and in that sense a mere root may be denied the dignity of a word. But as soon as a root is used for predication, it becomes a word, whether outwardly it is changed or not. What in Chinese is effected by position or by tone, namely, the adaptation of a root to serve the purposes of words, is in the Aryan languages

---

* *Ægypten*, i. 324.
† Sayce, *Introduction*, &c., i. 119, 120.

achieved by means of suffixes and terminations, though often also by change of tone. We saw that, in an earlier stage, the Aryan languages, too, could raise a root into a word, without the aid of suffixes, and that, for instance, *yudh*, to fight, could be used in the five senses of the act of fighting, the agent of fighting, the instrument of fighting, the place of fighting, and the result of fighting. For the sake of distinction, however, as soon as the necessity began to be felt, the Aryan language introduced derivative elements, mostly demonstrative or pronominal."

"The imperative may truly be called the most primitive sentence, and it is important to observe how little in many languages it deviates from what has been fixed upon as the true form of a root. . . . *va*, weave, whether as a reminder or as a command, would have as much right to be called a sentence as when we say, 'Work,' *i.e.* 'Let us work.' . . . From the use of a root in the imperative, or in the form of a general assertion, there is a very easy transition to its employment in other senses and for other purposes. . . . A master requiring his slaves to labour, and promising them their food in the evening, would have no more to say than 'Dig—Feed,' and this would be quite as intelligible as 'Dig, and you shall have food,' or, as we now say, 'If you dig, you shall have food.' " *

Thus we may lay it down as a general doctrine or well-substantiated principle of philological research, that " Language begins with sentences; not with single words ; " † or that originally every word in and of itself required to convey a meaning, after the manner of the early utterances of children. " The sentence is the only unit which language can know, and the ultimate starting-point of all our linguistic researches. . . . If the sentence is the unit of significant speech, it is evident that all individual words must once have been sentences; that is to say, when first used they must each have implied or represented a sentence." ‡

---

* *Science of Thought,* 423–440.
† Sayce, *Introduction, &c.,* i. 111.     ‡ *Ibid.,* i. 113, 114.

"The making of words as distinct from sentences was a long and laborious process, and there are many languages, like those of North America, in which the process has hardly yet begun. A dictionary is the result of reflection, and ages must elapse before a language can enter upon its reflective stage." [*]

Or, to give only one more quotation, as Professor Max Müller says, "it is difficult for us to think in Chinese, or in any radical language, without transferring to it our categories of thought. But if we watch the language of a child, which is really Chinese spoken in English, we see that there is a form of thought, and of language, perfectly rational and intelligible to those who have studied it, in which, nevertheless, the distinction between noun and verb, nay, between subject and predicate, is not yet realized." [†]

Starting, then, from this undifferentiated condition of language, let us next see how the "parts of speech" became evolved.

There appears to be no doubt that one of the earliest parts of speech to become differentiated was the pronoun. Moreover, all the pronouns (or "pronominal elements") as originally differentiated were indistinguishable from what we should now call adverbs; and they were all concerned with denoting relations of place. [‡] No exception to this general statement can be made even as regards the personal pronouns. "*Hic, iste, ille,* are notoriously a sort of correlatives to *ego, tu, sui,* and, if the custom of the languages had allowed it, might, on every occasion, be substituted for them." [§] Now, there is very good reason to conclude that these pronominal adverbs, or adverbial pronouns, were in the first instance what may be termed articulate translations of gesture-signs—*i.e.* of a pointing to place-relations. *I* being equivalent to *this one, he* or *she* or *it* to *that one,* &c., we find it easy to supply the indicative gestures out of which these denotative terms arose ; and although we are not now able to supply the phonetic

---

[*] Sayce, *Introduction, &c.,* i. 121.    [†] *Science of Thought,* p. 242.
[‡] Garnett, *Philolo. Essays,* p. 87.    [§] *Ibid.,* 77, 78.

source of these highly ancient "pronominal" or "demonstrative elements," it is easy to imagine that they may have arisen in the same apparently spontaneous way as very young children will now devise arbitrary sounds, both as proper names and as adverbs of position. That we should not err in thus comparing the grade of mental evolution exhibited by the earliest framers of spoken language with that of a young child, is rendered apparent by the additional and highly interesting fact, that, just as a young child begins by speaking of the *Ego* in the third person, so it was with early man in his use of personal pronouns. "Man regarded himself as an object before he learnt to regard himself as a subject; and hence 'the objective cases of the personal as well as of the other pronouns are always older than the subjective;' and the Sanskrit *mâm*, *ma* (Greek με, Latin *me*) is earlier than *aham* (ἐγών and *ego*)." *

Lest it should be thought that I am assuming too much in thus referring the origin of pronominal elements to gesture-signs, I will here quote the opinion of Professor Max Müller, who of all philologists is least open to suspicion of bias

---

* Farrar, *Origin of Language*, p. 99. The passage continues, "We might have conjectured this from the fact already noticed, that children learn to speak of themselves in the third person—*i.e.* regard themselves as objects—long before they acquire the power of representing their material selves as the instrument of an abstract entity." He also alludes to "some admirable remarks to this effect in Mr. F. Whalley Harper's excellent book on the *Power of Greek Tenses;*" and recurs to the subject in his more recently published *Chapters on Language*, p. 62. I could quote other authorities who have commented upon this philological peculiarity of early pronouns; but will only add the following in order to show how the peculiarity in question may continue to survive even in languages still spoken. "The Malay *ulun*, 'I,' is still 'a man' in Lampong, and the Kawi *ugwang*, 'I,' cannot be separated from *nwang*, 'a man'" (Sayce, *Introduction*, ii. 26). Lastly, Wundt has pointed out that this impersonal form of speech is distinctive, not only of early pronominal elements, but also of early forms of predication. For instance, "Die ersten Urtheile, die in das Bewusstsein hereinbrechen, *subjektlose* Urtheile sind, und dass die Prädikate derselben stets eine sinnliche Vorstellung ausdrücken. 'Es leuchtet es glänzt, es tönt,'—solcher Art sind die Urtheile, die der Mensch zuerst denkt und zuerst ausspricht. Jenes Prädikat, dass sogleich bei der Wahrnehmung eines Gegenstandes sich aufdrängt, wird zur Bezeichnung des Gegenstandes selber. 'Das Leuchtende, Glänzende, Tönende,'—solcher Art sind die Wörter, die ursprünglich in der Sprache gebildet werden" (*loc. cit.*, ii. 377).

towards my side of the present argument. Speaking of these " demonstrative elements, which point to an object in space and time, and express what we now express by *then, this* [ = I], *that* [ = there, he, she, it, &c.], near, far, above, below, &c.; " he says, " in their primitive form and intention they are addressed to the senses rather than to the intellect : they are sensuous, not conceptual." \* And elsewhere he adds, " I see no reason why we should not accept them as real survivals of a period of speech during which pantomime, gesture, pointing with the fingers to actual things were still indispensable ingredients of all conversation." † Again, " it was one of the characteristic features of Sanskrit, and the other Aryan languages, that they tried to distinguish the various applications of a root by means of what I have called demonstrative roots or elements. If they wished to distinguish the mat as the product of their handiwork, from the handiwork itself, they would say ' Platting—there ; ' if they wished to encourage the work they would say, ' Platting—they, or you, or we.' We found that what we call demonstrative roots or elements must be considered as remnants of the earliest and almost pantomimic phase of language, in which language was hardly as yet what we mean by language, namely *logos*, a gathering, but only a pointing." ‡

It is the opinion of some philologists, however, that these demonstrative elements were probably " once full or predicative words, and that if we could penetrate to an earlier stage of language, we should meet with the original forms of which they are the maimed half-obliterated representatives." §

---

\* *Science of Thought*, p. 221.

† *Ibid.*, p. 554.

‡ *Ibid.*, 241.

§ Sayce, *Introduction, &c.*, ii. 25 ; see also to the same effect, Bleek, *Ursprung der Sprache*, 70–72 ; F. Müller, *Grundriss der Sprachwissenshaft*, I., i., s. 40 ; and Noiré, *Logos*, p. 186. The chief ground of this scepticism is that it is difficult to conceive how a word could ever have gained a footing if it did not from the first present some independent predicative meaning. But it seems to me that the force of this objection is removed if we remember the sounds which are arbitrarily invented by young children and uneducated deaf-mutes, not to mention the inarticulate clicks of the Bushmen. Moreover, there is nothing inimical to the

But as even these philologists do not question that all originally "predicative words" would be found to have had their predicative value determined by gesture, "if we could penetrate to an earlier stage of language," the question whether such demonstrative elements as have come down to us were or were not themselves of originally predicative value, is not of vital importance in the present connection. For there is no doubt that pronominal elements which really were aboriginal as such, depended on accompanying gesture-signs for a conveyance of their predicative meaning; and although, as we might expect, there is a necessary absence of proof in particular cases whether these elements have come down to us in a practically aboriginal form, or whether they have done so as the worn-out remnants of independently predicative words, the general principles on which we are now engaged are not really affected by any such philological uncertainties in matters of detail. For even the authority just quoted as doubting whether we have evidence enough to conclude that demonstrative elements which have come down to us were never themselves predicative words, elsewhere says of early predicative utterance in general,—" It is certain that there was a time in the history of speech when the articulate, or semi-articulate, sounds uttered by primitive man were made the significant representatives of thought by the gestures with which they were accompanied; and this complex of sound and gesture—a complex in which, be it remembered, the sound had no meaning apart from the gesture—was the earliest sentence." * And, after giving examples from languages of Further India, he adds,—" But an inflectional language does not permit us to watch the word-making process so clearly as do those savage jargons, in which a couple of sounds, like the Grebo *ni ne,* signify 'I do it,' or

pronominal theory in the supposition that pronominal elements, even of the most aboriginal kind, were survivals of still more primitive sentence-words—a supposition which would of course remove the difficulty in question. But, as explained in the text, this difficulty, even if it could not be thus met, would really not be one of any importance to my exposition.

\* *Introduction, &c.,* i. 117.

'You do not,' according to the context and the gestures of the speaker. Here by degrees, with the growth of consciousness and the analysis of thought, the external gesture is replaced by some portion of the uttered sounds which agrees in a number of different instances, and in this way the words by which the relations of grammar are expressed came into being. A similar process has been at work in producing those analogical terminations whereby our Indo-European languages adapt a word to express a new grammatical relation."

Therefore, not unduly to multiply quotations, we may take it as the now established doctrine of philology that, as even this more sceptical authority puts it, "Grammar has grown out of gesture and gesticulation." * Later on I will show in how interesting a manner early forms of articulate utterance follow in their structure the language of gesture already treated of in a previous chapter. It was for the sake of displaying this resemblance that I there occupied so much space with the syntax of gesture-language; and, therefore, it will now be my object to trace the family likeness between the constructions of primitive modes of utterance, and those of the parent gestures from which these constructions have been directly inherited. But in order to do this more completely, we must first consider the philology of predicative words.

The parts of speech which are primarily concerned in predication, and which, therefore, may be called *par excellence* predicative words, are substantives, adjectives, and verbs. I will, therefore, begin by briefly stating what is known touching the evolution of these parts of speech.

We have abundant evidence to show that originally there was no distinction between substantives and adjectives, or object-words and quality-words. Nor is this at all surprising when we remember that even in fully developed forms of speech one and the same word may stand as a substantive or an adjective according to its context. "Cannon" in "cannon-

---

* *Introduction*, &c., ii. 301. Or, as Wundt puts it, "Die demonstrative Wurzel ist daher eine demonstrirende Pantomime in einen Laut übersetzt" (*Vorlesungen*, &c., ii. 392).

ball," or "pocket" in "pocket-book," &c., are adjectives in virtue of position—*i.e.* of *apposition* with the substantives which they thus serve to qualify.

Similarly as regards the genitive case. This, also, is of an attributive quality, and, therefore, like the now independent adjective, originally had no independent existence. When the force of the genitive had to be conveyed, it was conveyed by this same device of apposition. And, lastly, the same device was resorted to for purposes of predication. Or, to quote these important facts from responsible sources, Professor Sayce says :—" Even the genitive case, necessary as it appears to us to be, once had no existence, as indeed it still has none in groups of languages like the Taic or the Malay. Instead of the genitive, we here have two nouns placed in apposition to one another, two individuals, as it were, set side by side without any effort being made to determine their exact relations beyond the mere fact that one precedes the other, and is therefore thought of first. . . . Now, this apposition of two nouns, which still serves the purpose of the genitive in many languages, might be regarded as attributive or as predicative. If predicative, then the two contrasted nouns formed a complete sentence, ' Cup gold,' for instance, being equivalent to ' The cup is gold.' If attributive, then one of the two nouns took the place of an adjective, ' gold cup ' being nothing more than 'a golden cup.' " * Then, after giving examples from different languages of the artificial contrivances whereby in course of time these three grammatical differentiations originated (namely, by conventional changes of position between the words apposed, in some cases the form of predication being A B, and that of attribution or possession B A, while in other languages the reverse order has obtained), Professor Sayce goes on to say :— " These primitive contrivances for distinguishing between the predicate, the attribute, and the genitive, when the three ideas had in the course of ages been evolved by the mind of the

---

* Sayce, *Introduction, &c.*, i. 415. See also F. Müller, *loc. cit.*, I. i. 2, p. 2, or another statement of the same facts referred to by Sayce.

speaker, gradually gave way to the later and more refined machinery of suffixes, auxiliaries, and the like." *

For the sake of putting this point beyond the reach of question, I will quote another and independent authority to the same general effect.

"It is a curious fact hitherto overlooked by grammarians and logicians, that the definition of a noun applies strictly only to the nominative case. The oblique cases are really attribute-words, and the inflection is practically nothing but a device for turning a noun into an adjective or adverb. This is perfectly clear as regards the genitive, and, indeed there is historical evidence to show that the genitive in Aryan languages was originally identical with an adjective ending; 'man's life' and 'human life' being expressed in the same way. It is also clear that 'noctem' in 'flet noctem' is a pure adverb of time. It is not so easy to see that the accusative in such sentences as 'He beats the boy' is also a sort of adverb, because the connection between verb and object is so intimate as almost to form one simple idea, as in the case of noun-composition. But it is clear that if 'boy' in the compound 'boy-beating' is an attribute-word, it can very well be so also when 'beating' is thrown into the verbal form without any change of meaning." †

Lastly, upon this point Professor Max Müller says, while speaking of Aryan adjectives:—" These were not used for the first time when people said 'The sun is bright,' but when they predicated the quality of brightness, or the act of shooting out light, and said, as it were, 'Brightness-here.' Adjectives, in fact, were formed, at first, exactly like substantives, and many of them could be used in both characters. There are languages in which adjectives are not distinguished from substantives. But though outwardly alike, they are conceived as different from substantives the moment they are used in a sentence for the purpose of predicating or of qualifying a substantive." ‡

* Sayce, *Introduction, &c.*, i. 416.
† Sweet, *Words, Logic, and Grammar*, in *Trans. Philo. Soc.*, 1867, p. 493.
‡ *Science of Thought*, p. 442.

So much, then, for substantives and adjectives : it cannot be said that there is any evidence of historical priority of the one over the other ; but rather that so soon as the denotative meanings of substantives became fixed, they admitted of having imparted to them the meanings of adjectives, genitives, and predicates, by the simple expedient of apposition—an expedient which, as we have seen in earlier chapters, is rendered inevitable by the laws of association and "the logic of events :" it is an expedient that must have been furnished *to* the mind, and therefore need never have been intentionally devised *by* it.

Turning next to the case of verbs, or the class of words upon which more especially devolves the office of predication, it is the opinion of some philologists that these arose through the apposition of substantives with the genitives of pronouns.* And there can be no doubt that in many actually existing languages the functions of predication are still discharged in this way, without the existence of any verbs at all, as we shall see later on. But, on the other hand, it is shown that a great many Aryan substantives were formed by joining pronominal elements to previously existing verbal roots, in a manner so strongly suggestive of pointing-gestures, that it is difficult to doubt the highly primitive source of the construction. For example "digging-he"=labourer, "digging-it"=spade, "digging-here"=labour, "digging-there" = hole,† &c. Or again, "'The hole is dark' would have been expressed originally (in Aryan) by 'digging-it,' 'hiding here,' or, 'hiding-somewhere.' 'Hiding-here' might afterwards be used in the sense of a hiding-place. But when it was used as a mere qualifying predicate in a sentence in which there was but one subject, it assumed at once the character of an adjective." ‡

To me it appears evident that there is truth in both these views, which, therefore, are in no way contradictory to one another. We have evidence that many substantives were of

* See especially Garnett, *On the Nature and Analysis of the Verb.*
† *Science of Thought*, p. **223**.
‡ *Ibid.*, p. **442**.

later origin than many verbs, and *vice versâ;* but this does not show which of these two parts of speech preceded the other as a whole. Nor does it appear that we are likely to obtain any definite evidence upon the point. On psychological grounds, and from the analogy furnished by children, we might be prepared to think it most probable that substantives preceded verbs ; and this view is no doubt corroborated by the remarkable paucity of verbs in certain savage languages of low development. But as a matter of pure philology "we cannot derive either the verb from the noun, or the noun from the verb." * This writer goes on to say, " they are co-existent creations, belonging to the same epoch and impulse of speech." But whether or not this inference represents the truth is a matter of no importance for us. With or without verbs, primitive man would have been able to predicate—in the one case after the manner of children who have just begun to learn the use of them, and in the other case after the manner of those savages recently mentioned, who throw upon their nouns, in conjunction with pronouns, the office of verbs.

Seeing that my psychological opponents have laid so much stress upon the substantive verb as this is used by the Romance languages in formal predication, I will here devote a paragraph to its special consideration from a philological point of view. It will be remembered that I have already pointed out the fallacy which these opponents have followed in confounding the substantive verb, as thus used, with the copula—it being a mere accident of the Romance languages that the two are phonetically identified. Nevertheless, even after this fallacy has been pointed out to them, my opponents may seek to take refuge in the substantive verb itself: forced to acknowledge that it has nothing especially to do with predication, they may still endeavour to represent that elsewhere, or in itself, it represents a high order of conceptual thought. This, of course, I allow; and if, as my opponents assume, the substantive verb belonged to early, not to say

* Sayce, *Introduction, &c.*

primitive modes of speech, I should further allow that it raises a formidable difficulty in the otherwise even path of evolutionary explanation. But, as a matter of fact, these writers are no less mistaken about the primitive nature of the substantive verb itself, than they are upon the function which it accidentally discharges in copulation.* In order to prove this, or to show that the substantive verb is really very far from primitive, I will furnish a few extracts from the writings of philological authorities upon the subject.

"Whatever our *a priori* estimate of the power of the verb-substantive may be, its origin is traced by philology to very humble and material sources. The Hebrew verbs הָוָה (*houa*) or הָיָה (*haia*) may very probably be derived from an onomatopœia of respiration. The verb *kama*, which has the same sense, means primitively 'to stand out,' and the verb *koum*, 'to stand,' passes into the sense of 'being.' In Sanskrit, *as-mi* (from which all the verbs-substantives in the Indo-European languages are derived, as εἰμὶ, *sum*, am ; Zend, *ahmi* ; Lithuanic, *esmi*, Icelandic, *em*, &c.) is, properly speaking, no verbal root, but 'a formation on the demonstrative pronoun *sa*, the idea meant to be conveyed being simply that of local presence.' And of the two other roots used for the same purpose, namely, *bhu* (φύω, *fui*, &c.) and *sthâ* (*stare* &c.), the first is probably an imitation of breathing, and the second notoriously a physical verb, meaning 'to stand up.' May we not, then, ask with Bunsen, 'What is *to be* in all languages but the spiritualization of *walking* or *standing* or *eating?*'" †

Again, to quote only one other authority :—"In closing, for the present, the discussion of this extensive subject, it is proposed to make a few remarks upon the so-called verb-substantive, respecting the nature and functions of which there has perhaps been more misapprehension than about any other element of language. It is well known that many

---

\* I refer the reader to what is said on both these aspects of the verb in question by my opponents (see pp. 165–167.)

† Farrar, *Origin of Language*, pp. 105, 106.

grammarians have been accustomed to represent this element as forming the basis of all verbal expression, and as a necessary ingredient in every logical proposition. It would seem to follow, from this statement, that nations so unfortunate as to be without it, could neither employ verbal expression nor frame a logical proposition. How far this is the case will be seen hereafter : at present we shall make some brief remarks on this verb, and on the substitutes usually employed in dialects where it is formally wanting. It will be sufficient to produce a few prominent instances, as the multiplying of examples from all known languages would be a mere repetition of the same general phenomena.

" In the portion of the essay relating to the Coptic, it was observed : ' What are called the auxiliary and substantive verbs in Coptic are still more remote from all essential verbal character (than the so-called verbal roots). On examination they will almost invariably be found to be articles, pronouns, particles, or abstract nouns, and to derive their supposed verbal functions entirely from their accessories, or from what they imply.' In fact any one who examines a good Coptic grammar or dictionary will find that there is nothing formally corresponding to our *am, art, is, was,* &c., though there is a counterpart to Lat. *fieri* (*sthopi*) and another to *poni* (*chi*, neuter passive of *che*); both occasionally rendered *to be,* which, however, is not their radical import. The Egyptians were not, however, quite destitute of resources in this matter, but had at least half a dozen methods of rendering the Greek verb-substantive when they wished to do so. The element most commonly employed is the demonstrative *pe, te, ne ;* used also in a slightly modified form for the definite article ; *pe* = is, having reference to a subject in the singular masculine ; *te,* to a singular feminine ; and *ne* = are, to both genders in the plural. The past tense is indicated by the addition of a particle expressing remoteness. Here, then, we find as the counterpart of the verb-substantive an element totally foreign to all the received ideas of a verb ; and that instead of its being deemed necessary to say in formal terms

'Petrus est,' 'Maria est,' 'Homines sunt,' it is quite sufficient, and perfectly intelligible, to say, 'Petrus hic,' 'Maria hæc,' 'Homines hi.' The above forms, according to Champollion and other investigators of ancient hieroglyphics, occur in the oldest known monumental inscriptions, showing plainly that the ideas of the ancient Egyptians as to the method of expressing the category *to be*, did not exactly accord with those of some modern grammarians. . . . Every Semitic scholar knows that personal pronouns are employed to represent the verb-substantive in all the known dialects, exactly as in Coptic, but with less variety of modification. In this construction it is not necessary that the pronoun should be of the same person as the subject of the proposition. It is optional in most dialects to say either *ego ego, nos nos*, for *ego sum, nos sumus*, or *ego ille, nos illi*. The phrase 'Ye are the salt of the earth,' is, in the Syriac version, literally 'You they (*i.e.* the persons constituting) the salt of the earth.' Nor is this employment of the personal pronoun confined to the dialects above specified, it being equally found in Basque, in Galla, in Turco-Tartarian, and various American languages. . . . . It is true that the Malayan, Javanese, and Malagassy grammarians talk of words signifying *to be;* but an attentive comparison of the elements which they profess to give as such, shows clearly that they are no verbs at all, but simply pronouns or indeclinable particles, commonly indicating the time, place, or manner of the specified action or relation. It is not therefore easy to conceive how the mind of a Philippine islander, or of any other person, can supply a word totally unknown to it, and which there is not a particle of evidence to show that it was ever thought of. . . . A verb-substantive, such as is commonly conceived, vivifying all connected speech, and binding together the terms of every logical proposition, is much upon a footing with the phlogiston of the chemists of the last generation, regarded as a necessary pabulum of combustion, that is to say, *vox et præterea nihil*. . . . If a given subject be 'I,' 'thou,' 'he,' 'this,' 'that,' 'one ;' if it be 'here,' 'there,' 'yonder,' 'thus,' 'in,' 'on,' 'at,'

21

by ;' if it 'sits,' 'stands,' 'remains,' or 'appears,' we need
no ghost to tell us that it *is*, nor any grammarian or
metaphysician to proclaim that recondite fact in formal
terms." *

Having thus briefly considered the philology of predicative
words, we must next proceed to the not less important matter
of the philology of predication itself. And here we shall find
that the evidence is sufficiently definite. We have already
seen good reason for concluding that what Grimm has called
the "antediluvian" pronominal roots were the phonetic
equivalents of gesture-signs—or rather, that they implied
accompanying gesture-signs for the conveyance of their
meaning. Now, it is on all hands allowed that these
pronominal roots, or demonstrative elements, afterwards
became attached to nouns and verbs as affixes or suffixes,
and so in older languages constitute the machinery both of
declension and conjugation. Thus, we can trace back, stage
by stage, the form of predication as it occurs in the most
highly developed, or inflective, languages, to that earliest
stage of language in general, which I have called the
indicative. In order to show this somewhat more in detail,
I will begin by sketching these several stages, and then
illustrate the earliest of them that still happen to survive by
quoting the modes of predication which they actually present.

As we thus trace language backwards, its structure is
found to undergo the following simplification. First of all,
auxiliary words, suffixes, affixes, prepositions, copulas,
particles, and, in short, all inflections, agglutinations, or
other parts of speech which are concerned in the indication
of *relationship* between the other component parts of a
sentence, progressively dwindle and disappear. When these,
which I will call relational words, are shed, language is left
with what may be termed object-words (including pronominal
words), attributive-words, action-words, and words expressive
of states of mind or body, which, therefore, may be designated

* Garnett, *On the Nature and Analysis of the Verb, Proc. Philo. Soc.,* vol. iii.

condition-words. Roughly speaking, this classification corresponds with the grammatical nouns, pronouns, adjectives,
active verbs, and passive verbs ; but as our regress through
the history of language necessitates a total disregard of all
grammatical forms, it will conduce to clearness in my
exposition if we consent to use the terms suggested.

The next thing we notice is that the distinction between
object-words and attributive-words begins to grow indistinct,
and eventually all but disappears: substantives and adjectives
are fused in one, and whether the resulting word is to be
understood as subject or predicate—as the name of the object
or the name of a quality—depends upon its position in the
sentence, upon the tone in which it is uttered, or, in still
earlier stages, upon the gestures by which it is accompanied.
Thus, as Professor Sayce remarks, "the apposition of two
substantives [and, *a fortiori*, of two such partly or wholly
undifferentiated words as we are now contemplating] is the
germ out of which no less than three grammatical conceptions
have developed—those of the genitive, of the predicate, and
of the adjective." *

While this process of fusion is being traced in the case of
substantives and adjectives, it becomes at the same time
observable that the definition of verbs is gradually growing
more and more vague, until it is difficult, and eventually
impossible, to distinguish a verb at all as a separate part of
speech.

Thus we are led back by continuous stages, or through
greater and greater simplifications of language-structure, to a
state of things where words present what naturalists might
term so generalized a type as to include, each within itself, all
the functions that afterwards severally devolve upon different
parts of speech. Like those animalcules which are at the same
time but single cells and entire organisms, these are at the
same time single words and independent sentences. Moreover, as in the one case there is life, in the other case there
is meaning; but the meaning, like the life, is vague and

* Sayce, *Introduction, &c.*, i. 415.

unevolved : the sentence is an organism without organs, and is generalized only in the sense that it is protoplasmic. In view of these facts (which, be it observed, are furnished by languages still existing, as well as by the philological record of languages long since extinct) it is impossible to withhold assent from the now universal doctrine of philologists— "language diminishes the farther we look back in such a way, that we cannot forbear concluding it must once have had no existence at all." *

From all the evidence which has now been presented showing that aboriginally words were sentences, it follows that aboriginally there can have been no distinction between terms and propositions. Nevertheless, although this follows deductively from the general truth in question, it is desirable that we should study in more detail the special application of the principle to the case of formal predication, seeing that, as so often previously remarked, this is the place where my opponents have taken their stand. The reader will remember that I have already disposed of their assertions with regard to the copula. It will now be my object to show that their analysis is equally erroneous where it is concerned with both the other elements of which a formal proposition consists. Not having taken the trouble to acquaint themselves with the results of linguistic research, and therefore relying only on what may be termed the accidents of language as these happen to occur in the Aryan branch of the great language-tree, these writers assume that a proposition must always and everywhere have been thrown into the precisely finished form in which it was analyzed by Aristotle. As a matter of fact, however, it is now well known that such is not the case ; that the form of predication as we have it in our European languages has been the outcome of a prolonged course of evolution ; and that in its most primitive stage, or in the earliest stage which happens to have been preserved in the palæontology of language, predication can scarcely be said to have been differentiated

* Geiger, *Development of the Human Race*, English trans., p. 22.

from what I have called indication. For the sake of placing this important fact beyond the reach of doubt, I will begin by quoting the statements of a few among the leading authorities upon the philology of the subject.

"Primitive man would not trouble himself much with such propositions as 'Man is mortal,' 'Gold is heavy,' which are a source of such unfailing delight to the formal logician ; but if he found it necessary to employ permanent attribute-words, would naturally throw them into what is called the attributive form, by placing them in immediate proximity with the noun, whose inflections they would afterwards assume. And so the verb gradually came to assume the purely formal function of predication. The use of verbs denoting action necessitated the formation of verbs to denote 'rest,' 'continuance in state,' and when, in course of time, it became necessary in certain cases to predicate permanent as well as changing attributes, these words were naturally employed for the purpose, and such a sentence as 'The sun continues bright' was simply 'The bright sun' in another form. By degrees these verbs became so worn away in meaning, gradually coming to signify simple existence, that at last they lost all vestiges of meaning whatever, and came simply to be marks of predication. Such is the history of the verb 'to be,' which in popular language has entirely lost even the sense of 'existence.' Again, in a still more advanced state, it was found necessary to speak, not only of things, but of their attributes. Thus such a sentence as 'Whiteness is an attribute of snow,' has identically the same meaning as 'Snow is white' and 'White snow ;' and the change of 'white' into 'whiteness' is a purely formal device to enable us to place an attribute-word as the subject of a proposition." *

"Now comes a very important consideration, that not only is the order of subject and predicate to a great extent conventional, but that the very idea of the distinction between subject and predicate is purely linguistic, and has no foundation in the mind itself. In the first place, there is no

---

\* Sweet, *Words, Logic, and Grammar*, in *Trans. Philol. Soc.*, 1876, pp. 486, 487.

necessity for a subject at all : in such a sentence as 'It rains,' there is no subject whatever, the *it* and the terminal *s* being merely formal signs of predication. 'It rains : therefore I will take my umbrella,' is a perfectly legitimate train of reasoning, but it would puzzle the cleverest logician to reduce it to any of his figures. Again, the mental proposition is not formed by thinking first of the subject, then of the copula, and then of the predicate ; it is formed by thinking of the three simultaneously. When we formulate in our minds the proposition 'All men are bipeds,' we have two ideas, 'all men' and 'an equal number of bipeds,' or, more tersely, 'as many men, as many bipeds,' and we think of the two ideas simultaneously [*i.e.* in *apposition*], not one after the other, as we are forced to express them in speech. The simultaneity of conception is what is expressed by the copula in logic, and by the various forms of sentences in language. It by no means follows that logic is entirely destitute of value, but we shall not arrive at the real substratum of truth until we have eliminated that part of the science which is really nothing more than an imperfect analysis of language." *

Again, as a result of his prolonged study of some of the most primitive forms of language still extant among the Bushmen of South Africa, Dr. Bleek entertains no doubt whatever that aboriginally the same word, without alteration, implied a substantival or a verbal meaning, and could be used indifferently also as an adjective, adverb, &c.† That is to say, primitive words were sentence-words, and as such were used by early man in just the same way as young children use their hitherto undifferentiated signs, *Byby* = *sleep, sleeping, to sleep, sleeper, asleep, sleepy,* &c. ; and, by connotative extension, *bed, bolster, bed-clothes,* &c.

Lastly, as already indicated, we are not left to mere inference touching the aboriginal state of matters with regard to predication. For in many languages still existing we find the forms of predication in such low phases of development, that

---

* Sweet, *loc. cit.*, pp. 489, 490.
† Bleek, *Ursprung der Sprache*, s. 69, 70.

they bring us within easy distance of the time when there can
have been no such forms at all. Even Professor Max Müller
allows that there are still existing languages "in which there
is as yet no outward difference between what we call a root,
and a noun or a verb. Remnants of that phase in the growth
of language we can detect even in so highly developed a
language as Sanskrit." Elsewhere he remarks :—" A child
says, ' I am hungry,' without an idea that *I* is different from
*hungry*, and that both are united by an auxiliary verb. . . .
A Chinese child would express exactly the same idea by one
word, ' Shi,' *to eat,* or *food,* &c. The only difference would be
that a Chinese child speaks the language of a child, an
English child the language of a man." *

It is no doubt remarkable that the Chinese should so long
have retained so primitive a form ; but, as we know, the
functions of predication have here been greatly assisted by
devices of syntax combined with conventionally significant
intonation, which really constitute Chinese a well-developed
language of a particular type. Among peoples of a much
lower order of mental evolution, however, we are brought into
contact with still more rudimentary forms of predication,
inasmuch as these devices of syntax and intonation have not
been evolved. As previously stated, the most primitive of
all actually existing forms of predication where articulate
language is concerned, is that wherein the functions of a verb
are undertaken by the apposition of a noun with what is
equivalent to the genitive case of a pronoun. Thus, in
Dayak, if it is desired to say, " Thy father is old," " Thy father
looks old," &c., in the absence of verbs it is needful to frame
the predication by mere apposition, thus :—" Father-of-thee,
age-of-him." Or, to be more accurate, as the syntax follows
that of gesture-language in placing the predicate before the
subject, we should translate the proposition into its most
exact equivalent by saying, " His age, thy father." Similarly,
if it is required to make such a statement as that " He is
wearing a white jacket," the form of the statement would be,

* *Science of Thought,* p. 241.

"He-with-white with-jacket," or, as we might perhaps more tersely translate it, "He jackety whitey." *

Again, in Feejee language the functions of a verb may be discharged by a noun in construction with an oblique pronominal suffix, *e.g.*, *loma-qu* = heart or will-of-me, = I will.†

So likewise, "almost all philologists who have paid attention to the Polynesian languages, concur in observing that the divisions of parts of speech received by European grammarians are, as far as external form is concerned, inapplicable, or nearly so, to this particular class. The same element is admitted to be indifferently substantive, adjective, verb, or particle." ‡ "I will eat the rice," would require to be rendered, "The-eating-of-me-the-rice = My eating will be of the rice." "The supposed verb is, in fact, an abstract noun, including in it the notion of futurity of time in construction with an oblique pronominal suffix ; and the ostensible object of the action is not a regimen in the accusative case, but an apposition. It is scarcely necessary to say how irreconcilable this is with the ordinary grammatical definition of a transitive verb ; and that, too, in a construction where we should expect that true verbs would be infallibly employed, if any existed in the language." § And, not to overburden the argument with illustrations, it will be enough to add with this writer, "there can be no question that nouns in conjunction with oblique cases of pronouns may be, and, in fact, are employed as verbs. Some of the constructions above specified admit of no other analysis ; and they are no accidental partial phenomena, but capable of being produced by thousands." ‖

It would be easy to multiply quotations from other authorities to the same effect ; but these, I think, are enough to show how completely the philology of predication destroys the philosophy of predication, as this has been presented by

* Steinthal, *Charakteristik, &c.*, 165, 173.
† Garnett, *Philological Essays*, p. 310.
‡ *Ibid.*, p. 311.
§ *Ibid.*, p. 312.
‖ *Ibid.*, p 314.

my opponents. Not only, as already shown, have they been misled by the verbal accident of certain languages with which they happen to be familiar identifying the copula with the verb "to be" (which itself, as we have also seen, has no existence in many languages); but, as we now see, their analysis is equally at fault where it deals with the subject and predicate. Such a fully elaborated form of proposition as "A negro is black," far from presenting "the simplest element of thought," is the demonstrable outcome of an enormously prolonged course of mental evolution; and I do not know a more melancholy instance of ingenuity misapplied than is furnished by the arguments previously quoted from such writers, who, ignoring all that we now know touching the history of predication, seek to show that an act of predication is at once "the simplest element of thought," and so hugely elaborate a process as they endeavour to represent. The futility of such an argument may be compared with that of a morphologist who should be foolish enough to represent that the Vertebrata can never have descended from the Protozoa, and maintain his thesis by ignoring all the intermediate animals which are known actually to exist.

Take an instance from among the quotations previously given. It will be remembered that the challenge which my opponents have thrown down upon the grounds of logic and psychology, is to produce the brute which "can furnish the blank form of a judgment—the 'is' in 'A is B.'" *

Now, I cannot indeed produce a brute that is able to supply such a form; but I have done what is very much more to the purpose: I have produced many nations of still existing men, in multitudes that cannot be numbered, who are as incapable as any brute of supplying the blank form that is required. Where is the "is," in "Age-of-him Father-of-thee" = "His-age-thy-father" = "Thy-father-is-old"? Or, in still more primitive stages of human utterance, how shall we extract the blank form of predication from a "sentence-word," where there is not only an absence of any

* See Chapter on Speech, p. 166.

copula, but also an absence of any differentiation between the subject and the predicate? The truth, in short, is, as now so repeatedly shown, that not only the brute, but likewise the young child—and not only the young child, but likewise early man—and not only early man, but likewise savage man —are all and equally unable to furnish the blank form of predication, as this has been slowly elaborated in the highest ramifications of the human mind.

Of course all this futile (because erroneous) argument on the part of my opponents, rests upon the analysis of the proposition as this was given in the Aristotelian system of logic—an analysis which, in turn, depends on the grammar of the Greek language. Now, it goes without saying that the whole of this system is obsolete, so far as any question of the *origin* either of thought or of speech is concerned. I do not doubt the value of this grammatical study, nor of the logic which is founded upon it, provided that inferences from both are kept within their legitimate sphere. But at this time of day to regard as primitive the mode of predication which obtained in so highly evolved a language as the Greek, or to represent the "categories" of Aristotle's system as expressive of the simplest elements of human thought, appears to me so absurd that I can only wonder how intelligent men can have committed themselves to such a line of argument.*

---

* I may remark that it was Aristotle who first fell into the error of identifying the copula with the verb *to be*, by which it happens to be expressed in Greek. For many centuries afterwards this error was a fruitful source of endless confusions; but it is curious to find a wholly new fallacy springing from it in the latter half of the nineteenth century. Touching the subject and predicate, Aristotle, of course, never contemplated any more primitive relation between them than that which obtained in the only forms of speech with which he was acquainted. As regards his "categories" the following remarks by Professor Max Müller are worth quoting :—

"These categories, which proved of so much utility to the early grammarians, have a still higher interest to the students of the science of language and thought. Whereas Aristotle accepted them simply as the given forms of predication in Greek, after that language had become possessed of the whole wealth of its words, we shall have to look upon them as representing the various processes by which those Greek words, and all our own words and thoughts, too, first assumed a settled form. While Aristotle took all his words and sentences as given, and

Quitting, then, all these old-world fallacies which were based on an absence of information, we must accept the analysis of predication as this has been supplied to us by the advance of science. And this analysis has proved to demonstration, that "the division of the sentence into two parts, the subject and the predicate, is a mere accident; it is not known to the polysynthetic languages of America, which herein reflect the condition of primeval speech. . . . So far as the act of thought is concerned, subject and predicate are one and the same, and there are many languages in which they are so treated." * Consequently, it appears to me that the only position which remains for my opponents to adopt is that of arguing in some such way as follows.

Freely admitting, they may say, that the issue must be thrown back from predication as it occurs in Greek to predication as it occurs in savage languages of low development, still we are in the presence of predication all the same. And even when you have driven us back to the most primitive possible form of human speech, wherein as yet there are no parts of speech, and predication therefore requires to be conducted in a most inefficient manner, still most obviously it *is* conducted, inasmuch as it is only for the purpose of conducting it that speech can have ever come into existence at all.

Now, in order to meet this sole remaining position, I must begin by reminding the reader of some of the points which have already been established in previous chapters.

simply analyzed them in order to discover how many kinds of predication they contained, we ask how we ever came into possession of such words as *horse, white, many, greater, here, now, I stand, I fear, I cut, I am cut.* Anybody who is in possession of such words can easily predicate, but we shall now have to show that every word by itself was from the first a predication, and that it formed a complete sentence by itself. To us, therefore, the real question is, how these primitive sentences, which afterwards dwindled away into mere words, came into existence. The true categories, in fact, are not those which are taught by grammar, but those which produced grammar, and it is these categories which we now proceed to examine " (*Science of Thought*, p. 439).

* Sayce, *Introduction, &c.*, ii. 229. He adds, " Had Aristotle been a Mexican, his system of logic would have assumed a wholly different form."

First of all, when seeking to define "the simplest element of thought," I showed that this does not occur in the fully formed proposition, but in the fully formed concept; and that it is only out of two such concepts as elements that full or conceptual propositions can be formed as compounds. Or, as this was stated in the chapter on Speech, "conceptual names are the ingredients out of which is formed the structure of propositions; and, in order that this formation should take place, there must be in the ingredients that element of conceptual ideation which is already present in every denominative term." Or, yet again, as the same thing was there quoted from Professor Sayce, "it is a truism of psychology that the terms of a proposition, when closely interrogated, turn out to be nothing but abbreviated judgments." *

Having thus defined the simplest element of thought as a concept, I went on to show from the psychogenesis of children, that before there is any power of forming concepts—and therefore of bestowing names as denominative terms, or, *a fortiori*, of combining such terms in the form of conceptual propositions—there is the power of forming recepts, of naming these recepts by denotative terms, and even of placing such terms in apposition for the purpose of conveying information of a pre-conceptual kind. The pre-conceptual, rudimentary, or unthinking propositions thus formed occur in early childhood, prior to the advent of self-consciousness, *and prior, therefore, to the very condition which is required for any process of conceptual thought.* Moreover, it was shown that this pre-conceptual kind of predication is itself the product of a gradual development. Taking its origin from the ground of gesture-signs, when it first begins to sprout into articulate utterance there is absolutely no distinction to be observed between "parts of speech." Every word is what we now know as a "sentence-word," any special applications of which can only be defined by gesture. Next, these sentence-words, or others that are afterwards acquired, begin to be imperfectly differentiated into denotative names of objects, qualities, actions, and states; and

* *Introduction, &c.,* i. 15.

the greater the definition which they thus acquire as parts of speech, the more do they severally undergo that process of connotative extension as to meaning which is everywhere the index of a growing appreciation of analogies. Lastly, object-words and attributive-words (*i.e.* denotative names of things and denotative names of qualities or actions), come to be used in apposition. But the rudimentary or unthinking form of predication which results from this is due to merely sensuous associations and the external " logic of events ; " like the elements of which it is composed, it is not conceptual, but pre-conceptual. With the dawn of self-consciousness, however, predication begins to become truly conceptual ; and thus enters upon its prolonged course of still gradual development in the region of introspective thought.

All these general facts, it will be remembered, were established on grounds of psychological observation alone ; I nowhere invoked the independent witness of philology. But the time having now come for calling in this additional testimony, the corroborating force of it appears to me overwhelming. For it everywhere proves the growth of predication to have been the same in the race as we have found it to be in the individual. Therefore, as in the latter case, so in the former, I now ask—Will any opponent venture to affirm that pre-conceptual ideation is indicative of judgment ? Or, which is the same thing, will he venture to deny that there is an all-important distinction between predication as receptual and predication as conceptual ? Will he still seek to take refuge in the only position now remaining, and argue, as above supposed, that not only in the childish appositions of denotative names, but even in the earlier and hitherto undifferentiated protoplasm of a " sentence-word," we have that faculty of predication on which he founds his distinction between man and brute ? Obviously, if he will not do this, his argument is at an end, seeing that in the race, as in the individual, there is now no longer any question as to the continuity between the predicative germ in a sentence-word, and the fully evolved structure of a formal proposition. On the other hand, if he does elect to argue thus, the following brief considerations will effectually dislodge him.

If the term "predication" is extended from a conceptual proposition to a sentence-word, it thereby becomes deprived of that distinctive meaning upon which alone the whole argument of my opponents is reared. For, when used by a young child (or primitive man), sentence-words require to be supplemented by gesture-signs in order to particularize their meaning, or to complete the "predication." But, where such is the case, there is no longer any psychological distinction between *speaking* and *pointing:* if this is called predication, then the predicative "category of language" has become identified with the indicative : man and brute are conceded to be "brothers."

Take an example. At the present moment I happen to have an infant who has not yet acquired the use of any one articulate word. Being just able to toddle, he occasionally comes to grief in one way or another ; and when he does so he seeks to communicate the nature of his mishap by means of gesture-signs. To-day, for instance, he knocked his head against a table, and forthwith ran up to me for sympathy. On my asking him where he was hurt, he immediately touched the part of his head in question—*i.e. indicated* the painful spot. Now, will it be said that in doing this the child was *predicating* the seat of injury ? If so, all the distinctive meaning which belongs to the term predicating, or the only meaning on which my opponents have hitherto relied, is discharged. The gesture-signs which are so abundantly employed by the lower animals would then also require to be regarded as predicatory, seeing that, as before shown at considerable length, they differ in no respect from those of the still speechless infant.

Therefore, whether my opponents allow or disallow the quality of predication to sentence-words, alike and equally this argument collapses. Their only logical alternative is to vacate their argument altogether ; no longer to maintain that "Speech is the Rubicon of Mind," but to concede that, as between the indicative phase of language which we share with the lower animals, and the truly predicative phase which belongs only to man, there is no distinction of kind to be attributed ; seeing that, on the contrary, whether we look to the psychogenesis of the individual or to that of the race, we alike find a demonstrable continuity of evolution from the lowest to the highest level of the sign-making faculty.

## CHAPTER XV.

### THE WITNESS OF PHILOLOGY (*continued*).

IN the last chapter we have been concerned with the philology of predication. In the present chapter I propose to consider the philology of conception. Of course the distinction is not one that can be very sharply drawn, because, as fully shown in my chapter on Speech, every concept embodies a judgment, and therefore every denominative term is a condensed proposition. Nevertheless, as my opponents have laid so much stress on full or formal predication, as distinguished from conception, I have thought it desirable, as much as possible, to keep these two branches of our subject separate. Therefore, having now disposed of all opposition that can possibly be raised on the ground of formal predication, I will conclude by throwing the light of philology on the origin of material predication, or the passage of receptual denotation into conceptual denomination, as this is shown to have occurred in the pre-historic evolution of the race.

It will be remembered that, under my analysis of the growth of predication, much more stress has been laid in the last chapter than in previous chapters on what I have called the protoplasm of predication as this occurs in the hitherto undifferentiated " sentence-word." While treating of the psychology of predication in the chapter on Speech, I did not go further back in my analysis than to point out how the " nascent " or " pre-conceptual " propositions of young children are brought about by the mere apposition of denotative terms —such apposition having been shown to be due to sensuous association when under the guidance of the "logic of events." But when I came to deal with the philology of predication, it became evident that there was even an earlier phase of the faculty in question than that of apposing denotative terms by sensuous association. For, as we have so recently seen, philologists have proved that even before there were any denotative terms respectively significant of objects, qualities, actions, states, or relations, there were sentence-words which combined in one vague mass the meanings afterwards apportioned to substantives, adjectives, verbs, prepositions, &c., with the consequence that the only kind of apposition which could be called into play for the purpose of indicating the particular significance intended to belong to such a word on particular occasions, was the apposition of gesture-signs. Now, I had two reasons for thus postponing our consideration of what is undoubtedly the earliest phase of articulate sign-making. In the first place, it seemed to me that I might more easily lead the reader to a clear understanding of the subject by beginning with a phase of predication which he could most readily appreciate, than by suddenly bringing him into the presence of a germ-like origin which is far from being so readily intelligible. But over and above this desire to proceed from the familiar to the unfamiliar, I had, in the second place, a further and a better reason for not dealing with the ultimate germ of articulate sign-making so long as I was dealing only with the psychology of our subject. This reason was, that in the development of speech as exhibited by the growing child—which, of course, furnishes our only material for a study of the subject from a psychological point of view—the original or germinal phase in question does not appear to be either so marked, so important, or, comparatively speaking, of such prolonged duration as it was in the development of speech in the race. To use biological terms, this the earliest phase in the evolution of speech has been greatly foreshortened in the ontogeny of mankind, as compared with what it appears to have been in the phylogeny. The result, of course, is that we should gain but an inadequate idea of its

22

importance, were we to estimate it by a merely psychological analysis of what we now find in the life-history of the individual.

It is perfectly true, as Professor Max Müller says, that "if an English child says 'Up,' that *up* is, to his mind, noun, verb, and adjective, all in one." Nevertheless, in a young child, from the very first, there is a marked tendency to observe the distinctions which belong to the principal parts of speech. The earliest words uttered by my own children have always been nouns and proper names, such as " Star," " Mamma," " Papa," " Ilda," &c. ; and although, later on, some of these earliest words might assume the functions of adjectives by being used in apposition with other nouns subsequently acquired (such as " Mamma-ba," for a sheep, and " Ilda-ba " for a lamb), neither the nouns nor the adjectives came to be used as verbs. It has been previously shown that the use of adjectives is acquired almost as soon as that of substantives ; and although the poverty of the child's vocabulary then often necessitates the adjectives being used as substantives, the substantives as adjectives, and both as rudimentary pro-positions, still there remains a distinction between them as object-words and quality-words. Similarly, although action-words and condition-words are often forced into the position of object-words and quality-words, it is apparent that the primary idea attaching to them is that which properly belongs to a verb. And, of course, the same remarks apply to relation-words, such as " Up."

Take, for instance, the cases of pre-conceptual predication which were previously quoted from Mr. Sully, namely, " Bow-wow " = " That is a dog ; " " Ot " = " This milk is hot ; " " Dow "=" My plaything is down ; " " Dit ki "=" Sister is crying ; " " Dit naughty "=" Sister is naughty ; " " Dit dow ga " =" Sister is down on the grass." In all these cases it is evident that the child is displaying a true perception of the different functions which severally belong to the different parts of speech ; and so far as psychological analysis alone could carry us, there would be nothing to show that the forcing of one part of speech into the office of another, which so frequently occurs at this age, is due to anything more than the exigencies of expression where as yet there are scarcely any words for the conveyance of meaning of any kind. Therefore, on grounds of psychological analysis alone, I do not see that we are justified in arguing from these facts that a young child has no appreciation of the difference between the functions of the different parts of speech—any more than we should were we to argue that a grown man has no such appreciation when he extends the meaning of a substantive (such as "pocket") so as to embrace the function of an adjective on the one hand (*e.g.* "pocket-book"), and of a verb on the other (*e.g.* "he *cannoned* off the white, and *pocketed* the red "). What may be termed this grammatical abuse of words becomes an absolute necessity where the vocabulary is small, as we well know when trying to express ourselves in a foreign language with which we are but slightly acquainted. And, of course, the smaller the vocabulary, the greater is such necessity ; so that it is greatest of all when an infant is only just emerging from its infancy. Therefore, as just remarked, on grounds of psychological analysis alone, I do not think we should be justified in concluding that the first-speaking child has no appreciation of what we understand by parts of speech ; and it is on account of the uncertainty which here obtains as between necessity and incapacity, that I reserved my consideration of "sentence-words" for the independent light which has been thrown upon them by the science of comparative philology.

Now, when investigated by this light, it appears, as already observed, that the protoplasmic condition of language prior to its differentiation into parts of speech was of much longer duration in the race than, relatively speaking, it is in the individual. Moreover, it appears to have been of relatively much greater importance to the subsequent development of language. How, then, is this difference to be explained ? I think the explanation is sufficiently simple. An infant of to-day is born into the medium of already-spoken language ;

and long before it is itself able to imitate the words which it hears, it is well able to understand a large number of them. Consequently, while still literally an *infant*, the use of grammatical forms is being constantly borne in upon its mind ; and, therefore, it is not at all surprising that, when it first begins to use articulate signs, it should already be in possession of some amount of knowledge of their distinctive meanings as names of objects, qualities, actions, states, or relations. Indeed, it is only as such that the infant has acquired its knowledge of these signs at all ; and hence, if there is any wonder in the matter, it is that the first-speaking child should exhibit so much vagueness as it does in the matter of grammatical distinction.

But how vastly different must have been the case of primitive man ! The infant, as a child of to-day, finds a grammar already made to its use, and one which it is bound to learn with the first learning of denotative names. But the infant, as an adult in primeval time, was under the necessity of slowly elaborating his grammar together with his denotative names ; and this, as we have previously seen, he only could do by the aid of gesture and grimace. Therefore, while the acquisition of names and forms of speech by infantile man must have been thus in chief part dependent on gesture and grimace, the acquisition by the infantile child is now not only independent of gesture and grimace, but actively inimical to both. The already-constructed grammar of speech is the evolutionary substitute of gesture, from which it originally arose ; and, hence, so soon as a child of to-day begins to speak, gesture-signs begin at once to be starved out by grammatical forms. But in the history of the race gesture-signs were the nursing-mothers of grammatical forms ; and the more that their progeny grew, the greater must have been the variety of functions which the parents were called upon to perform. In other words, during the infancy of our race the growth of articulate language must not only have depended, but also re-acted upon that of gesture-signs—increasing their

number, their intricacy, and their refinement, up to the
time when grammatical forms were sufficiently far evolved
to admit of the gesture-signs becoming gradually dispensed
with. Then, of course, Saturn-like, gesticulation was devoured
by its own offspring ; the relations between signs appealing to
the eye and to the ear became gradually reversed ; and,
as is now the case with every growing child, the language
of formal utterance sapped the life of its more informal progenitor.

We are now in a position to consider the exact psychological relation of sentence-words to denotative and receptually connotative words. It will be remembered that I have
everywhere spoken of sentence-words as representing an even
more primitive order of ideation than denotative words, and,
*a fortiori*, than receptually connotative words. On the other
hand, in earlier parts of this treatise I showed that both the
last-mentioned kinds of words occur in children when they
first begin to speak, and may even be traced so low down in
the psychological scale as the talking birds. This apparent
ambiguity, therefore, now requires to be cleared up. Can
anything, it may be reasonably asked, in the shape of spoken
language be more primitive than the very first words which
are spoken by a child, or even by a parrot? But, if not,
how can I agree with those philologists who conclude that
there is an even still more primitive stage of conceptual
evolution to be recognized in sentence-words ?

Briefly, my answer to these questions is that in the
young child and the talking bird denotative-words, conno-
tative-words, and sentence-words are all equally primitive ;
or, if there is any priority to be assigned, that it must be
assigned to the first-named. But the reason of this, I hold
to be, is, that the child and the bird are both living in an
already-developed medium of spoken language, and, therefore, as recently stated, have only to learn their denotative names by special association, while primitive man
had himself to fashion his names out of the previously
inarticulate materials of his own psychology. Now this,

as we have also seen, he only could do by such associations
of sounds and gestures as in the first instance must have
conveyed meanings of a pre-conceptually predicative kind.
In the absence of any sounds already given—and therefore
already *agreed upon*—as denotative names, there could be no
possibility of primitive man arbitrarily *assigning* such names ;
and thus there could have been no parallel to a young
child who receptually *acquires* them.    In order that he
should assign names, primitive man must first have had
occasion to make his pre-conceptual statements about the
objects, qualities, &c., the names of which afterwards grew
out of these statements, or sentence-words.    Adam, indeed,
gave names to animals ; but Adam was already in possession
of conceptual thought, and therefore in a psychological
position to appreciate the importance of what he was about.
But the " pre-Adamite man " who is now before us could
not possibly have invented names for their own sakes,
unless he were already capable of thinking about names
*as* names, and, therefore, already in possession of that very
conceptual thought which, as we have now so often seen,
depends upon names for its origin.    Even with all our
own fully developed powers of conceptual thought, we
cannot *name* an object when in the society of men with
whose language we are totally unacquainted, without *predicating* something about that object by means of gestures or
other signs.    Therefore, without further discussion, it must
be obvious—not only, as already shown, that there is here
no exact parallel between ontogenesis and phylogenesis,
and that we have thus a full explanation why sentence-
words were of so much more importance to the infant
man than they are to the infant child, but further and
consequently—that the question whether sentence-words are
more primitive than denotative words is not a question
that is properly stated, unless it be also stated whether
the question applies to the individual or to the race.    As
regards the individual of to-day, it cannot be said that
there is any priority, historical or psychological, of sentence-

words over denotative words, or even over receptually connotative words of a low order of extension. Nay, we have seen
that the leading principles of grammatical form admit of
being acquired by the child together with his acquisition of
words of all kinds, and that even talking birds are able to
distinguish between names as severally names of objects,
qualities, states, or actions.

Thus we find that to almost any order of intelligence
which is already surrounded by the medium of spoken
language, the understanding—and, in the presence of any
power of imitative utterance, the acquisition—of denotative
names as signs or marks of corresponding objects, qualities,
&c., is, if anything, a more primitive act than that of using a
sentence-word; but that in the absence of such an already-
existing medium, sentence-words are more primitive than
denotative names. Nevertheless, it is of importance to note
how low an order of receptual ideation is capable of learning
a denotative name by special association, because this fact
proves that as soon as mankind advanced to the stage where
they first began to coin their sentence-words, they must
already have been far above the psychological level required
for the acquisition of denotative words, *if only such words had
previously been in existence.* Consequently, we can well understand how such words would soon have begun to come into
existence through the habitual employment of sentence-words
in relation to particular objects, qualities, states, actions, &c.;
by such special associations, sentence-words would readily
degenerate into merely semiotic marks. How long or how
short a time this genesis of relatively "empty words" out of
the primordially "full words" may have occupied, it is now
impossible to say; but the important thing for us to notice
is, that during the whole of this time—whatever it may have
been—the mind of primitive man was already far above the
psychological level which is required for the apprehension
of a denotative name.*

* In these considerations I find myself able largely to reconcile what has
always been regarded as a contradiction between the views of Professor Whitney

So much, then, for the first class of considerations which has been opened up by throwing upon the results of our psychological analysis the independent light of philological research. I will now pass on to a second class, which is even of more importance.

From the fact that sentence-words played so all-important a part in the origin of speech, and that in order to do so they essentially depended on the co-operation of gestures with which they were accompanied, so that in the resulting "complex of sound and gesture the sound had no meaning apart from the gesture;" from these now well-established facts, we may gain some additional light on a question previously considered—namely, the extent to which primitive words were "abstract" or "concrete," "particular" or "general," and, therefore, "receptual" or "conceptual." According to Professor Max Müller, "the science of language has proved by irrefragable evidence that human thought, in the true sense of that word— that is, human language—did not proceed from the concrete to the abstract, but from the abstract to the concrete. Roots, the elements out of which all language has been constructed, are abstract, never concrete ; and it is by predicating these abstract concepts of this or that, by localizing them here or there, in fact by applying the category of οὐςία, or substance, to the roots, that the first foundation of our language and our thought were laid." *

Here, to begin with, there is an inherent contradiction.

---

and those of other philologists on the subject of sentence-words. Partly following Schleicher—who maintains the doctrine still more unequivocally—he regards the word as having been historically prior to the sentence. This, of course, is in contradiction to the doctrine of the sentence having been historically prior to the word, which, as we have seen, is the doctrine now held by philologists in general. But, now, what the latter doctrine really amounts to is, that words were sentences before they were names—predicative before they were nominative ; and, as I understand it, Whitney's objection to this doctrine is really raised on grounds of psychology. If so, the above considerations show that he is perfectly right. Intellectually, primitive man was fully capable of acquiring the use of words as names ; and, therefore, psychologically considered, it was only an accident of social environment which prevented him from so doing.

* *Science of Thought*, pp. 432, 433.

When it is said that the roots in question already presented abstract concepts, it becomes a contradiction to add that "the first foundations of language and thought were laid by applying the category of substance to the roots." For, if these roots already presented abstract concepts, they already presented the distinctive feature of human "thought," whose "foundations," therefore, must have been "laid" somewhere further back in the history of mankind. But, besides this inherent contradiction, we have here an emphatic re-statement of the two radical errors which I previously mentioned, and which everywhere mar the philosophical value of Professor Max Müller's work. The first is his tacit assumption that the roots of Aryan speech represent the original elements of articulate language. The second is that, upon the basis of this assumption, the science of language has proved, by irrefragable evidence, that human thought proceeded from the abstract to the concrete—or, in other words, that it sprang into being Minerva-like, already equipped with the divine inheritance of conceptual wisdom. Now, in entertaining this theory, Professor Max Müller is not only in direct conflict with all his philological brethren, but likewise, as we have previously seen, often compelled to be irreconcilably inconsistent with himself.* Moreover, as we have likewise seen, his assumption as to the aboriginal nature of Aryan roots, on which his transcendental doctrine rests, is intrinsically absurd, and thus does not really require the united voice of professed philologists for its condemnation. Therefore, what the science of language *does* prove "by irrefragable evidence" is, *not* that these roots of the Aryan branch of language are the aboriginal elements of human speech, or indices of the aboriginal condition of human ideation; but that, being the survivals of incalculably more primitive and immeasurably more remote phases of word-formation, they come before us as the already-matured products of conceptual thought—and, *a fortiori*, that on the basis of these roots alone *the science of language has absolutely no evidence at all to*

* Pp. 281, 282, note.

*furnish* as touching the matter which Professor Max Müller here alludes to in such positive terms. In this connection there can be no possible escape from the tersely expressed conclusion previously quoted from Geiger, and unanimously entertained as an axiom by philologists in general:—" These roots are not the primitive roots : we have perhaps in no one single instance the first aboriginal articulate sound—just as little, of course, the aboriginal signification." *

But the point which I now wish to bring forward is this. We have previously seen the source of these unfortunate utterances in Professor Max Müller's philology appears to reside in certain prepossessions which he exhibits in the domain of psychology. For he adopts the assumption that there can be no order of words which do not, by the mere fact of their existence, imply concepts : he does not sufficiently recognize that there may be a power of bestowing names as signs, without the power of thinking these signs as names. Consequently, the distinction which, on grounds of comparative psychology, appears to me so obvious and so necessary— *i.e.* between names as merely denotative marks due to pre-conceptual association, and denominative judgments due to conceptual thought—has escaped his sufficient notice. Consequently, also, he has failed to distinguish between ideas as "general" and what I have called "generic;" or between an idea that is general because it is born of an intentional synthesis of the results of a previous analysis, and an idea that is *generalized* † because not yet differentiated by any intentional analysis, and therefore representing simply an absence of conceptual thought. My child on first beginning to speak had a generalized idea of similarity between all kinds of brightly shining objects, and therefore called them

---

* *Ursprung der Sprache*, s. 65. For the original German, see the passage as previously quoted on page 273, note.

† As pointed out in a previous chapter, curious ambiguity attaches to this term. For, as used in biology, it means the *hitherto undifferentiated*, while in psychology and elsewhere a "generalization" means the *synthetically integrated*. But, as psychologists never speak of ideas as "generalized," I here use the word in its biological sense. See also above, pp. 277–280.

all by the one denotative name of "star." The astronomer has a general idea answering to his denominative name of "star;" but this has been arrived at after a prolonged course of mental evolution, wherein conceptual analysis has been engaged in conceptual classification in many and various directions : it therefore represents the psychological antithesis of the generalized idea, which was due to the merely sensuous associations of pre-conceptual thought. Ideas, then, as general and as generic severally occupy the very antipodes of Mind.

All this we have previously seen. My object in here recurring to the matter is to show that much additional light may be thrown upon it by the philological doctrine of "sentence-words," which Professor Max Müller, in common with other philologists, fully accepts.

Of all the writers on primitive modes of speech as represented by existing savages, no one is entitled to speak with so much authority as Bleek. Now, as a result of his prolonged and first-hand study of the subject, he is strongly of opinion that aboriginal words were expressive "not at all of an abstract or general character, but exclusively concrete or individual." By this he means that primitive ideas were what I have called generic. For he says that had a word been formed from imitation of the sound of a cuckoo, for instance, it could not possibly have had its meaning limited to the name of that bird ; but would have been extended so as to embrace "the whole situation so far as it came within the consciousness of the speaker." That is to say, it would have become a generic name for the whole recept of bird, cry, flying, &c., &c., just as to our own children the word *Ba*=sheep, bleating, grazing, &c. Now, this process of comprising under one denotative term the hitherto undifferentiated perceptions of "a whole situation so far as it comes within the consciousness of the speaker," is the very opposite of the process whereby a denominative term is brought to unify, by an act of "generalization," the previously well-differentiated concepts between which some analogy is afterwards discovered.

Therefore the absence of any parts of speech in primitive language is due to a generic order of ideation, whereas the unions of parts of speech in any languages which present them is due to the generalizing order of ideation. Or, as Bleek puts it while speaking of the comparatively undifferentiated condition of South African languages, "this differs entirely from the principle which prevails in modern English, where a word, without undergoing any change of form, may nevertheless belong to different parts of speech. For in English the parts of speech, though not always differing in sound, are always accurately distinguished in concept; while in the other case there was as yet no consciousness of any difference, inasmuch as neither form nor position had hitherto called attention to anything of the kind. For forms had not yet made their appearance, and determinate position [*i.e.* significance expressed by syntax], as, for example, in Chinese, could only arise in a language of highly advanced internal formation." *

Indeed, if we consider the matter, it is not conceivable that the case could be otherwise. No one will maintain that the sentence-words of young children exhibit the highest elaborations of conceptual thought, on the ground that they present the highest degree of "generality" which it is possible for articulate sounds to express. But if this is not to be suggested as regards the infant child, what possible ground can there be for suggesting it as regards the infant man, or for inferring that aboriginal speech must have been expressive of "general" and "abstract" ideas, merely because the further backwards that we trace the growth of language the less organized do we find its structure to be? Clearly, the contradiction arises from a confusion between ideas as generic and general, or between the extension which is due to original vagueness and that which is laboriously acquired by subsequent precision. An Amœba is morphologically more "generalized" than a Vertebrate; but for this very reason it is the less highly evolved as an organism. The philology of

* *Ursprung der Sprache,* s. 69, 70.

sentence-words, therefore, leads us back to a state of ideation wherein as yet the powers of conceptual thought were in that nascent condition which betokens what I have called their pre-conceptual stage—or a stage which may be observed in a comparatively foreshortened state among children before the dawn of self-consciousness.

There can be no reasonable doubt that during this stage of mental evolution sentence-words arose in the race as they now do in the individual, the only difference being that then they had to be invented instead of learnt. This difference would probably have given a larger importance to the principle of onomatopœia,* and certainly a much larger importance to the co-operation of gesture, than now obtains in the otherwise analogous case of young children. But in the one case as in the other, I think there can be no reasonable question that sentence-words must have owed their origin to receptual and pre-conceptual apprehensions of all kinds, whether of objects, qualities, actions, states, relations, or of any two or more of these "categories" as they may happen to have been blended in the hitherto undifferentiating perceptions of aboriginal man.

I must now allude to the results of our previous inquiry touching "the syntax of gesture-language." For comparison will show that in all essential particulars the semiotic construction of this the most original and immediately graphic mode of communication, bears a striking resemblance to that which is presented by the earliest forms of articulate language, both as revealed by philology and in "baby-talk." † Thus, as we saw, "gesture-language has no grammar properly so called. The same sign stands for 'walk,' 'walkest,' 'walking,' 'walked,' 'walker.' Adjectives and verbs are not easily distinguished by the deaf and dumb. Indeed, our elaborate system of parts of speech is but little applic-

---

* Bleek entertains no doubt on this point.

† Compare also close of Chapter VII. (pp. 138–144), where the children mentioned by Dr. Hale are shown to have adopted the syntax of gesture-language in their spontaneously devised spoken language.

able to the gesture-language." Next, to quote again only one of the numerous examples previously given to show the primitive order of apposition, whereby the language of gesture serves to convey a predication, "I should be punished if I were lazy and naughty" would be put, "I lazy, naughty, no!—lazy, naughty, I punished; yes!" Again, "to make is too abstract for the deaf-mute; to show that the tailor makes the coat, or that the carpenter makes the table, he would represent the tailor sewing the coat and the carpenter sawing and planing the table. Such a proposition as 'Rain makes the land fruitful' would not come into his way of thinking: 'Rain, fall; plants, grow,' would be his pictorial (*i.e.* receptual) expression." Elsewhere this writer remarks that the absence of any distinction between substantive, adjective, and verb, which is universal in gesture-language, is customary in Chinese, and not unknown even in English. "To *butter* bread, to *cudgel* a man, to *oil* machinery, to *pepper* a dish, and scores of such expressions, involve action and instrument in one word, and that word a substantive treated as the root or crude form of a verb. Such expressions are concretisms, picture-words, gesture-words, as much as the deaf-and-dumb man's one sign for 'butter' and 'buttering.'" And similarly as to the substantive-adjective, in such words as *iron-stone*, *feather-grass*, *chesnut-horse*, &c.; here the mere apposition of the words constitutes the one an attribution of the other, as is the case in gesture-language. And not only in Chinese, but as shown in the last chapter, in a great number and variety of savage tongues this mode of construction is habitual. In all these cases distinctions between parts of speech can be rendered only by syntax; and this syntax is the syntax of gesture.

I will ask the reader to refer to the whole passage in which I previously treated of the syntax of gesture,* giving special attention to the points just noted, and also to the following:—invariable absence of the copula, and frequent absence of the verb (as "Apple-father-I"="My father gave

* Chapter VI., pp. 114–120.

me an apple?"); resemblance of sentences to the polysynthetic or unanalyzing type (as "I-Tom-struck-a-stick" =
"Tom struck me with a stick"); the device whereby syntax,
or order of apposition, is made to distinguish between predicative, attributive, and possessive meanings, and therefore
also between substantives and adjectives ; the importance of
grimace in association with gesture (as when a look of inquiry
converts an assertion into a question); the highly instructive
means whereby relational words, and especially pronouns, are
rendered in the gestures of pointing ; the no less instructive
manner whereby a general idea is rendered in a summation
of particular ideas (as "Did you have soup? did you have
porridge?" &c. = "What did you have for dinner?"); and the
receptual or sensuous source of all gesture-signs which are
concerned in expressing ideas presenting any degree of
abstraction (as striking the hand to signify "hard," &c.).

Hence, we may everywhere trace a fundamental similarity
between the comparatively undeveloped form of conceptual
thought as displayed in gesture, and that which philology has
revealed as distinctive of early speech. Of course in both
cases conceptual thought is there : the ideation is human,
though, comparatively speaking, immature. But the important point to notice is the curiously close similarity between
the forms of language-structure as revealed in gesture and in
early speech. For no one, I should suppose, can avoid
perceiving the ideographic character of gesture-language,
whereby it is more nearly allied to the purely receptual
modes of communication which we have studied in the
lower animals, than is the case with our fully evolved forms
of predication. It therefore seems to me highly suggestive
that the earliest forms and records of spoken language that
we possess (notwithstanding that they are still far from
aboriginal), follow so closely the model which is still supplied
to us in the ideographic gestures of deaf-mutes. Such syntax
as there is—*i.e.* such *a putting in order* as is expressive of the
mode of ideational grouping—so nearly resembles the syntax
of gesture-language, that we can at once perceive their

common psychological source. It is on account of this structural resemblance between gesture and early speech that I have devoted so much space to our consideration of the former ; and if I do not now dwell at greater length upon the significance of the analogy, it is only because this significance appears too obvious to require further treatment.

There is, however, one point with reference to this analogy on which a few words must here be said. If there is any truth at all in the theory of evolution with reference to the human mind, we may be quite sure, from what has been said in earlier chapters, that tone, gesture, and grimace preceded articulation as the medium of pre-conceptual utterance. Therefore, the structural similarity between existing gesture-language and the earliest records of articulate language now under consideration, is presumably due, not only to a similarity of psychological conditions, but also to direct continuity of descent. Or, as Colonel Mallery well puts it, while speaking of the presumable origin of spoken language, "as the action was then the essential, and the consequent or concomitant sound the accident, it would be expected that a representation, or feigned reproduction of the action, would have been used to express the idea before the sound associated with that action could have been separated from it. The visual onomatopœia of gestures, which even yet have been subjected to but slight artificial corruption, would therefore serve as a key to the audible. It is also contended that in the pristine days, when the sounds of the only words yet formed had close connection with objects and the ideas directly derived from them, signs were as much more copious for communication than speech as the sight embraces more and more distinct characteristics of objects than does the sense of hearing." *

All the foregoing and general conclusions thus reached,

---

* *Sign-Language*, &c., p. 284. On page 352, this writer further supplies a most interesting comparison between gesture and spoken language as both are used by the North American Indians—showing that the syntax in the two cases is identical.

touching the genesis of conceptual from pre-conceptual ideation, admit of being strikingly corroborated through another line of philological research. On antecedent grounds the evolutionist would suppose that "the first language-signs must have denoted those physical acts and qualities which were directly apprehensible by the senses ; both because these alone are directly significable, and because it was only they that untrained human beings had the power to deal with or the occasion to use." * In other words, if, as we suppose, language had its origin in merely denotative sign-making, which gradually became more and more connotative and thus gradually more and more predicative ; obviously the original denotations must have referred only to objects (or actions, states, and qualities) of merely receptual significance —*i.e.* "those physical acts and qualities which are directly apprehensible by the senses." And, no less obviously, the connotative extension of such denotative names must, for an enormously long period, have been confined to a pre-conceptual cognizance of the most obvious analogies—*i.e.* such analogies as would necessarily thrust themselves upon the merely sensuous perception by the force of direct association.

Now, if this were the case, what would the evolutionist expect to find in language as it now exists ? Clearly, he would expect to find more or less well-marked traces, in the fundamental constitution of all languages, of what has been called "fundamental metaphor"—by which is meant an intellectual extension of terms that originally were of no more than sensuous signification. And this is precisely what we do find. "The whole history of language, down to our

---

* Whitney, *Encyclo. Brit.*, *loc. cit.*, p. 770. It is interesting to note that the psychological importance of this principle was clearly enunciated by Locke :—" It may lead us a little towards the original of all our notions and knowledge, if we remark how great a dependence our words have on common sensible ideas ; and how those which are made use of to stand for actions and notions quite removed from sense, have their rise from thence, and from obvious sensible ideas are transferred to more abstruse significations, and made to stand for ideas that come out under the cognizance of our senses " (*Human Understanding*, iii. i. 5).

23

own day, is full of examples of the reduction of physical terms and phrases to the expression of non-physical conceptions and relations ; we can hardly write a line without giving illustrations of this kind of linguistic growth. So pervading is it, that we never regard ourselves as having read the history of any intellectual or moral term till we have traced it back to its physical origin." *

Now, I hold that this receptual nucleus of all our conceptual terms furnishes the strongest possible evidence, not only of the historical priority of the former, but also of what Professor Max Müller calls their "dire necessity" to the growth of the latter.† In other words, the facts appear conclusively to show that conceptual connotation (denomination) has always had—*and can only have had*—a receptual core (denotation) around which to develop. Psychological analysis has already shown us the psychological priority of the recept ; and now philological research most strikingly corroborates this analysis by *actually finding the recept in the body of every concept.*

How this large and general fact is to be met by my antagonists I know not. It certainly does not satisfy the case to say, with Professor Max Müller, ‡ Noiré, § and those who

---

* Whitney, *Encyclo. Brit.*, p. 770. See also Nodier, *Notions de Linguistique*, p. 39; Garnett, *Essays*, p. 89 ; Grimm, *Gesch. d. d. Sprache*, s. 56 *et seq. ;* Pott, *Metaphern vom Leben, &c.*, *Zeitschr. fur Vergl. Sprachf. Jahrg.*, ii., heft 2 ; Heyse, *System, &c.*, s. 97 ; and Farrar, *Origin of Language*, 130; *Chapters on Language*, pp. 67, 133, 204–246. He refers to the above, and quotes the following passages from Emerson and Carlyle :—" As the limestone of the Continent consists of infinite masses of shells of animalcules, so language is made up of images and tropes, which now, in their secondary use, have long ceased to remind us of their poetic origin " (*Essays on the Poets*). "Language is the flesh-garment of Thought. I said that Imagination wore this flesh-garment ; and does she not ? Metaphors are her stuff. Examine Language. What, if you except a few primitive elements of natural sound, what is it all but metaphors recognized as such, or no longer recognized ; still fluid and florid, or now solid-grown and colourless ? If those same primitive elements are the osseous fixtures in the flesh-garment of Language—then are metaphors its muscles, its tissues, and living integuments. An unmetaphorical style you shall in vain seek for : is not your very *attention* a *stretching-to* ? " (*Sartor Resartus*, ch. x.).

† *Science of Thought*, p. 329.
‡ *Science of Language*, p. 123.
§ *Logos*, p. 258, *et seq.*

think with them, that in no other way could the growth of conceptual thought have been possible ; for this is merely to reiterate on *a priori* grounds the conclusion which I have reached *a posteriori.* And the more that this historical priority of denotation can thus be shown an *a priori* necessity to the subsequent genesis of denomination, the greater becomes the cogency of our evidence *a posteriori* that, as a matter of fact, such has been invariably the order of historical succession. For, if conceptual ideation differs from receptual in kind, why this necessity for the historical priority of the latter ? Why should denotation thus always require to precede denomination—or receptual connotation thus always require to precede conceptual predication—unless it be that the one is a further and a continuous development of the other ? Surely as well might the botanist institute a specific distinction between the root and the flower of the self-same plant, as the psychologist, with these results of philological research before him, still persist in drawing a distinction of kind between the receptual denotation of " radical elements," and the full efflorescence of conceptual thought.

A single illustration may serve to convey the force of this argument more fully than any abstract discussion of it. But I will introduce the illustration with an analogous case. The following well-established fact I quote from Geiger :—

" Man had language before he had tools. . . . On considering a word denoting an activity carried on with a tool, we shall invariably find that this was not its original meaning, but that it previously implied a similar activity requiring only the natural organs. . . . This fact of the activity with implements deriving its name from one more simple, ancient, and brute-like, is quite universal, and I do not know how otherwise to account for it but that the name is older than the activity with tools which it denotes at the present time—that, in fact, the word was already extant before men used any other organs but the native and natural ones. . . . . The vestiges of his earliest conceptions still preserved in language proclaim it loudly and distinctly that man has developed from a state in which he had solely to rely on the aid of his organs—a state, therefore, in which he differed little in his habits from the brute creation, and with respect to the enjoyment of his existence, nay, to his preservation, depended almost entirely on whatever lucky chance presented to him." *

Now, to this special illustration on the general principle of "fundamental metaphor" it will doubtless be said—Very interesting in itself; but, after all, it merely amounts to a philological proof that tools are younger than words; that men did not always possess tools; that tools were gradually invented; and that, when invented, they were named by a metaphorical application of words previously in use.—Well, if we are all agreed so far, I will proceed to adduce my illustration.

Judging from the now extensive literature which is opposed to evolutionary teaching in the case of man, I gather that the great majority of writers are quite as much impressed by the moral and religious aspects of human psychology as they are by the intellectual. Now, as already stated in the Preface, I reserve for a future volume a full consideration of these distinctively human faculties. In the present part of my work I am concerned exclusively with the question as to the origin of those powers of conceptual thought which, under any point of view, must be regarded as the necessary and antecedent condition to the possibility both of conscience and religion. Nevertheless, merely for the sake of supplying an illustration touching the point now before us, I may here forestall a little of what I shall hereafter have to present in detail touching the evidence that we have of the genesis of conscience. And this I will do by another quotation from the same philologist, seeing that he is an authority whom none of my opponents can afford to ignore.

"If we examine the words, those oldest pre-historic testimonies, we shall find that all moral notions contain

---

* Geiger, *Address delivered before the International Congress for Archæology and History at Bonn*, 1868.

something morally indifferent." That is to say, they all contain what I have termed a "receptual core," expressive of some simple physical process, or condition, the name of which has been afterwards transferred, by "fundamental metaphor," to the moral "concept." Omitting the illustrations, the passage continues as follows :—" But why have not the morally good and bad their own names in language ? Why do we know them from something else that previously had its appellation ? Evidently because language dates from a period when a moral judgment, a knowledge of good and evil, had not yet dawned in the human mind." *

Now, at present I am not concerned with this conclusion, further than to remark that I do not see how it is to be obviated, if our previous agreement is to stand with regard to the precisely analogous case of the names of tools. That is to say, if any one allows that the philological evidence is sufficient to prove the priority of words to the tools which they designate, consistency must constrain him also to allow that the fundamental concepts of morality are of later origin than the names by which they have been baptized, and in virtue of which they must be regarded as having become concepts at all. These names—just like the names of tools—were all originally of nothing more than pre-conceptual significance, serving to denote such obvious physical states or activities as were immediately cognizable by the powers of sensuous perception and direct association. Then, as the moral sense began to dawn, and the utilitarian significance of conduct as ethical began to be appreciated, the principles of " fundamental metaphor " were applied to the naming of these newly found concepts—presumably at about the same time as these same principles were applied to the naming of newly found tools.

Now, this is only one illustration out of a practically infinite number of others which it would be easy to quote—seeing, indeed, as Whitney observes, that " we can hardly write a line without giving illustrations of this kind of linguistic growth." And whatever may be thought (at this premature

* Geiger, *A Lecture to the Commercial Club of Frankfort-on-the-Main* (1869).

stage of our inquiry) concerning the application of the
general principle before us to the special case of conscience,
it appears to me there can be no question at all that this
general principle of " fundamental metaphor " reveals the fact
of an intellectual growth from what I have called the pre-
conceptual to the conceptual phase ; and, moreover, that it
proves such a growth to have been the universal characteristic
of human faculty in those pre-historic times of which language
preserves to us the only record.*

There still remains one other department of philological

---

* Perhaps the most interesting department of fundamental metaphor is that
wherein the metaphor is found by philological research to have reference, not to
any natural object, quality, &c., but to a pre-existing action or gesture as already
made by man himself for the purpose of conveying information, expressing his
emotions, &c. For fundamental metaphor of this kind obviously brings us within
seeing distance of the time when the audible signs of articulations were born of
the visible signs of gesture and grimace. In illustration of this branch of our
subject I will only quote one passage ; but the reader will at once perceive how
easy it would be to furnish many other instances from the etymology of words now
in habitual use.

" The further a language has been developed from its primordial roots, which
have been twisted into forms no longer suggesting any reason for their original
selection, and the more the primitive significance of its words has disappeared, the
fewer points of contact can it retain with signs. The higher languages are more
precise because the consciousness of the derivation of most of their words is lost,
so that they have become counters, good for any sense agreed upon and for no other.

" It is, however, possible to ascertain the included gesture even in many English
words. The class represented by the word *supercilious* will occur to all readers,
but one or two examples may be given not so obvious and more immediately connected with the gestures of our Indians. *Imbecile*, generally applied to the weakness
of old age, is derived from the Latin *in*, in the sense of on, and *bacillum*, a staff,
which at once recalls the Cheyenne sign for *old man* [previously mentioned]. So
*time* appears more nearly connected with τείνω, to stretch, when information is
given of the sign for *long time*, in the Speech of Kin Chē-ĕss, in this paper, namely,
placing the thumbs and forefingers in such a position as if a small thread was held
between the thumb and forefinger of each hand, the hands first touching each other,
and then moving slowly from each other, as if *stretching* a piece of gum-elastic "
(Mallery, *Sign-Language, &c.*, p. 350). This writer also says, with reference to the
uncivilized languages which he has specially studied, " In the languages of North
America, which have not become arbitrary, to the degree exhibited by those of civilized man, the connection between the idea and the word is only less obvious than that
still unbroken connection between the idea and the sign, and they remain strongly
affected by the concepts of outline, form, place, position, and feature on which

inquiry to be considered, and its consideration will tend yet
further and most forcibly to corroborate all the general conclusions already attained. Hitherto we have been engaged
for the most part on what I have already called the palæontology of human thought as revealed, fossil-like, in the linguistic
petrifactions of pre-historic man. But the science of comparative philology is not confined in its researches upon early
forms of speech to the bygone remnants of a distant age. On
the contrary, just like the science of comparative anatomy,
it is furnished with still existing materials for study, which are
of the nature of living organisms, and which present so many
grades of evolution that the lowest members of the series
bring us within easy distance of those aboriginal forms which
can only be studied in the fossil state. Hitherto I have
considered these lowest existing languages only with reference to their forms of predication. Here I desire to consider
them with reference to the quality of ideation that they
betoken.

In the next instalment of my work I shall have to treat of
the psychology of savages, and then it will become apparent
that there is no very precise relation to be constantly traced
between grades of mental evolution in general, and of
language-development in particular. Nevertheless there is a
general relation: and therefore it is among the lowest savages
that we meet with the lowest types of language-structure.*

gesture is founded, while they are similar in their fertile combination of radicals.
Indian language consists of a series of words that are but slightly differentiated
parts of speech following each other in the order suggested in the mind of the
speaker without absolute laws of arrangement, as its sentences are not completely
integrated. The sentence necessitates parts of speech, and parts of speech are
possible only when a language has reached that stage where sentences are logically
constructed. The words of an Indian tongue, being synthetic or undifferentiated
parts of speech, are in this respect strictly analogous to the gesture elements
which enter into a sign-language. The study of the latter is therefore valuable
for comparison with the words of the former. The one language throws much
light upon the other, and neither can be studied to the best advantage without a
knowledge of the other."

* There are certain writers, such as Du Ponceau, Charlevoix, James, Apple-
yard, Threlkeld, Caldwell, &c., who have sought to represent that the languages
of even the lowest savages are "highly systematic and truly philosophical," &c.

In the present connection I shall have to treat of these languages only in so far as they throw light upon the quality of ideation with which they are concerned, or so far as they are related to the general principles with which we have already been occupied. And, even as thus limited, I will endeavour to make my exposition as brief as possible.

I will begin by supplying a few quotations from the more competent authorities who have written upon the subject from a linguistic point of view.

"It requires but the feeblest power of abstraction — a power even possessed by idiots — to use a name as the sign of a conception, *e.g.* to say 'sun'; *—to say 'sheen,' as the description of a phenomenon common to all shining objects, is a higher effort, and to say 'to shine' as expressive of the state or act is higher still. Now, familiar as such efforts may be to us, there is ample proof that they could not have been so to the inventors of language, because they are not so, even now, to some nations of mankind after all their long millenniums of existence. Instances of this fact have been repeatedly adduced." † Thus, for example, the Society Islanders have separate words for

---

But this opinion rests on a radically false estimate of the criteria of system and philosophy in a language. For the criteria chosen are exuberance of synonyms, intricacies or complications of forms, &c., which are really works of a low development. The fallacy is now acknowledged to be such by all philologists. Even Farrar, who at first himself fell into this error (*Origin of Language*, p. 28), in his subsequent work writes :— "Further examination has entirely removed this belief. For this apparent wealth of synonyms and grammatical forms is chiefly due *to the hopeless poverty of the power of abstraction.* It would not only be no advantage, but even an impossible encumbrance to a language required for literary purposes. The transnormal character of these tongues only proves that they are the work of minds incapable of all subtle analysis, and following in one single direction an erroneous and partial line of development. . . . If language proves anything, it proves that these savages must have lived continuously in a savage condition " (Farrar, *Chapters on Language*, pp. 53, 54, who also refers to numerous authorities).

* The term "conception" here is, of course, equivalent to my term "preconception." When my daughter uttered her first denotative word "star," she was, indeed, bestowing a name; but it was the name of a recept, not of a concept.

† Farrar, *Chapters on Language*, pp. 198, 199.

dog's-tail, bird's-tail, sheep's-tail, &c., but no word for tail itself—*i.e.* tail in general.* The Mohicans have words to signify different kinds of cutting, but no verb "to cut;" and forms for "I love him," "I love you," &c., but no verb "to love;" while the Choctanis have names for different species of oak, but no word for the genus oak.† Again, the Australians have no word for tree, or even for bird, fish, &c.; ‡ and the Eskimo, although he has verbs which signify to fish-seal, to fish-whale, &c., has not any verb "to fish." " Ces langues," Du Ponceau remarks, " généralisent rarement ; " and he shows that they have not even any verb to imply "I will," or "I wish," although they have separate verbal forms for "I wish to eat meat," "I wish to eat soup ;" neither have they any general noun-substantive which means "a blow," although they have a variety which severally mean blows with as many different kinds of instruments. § Similarly, Mr. Crawford tells us, "the Malay is very deficient in abstract words ; and the usual train of ideas of the people who speak it does not lead them to make a frequent use even of the few they possess. With this poverty of the abstract is united a redundancy of the concrete,"—and he gives many instances of the same kind as those above rendered from other languages. ‖ So, likewise, we are told, "the dialect of the Zulus is rich in nouns denoting different objects of the same genus, according to some variety of colour, or deficiency of members, or some other peculiarity," such as "white-cow," "red-cow," "brown-cow ;"¶ and the Sechuâna has no fewer than ten words all meaning "horned cattle." ** Cheroki presents thirteen different verbs to signify different

---

* *Mithridates*, iii. 325, 397.   See also Pott, *Etym. Forsch.*, ii. 167 ; and Heyse, *System*, 132.
† Latham, *Races of Man*, p. 376.
‡ Quatrefages, *Rev. des Deux Mondes*, Dec. 15, 1860; Maury, *La Terre et l'Homme*, p. 433.
§ *Mem. sur le Syst. Gram.*, &c., p. 120.
‖ *Malay Grammar*, i., p. 68, *et seq.*
¶ *Journl. Ameri. Orient, Soc.*, i. No. 4, p. 402.
** Casalis, *Grammar*, p. 7.

kinds of washing, without any to indicate "washing" itself; *
and Milligan says that the aborigines of Tasmania had
"no words representing abstract ideas; for each variety of
gum-tree, wattle-tree, &c., they had a name, but they had
no equivalent for the expression of 'a tree;' neither could
they express abstract qualities, such as hard, soft, warm, cold,
long, short, round." †

Lastly, to give only one other example, Dr. Latham
states that a Kurd of the Zaza tribe, who furnished Dr.
Sandwith with a list of native words, was not "able to
conceive a hand or father, except so far as they were
related to himself, or something else; and so essentially
concrete rather than abstract were his notions, that he
combined the pronoun with the substantive whenever he
had a part of the human body or a degree of consanguinity
to name," saying *sere-min*, "my head," and *pie-min*, "my
father."

Thus, as Professor Sayce remarks, after alluding to
some of the above facts, "we may be sure that it was not
"the 'ideas of prime importance' which primitive man
struggled to represent, but those individual objects of which
his senses were cognizant."‡ And, without further multiplying testimony, we may now be prepared to accept
from him the general statement that, "all over the world,
indeed, wherever we come across a savage race, or an
individual who has been unaffected by the civilization
around him, we find this primitive inability to separate
the particular from the universal by isolating the individual
word, and extracting it, as it were, from the ideas habitually
associated with it." § Or, in my own phraseology, among
all primitive races still existing, we meet with what must
seem to my opponents a wholly unintelligible incapacity
to evolve a concept from any number of recepts, notwith-

---

* Pickering, *Indian Languages*, p. 26.
† *Vocabulary of the Dialects of some of the Aboriginal Tribes of Tasmania* p. 34.
‡ *Introduction, &c.*, vol. ii., p. 6.
§ *Ibid.*, vol. i., p. 379.

standing that the latter may all be most nearly related together, and severally named by as many denotative signs : even with their numberless already-formed words for different kinds of trees, the aborigines of Tasmania could not designate "a tree." Of course they must have had a recept of a tree, or a generic image formed out of innumerable perceptions of particular trees—so that, for instance, it would doubtless have surprised a Tasmanian could he have seen a tree (even though it were a new species for which he had no name) standing inverted with its roots in the air and its branches in the ground. In just the same way a dog is surprised when it first sees a man walking on his hands : the dog will bark at such an object because it conflicts with the generic image which has been automatically formed by numberless perceptions of individual men walking on their feet. But, in the absence of any name for trees in general, there is nothing to show that the savage has a concept answering to "tree," any more than that the dog has a concept answering to "man." Indeed, unless my opponents vacate the basis of Nominalism on which their opposition is founded, they must acknowledge that in the absence of any *name* for tree there *can be no conception* of tree.

So much, then, for what Archdeacon Farrar has called "*the hopeless poverty of the power of abstraction*" in savages. Their various languages unite, in verbal testimony, to assure us that human thought does *not* "proceed from the abstract to the concrete;" but, on the contrary, that in the race, as in the individual, receptual ideation is the precursor of conceptual—denotation the antecedent of denomination, as in still earlier stages it was itself preceded by gesticulation. Such being the case with regard to names, it is no wonder, as we previously found, that low savages are so extraordinarily deficient in their forms of predication.

The palæontology of human thought, then, as recorded in language, incontestibly proves that the origin and progress of ideation in the race was psychologically identical with what we now observe in the individual. All the stages of ideation which we have seen to be characteristic of psychogenesis in a child, are thus revealed to us as having been characteristic of psychogenesis in mankind.

First there was the indicative stage. This is proved in two ways. On the one hand, all philologists will now agree with Geiger—" But, what says more than anything, language diminishes the further we look back, in such a way that we cannot forbear concluding it must once have had no existence at all." * On the other hand, even if we tap the tree of language as high up in its stem as the pronominal roots of Sanskrit, what is the kind of ideational sap which flows therefrom ? It is, as we have already seen, so strongly suggestive of gesture and grimace that even Professor Max Müller allows that in it we have "remnants of the earliest and almost pantomimic phase of language, in which language was hardly as yet what we mean by language, namely *logos*, a gathering, but only a pointing." †

Secondly, we have clear evidence of sentence-words, as well as of what I have called the denotative phase, or the naming of simple recepts—whether only of actions, or, as we may safely assume, likewise also of objects and qualities; and whether arbitrarily, or, as seems virtually certain, in chief part by onomatopœia. Both these subordinate points, however— which are rendered more doubtful on account of the struggle for existence among words having proved favourable to denotative terms expressive of actions, and unfavourable to the survival of onomatopœia—are of comparatively little moment to us; the important fact is the one which is most clearly testified to by the philological record, namely, that the lowest strata of this record yield fossils of the lowest order of development: the " 121 concepts," appear to be, for the most part, denotations of simple recepts.

Thirdly, higher up in the stratified deposits, we meet with

* *A Lecture delivered at Frankfort,* 1869.
† *Science of Thought,* p. 245.

overwhelming evidence of the connotative extension of these denotative terms. Indeed, many of these terms have probably undergone a certain amount of connotative extension as the condition to their having survived as roots ; and, therefore, in these lowest deposits it is difficult to be sure that an apparently denotative term is not really a term which has undergone the earlier stages of connotative extension. If such were the case, we can understand the loss of any onomatopoetic significance which it may originally have presented. But, however this may be, there is an endless mass of evidence to prove the subsequent and continuous growth of connotative extension throughout the whole range of philological time.

Lastly, as regards the predicative phase, we have seen that philology shows the same order and method to have been followed in the race as in the child. In the growing child, as we have seen, pre-conceptual predication is contemporary with—or occupies the same psychological level as—the connotative extension of denotative terms. Indeed, the very act of connotation is in itself an act of predication—if in the conceptual sphere, of conceptual predication (denomination) ; if in the pre-conceptual, of pre-conceptual. Again, in the psychogenesis of the child we noted how important a part is played in the development of pre-conceptual predication by the mere apposition of connotative terms—such apposition being rendered inevitable by the laws of association. If A is the connotative name for $A$, B the connotative name for $B$, when the young child sees that $A$ and $B$ occur together, the statement A B is rendered inevitable by "the logic of events ; " and this statement is a pre-conceptual proposition. Now, in both these respects philology yields abundant parallels. The quotations which I have given conclusively prove that "every word must originally have been a sentence ; " or, in my own terminology, a pre-conceptual proposition of precisely the same kind as that which is employed by a young child. If it be replied that the young child is without self-consciousness, while the primitive man was not without self-consciousness, this would merely be to beg the whole question on which we are engaged, and, moreover, to beg it in the teeth of every antecedent probability, as well as of every actual analogy, to which appeal can possibly be made. If it be true—and who will venture to doubt it?—that "language diminishes the further we look back, in such a way that we cannot forbear concluding it must once have had no existence at all," will it be maintained that the man-like being who was then unable to communicate with his fellows by means of any words at all was gifted with self-consciousness? Should so absurd a statement be ventured, it would be fatal to the argument of my adversaries; for the statement would imply, either that concepts may exist without names, or that self-consciousness may exist without concepts. The truth of the matter is that philology has proved, in a singularly complete manner, the origin and gradual development in time, first of pre-conceptual communication, and next of the self-consciousness which supplied the basis of conceptual predication. No wonder, therefore, as Professor Max Müller somewhat naively observes, " it may be said that the first step in the formation of names and concepts is very imperfect. So it is." Truly "to name the act of carrying by a root formed from sounds which accompany the act of carrying a heavy load, is a far more primitive act than to fix an attribute by a name " conceptually applied. So primitive, indeed, is nomination of this kind, that I defy any one to show wherein it differs psychologically from what I have called the denotation of a young child, or even of a talking bird.

And, having reduced the matter to this issue so far as the results of philology are concerned, I may fitly conclude by briefly indicating the principal point which appears to divide my opinions from those of the eminent philologist just alluded to—if not also from those of the majority of my psychological opponents. Briefly, the point is that on the other side an unwarrantable assumption is made—to wit, that conceptual thought is an antecedent condition, *sine quâ non,* to any and every act of bestowing a name; and, *a fortiori,* to any and every act of predication. This is the fundamental assumption, which, whether openly expressed or covertly implied, serves as the basis of the whole superstructure of my opponents' argument. Now, I claim to have shown, by a complete inductive proof, that this assumption is not only unwarrantable in theory, but false in fact. There are names and names. Not every name that is bestowed betokens conceptual thought on the part of the namer. Alike from the case of the talking bird, of the young child, and of early man (so far as he has left any traces of his psychology in the structure of language), I have demonstrated that prior to the stage of denomination there are the stages of indication, denotation, and receptual connotation. These are the psychological stepping-stones across that "Rubicon of Mind," which, owing to their neglect, has seemed to be impassable. The Concept (and, *a fortiori*, the Proposition) is not a structure of ideation which is presented to us without a developmental history. Although it has been uniformly assumed by all my opponents "that the simplest element of thought" can have had no such history, the assumption is, as I have said, directly contradicted by observable fact. Had the case been otherwise—had the concept really been without father and without mother, without beginning of days or end of life— then truly a case might have been shown for regarding it as an entity *sui generis*, destitute of kith or kin among all the other faculties of mind. But, as we have now so fully seen, no such unique exception to the otherwise uniform process of evolution can here be maintained : the phases of development which have gradually led up to conceptual thought admit of being as clearly traced as those which have led to any other product, whether of life or of mind.

Here, then, I bring to a close this brief and imperfect rendering of the "Witness of Philology." But, brief and imperfect as the rendering is, I am honestly unable to see how it is conceivable that the witness itself could have been more uniform as to its testimony, or more multifarious as to its facts—more consistent, more complete, or more altogether overwhelming than we have found it to be. In almost every single respect it has corroborated the results of our psychological analysis. It has come forward like a living thing, which, in the very voice of Language itself, directly and circumstantially narrates to us the actual history of a process the constituent phases of which we had previously inferred. It has told us of a time when as yet mankind were altogether speechless, and able to communicate with one another only by means of gesticulation and grimace. It has described to us the first articulate sounds in the form of sentence-words, without significance apart from the pointings by which they were accompanied. It has revealed the gradual differentiation of such a protoplasmic form of language into " parts of speech ; " and declared that these grammatical structures were originally the offspring of gesture-signs. More particularly, it has shown that in the earliest stages of articulate utterance pronominal elements, and even predicative words, were used in the impersonal manner which belongs to a hitherto undeveloped form of self-consciousness—primitive man, like a young child, having therefore spoken of his own personality in objective terminology. It has taught us to find in the body of every conceptual term a pre-conceptual core ; so that, as the learned and thoughtful Garnett says, "*nihil in oratione quod non prins in sensu* may now be regarded as an incontrovertible axiom." * It has minutely described the whole of that wonderful aftergrowth of articulate utterance through many lines of divergent evolution, in virtue of which all nations of the earth are now in possession, in one degree or another, of the god-like attributes of reason and of speech. Truly, as Archdeacon Farrar says, " to the flippant and the ignorant, how ridiculous is the apparent inadequacy of the origin to produce such a result." † But here, as elsewhere, it is the method of evolution to bring to nought the things that are mighty by the things that are of no reputation ; and when we feel disposed to boast ourselves in that we alone may claim the Logos, should we not do well to pause and remember in what it was that this our high prerogative arose ?   " So hat

* *Essays*, p. 89.        † *Chapters on Language*, p. 133.

auch keine Sprache ein abstractum, zu dem sie nicht durch Ton und Gefühl gelangt wäre." * To my mind it is simply inconceivable that any stronger proof of mental evolution could be furnished, than is furnished in this one great fact by the whole warp and woof of the thousand dialects of every pattern which are now spread over the surface of the globe. We cannot speak to each other in any tongue without declaring the pre-conceptual derivation of our speech ; we cannot so much as discuss the " origin of human faculty " itself, without announcing, in the very medium of our discussion, what that origin has been. It is to Language that my opponents have appealed : by Language they are hopelessly condemned.

* Herder, *Abhandl.*, s. 122.

# CHAPTER XVI.

## THE TRANSITION IN THE RACE.

AT this point I shall doubtless be expected to offer some remarks on the probable mode of transition between the brute and the human being. Having so fully considered both the psychology and philology of ideation, it may be thought that I am now in a position to indicate what I suppose to have been the actual stepping-stones whereby an intelligent species of ape can be conceived to have crossed " the Rubicon of Mind." But, if I am expected to do this, I might reasonably decline, for two reasons.

In the first place, the attempt, even if it could be successful, would be superfluous. The only objection I have had to meet is one which has been raised on grounds of psychology. This objection I have met, and met upon its own grounds. If I have been successful, for the purposes of argument nothing more remains to be said. If I have not been successful, it is obviously impossible to strengthen my case by going beyond the known facts of mind, as they actually exist before us, to any hypothetical possibilities of mind in the dim ages of an unrecorded past.

In the second place, any remarks which I have to offer upon this subject must needs be of a wholly speculative or unverifiable character. As well might the historian spend his time in suggesting hypothetical histories of events known to have occurred in a pre-historic age : his evidence that such and such events must have occurred may be conclusive, and yet he may be quite in the dark as to the precise conditions which led up to them, the time which was occupied by them, and the particular method of their occurrence. In such cases it often happens that the more certain an historian may be that such and such an event did take place, the greater is the number of ways in which he sees that it might have taken place. Merely for the sake of showing that this is likewise the case in the matter now before us, I will devote the present chapter to a consideration of three alternative—and equally hypothetical—histories of the transition. But, from what has just been said, I hope it will be understood that I attach no argumentative importance to any of these hypotheses.

Sundry German philologists have endeavoured to show that speech originated in wholly meaningless sounds, which in the first instance were due to merely physiological conditions. In their opinion the purely reflex mechanisms connected with vocalization would have been sufficient to yield not only many differences of tone under different states as to suffering, pleasure, effort, &c., but even the germ of articulation in the meaningless utterance of vowel sounds and consonants. Thus, for example, Lazarus says :— " Der Process der eigen-thümlich menschlichen Laut-Erzeugung, die Articulation der Ton, die Hervorbringung von Vocalen und Consonanten, ist demnach auf rein physiologischem Boden gegeben—in der urprünglichen Natur des menschlichen physischen bewegten Organismus begründet, und wird vor aller Willkür und Absicht also ohne Einwirkung des Geistes obwohl auf Veranlassung von Gefühlen und Empfindungen vollzogen." *

This, it will be observed, is the largest possible extension of the interjectional theory of the origin of speech. It assumes that not only inarticulate, but also articulate sounds were given forth by the " sprachlosen Urmenschen," in the way of instinctive cries, wholly destitute of any semiotic intention. By repeated association, however, they are supposed to have acquired, as it were automatically, a semiotic value. For,

* *Das Leben der Seele*, ii. 47.

to quote Professor Friedrich Müller, "Sie sind zwar Anfangs bedeutungslos : sie können aber bedeutungsvoll werden. Alles, was in unserem Inneren vorgeht, wird von der Seele wahrgenommen. Sobald durch gewisse aüssere Einflüsse in Folge einer Combination mehrerer Empfindungen eine Anschauung entsteht, nimmt die Seele dieselbe an, Diese Anschauung hat—in Folge der durch eine der Empfindungen hervorgebrachten Reflexbewegung in den Stimmorganen— einen Laut zum Begleiter, welcher in gleicher Weise wie die Anschauung von der Seele wahrgenommen wird, diese beiden Wahrnehmungen, nämlich jene der Anschauung und jene des Lautes, *verbinden* sich miteinander vermöge ihrer· *Gleichzeitigkeit* im menschlichen Bewusstsein, es findet also eine *Association* der Laut-Anschauung mit jener der *Sach-* Anschauung statt, die Elemente der Sach-Anschauung bekommen an der Laute-Anschauung einen *festen* Mittelpunkt, durch den die *Anschauung* zur *Vorstellung* sich entwickelt. Wir sind damit bei der menschlichen Sprache angelangt, welche also ihrem Wesen nach auf der *Substituirung* eines *Klang*-oder *Ton*bildes für das Bild einer Anschauung beruht." *

Now, without at all doubting the important part which originally meaningless sounds may have played in furnishing material for vocal sign-making, and still less disputing the agency of association in the matter, I must nevertheless refuse to accept the above hypothesis as anything like a full explanation of the origin of speech. ₁For it manifestly ignores the whole problem which stands to be solved—namely, the genesis of those powers of ideation which first put a soul of meaning into the previously insignificant sounds. Nearly all the warm-blooded animals so far share with mankind the same physiological nature as to give forth a variety of vocal sounds under as great a variety of mental states. Therefore, if in accordance with the above hypothesis we regard all such sounds as meaningless (or arising from the "purely physiological basis" of reflex movement), the question obviously

* *Grundriss der Sprachwissenschaft*, i. 35, 36.

presents itself, Why have not the lower animals developed speech? According to the above doctrine, aboriginal and hitherto speechless man started without any superiority in respect of the sign-making faculty, and thus far precisely resembled what is taken to be the present psychological condition of the lower animals.* Why, then, out of the same original conditions has there arisen so enormous a difference of result? If, in the case of mankind, associations of meaningless sounds with particular states, objects, &c., led to a substitution of the former for the latter, and thus gave to them the significance of names, how are we to account for the total absence of any such development in brutes? To me it appears that this is clearly an unanswerable difficulty; and therefore I do not wonder that the so-called interjectional theory of the origin of speech has brought discredit on the whole philosophy of the subject. But, as so often happens in philosophical writings, we have here a case where an important truth is damaged by imperfect or erroneous presentation. All the principles set forth in the above hypothesis are sound in themselves, but the premiss from which they start is untrue. This premiss is, that aboriginal man presented no rudiments of the sign-making faculty —that this faculty itself required to be originated *de novo* by accidental associations of sounds with things. But, as we now well know from all the facts previously given, even the lower animals present the sign-making faculty in no mean degree of development; and, therefore, it is perfectly certain that the "Urmenschen," at the time when they were "sprachlosen," were not on this account *zeichenlosen*. The psychological germ of communication, which probably could not have been created by merely accidental associations between sounds and things, must already have been given in those psychological conditions of receptual ideation which are common to all intelligent animals.

But to this all-essential germ, as thus given, I doubt not that the soil of such associations as the interjectional theory

* See, for example, F. Müller, *loc. cit.*, i. 36, 37.

has in view must have been of no small importance ; for this would naturally help to nourish its semiotic nature. And the reason why the similar germ of sign-making which occurs in the brute creation has not been similarly nurtured, I have already considered in Chapter VIII. For, it is needless to add, on every ground I disagree with the above quotations where they represent articulate sounds as having been aboriginally uttered by " Urmenschen " in the way of instinctive cries, without any vestige of semiotic intention.*

I will now pass on to consider the two other hypotheses ; and by way of introduction to both we must remember that our materials of study on the side of the apes is very limited. I do not mean only that no single representative of any of the anthropoid apes has ever been made the object of even so much observation with respect to its intelligence as I bestowed upon a cebus. Yet this, no doubt, is an important point, because we know that of all quadrumana—and, there-fore, of all existing animals—the anthropoid apes are the most intelligent, and, therefore, if specially trained would probably display greater aptitude in the matter of sign-making than is to be met with in any other kind of brute. But I do not press this point. What I now refer to is the fact that the existing species of anthropoid apes are very few in number, and appear to be all on the high-road to extinction. Moreover, it is certain that none of these existing species can have been the progenitor of man ; and, lastly, it is equally certain that the extinct species (or genus) which did give origin to man must have differed in several

---

* Some of the supporters of the interjectional theory in this extreme, not to say extravagant form, appear to go on the assumption that primitive and hitherto speechless man already differed from the lower animals in presenting conceptual thought. This assumption would, of course, explain why man alone began to invest his instinctive cries, &c., with the character of names. But, from a psychological point of view, any such assumption is obviously a putting of the cart before the horse. I make this remark in order to add that the objection would not apply if the ideation were supposed to be *pre-conceptual—i.e.* beyond the level reached by any brute, though not yet distinctively human. Later on, I myself espouse a theory to this effect.

important respects from any of its existing allies. In the first place, it must have been more social in habits ; and, in the next place, it was probably more vociferous than the orang, the gorilla, or the chimpanzee. That there is no improbability in either of these suppositions will be at once apparent if we remember that both are amply sustained by analogies among existing and allied species of the monkey tribe. Or, to state these preliminary considerations in a converse form, when it is assumed * that because the few existing and expiring species of anthropoid apes are unsocial and comparatively silent, therefore the simian ancestors of man must have been so, it is enough to point to the variability of both these habits among certain allied genera of monkeys and baboons, in order at the same time to dispose of the assumption, and to indicate the probable reasons why one genus of ape gradually became evolved into *Homo*, while all the allied genera became, or are still becoming, extinct.

Again, and still by way of preliminary consideration, we must remember that the analogy of the growing child, although most valuable up to a certain point, is not to be unreservedly followed where we have to deal with the genesis of speech. For, as previously noted, to the infancy of the individual language is supplied from without, and has only to be learnt ; while to the infancy of the race language was not supplied, but had to be made. Therefore, even apart from any question of heredity, we have here an immense difference in the psychological conditions between the case of a growing child and that of aboriginal man. Only in so far as the growing child displays the tendency on which I have dwelt of spontaneously extending the significance of denotative words, or of spontaneously using such words in apposition for the purpose of pre-conceptual predication—only to this extent may we hope to find any true analogy between the individual and the race in respect of that "transition" from receptual to conceptual ideation with which we are now concerned.†

* *E.g.* by Mr. Ward, in his *Dynamical Sociology.*
† Differences of opinion are entertained by philologists concerning the value

There is another preliminary consideration which I think is well worth mentioning.  The philologist Geiger is led by his study of language to entertain, and somewhat elaborately to sustain, the following doctrine.  First he points out that man, much more than any other animal, uses the sense of sight for the purposes of perceptual life.  By this he does not mean that man possesses a keener vision than any other animal, but merely that of all his special senses that of sight is most habitually used for taking cognizance of the external world.  And this, I think, must certainly be admitted.  Even a hitherto speechless infant may be seen to observe objects at great distances, carefully to investigate objects which it holds in its hands, and generally to employ its eyes much more effectively than any of the lower animals at a comparable stage of development.  Now, from this relative superiority of the sense of sight in man, Geiger argues that before the origin of articulate speech he, more than any other animal, must have been accustomed to communicate with his fellows by means of signs which appealed to that sense—*i.e.* by gesture and grimace.  But, if this be admitted, it follows that from the time when a particular species of the order Primates began to use its eyesight more than the allied species, a condition was given favourable to the subsequent and gradual development of a gesticulating form of ape-like creature.  Here grimace also would have played an important part, and where attention was particularly directed towards movements of the mouth for semiotic purposes, articulate sounds would begin to acquire more or less conventional significations.  In this way Geiger supposes that the conditions required for the origin of articulate signs were laid down ; and, in view of all that he says, it certainly is suggestive that the animal which relies most upon the sense of sight is also the animal which has

of "nursery-language," or "baby-talk," as a guide to the probable stages of language-growth in primitive man.   Without going into the arguments upon this question on either side, it appears to me that the analogy as above limited cannot be objected to even by the most extreme sceptics upon the philological value of infantile utterance.   And it is only to this extent that I anywhere use the analogy.

made so prodigious an advance in the faculty of sign-making. In this greater reliance on the sense of sight, therefore, we probably have another among the many and complex conditions which determined the difference in respect of sign-making between the remote progenitors of man and their nearest zoological allies—a difference which would naturally become more and more pronounced the more that vision and gesticulation acted and reacted on one another.

It appears to me that this suggestion of Geiger admits of being strikingly supported by certain facts which are known to obtain in the case of deaf-mutes. Even when wholly uneducated, the born mute, as we have previously seen, habitually invents articulate sounds as his own names of things. These sounds are, of course, unheard by the mute himself, and their use must be ascribed—as I have already ascribed it—to the hereditary transmission of an acquired propensity. But the point now is that, although the majority of these articulate sounds appear to be wholly arbitrary (*e.g. ga* for " one," *schuppatter* for " two," *riecke* for " I will not "), a certain proportion are often clearly traceable to vocalizations incidental to movements of the mouth in performing the actions signified (*e.g. mumm* for " eating," *schipp* for "drinking ").* Similarly, observation of a dog's mouth, while in the act of barking, leads to an imitative action on the part of a mute as his sign for a dog, and this in turn may lead to the utterance of such an articulate sound as *be-yer*, which the mute afterwards uses as his name for a dog.† Now, if words may thus be coined even by deaf-mutes as a result of observing movements of the mouth, much more is this likely to have been the case among the " Urmenschen," who were able not only to see the movements, but also to hear the sounds.

I will now adduce the two hypotheses above alluded to as conceivable suggestions touching the mode of transi-

* For cases, see Heinieke, *Beobachtungen über Stumme,* s. 137, &c.
† *Ibid.,* s. 73.

tion.  First, let us try to imagine an anthropoid ape, social in habits, using its voice somewhat extensively as an organ of sign-making after the manner of all other species of social quadrumana, and possibly somewhat more sagacious than the orang-outang mentioned in my previous work,* or the remarkable chimpanzee now in the Zoological Gardens, which, in respect of intelligence as well as comparative hairlessness and carnivorous propensities, appears to be the most human-like of animals hitherto discovered in the living state.† It does not seem to me difficult further to imagine that such an animal should extend the vocal signs which it habitually employs in the expression of its emotions and the logic of its recepts, to an association with gesture-signs, so as to constitute sentence-words indicative of such simple and often-repeated ideas as the presence of danger, discovery of food, &c. Nay, I do not think it is too much to suppose that such an animal may even have gone so far as to make sounds which were denotative of a few of the most familiar objects, such as food, child, enemy, &c., and also, possibly, of frequently repeated forms of activity ; for this, as I have shown at considerable length, is no more than we actually observe to be done by animals which are lower in the scale of intelligence ; and although it is not done by articulate signs (except in the psychologically poor instance of talking birds), this, as I have also shown, is a matter of no psychological

---

* *Mental Evolution in Animals*, p. 238.

† The carnivorous habits of this animal (which is named as a new species) are most interesting.  It is surmised that in its wild state it must live upon birds ; but in the Zoological Gardens it is found to show a marked preference for cooked meat over raw.  It dines off boiled mutton-chops, the bones of which it picks with its fingers and teeth, being afterwards careful to clean its hands.  It mixes a little straw with the mutton as vegetables, and finishes its dinner with a dessert of fruits. But a more important point is that this animal answers its keeper in vocal tones— or rather grunts—when he speaks to it, and these tones are understood by the keeper as indicative of different mental states.  I have spent a great deal of time in observing this animal, but the publicity and other circumstances render it difficult to do much in the way of experiment or tuition.  With regard to teaching her to count, see above, p. 58 ; and with regard to her understanding of words, p. 126.

import. Whether the denotative stage of language in the ape was first reached by articulation, or (as I think is very much more probable) by vocal sounds of other kinds assisted by gestures and grimace, is similarly immaterial. In either case the advance of intelligence which would thus have been secured would in time have reacted upon the sign-making faculty, and so have led to the extension of the vocabulary, both as to sounds and gestures. Sooner or later the vocal signs—assisted out by gestures and ever leading to a gradual advance of intelligence—would have become more or less conventional, and so, in the presence of suitable anatomical and social conditions, articulate. Thus far I cannot see anything to stumble over, when we remember all that has been said upon the conventional signs which are used by the more intelligent of our domesticated animals, and even by talking birds.*

This is the hypothesis which is countenanced by Mr. Darwin in his *Descent of Man.* He says :—" I cannot doubt that language owes its origin to the imitation and modification of various natural sounds, the voices of other animals, and man's own instinctive cries, aided by signs and gestures. . . . Since monkeys certainly understand much that is said to them by man, and, when wild, utter signal-cries of danger to their fellows ; and since fowls give distinct warnings for danger on the ground, or in the sky from hawks (both, as well as a third cry, intelligible to dogs),† may not some unusually wise ape-like animal have imitated the growl of a beast of prey, and thus told his fellow-monkeys the nature of the expected danger ? This would have been a first step in the formation of a language." ‡

---

* " If there once existed creatures above the apes and below man, who were extirpated by primitive man as his especial rivals in the struggle for existence, or became extinct in any other way, there is no difficulty in supposing them to have possessed forms of speech, more rudimentary and imperfect than ours " (Professor Whitney, Art. *Philology, Ency. Brit.*, vol. xviii., p. 769).

† Houzeau gives a very curious account of his observations on this subject in his *Facultés Mentales des Animaux*, tom. ii., p. 348.

‡ *Descent of Man*, p. 87.

But Mr. Darwin adds another feature to the hypothesis now under consideration, as follows :—

"When we treat of sexual selection we shall see that primæval man, or rather some early progenitor of man, probably first used his voice in producing true musical cadences, that is in singing, as do some of the gibbon-apes at the present day; and we may conclude, from a widely spread analogy, that this power would have been especially exerted during the courtship of the sexes,—would have expressed various emotions, such as love, jealousy, triumph,— and would have served as a challenge to rivals. It is, there-fore, probable that the imitation of musical cries by articulate sounds may have given rise to words expressive of various complex emotional states." *

Such, then, is one way in which it appears to me quite conceivable that the faculty of articulate sign-making might have taken the first step towards the formation of speech. But, not to go further than this first step, I can see another possibility as to the precise method of attainment, and one which I think is still more probable. It is the opinion of some authorities in anthropology that speech was probably, and comparatively speaking, late in making its appearance; so that our ancestors in whom it did first appear were already more human than simian, and as such deserving of the name *Homo alalus.*† Now, if this were the case, the

---

* *Descent of Man*, p. 87.

† This term is used by Haeckel as synonymous with *Pithecanthropoi*, or the ape-like men, who are supposed to have immediately preceded *Homo sapiens* (*History of Evolution*, English trans., vol. ii., p. 293). In the next instalment of work I will consider what has to be said in favour of this view from the side of my anthropology. Meanwhile, it is sufficient to bear in mind that, as previously stated, great as is the psychological difference introduced by the faculty of speech, for the attainment of this faculty anatomical changes so minute as to be imperceptible were all that seem to have been required. "The argument, that because there is an immense difference between a man's intelligence and an ape's, therefore there must be an equally immense difference between their brains, appears to me to be about as well based as the reasoning by which one should endeavour to prove that, because there is a 'great gulf' between a watch that keeps accurate time and another that will not go at all, there is therefore a great

course of our hypothetical history would be even more easy to imagine than it was under the supposition previously considered. For, under the present supposition, we start with an already man-like creature, erect in attitude, much more intelligent than any other animal, shaping flints to serve as tools and weapons, living in tribes or societies, and able in no small degree to communicate the logic of his recepts by means of gesture-signs, facial expressions, and vocal tones. Clearly, from such an origin, the subsequent evolution of sign-making in the direction of articulate sounds would be an even more easy matter to imagine than under the previous hypothesis. For, let us try to imagine a community of *Homo alalus*, considerably more intelligent than the existing anthropoid apes, although still considerably below the intellectual level of existing savages. It is certain that in such a community natural signs of voice, gesture, and grimace would be in vogue to a greater or less extent.* As their numbers increased (and, consequently, as natural selection laid a greater and greater premium on intelligent co-operation, as in the case of social insects),† such signs would require to become more and more conventional, or acquire more and more the character of sentence-words and denotative signs.‡ Now, where the signs were vocal, the only

structural hiatus between the two watches. A hair in the balance-wheel, a little rust on a pinion, a bend in a tooth of the escapement, a something so slight that only the practised eye of the watchmaker can discover it, may be the source of all the difference. And believing, as I do, with Cuvier, that the possession of articulate speech is the grand distinctive character of man (whether it be absolutely peculiar to him or not), I find it very easy to comprehend, that some equally inconspicuous structural difference may have been the primary cause of the immeasurable and practically infinite divergence of the human from the simian stirps" (Huxley, *Man's Place in Nature*, p. 103).

* Here I will ask the reader to bear in mind the considerations above adduced from Geiger, as to the encouragement which must have been given to a semiotic use of vocal sounds by habitual attention being given to the movements of the mouth in significant grimace—such attention being naturally bestowed in larger measure by an intelligent ape-like creature which was accustomed to depend chiefly on its sense of sight, than it would be by any of the existing quadrumana.

† For sign-making among the social insects, see above, pp. 88–95.

‡ Here, be it observed, the element of truth which belongs to the first of the three hypotheses that we are considering comes in. Compare foot-note on page

ways in which they could be developed so as to meet this need would be, (1) conventional modulations of intensity, (2) of pitch, and (3) of time-intervals. But clearly, neither modulations of intensity nor of pitch could carry improvement very far, seeing that the human voice does not admit of any great range of either. Consequently, if any improvement at all were to be effected—and it was bound to be effected, if possible, by natural selection,—it could only be so in the direction of modulating time-intervals between vocal sounds. Now, such a modulation of time-intervals is the beginning of *articulation.*

That is to say, the first articulation probably consisted in nothing further than a semiotic breaking of vocal tones, in a manner resembling that which still occurs in the so-called "chattering" of monkeys—the natural language for the expression of their mental states. The great difference would be that the semiotic value of such incipient articulation must have been more largely intellectual, or less purely emotional: it must have partaken less of the nature of cries, and more of the nature of names. It seems probable that, as all natural cries are given forth by the throat and larynx, with little or no assistance from the tongue and lips, these first efforts at articulation would have been mainly restricted to vowel sounds, sparsely supplemented by guttural and labial consonants. This state of matters might have lasted for an enormous length of time, during which the liquid, and lastly the lingual consonants would perhaps have begun to be used. This is the order in which we might expect the consonants to arise, in view of the consideration that the gutturals and labials would probably have admitted of more easy pronunciation than the liquids and linguals by an almost speechless *Homo.** From this point onwards, the further

---

364: *Homo alalus*, though not yet a conceptual thinker, is nevertheless in possession of a higher receptual life than has ever been attained by a brute, and is correspondingly more capable of utilizing as signs interjectional or other sounds which emanate from the "purely physiological grounds" of his own organization.

&ast; See Preyer, *loc. cit.*, for a detailed account of the order in which the consonants are developed in the growing child. Also Professor Holden, on the

development of articulation would only be a matter of time and mental growth; but I think it is highly probable that the initial stages thus sketched probably occupied a lapse of time out of all proportion to that which was afterwards required for the higher developments.

Moreover, in this connection we must not neglect to notice the "clicks" of the African Bushmen and Hottentots, which appear to furnish us with direct evidence of the survival among these low races of a primordially inarticulate system of sign-making.* No one has studied the languages of these peoples with so much labour or so much result as the philosophically minded Dr. Bleek, and he says that the clicks which occur in the great majority of their words, "must be made an object of special attention if we would arrive at even an approximate idea of the original vocal elements from which human language sprang."

The clicks in question are four in number, or, according to Bleek, "at least six." They are called the dental, palatal, cerebral, and lateral. The lateral click is the same as that which is employed by our own grooms when urging a horse. The dental is also used by European races as a sound expressive of disappointment, unspeakable contempt, &c. In

*Vocabularies of Children,* in *Proc. Amer. Philolo. Ass.*, 1877. There can be no doubt that vowel sounds must have been of early origin in the race; but in what order the consonants may have followed is much more doubtful. For different races now exhibit great differences with regard to the use—and even to the capability of using—consonantal sounds; the Chinese, for instance, changing *r* into *l*, while the Japanese change *l* into *r*. And, of course, the whole science of comparative philology may be said to be based upon a study of the laws of " phonetic change." But it is obviously a matter of no importance in what particular order the different articulate sounds were first evolved. According to Prince Lucien Bonaparte, who has investigated the matter with much care, the total number of these sounds that can be possibly made by the human organs of vocalization is 385. See, also, Ellis, on *Early English Pronunciation;* and, for the limitation of consonants in various languages of existing races, Hovelaque, *Science of Language,* English trans., pp. 49, 61, 81.

* "When we remember the inarticulate clicks which still form part of the Bushman's language, it would seem as if no line of division could be drawn between man and beast, even when language is made the test" (Sayce, *Introduction, &c.*, ii., p. 302).

† *Ursprung der Sprache,* s. 52.

books it is usually written "tut, tut," which serves to show how hopeless is any attempt at translating a click into any articulate equivalent. The other two clicks are formed by the tongue operating upon the roof of the mouth. Some remote idea of the difficulty of rendering a language of this kind into any alphabetical form, may be gained by trying to pronounce one of the words which are printed in our European treatises upon them. For example, the Hottentot word for "moon" is printed ‖ *khăp*, where ‖ stands for the lateral click, *kha* for a guttural consonant, and ˜ for a nasal twang.

With reference to this inarticulate kind of sign-making, which thus so largely prevails among the languages of low races in close organic connection with articulate, it seems worth while to record the following observation which was communicated by Professor Haeckel to Dr. Bleek, and published by the latter in his work already quoted :—

"The language of apes has not hitherto received from zoologists the attention which it deserves, and there are no accurate descriptions of the sounds uttered by them. They are sometimes called 'howls,' sometimes 'cries,' 'clicks,' 'roars,' &c. Now, I have myself frequently heard in zoological gardens, from apes of very different species, remarkable clicking sounds, which are produced with the lips, and also, though not so often, with the tongue ; but I have nowhere been able to find any account of them."

Upon the whole, then, it appears to me extremely probable that in these clicks we have survivals, in lowly developed languages, of a formerly inarticulate condition of mankind ; or, as Professor Sayce remarks from a philological point of view, "the clicks of the Bushmen still survive to show us how the utterances of speechless man could be made to embody and convey thought." *

In its main outlines the hypothetical sketch which I have given follows that which Mr. Darwin has drawn in his *Descent*

---

* *Introduction*, &c., ii., 302 : by "thought" of course he means what I mean by recepts.

*of Man.* As we have already seen, however, there is this important difference. Mr. Darwin entertains only the second of the three alternative hypotheses here presented, or the hypothesis which assumes that the rudiments of articulate speech began in the "ape-like," or "early progenitors" of man. He does not seem to have entertained the idea of *Homo alalus* as a connecting link between these early progenitors and *Homo sapiens.* I may, therefore, here briefly give my reasons for thinking it probable that this connecting link had an actual existence.

Let it be observed, in the first place, that there is no antagonism between the two hypotheses in question—the latter, indeed, being merely an extension of the former. For the latter adopts all Mr. Darwin's views as to the importance of instinctive cries, danger-signals, &c., for the higher development of sign-making in that "ape-like animal" which was the brutal progenitor of *Homo alalus.** Moreover, our hypothesis is entitled to assume, with Mr. Darwin's, that this anthropoid ape was presumably not only more intelligent than any of the few surviving species, but also much more social. And this is an important point to insist upon, because it is obvious that the conditions of social life are also the prime conditions to any considerable advance upon the sign-making faculty as this occurs in existing apes. The only respect, therefore, in which the two hypotheses differ is in the one supposing that the faculty of articulate sign-making was a much later product of evolution than it is taken to have been by the other. That is to say, while Mr. Darwin's hypothesis regards the commencement of articulation as a necessary condition to any considerable advance upon the receptual intelligence of our brutal ancestry, the present hypothesis regards it as more probable that this receptual intelligence was largely developed by gesture and vocal signs, before the latter can be said to have become

---

* Here also compare the first of the three hypotheses, the important elements of truth in which are, as I have already more than once observed, to be considered as adopted by Mr. Darwin's hypothesis, and therefore also by the present one.

25

properly articulate—the result being that a creature rather more human than "ape-like" was evolved, who, nevertheless, was still able to communicate with his fellows only by means of gesture-signs and vocal tones.

My reasons for regarding this hypothesis as more probable than the other are these.

First of all, on grounds of psychology, I see no reason to doubt that the receptual intelligence of an already intelligent and highly social species of anthropoid ape would admit of considerable advance upon that of any existing species without the aid of articulation—social habits making all the difference as to the development of sign-making with its consequent reaction upon mental development. Next, for these early stages of advance, I do not see that articulate sign-making would have conferred any considerable advantage over a further development of the more natural systems. For, so long as the only co-operation required had reference to comparatively simple actions, the language of tone and gesture would have admitted of sufficient development to have met all requirements. Lastly, if we take the growing child as an index of psychogenesis in the race, there can be no doubt that it points to a comparatively late origin of the faculty of articulation. Remembering the general tendency of ontogenesis to foreshorten the history of phylogenesis, it is, I think, most suggestive that—notwithstanding its readiness to imitate, and notwithstanding its being surrounded by spoken language—the infant does not begin to use articulate signs until long after it has been able to express many of its receptual ideas in the language of tone and gesture. It will be remembered that I have already laid stress upon the astonishing degree of elaboration which this form of language undergoes in the case of children who are late in beginning to speak (see pp. 220). And although it might be scarcely justifiable to take these cases as possibly representative of the semiotic language of *Homo alalus* (seeing that the child of to-day inherits the cerebrum of *Homo sapiens*); still I think it is no less certain that we should err on the opposite side, if we were to take the case of a child who is precocious in the matter of speech as a fair index of the grade of mental evolution at the time when articulation first began in the race (seeing that the history of the latter is probably foreshortened in that of the former). Yet, even if we were to do this, for the sake of argument, the result would still be most strongly to indicate that long before our remote ancestors were able to use articulate speech, they were immeasurably in advance of all existing brutes in their semiotic use of tone and gesture. For even a precocious child does not begin to make any considerable use of words as signs until it is well on into its second year, while usually this stage is not reached until the third. And, at whatever age it is reached, the general intelligence of the child is not only much in advance of that of any existing brute, but the direction in which this advance is most conspicuous is just the direction where, in the present connection, it is most suggestive—namely, in that of natural sign-making by tone and gesture.

In view, then, of these several considerations, I am disposed to think that the progress of mental evolution from the brute to the man most probably took place by some such stages as the following.

Starting from the highly intelligent and social species of anthropoid ape as pictured by Darwin, we can imagine that this animal was accustomed to use its voice freely for the expression of its emotions, uttering of danger-signals, and singing.* Possibly enough, also, it may have been sufficiently intelligent to use a few imitative sounds in the arbitrary way

---

* The song of the gibbon has already been alluded to in a quotation from Darwin. I may here add that the chimpanzee "Sally" not unfrequently executes an extraordinary performance of an analogous kind. The song, however, is by no means so "musical." It is sung without any regard to notation, in a series of rapidly succeeding howls and screams—very loud, and accompanied by a drumming of the legs upon the ground. She will only thus "break forth into singing" after more or less sustained excitement by her keeper; but more often than not she refuses to be provoked by any amount of endeavour on his part.

that Mr. Darwin suggests; and certainly sooner or later the receptual life of this social animal must have advanced far enough to have become comparable with that of an infant at about two years of age. That is to say, this animal, although not yet having begun to use articulate signs, must have advanced far enough in the conventional use of natural signs (or signs with a natural origin in tone and gesture, whether spontaneous only or intentionally imitative), to have admitted of a tolerably free exchange of receptual ideas, such as would be concerned in animal wants, and even, perhaps, in the simplest forms of co-operative action.* Next, I think it probable that the advance of receptual intelligence which would have been occasioned by this advance in sign-making, would in turn have led to a further development of the latter—the two thus acting and re-acting on one another, until the language of tone and gesture became gradually raised to the level of imperfect pantomime, as in children before they begin to use words. At this stage, however, or even before it, I think very probably vowel-sounds must have been employed in tone-language, if not also a few of the consonants. And I think this not only on account of the analogy furnished by an infant already alluded to, but also because in the case of a " singing " animal, intelligent enough to be constantly using its voice for semiotic purposes, and therefore employing a variety of more ,or less conventional tones, including clicks, it seems almost necessary that some of the vowel sounds—and possibly also some of the consonants—should have been brought into use. But, be this as it may, eventually the action and re-action of receptual intelligence and conventional sign-making must have ended in so far developing the former as to have admitted of the breaking up (or articulation) of vocal sounds, as the only direction in which any further improvement of vocal sign-making was possible. I think it not improbable that this important stage in the development of speech was greatly assisted by the

---

* Compare quotations from the German philologists in support of the first hypothesis, pp. 361, 362.

already-existing habit of articulating musical notes, supposing our progenitors to have resembled the gibbons or the chimpanzees in this respect. But long after this first rude beginning of articulate speech, the language of tone and gesture would have continued as much the most important machinery of communication : the half-human creature now before our imagination would probably have struck us as a wonderful adept at making significant sounds and movements both as to number and variety; but in all probability we should scarcely have been able to notice the already-developing germ of articulation. Nor do I believe that, if we were able to strike in again upon the history thousands of years later, we should find that pantomime had been superseded by speech. On the contrary, I believe we should find that although considerable progress had been made in the former, so that the object then before us might appear deserving of being classed as *Homo*, we should also feel that he must needs still be distinguished by the addition *alalus* Lastly, I believe that this most interesting creature probably lived for an inconceivably long time before his faculty of articulate sign-making had developed sufficiently far to begin to starve out the more primitive and more natural systems ; and I believe that, even after this starving-out process did begin, another inconceivable lapse of time must have been required for such progress to have eventually transformed *Homo alalus* into *Homo sapiens*.

It is now time to consider a branch of this hypothesis which has been suggested by the philologist Professor Noiré, to which allusion has already been made in an earlier chapter.*

Before Mr. Darwin had published his views, Professor Noiré had elaborated a theory of the origin of speech which was substantially the same as that which I have already quoted from the *Descent of Man*.† The only difference between

---

* See pp. 288–290.

† *Welt als Entwickelung der Geists*, s. 255. This book, however, was not published until 1874—*i.e.* some years after the *Descent of Man*.

the two was that, while Darwin referred the origin of articulate speech from instinctive cries, &c., to the anthropoid apes, Noiré referred it to a being already human.   In other words, Noiré adopted what I have here called the third hypothesis, which assumes a speechless form of man as anterior to the existing form.*   But, as a result of further deliberation, Noiré came to the conclusion that "the objects of fear and trembling and dismay are even now the least appropriate to enter into the pure, clear, and tranquil sphere of speech-thought, or to supply the first germs of it."   Accordingly, he discarded the view that these germs were to be sought in instinctive cries and danger calls, in favour of the hypothesis that articulation had its origin in sounds which are made by bodies of men when engaged in common occupations. Having already explained the elements of this Yo-he-ho theory, it will here be enough to repeat that I think there is probably some measure of truth in it ; although I likewise think it self-evident that this cannot have been the only source of aboriginal speech.   In what proportion this branch of onomatopœia was concerned in the genesis of aboriginal words— supposing it to have been concerned at all—we have now no means of even conjecturing.   But seeing that there are so many other sources of onomatopœia supplied by Nature, and that these other sources are so apparent in all existing languages, while the one suggested by Noiré has not left a record of its occurrence in any language,—seeing these things, I conclude, as before stated, that at best the Yo-he-ho principle can be accredited with but a small proportional part in the aboriginal genesis of language.†   Therefore, with respect to this hypothesis I have only three remarks to make: (1) that it is

---

* This is likewise the view that was ably supported by Geiger on philological grounds, *Ursprung der Sprache*, 1869 ; and by Haeckel on grounds of general reasoning, *History of Creation*, English trans., 1876.

† "How many of the roots of language were formed in this way it is impossible to say ; but when we consider that there is no modern word which we can derive from such cries as the sailor makes when he hauls a rope, or the groom when he cleans a horse, it does not seem likely that they can have been very numerous" (Sayce, *Introduction, &c.*, i., p. 110).

plainly but a special branch of the general onomatopoetic theory; (2) that, as such, it not improbably presents some measure of truth; and (3) that, consequently, it ought to be regarded—not as it is regarded by its author Noiré and its advocate Max Müller, namely, as the sole explanation of the origin of speech, but—as representing only one among many other ways in which, during many ages, many communities of vociferous though hitherto speechless men may have slowly evolved the art of making articulate signs.

Probably it will be objected to this third hypothesis, in all its branches, that it amounts to a *petitio principii*: *Homo alalus*, it may be said, is *Homo postulatus*. To this I answer, Not so. The question raised has been raised expressly and exclusively on the faculty of conceptual speech, and it is conceded that of this faculty there can have been no earlier phase than that of articulation. Consequently, if my opponents assume that prior to the appearance of this earliest phase it is impossible that any hitherto speechless animal should have been erect in attitude, intelligent enough to chip flints, or greatly in advance of other animals in the matter of making indicative gesture-signs, assisted by vocal tones,—if my opponents assume all this, it is *they* who are endeavouring to beg the question. For they are merely assuming, in the most arbitrary way, that the faculty of conceptual thought is necessary in order that an animal already semi-erect, should become more erect; in order that an animal already intelligent enough to use stones for cracking nuts and opening oysters, should not only (as at present) choose the most appropriate stones for the purpose, but begin to fashion them for these or other purposes; in order that an animal already more apt than any other in the use of gesture and vocal signs, should advance considerably along the same line of psychical improvement.* The hypothesis that such a considerable advance

* With regard to the erect attitude, we must remember that, although the chimpanzee and orang never adopt it, the only other kinds of anthropoid apes— namely, gorilla and gibbon—frequently do so when progressing on level surfaces.

might have gradually taken place, up to the psychological level supposed, may or may not be true ; but, at least, it does not beg the question.   The question is whether the distinctively human faculty of conceptual ideation differs in kind or in degree from the lower faculty of receptual ideation ; and my present suggestion amounts to nothing more than a supposition that receptual ideation may have been developed in the animal kingdom to some such level as it reaches in a child who is late in beginning to speak.*   If any opponent should object to this suggestion on the score of its appearing to beg the question, he must remember that this question only arises—in accordance with his own argument—at the place where the faculty of sign-making ministers to that of introspective thought.   The question as to how far the lower faculties of mind admit of being developed apart from (or, as I believe, antecedent to) the occurrence of introspective thought, is obviously quite a distinct question.   And it is a question that can only be answered by observation.   Now, I have already shown that in the case of intelligent animals —and still more in that of a growing child—the faculties of receptual ideation do admit of being wrought up to an astonishing degree of adaptive efficiency, without the possibility of their having been in any way indebted to the distinctively human faculty of conceptual thought.

On the whole, then, it seems to me probable, on grounds

---

In the case of the gorilla, indeed, although the fore-limbs quit the ground and the locomotion thus becomes bipedal, the body is never fully straightened up ; but in the case of the gibbon the erect attitude may be said to be complete when the animal is walking.   (Huxley, *Man's Place in Nature*, pp. 36–49).   With regard to the selection and use of stones as tools, Commander Alfred Carpenter, R.N., thus describes the *modus operandi* of monkeys inhabiting islands off S. Burmah :— " The rocks at low-water are covered with oysters.   The monkeys select stones of the best shape for their purpose from shingle of the beach, and carry them to the low-water mark, where the oysters live, which may be as far as eighty yards from the beach.   This monkey has chosen the easiest way to open the rock-oyster, namely, to dislocate the valves by a blow on the base of the upper one, and to break the shell over the attaching muscle " (*Nature*, vol. xxxvi., p. 53.   In connection with this subject see also *Animal Intelligence*, p. 481).

* See above, p. 220.

of psychology alone, that the developmental history of intelligence in our race so far resembled this history in the growing child that, prior to the advent of speech, receptual ideation had attained a much higher level of perfection than it now presents in any animal—so much so, indeed, that the adult creature presenting it might well have merited the name of *Homo alalus.* And, as we shall see in my next volume, this inference on psychological grounds is corroborated by certain inferences which may reasonably be drawn from some other classes of facts. But in now for the present taking leave of this question, I desire again to repeat, that it has nothing to do with my main argument. For it makes no essential difference to my case whether the faculty of speech was early or late in making its first appearance. Under either alternative, so soon as the denotative stage of articulation had been reached by our progenitors in the way already sketched on its psychological side, the next stage would have consisted in an extension of denotative signs into connotative signs. As we have now seen, by a large accumulation of evidence, this extension of denotative into connotative signs is rendered inevitable through the principle of sensuous association. In other words, I have adduced what can only be deemed a superabundance of facts to prove that, in the first-talking child and even in the parrot, originally denotative names of particular objects are spontaneously extended to other objects sensuously perceived to be like in kind. And no less superabundantly have I proved that this process of connotative extension is antecedent to the rise of conceptual thought, and, therefore, to that of true denomination. The limits to which such purely receptual connotation may extend, I have shown to be determined by the degree of development which has been reached by the faculties of purely receptual apprehension. In the parrot this degree of development is but low ; in the dog and monkey considerably higher (though, unfortunately, these animals are not able to give any articulate expression to their receptual apprehensions); in the child of two years it is higher still. But, as before shown, no antagonist can afford to allege that in any of these cases there is a difference of kind between the mental faculties that are respectively involved ; because his argument on psychological grounds can only stand upon the basis of conceptual cognition, which, in turn, can only stand upon the basis of self-consciousness ; and this is demonstrably absent in the child until long after the time when denotative names are connotatively extended by the receptual intelligence of the child itself.

Thus, there can be no reasonable question that it is psychologically possible for *Homo sapiens* to have had an ancestry, which—whether already partly human or still simian —was able to carry denotation to a high level of connotation, without the need of cognition belonging to the order conceptual. Whether the signs were then made by tone and gesture alone, or likewise by articulate sounds, is also, psychologically considered, immaterial. In either case connotation would have followed denotation up to whatever point the higher receptual ("pre-conceptual") intelligence of such an ancestry was able to take cognizance of simple analogies. And this psychological possibility becomes on other grounds a probability of the highest order, so soon as we know of any independent evidence touching the corporeal evolution of man from a simian ancestry.

Now, we have already seen that pre-conceptual connotation amounts to what I have termed pre-conceptual judgment. The qualities or relations thus connotated are not indeed contemplated *as* qualities or *as* relations ; but in the mere act of such a connotative classification the higher receptual intelligence is virtually judging a resemblance, and virtually predicating its judgment. Therefore I think it probable that the earliest forms of such virtual predication were those which would have been conveyed in single words. And, as we have seen in the foregoing chapters, there is abundant and wholly independent evidence to show, that this form of nascent predication continued to hold an important place until so late in the intellectual history of our race as to leave a permanent record of its occurrence in the structure of all languages now extant.

The epoch during which these sentence-words prevailed was probably immense; and, as we have before seen, far from having been inimical to gesticulation, must have greatly encouraged it — raising, in fact, the indicative phase of language to the level of elaborate pantomime. Out of the complex of sentence-words and gesture-signs thus inaugurated, grammatical forms became slowly evolved, as we know from the independent witness of philology. But long before grammatical forms of any sort began to be evolved, a kind of uncertain differentiation must have taken place in this protoplasmic material of speech, in such wise that some sentence-words would have tended to become specially denotative of particular objects, others of particular actions, states, qualities, and relations. This "primitive streak," as it were, of what was afterwards to constitute the vertebral column of articulated language in the independent yet mutually related "parts of speech," must in large measure have owed its development to gesture. Now, by this time, gesture itself must already have acquired an elementary kind of syntax, such as belongs even to semiotic movements of an infant who happens to be late in beginning to speak.* This elementary kind of syntax would necessarily be taken over by, or impressed upon, the growing structure of speech, at all events so far as the principles and the order of apposition were concerned. Moreover, this sign-making value of apposition would at the same time have been promoted within the sphere of articulate signs themselves. For, as we have previously seen, as soon as words become in any measure denotative, they immediately begin to undergo a connotative extension ; † and with this progressive widening of signification, words require to be more and more frequently used in apposition. Quite independently of any as yet non-existing powers of introspective thought, the external "logic of events" must have constantly determined such apposition of receptually connotative terms, as we have already so fully seen in the case of the growing child. Thus the conditions were laid for the tripartite division—the genitive case, the

* See pp. 220–222.  † See pp. 179–181.

adjective, and the verb. Not till long subsequent ages, however, would this division have taken place in its fulness. During the time which· we are now contemplating, there could have been no distinction at all between the genitive case and the adjective; neither could there have been any verbs as independent parts of speech. Nevertheless, already some of the denotative signs would have been used as names of particular objects, others of particular qualities, and yet others of particular actions, states, and relations. Not yet deserving to be regarded as fully differentiated parts of speech, these object-words, quality-words, &c., would have resembled those with which we are all well acquainted in nursery language, and which still survive, in a remarkably large measure, among many dialects of a low order of development. Now, as soon as these denotative names became at all fixed in meaning within the limits of the same community, those which respectively signified objects, qualities, actions, states, and relations, must necessarily have been often used in apposition; and, as often as they were thus used, would have constituted nascent or pre-conceptual propositions.

The probability certainly is that immense intervals of time would have been consumed in the passage through these various grades of mental evolution; but when we remember the great importance of this kind of evolution to the species which had once begun to travel in that direction, we cannot wonder that survival of the fittest should have placed a high premium upon the instrument of its attainment or, in other words, that the faculty of sign-making, when once happily started, should have been successively pushed onwards through ascending grades of efficiency, so that it should soon become as unique in the mammalian series as, for analogous reasons, are the flying powers of the Chiroptera. But however long or however short the time may have been that was required for our early progenitors to pass from one of these stages of sign-making to another, so soon as the denotative name of an object was brought into apposition with the denotative name of a quality or an action, so soon was there uttered the virtual statement of a virtual judgment, even though the mind which formed it was very far indeed from being able either to think about its judgment as a judgment, or to state a truth as true.

Thus we perceive that two different principles were presumably concerned in the genesis of what I have called pre-conceptual predication. The first consists in the natural and inevitable extension of denotative into connotative terms, through the force of merely receptual association. The second consists in the no less natural and inevitable apposition of denotative terms themselves, whereby a receptually perceived relation is virtually—though not conceptually—predicated as subsisting between the objects, qualities, states, actions, or relations which are denoted. Of course it is evident that these two modes of development must have mutually assisted one another : the more that denotative signs underwent connotative extension, the greater must have been their predicative value when used in apposition ; and the more frequently denotative signs were used in apposition, the greater must have become the extension of their connotative value.

Lastly, it is desirable throughout all this hypothetical discussion to remember that we have the positive evidence of philology touching two points of considerable importance. The first point is that, as in the aboriginal sentence-words there was no differentiation of, or distinction between, subject and predicate ; so, until very late in the evolution of predicative utterance, there was—and in very many languages still continues to be— an absence of the copula. Nay, even the substantive verb, which has been unwittingly confounded with the copula by some of my opponents, was also very late in making its appearance.

The second point is that, although " pronominal elements " —or verbal equivalents of gesture-signs indicative of space-relations—were among the earliest of verbal differentiations, it was not until after æons of ages had elapsed that any pronouns arose as specially indicative of the first person.*

* See above, pp. 300, 301.

Now, this point I consider one of prime importance. For it furnishes us with direct evidence of the fact that, long after mankind had begun to speak, and even long after they had gained considerable proficiency in the art of articulate language, the speakers still continued to refer to themselves in that same kind of objective phraseology as is employed by a child before the dawn of self-consciousness. This, of course, is what on antecedent or theoretical grounds we should infer *must have been* the case ; but it is surely a matter of great moment that our inference on this point should admit of such full and independent verification at the hands of philological research. As we have now so repeatedly seen, the distinction between ideas as receptual and conceptual turns upon the presence or absence of self-consciousness, in the full or introspective signification of that term. And, as we have likewise seen, the outward and visible sign of this inward and spiritual grace is given in the subjective use of pronominal words. But if these things admit of no question in the case of an individual human mind—if in the case of the growing child the rise of self-consciousness is demonstrably the condition to that of conceptual thought,—by what feat of logic can it be possible to insinuate that in the growing psychology of the race there may have been conceptual thought before there was any true self-consciousness? Obviously this cannot be insinuated without denying those identical principles of psychology on which my opponents themselves rely. Will it, then, be said that the criterion of self-consciousness which is valid for a child is not valid for the race—that although in the former the rise of self-consciousness is marked by the change from objective to subjective phraseology, in the latter a precisely similar change is not to be accredited with a similar meaning? If this were to be suggested, it would not merely be quite gratuitous as a suggestion, but directly opposed to the whole of an otherwise perfectly parallel analogy. In point of fact, then, there is obviously no escape from the conclusion that in the race, as in the individual, the development of true, or

"inward," from receptual, or "outward," self-consciousness
was a gradual process; that its birth in the former is not
merely a matter of inference—overpowering though this
inference be,—but a matter of actual fact which is recorded
in the archives of Language itself; and, therefore, that the
central question upon which the whole of the present treatise
has been engaged cannot any longer be regarded as an open
question. It has been closed, part by part, as the witness
of philology has verified, stage by stage, the results of our
psychological analysis; and now, eventually, the verification
has extended to the central core of the matter, revealing in
all its naked simplicity the one decisive fact, that in the
childhood of the world, no less than in that of the man, we
may see the fundamental change from sense to thought : in
the one as in the other do we behold that—

> " As he grows he gathers much,
> And learns the use of ' I,' and ' me,'
> And finds ' I am not what I see,
> And other than the things I touch.'
>
> " So rounds he to a separate mind
> From whence clear memory may begin,
> As thro' the frame that binds him in
> His isolation grows defined."

# CHAPTER XVII.

## GENERAL SUMMARY AND CONCLUDING REMARKS.

In the present treatise I take as granted the general theory of evolution, so far as it is now accepted by the vast majority of naturalists. That is to say, I assume the doctrine of descent as regards the whole of organic nature, morphological and psychological, with the one exception of man. Moreover, I assume this doctrine even in the case of man, so far as his bodily organization is concerned ; it being thus only with reference to the human mind that the exception to which I have alluded is made. And I make this exception in deference to the opinion of that small minority of evolutionists who still maintain that, notwithstanding their acceptance of the theory of descent as regards the corporeal constitution of man, they are able to adduce cogent evidence to prove that the theory fails to account for his mental constitution.

Such being my basis of assumption, we began by considering the state of the question *a priori*. If, in accordance with our assumption, the process of organic and of mental evolution has been continuous throughout the whole region of life and of mind, with the one exception of the mind of man, on grounds of an immensely large analogy we must deem it antecedently improbable that the process of evolution, elsewhere so uniform and ubiquitous, should have been interrupted at its terminal phase. And this antecedent presumption is still further strengthened by the undeniable fact that, in the case of every individual human being, the human mind presents to actual observation a process of gradual development, extending from infancy to manhood. For it is thus shown to be a matter of observable fact that, whatever may have been the origin or the history of human intelligence in the past, as it now exists—or, rather, as in every individual case it now comes into existence—it proves itself to be no exception to the general law of evolution : it unquestionably does admit of gradual growth from a zero level, and without such a gradual growth we have no evidence of its becoming. Furthermore, so long as it is passing through the lower stages of this growth, the human mind ascends through a scale of faculties which are parallel with those that are permanently presented by what I have termed the psychological species of the animal kingdom—a general fact which tends most strongly to prove that, at all events up to the time when the distinctively human qualities of ideation are attained, no difference of kind is apparent between human and brute psychology. Lastly, not only in the individual, but also in the race, the phenomena of mental evolution are conspicuous—so far, at least, as the records of the human race extend. Whether we have regard to actual history, to tradition, to antiquarian remains, or flint implements, we obtain uniform evidence of a continuous process of upward development, which is thus seen to be as characteristic of those additional attributes wherein the human mind now surpasses that of any other species as it is of those attributes which it shares with other species. Therefore, if the process of mental evolution was interrupted between the anthropoid apes and primitive man during the pre-historic period of which we have no record, it must again have been resumed with primitive man, after which it must have continued as uninterruptedly in the human species as it previously did in the animal species. This, to say the least, is a most improbable supposition. The law of continuity is proved to apply on both sides of a psychological interval, where there happens to be a necessary absence of historical information. Yet we are asked to believe that, in

26

curious coincidence with this interval, the law of continuity was violated — notwithstanding that in the case of every individual human mind such is known never to be the case.

In order to overturn so immense a presumption as is thus raised against the contention of my opponents on merely *a priori* grounds, it appears to me that they must be fairly called upon to supply some very powerful considerations of an *a posteriori* kind, tending to show that there is something in the constitution of the human mind which renders it virtually impossible to suppose that such an order of mental existence can have proceeded by way of genetic descent from mind of lower orders. I therefore next proceeded to consider the arguments which have been adduced in support of this thesis.

In order that the points of difference on which these arguments are founded might be brought out into clear relief, I began by briefly considering the points of resemblance between the human mind and mind of lower orders. Here we saw that so far as the Emotions are concerned no difference of kind has been, or can be, alleged. The whole series of human emotions have been proved to obtain among the lower animals, except those which depend on the higher intellectual powers of man—*i.e.* those appertaining to religion and perception of the sublime. But all the others—which in my list amount to over twenty—occur in the brute creation ; and although many of them do not occur in so highly developed a degree, this is immaterial where the question is one of kind. Indeed, so remarkable is the general similarity of emotional life in both cases—especially when we have regard to the young child and savage man—that it ought fairly to be taken as direct evidence of a genetic continuity between them.

And so, likewise, it is with Instinct. For although this occurs in a greater proportion among the lower animals than it does in ourselves, no one can venture to question the identity of all the instincts which are common to both. And this is the only point that here requires to be established.

Again, with respect to the Will, no argument can arise touching the identity of animal and human volition up to the point where the latter is alleged to take on the attribute of freedom—which, as we saw, under any view depends on the intellectual powers of introspective thought.

There remain, then, only these intellectual powers of introspective Thought, *plus* the faculties of Morality and Religion. Now, it is evident that, whatever we may severally conclude as touching the distinctive value of the two latter, we must all agree that a prime condition to the possibility of either resides in the former : without the powers of intellect which are competent to frame the abstract ideation that is concerned both in morals and religion, it is manifest that neither could exist. Therefore, in logical order, it is these powers of intellect that first fall to be considered. In subsequent parts of this work I shall fully deal both with morals and religion : in the present part I am concerned only with the intellect.

And here it is, as I have acknowledged, that the great psychological distinction is to be found. Nevertheless, even here it must be conceded that up to a certain point, as between the brute and the man, there is not merely a similarity of kind, but an identity of correspondence. The distinction only arises with reference to those super-added faculties of ideation which occur above the level marked 28 in my diagram—*i.e.* where the upward growth of animal intelligence ends, and the development of distinctively human faculty begins. So that in the case of intellect, no less than in that of emotion, instinct, and volition, there can be no doubt that the human mind runs exactly parallel with the animal, up to the place where these superadded powers of intellect begin to supervene. Therefore, upon the face of them, the facts of comparative psychology thus far, to say the least, are strongly suggestive of these superadded powers having been due to a process of continued evolution.

So much, then, for the points of agreement between animal and human psychology. Turning next to the points of difference, we had first to dispose of certain allegations which were either erroneous in fact or plainly unsound in theory. This involved a rejection *in toto* of the following distinctions—namely, that brutes are non-sentient machines ; that they present no rudiments of reason in the sense of perceiving analogies and drawing inferences therefrom ; that they are destitute of any immortal principle ; that they show no signs of progress from generation to generation ; that they never employ barter, make fire, wear clothes, use tools, and so forth. Among these sundry alleged distinctions, those which are not demonstrably false in fact are demonstrably false in logic. Whether or not brutes are destitute of any immortal principle, and whether or not human beings present such a principle, the science of comparative psychology has no means of ascertaining ; and, therefore, any arguments touching these questions are irrelevant to the subject-matter on which we are engaged. Again, the fact that brutes do not resemble ourselves in wearing clothes, making fire, &c., clearly depends on an absence in them of those powers of higher ideation which alone are adequate to yield such products in the way of intelligent action. All such differences in matters of detail, therefore, really belong to, or are absorbed by, the more general question as to the nature of the distinction between the two orders of *ideation.* To this, therefore, as to the real question before us, we next addressed ourselves. And here it was pointed out, *in limine,* that the three living naturalists of highest authority who still argue for a difference of kind between the brute and the man, although they agree in holding that only on grounds of psychology can any such difference be maintained, nevertheless upon these grounds all mutually contradict one another. For while Mr. Mivart argues that there must be a distinction of kind, because the psychological interval between the highest ape and the lowest man is so great ; Mr. Wallace argues for the same conclusion on the ground that this interval is not so great as the theory of a natural evolution would lead us to expect : the brain of a savage, he says, is so much more efficient an instrument than the mind to which it ministers, that its presence can only be explained as a preparation for the higher efficiency of mental life as afterwards exhibited by civilized man.  Lastly, Professor De Quatrefages contradicts both the English naturalists by vehemently insisting that, so far as the powers of intellect are concerned, there is a demonstrable identity of kind between animal intelligence and human, whether in the savage or civilized condition : he argues that the distinction only arises in the domain of morals and religion.  So that, if our opinion on the issue before us were to be in any way influenced by the voice of authority, I might represent the judgments of these my most representative opponents as mutually cancelling one another —thus yielding a zero quantity as against the enormous and self-consistent weight of authority on the other side.

But, quitting all considerations of authority, I proceeded to investigate the question *de novo*, or exclusively on its own merits.  To do this it was necessary to begin with a somewhat tedious analysis of ideation.  The general result was to yield the following as my classification of ideas.

1. Mere memories of perceptions, or the abiding mental images of past sensuous impressions.  These are the ideas which, in the terminology of Locke, we may designate Simple, Particular, or Concrete.  Nowadays no one questions that such ideas are common to animals and men.

2. A higher class of ideas, which by universal consent are also common to animals and men ; namely, those which Locke called Complex, Compound, or Mixed.  These are something more than the simple memories of particular perceptions ; they are generated by the mixture of such memories, and therefore represent a compound, of which " particular ideas " are the elements or ingredients.  By the laws of association, particular ideas which either resemble one another in themselves, or frequently occur together in experience, tend to coalesce and blend into one : as in a " composite photograph " the sensitive plate is able to unite many more or less similar images into a single picture, so the sensitive tablet of

the mind is able to make of many simple or particular ideas, a complex, a compound, or, as I have called it, a *generic* idea. Now, a generic idea of this kind differs from what is ordinarily called a general idea (which we will consider in the next paragraph), in that, although both are generated out of simpler elementary constituents, the former are thus generated as it were spontaneously or anatomically by the principles of merely perceptual association, while the latter can only be produced by a consciously intentional operation of the mind upon the materials of its own ideation, known as such. This operation is what psychologists term conception, and the product of it they term a concept. Hence we see that between the region of percepts and those of concepts there lies a large intermediate territory, which is occupied by what I have called generic ideas, or *recepts*. A recept, then, differs from a percept in that it is a compound of mental representations, involving an orderly grouping of simpler images in accordance with past experience ; while it differs from a concept in that this orderly grouping is due to an unintentional or automatic activity on the part of the percipient mind. A recept, or generic idea, is *imparted to* the mind by the external "logic of events ; " while a general idea, or concept, is *framed by* the mind consciously working to a higher elaboration of its own ideas. In short, a recept is *received*, while a concept is *conceived*.

3. The highest class of ideas, which psychologists are unanimous in denying to brutes, and which, therefore, we are justified in regarding as the unique prerogative of man. These are the General, Abstract, and Notional ideas of Locke, or the Concepts just mentioned in the last paragraph. As we have there seen, they differ from recepts—and, *a fortiori*, from percepts, in that they are themselves the objects of thought. In other words, it is a peculiarity of the human mind that it is able to think about its own ideas as such, consciously to combine and elaborate them, intentionally to develop higher products out of less highly developed constituents. This remarkable power we found—also by common consent—to depend on the faculty of self-consciousness,

whereby the mind is able, as it were, to stand apart from itself, to render one of its states objective to others, and thus to contemplate its own ideas as such. Now, we are not concerned with the philosophy of this fact, but only with its history. How it is that such a faculty as self-consciousness is possible ; what it is that can thus be simultaneously the subject and the object of thought ; whether or not it is conceivable that the great abyss of personality can ever be fathomed ; these and all such questions are quite alien to the scope of the present work. All that we have here to do is to analyze the psychological conditions out of which, as a matter of observable fact, this unique peculiarity emerges—to trace the history of the process, and tabulate the results. Well, we have seen that here, again, every one agrees in regarding the possibility of self-consciousness to be given in the faculty of language. Whether or not we suppose that these two faculties are one—that neither could exist without the other, and, therefore, that we may follow the Greeks in assigning to them the single name of Logos,—at least it is as certain as the science of psychology can make it, that within the four corners of human experience a self-conscious personality cannot be led up to in any other way than through the medium of language. For it is by language alone that, so far as we have any means of knowing, a mind is rendered capable of so far fixing—or rendering definite to itself—its own ideas, as to admit of any subsequent contemplation of them as ideas. It is only by means of marking ideas by names that the faculty of conceptual thought is rendered possible, as we saw at considerable length in Chapter IV.

Such, then, was my classification of ideas. And it is a classification over which no dispute is likely to arise, seeing that it merely sets in some kind of systematic order a body of observable facts with regard to which writers of every school are nowadays in substantial agreement. Now, if this classification be accepted, it follows that the question before us is thrown back upon the faculty of language. This faculty, therefore, I considered in a series of chapters. First it was pointed out that, in its widest signification, "language" means the faculty of making signs. Next, I adopted Mr. Mivart's "Categories of Language," which, when slightly added to, serve to give at once an accurate and exhaustive classification of every bodily or mental act with reference to which the term can possibly be applied. In all there were found to be seven of these categories, of which the first six are admittedly common to animals and mankind. The seventh, however, is alleged by my opponents to be wholly peculiar to the human species. In other words, it is conceded that animals do present what may be termed the germ of the sign-making faculty; but it is denied that they be able, even in the lowest degree, to make signs of an intellectual kind—*i.e.* of a kind which consists in the bestowing of names as marks of ideas. Brutes are admittedly able to make signs to one another—and also to man—with the intentional purpose of conveying such ideas as they possess; but, it is alleged, no brute is able to name these ideas, either by gestures, tones, or words. Now, in order to test this allegation, I began by giving a number of illustrations which were intended to show the level that is reached by the sign-making faculty in brutes; next I considered the language of tone and gesture as this is exhibited by man; then I proceeded to investigate the phenomena of articulation, the relation of tone and gesture to words; and, lastly, the psychology of speech. Not to overburden the present summary, I will neglect all the subordinate results of this analysis. The main results, however, were that the natural language of tone and gesture is identical wherever it occurs; but that even when it becomes conventional (as it may up to a certain point in brutes), it is much less efficient than articulate language as an agency in the construction of ideas; and, therefore, that the psychological line between brute and man must be drawn, not at language, or sign-making in general, but at that particular kind of sign-making which we understand by "speech." Nevertheless, the real distinction resides in the intellectual powers; not in the symbols thereof. So that a man means, it matters not by what system of signs he expresses his meaning. In other words, although I endeavoured to prove that articulation must have been of unique service in developing these intellectual powers, I was emphatic in representing that, when once these powers are present, it is psychologically immaterial whether they find expression in gesture or in speech. In any case the psychological distinction between a brute and a man consists in the latter being able to *mean a proposition ;* and the kind of mental act which this involves is technically termed a "judgment." Predication, or the making of a proposition—whether by gesture, tone, speech, or writing,—is nothing more nor less than the expression of a judgment; and a judgment is nothing more nor less than the apprehension of whatever meaning it may be that a proposition serves to set forth.

Now, this is admitted by all my opponents who understand the psychology of the subject. Moreover, they allow that if once this chasm of predication were bridged, there would be no further chasm to cross. For it is universally acknowledged that, from the simplest judgment which it is possible to make—and, therefore, from the simplest proposition which it is possible to construct—human intelligence displays an otherwise uninterrupted ascent through all the grades of excellence which it afterwards presents. Here, therefore, we had carefully to consider the psychology of predication. And the result of our analysis was to show that the distinctively human faculty in question really occurs further back than at the place where a mind is first able to construct the formal proposition "A is B." It occurs at the place where a mind is first able to bestow a name, known as such, —to call A *A*, and B *B*, with a cognizance that in so doing it is performing an act of conceptual classification. Therefore, unless we extend the term "judgment" so as to embrace such an act of conceptual naming (as well as the act of expressing a relation between things conceptually named), we must conclude that "the simplest element of thought" is not a judgment, but a concept. It is needless again to go over

the ground of this proof; for, although in the course of it
I had to point out certain inexcusable errors in psychological
analysis on the part of some of my opponents, the proof
itself is too complete to admit of any question.

Thus, then, we were brought back to our original distinction between a concept and a recept. But now we were
in a position to show that, just as in the matter of conducting
"inferences," so in the matter of making signs, there is an
order of ideation that is receptual as well as one that is
conceptual. And, more particularly, even in that kind of
sign-making which consists in the bestowing of names, ideation of the receptual order may be concerned without any
assistance at all from ideation of the conceptual order. In
other words, there are names and names. Not every name
that is bestowed need necessarily be expressive of a concept,
any more than every "inference" that is conducted need
necessarily be the result of self-conscious thought. Not only
young children before they attain to self-conscious thought,
but even talking birds habitually name objects, qualities,
actions, and states. Nevertheless, while giving abundant
evidence of this fact, I was careful to point out that thus
far no argumentative implications of any importance were
involved. That a young child and a talking bird should be
able thus to learn the names of objects, qualities, &c., by
imitation—or even to invent arbitrary names of their own—
is psychologically of no more significance than the fact that
both the child and the bird will similarly employ gesture-
signs or vocal tones whereby to express the simple logic of
their · recepts. Nevertheless, it is needful in some way to
distinguish this non-conceptual kind of naming from that
kind which is peculiar to man after he has attained self-consciousness, and thus is able, not only to name, but to *know
that he names*—not only to call A *A*, but to *think A as his
symbol of* A. Now, in order to mark this distinction, I have
assigned the term *denotation* to naming of the receptual kind,
and applied the term *denomination* to naming of the conceptual kind. When a parrot calls a dog "Bow-wow" (as a

parrot, like a child, can easily be taught to do), it may be said in a sense to be naming the dog ; but obviously it is not *predicating* any characters as belonging to a dog, or performing any act of *judgment* with regard to a dog—as is the case, for example, with a naturalist who, by means of his name *Canis*, conceptually assigns that animal to a particular zoological genus. Although the parrot may never utter the name " Bow-wow " save when it sees a dog, this fact is attributable to the laws of association acting only in the receptual sphere : it furnishes no shadow of a reason for supposing that the bird ever thinks about the dog as a dog, or sets the concept Dog before its mind as a separate object of thought. Therefore, none of my opponents can afford to deny that in one sense of the word there may be names without concepts : whether as gestures or as words ("vocal gestures "), there may be signs of things without these signs presenting any vestige of predicative value. Now, it is in order not to prejudice the case of my opponents, and thus clearly to mark out the field of discussion, that I have instituted the distinction between names as receptual and conceptual, or denotative and denominative.

This distinction having been clearly understood, the next point was that both kinds of names admit of connotative extension—denotative names within the receptual sphere, and denominative within the conceptual. That is to say, when a name has been applied to one thing, its use may be extended to another thing, which is seen to belong to the same class or kind. The degree to which such connotative extension of a name may take place depends, of course, on the degree in which the mind is able to take cognizance of resemblances or analogies. Hence the process can go much further in the conceptual sphere than it does in the receptual. But the important point is that it unquestionably takes place in the latter within certain limits. Nor is this anything more than we should antecedently expect. For in the lengthy account and from the numerous facts which I gave of the receptual intelligence of brutes, it was abundantly proved that long before the differential engine of conception has come to the assistance of mind, mind is able to reach a high level in the distinguishing of resemblances or analogies by means of receptual discrimination alone.   Consequently, it is inevitable that non-conceptual or denotative names should undergo a connotative extension, within whatever limits these powers of merely receptual discrimination impose.   And, as a matter of fact, we found that such is the case.   A talking bird will extend its denotative name from one dog in particular to any other dog which it may happen to see; and a young child, after having done this, will extend the denotative name still further, so as to include images, and eventually pictures, of dogs.   Hence, if the receptual intelligence of a parrot were somewhat more advanced than it happens to be, we can have no doubt that it would do the same : the only reason why in this matter it parts company with a child so soon as it does, is because its receptual intelligence is not sufficiently deve-loped to perceive the resemblance of images and pictures to the objects which they are intended to represent.   But the receptual intelligence of a dog is higher than that of a parrot, and some dogs are able to perceive resemblances of this kind. Therefore if dogs, like parrots, had happened to be able to articulate, and so to learn the use of denotative names, there can be no doubt that they would have accompanied the growing child through a somewhat further reach of conno-tative utterance than is the case with the only animals which present the anatomical conditions required for the imitation of articulate sounds.   Both dogs and monkeys are able, in an extraordinary degree, to *understand* these sounds : that is to say, they can learn the meanings of an astonishing number of denotative names, and also be taught to apprehend a surprisingly large extension of connotative significance. Consequently, if they could but *imitate* these sounds, after the manner of a parrot, it is certain that they would greatly distance the parrot in this matter of receptual connotation.

But, lastly, we are not shut up to any such hypothetical case.   For the growing child itself furnishes us with evidence upon the point, which is no less cogent than would be the case if dogs and monkeys were able to talk. For, without argumentative suicide, none of my opponents can afford to suggest that, up to the age when self-consciousness dawns, the young child is capable of conceptual connotation ; yet it is unquestionable that up to that age a continuous growth of connotation has been taking place, which, beginning with the level that it shares with a parrot, is eventually able to construct what I have called "receptual propositions," the precise nature of which I will summarise in a subsequent paragraph. The evidence which I have given of this connotative extension of denotative names by children before the age at which self-consciousness supervenes—and, therefore, *prior to the very condition which is required for conceptual ideation*—is, I think, overwhelming. And I do not see how its place in my argument can be gainsaid by any opponent, except at the cost of ignoring my distinction between connotation as receptual and conceptual. Yet to do this would be to surrender his whole case. Either there is a distinction, or else there is not a distinction, between connotation that is receptual, and connotation that is conceptual. If there is no distinction, all argument is at an end : the brute and the man are one in kind. But I allow that there is a distinction, and I acknowledge that the distinction resides where it is alleged to reside by my opponents—namely, in the presence or absence of self-consciousness on the part of a mind which bestows a name. Or, to revert to my own terminology, it is the distinction between denotation and denomination.

Now, in order to analyze this distinction, it became needful further to distinguish between the highest level of receptual ideation that is attained by any existing brute, and those further developments of receptual ideation which are presented by the growing child, after it parts company with all existing brutes, but before it assumes even the lowest stage of conceptual ideation—*i.e.* prior to the dawn of self-consciousness. This subordinate distinction I characterized by the terms "lower recepts" and "higher recepts." Already I had instituted a distinction between "lower concepts" and "higher concepts," meaning by the former the conceptual naming of recepts, and by the latter a similar naming of other concepts. So that altogether four large and consecutive territories were thus marked out : (1) Lower Recepts, which are co-extensive with the psychology of existing animals, including a very young child ; (2) Higher Recepts, which occupy a psychological area between the recepts of animals and the first appearance of self-consciousness in man ; (3) Lower Concepts, which are concerned only with the self-conscious naming of recepts ; (4) Higher Concepts, which have to do with the self-conscious classification of other concepts known as such, and the self-conscious naming of such ideal integrations as may result therefrom.

Now, if all this is true of naming, clearly it must also be true of judging. If there is a stage of pre-conceptual naming (denotation), there must also be a stage of pre-conceptual judgment, of which such naming is the expression. No doubt, in strictness, the term judgment should be reserved for conceptual thought (denomination) ; but, in order to avoid an undue multiplication of terms, I prefer thus to qualify the existing word "judgment." Such, indeed, has already been the practice among psychologists, who speak of "intuitive judgments" as occurring even in acts of perception. All, therefore, that I propose to do is to institute two additional classes of non-conceptual judgment—namely, lower receptual and higher receptual, or, more briefly, receptual and pre-conceptual. If one may speak of an "intuitive," "unconscious," or "perceptual" judgment (as when we mistake a hollow bowl for a sphere), much more may we speak of a receptual judgment (as when a sea-bird dives from a height into water, but will not do so upon land), or a pre-conceptual judgment (as when a young child will extend the use of a denotative name without any denominative conception). In all, then, we have four phases of ideation to which the term judgment may be thus either literally or metaphorically applied—namely, the perceptual, receptual, pre-conceptual and conceptual. Of these the last only is judgment, properly so called. Therefore I do not say that a brute really judges when, without any self-conscious thought, it brings together certain reminiscences of its past experience in the form of recepts, and translates for us the result of its ideation by the performance of what Mr. Mivart calls "practical inferences." Neither do I say that a brute really judges when, still without self-conscious thought, it learns correctly to employ denotative names. Nay, I should deny that a brute really judges even if, after it is able to denote separately two different recepts (as is done by a talking bird), it were to name these two recepts simultaneously when thus combined in an act of "practical inference." Although there would then be the outward semblance of a proposition, we should not be strictly right in calling it a proposition. It would, indeed, be the *statement of a truth perceived;* but not the statement of a truth perceived *as true.*

Now, if all this be admitted in the case of a brute—as it must be by any one who takes his stand on the faculty of true or conceptual judgment,—obviously it must also be admitted in the case of the growing child. In other words, if it can be proved that a child is able to state a truth before it is able to state a truth as true, it is thereby proved that in the psychological history of every human being there is first the kind of predication which is required for dealing with receptual knowledge, or for the stating of truths perceived; and next the completed judgment which is required for dealing with conceptual knowledge, or of stating truths perceived as true. Of course the condition required for the raising of this lower kind of judgment and this lower kind of predication (if, for the sake of convenience, we agree to use these terms) into the higher or only true kind of judgment and predication, is the advent of self-consciousness. Or, in other words, the place where a mere statement of truth first passes into a real predication of truth, is determined by the place at which there first supervenes the faculty of introspective reflection. The whole issue is thus reduced to an analysis of self-consciousness.    To this analysis, therefore, we next addressed ourselves.

Seeing that the faculty in question only occurs in man, obviously it is only in the case of man that any material is supplied for the analysis of it. Moreover, as previously remarked, so far as this our analysis is concerned, we have only to deal with the psychology of self-consciousness : we are not concerned with its philosophy. Now, as a matter of psychology, no one can possibly dispute that the faculty in question is one of gradual development ; that during the first two or three years of the growing intelligence of man there is no vestige of any such faculty at all ; that when it does begin to dawn, the human mind is already much in advance of the mind of any brute ; but that, even so, it is much less highly developed than it is afterwards destined to become ; and that the same remark applies to the faculty of self-consciousness itself. Furthermore, it will be granted that self-consciousness consists in paying the same kind of attention to internal, or psychical processes, as is habitually paid to external, or physical processes—although, of course, the degrees in which such attention may be yielded are as various in the one case as in the other. Lastly, it will be further granted that in the minds of brutes, as in the minds of men, there is a world of images, or recepts ; and that the only reason why in the former case these images are not attended to unless called up by the sensuous association of their corresponding objects, is because the mind of a brute is not able to leave the ground of such merely sensuous association, so as to move through the higher and more tenuous region of intro-spective thought.    Nevertheless, I have proved that this image-world, even in brutes, displays a certain amount of internal activity, which is not wholly dependent on sensuous associations supplied from without.    For the phenomena of "home-sickness," pining for absent friends, dreaming, halluci-nation, &c., amply demonstrate the fact that in our more intelligent domesticated animals there may be an internal (though unintentional) play of ideation, wherein one image suggests another, this another, and so on, without the need of any immediate associations supplied from present objects of sense. Furthermore, I have pointed out that receptual ideation of this kind is not restricted to the images of sense-perception ; but is largely concerned with the mental states of other animals. That is to say, the logic of recepts, even in brutes, is sufficient to enable the mind to establish true analogies between subjective states and the corresponding states of other intelligences : animals habitually and accurately interpret the mental states of other animals, while also well knowing that other animals are able similarly to interpret theirs. Hence, it must be further conceded that intelligent animals recognize a world of ejects, as well as a world of objects : mental existence is known to them ejectively, though, as I allow, never thought upon subjectively. At this stage of mental evolution the individual—whether an animal or an infant—so far realizes its own individuality as to be informed by the logic of recepts that it is one of a kind, although of course it does not recognize either its own or any other individuality as such.

Nevertheless, there is thus given a rudimentary or nascent form of self-consciousness, which up to the stage of development that it attains in a brute or an infant may be termed receptual self-consciousness ; while in the more advanced stages which it presents in young children it may be termed pre-conceptual self-consciousness. Pre-conceptual self-consciousness is exhibited by all children after they have begun to talk, but before they begin to speak of themselves in the first person, or otherwise to give any evidence of realizing their own existence as such. Later on, when true self-consciousness does arise, the child, of course, is able to do this ; and then only is supplied the condition *sine quâ non* to a reflection upon its own ideas—hence to a knowledge of names as names, and so to a statement of truths as true. But long before this stage of true or conceptual self-consciousness is reached—whereby alone is rendered possible true or conceptual predication—the child, in virtue of its pre-conceptual

27

self-consciousness, is able to make known its wants, and otherwise to communicate its ideas, by way of pre-conceptual predication. I gave many instances of this pre-conceptual predication, which abundantly proved that the pre-conceptual self-consciousness of which it is the expression amounts to nothing more than a practical recognition of self as an active and feeling agent, without any introspective recognition of that self as an object of knowledge.

Given, then, this stage of mental evolution, and what follows ? The child, like the animal, is supplied by its logic of recepts with a world of images, standing as signs of outward objects ; with an ejective knowledge of other minds, and with that kind of recognition of self as an active, suffering, and accountable agent to which allusion has just been made. But, over and above the animal, the child has now at its command a much more improved machinery of sign-making, which, as we have before seen, is due to the higher evolution of its receptual ideation. Now among the contents of this ideation is a better apprehension of the mental states of other human beings, together with a greatly increased power of denotative utterance, whereby the child is able to name receptually such ejective states as it thus receptually apprehends. These, therefore, severally receive their appropriate denotations, and so gain clearness and precision as ejective images of the corresponding states experienced by the child itself. " Mamma pleased to Dodo" would have no meaning as spoken by a child, unless the child knew from his own feelings what is the state of mind which he thus ejectively attributes to his mother. Hence, we find that at the same age the child will also say " Dodo pleased to mamma." Now it is evident that we are here approaching the very borders of true or conceptual self-consciousness. The child, no doubt, is still speaking of himself in objective phraseology ; but he has advanced so far in the interpretation of his own states of mind as clearly to name them, in the same way as he would name any external objects of sense-perception. Thus is he enabled to fix these states before his mental vision as things which admit of being denoted by verbal signs, although as yet he has never thought about either the states of mind or his names for them *as such*, and, therefore, has not yet attained to the faculty of denomination. But the interval between denotation and denomination has now become so narrow that the step from recognizing "Dodo" as not only the object, but also the subject of mental changes, is rendered at once easy and inevitable. The mere fact of attaching verbal signs to mental states has the effect of focussing attention upon those states; and when attention is thus focussed habitually, there is supplied the only further condition which is required to enable a mind, through its memory of previous states, to compare its past with its present, and so to reach that apprehension of continuity among its own states wherein the full introspective, or conceptual consciousness of self consists.

Several subordinate features in the evolution of this conceptual from pre-conceptual self-consciousness were described; but it is needless again to mention them. Enough has been here said to show ample grounds for the conclusions which my chapter on "Self-consciousness" was mainly concerned in establishing—namely, that language is quite as much the antecedent as it is the consequent of self-consciousness; that pre-conceptual predication is indicative of a pre-conceptual self-consciousness; and that from these there naturally and inevitably arise those higher powers of conceptual predication and conceptual self-consciousness on which my opponents (disregarding the phases that lead up to them) have sought to rear their alleged distinction of kind between the brute and the man.

Thus, as a general result of the whole inquiry so far, we may say that throughout the entire range of mental phenomena we have found one and the same distinction to obtain between the faculties of mind as perceptual, receptual, and conceptual. Percept, Recept, and Concept; Perceptual Judgment, Receptual Judgment, and Conceptual Judgment; Indication, Denotation, and Denomination;—these are all manifestations, in different regions of psychological inquiry, of the same psychological distinctions. And we have seen that the distinction between a Recept and a Concept, which is thus carried through all the fabric of mind, is really the only distinction about which there can be any dispute. Moreover, we have seen that the distinction is on all hands allowed to depend on the presence or absence of self-consciousness. Lastly, we have seen that even in the province of self-consciousness itself the same distinction admits of being traced : there is a form of self-consciousness which may be termed receptual, as well as that which may be termed conceptual. The whole question before us thus resolves itself into an inquiry touching the relation between these two forms of self-consciousness : is it or is it not observable that the one is developmentally continuous with the other ? Can we or can we not perceive that in the growing child the powers of receptual self-conciousness, which it shares with a brute, pass by slow and natural stages into those powers of conceptual self-consciousness which are distinctive of a man ?

This question was fully considered in Chapter XI. I had previously shown that so far as the earliest, or indicative phase of language is concerned, no difference even of degree can be alleged between the infant and the animal. I had also shown that neither could any such difference be alleged with regard to the earlier stages of the next two phases—namely, the denotative and the receptually connotative. Moreover, I had shown that no difference of kind could be alleged between this lower receptual utterance which a child shares with a brute, and that higher receptual utterance which it proceeds to develop prior to the advent of self-consciousness. Lastly, I had shown that this higher receptual utterance gives to the child a psychological instrument whereby to work its way from a merely receptual to an incipiently conceptual consciousness of self. Such being the state of the facts as established by my previous analysis, I put to my opponents the following dilemma. Taking the case of a child about two years old, who is able to frame such a rudimentary, communicative, or pre-conceptual proposition as " Dit ki " (Sister is crying), I proceeded thus.

"Dit" is the denotative name of one recept, "ki" the denotative name of another : the object and the action which these two recepts severally represent happen to occur together before the child's observation : the child, therefore, denotes them simultaneously—*i.e.* brings them into *apposition.* The apposition in consciousness of these two recepts, with their corresponding denotations, is thus effected *for* the child by the logic of events : it is not effected *by* the child in the way of any intentional or self-conscious grouping of its ideas, such as we have seen to be the distinguishing feature of the logic of concepts. Here, then, comes the dilemma. For I say, either you here have conceptual judgment, or else you have not. If you say that this is conceptual judgment, you destroy the basis of your own distinction between man and brute, because then you must also say that brutes conceptually judge—the child as yet not having attained to conceptual self-consciousness. If, on the other hand, you say that here you have not conceptual judgment, inasmuch as you have not self-consciousness, I ask at what stage in the subsequent development of the child's intelligence you would consider conceptual judgment to arise. Should you answer that it first arises when conceptual self-consciousness first supplies the condition to its arising, I must refer you to the proof already given that the advent of self-consciousness is itself a gradual process, the precedent conditions of which are supplied far down in the animal series. But if this is so, where the faculty of stating a truth perceived passes into the higher faculty of perceiving the truth as true, there is a continuous series of gradations connecting the one faculty with the other. Up to the point where this continuous series of gradations begins, the mind of the child is, as I have already proved, indistinguishable from the mind of an animal by any one principle of psychology. Will you, then, maintain that up to this time the two orders of psychical existence are identical in kind, but that during its ascent through this final series of gradations the human intelligence becomes distinct in kind from that of animals, and *therefore also from its own previous self?* If so, your argument here ends in a contradiction.

In confirmation of this my general argument, two subsidiary considerations were then added. ˙The first was that although the advance to true self-consciousness from lower grades of mental development is no doubt a very great and important matter, still it is not so great and important in comparison with what this development is afterwards destined to become, as to make us feel that it constitutes any distinction *sui generis*—or even, perhaps, the principal distinction—between the man and the brute. For even when self-consciousness does arise, and has become fairly well developed, the powers of the human mind are still in an almost infantile condition. In other words, the first genesis of true self-consciousness marks a comparatively low level in the evolution of the human mind—as we might expect that it should, if its genesis depends upon, and therefore lies so near to, those precedent conditions in merely animal psychology to which I have assigned it. But, if so, does it not follow that, great as the importance of self-consciousness afterwards proves to be in the development of distinctively human ideation, in itself, or in its first beginning, it does not betoken any very perceptible advance upon those powers of pre-conceptual ideation which it immediately follows? There is thus shown to be even less reason for regarding the first advent of conceptual self-consciousness as marking a psychological difference of kind, than there would be so to regard the advent of those higher powers of conceptual ideation which subsequently—though as gradually—supervene between early childhood and youth. Yet no one has hitherto ventured to suggest that the intelligence of a child and the intelligence of a youth display a difference of kind.

The second subsidiary consideration which I adduced was, that even in the case of a fully developed self-conscious intelligence, both receptual and pre-conceptual ideation continue to play an important part. The vast majority of our verbal propositions are made for the practical purposes of communication, or without the mind pausing to contemplate the propositions in the light of self-consciousness. No doubt in many cases, or in those where highly abstract ideation is concerned, this independence of the two faculties is more apparent than real : it arises from each having undergone so much elaboration by the assistance which it has derived from the other, that both are now in possession of a large body of organized material on which to operate, without requiring, whenever they are exercised, to build up the structure of this material *ab initio*. When I say " Heat is a mode of motion," I am using what is now to me a mere verbal sign, which expresses an external fact : I do not require to examine my own ideas upon the abstract relation which the proposition sets forth, although for the original attainment of these ideas I had to exercise many and complex efforts of conceptual thought. But although I hold this to be the true explanation of the apparent independence of predication and introspection in all cases of highly abstract thought, I am convinced, on the ground of adequate reasons given, that in all cases where those lower orders of ideation are concerned to which I have so often referred as receptual and pre-conceptual, the independence is not only apparent, but real. Now, if the reasons which I have assigned for this conclusion are adequate—and they are reasons sanctioned by Mill,—it follows that the ideation concerned in ordinary predication becomes so closely affiliated with that which is expressed in the lower levels of sign-making, that even if the connecting links were not supplied by the growing child, no one would be justified, on psychological grounds alone, in alleging any difference of kind between one level and another. The object of all sign-making is communication, and from our study of the lower animals we know that communication first has to dó exclusively with recepts, while from our study of the growing child we know that it is the signs used in the communication of recepts which first lead to the formation of concepts. For concepts are first of all named recepts, known as such ; and we have seen in previous chapters that this kind of knowledge (*i.e.* of names as names) is rendered possible by introspection, which, in turn, is reached by the naming of self as an agent. But even after the power of conceptual introspection has been fully reached, demand is not always made upon it for the communication of merely receptual knowledge ; and therefore it is that not every proposition requires to be introspectively contemplated as such before it can be made. Given the power of denotative nomination on the one hand, and the power of even the lowest degree of connotative nomination on the other, and all the conditions are furnished to the formation of non-conceptual statements, which differ from true propositions only in that they do not themselves become objects of thought. And the only difference between such a statement when made by a young child, and the same statement when similarly made by a grown man, is that in the former case it is not even *potentially* capable of itself becoming an object of thought.

The investigation having been thus concluded so far as comparative psychology was concerned, I next turned upon the subject the independent light of comparative philology. Whereas we had hitherto been dealing with what on grounds of psychological analysis alone we might fairly infer were the leading phases in the development of distinctively human ideation, we now turned to that large mass of direct evidence which is furnished by the record of Language, and is on all hands conceded to render a kind of unintentional record of the pre-historic progress of this ideation.

The first great achievement of comparative philology has been that of demonstrating, beyond all possibility of question, that language as it now· exists did not appear ready-made, or by way of any specially created intuition. Comparative philology has furnished a completed proof of the fact that language, as we now know it, has been the result of a gradual evolution. In the chapter on " Comparative

Philology," therefore, I briefly traced the principles of language growth, so far as these are now well recognized by all philologists. It was shown, as a matter of classification, that the thousand or more existing languages fall into about one hundred families, all the members of each family being more or less closely allied, while members of different families do not present evidence of genetic affinity. Nevertheless, these families admit of being comprised under larger groups or "orders," in accordance with certain characteristics of structure, or type, which they present. Of these types all philologists are agreed in distinguishing between the Isolating, the Agglutinating, and the Inflectional. Some philologists make a similar distinction between these and the Polysynthetic, while all are agreed that from the agglutinative the Incorporating type has been derived, and from the inflectional the Analytic.

Passing on from classification to phylogeny, we had to consider the question of genetic relationship between the three main orders, *inter se*, and also between the Polysynthetic type and the Agglutinating. The conflict of authoritative opinion upon this question was shown to have no bearing upon the subject-matter of this treatise, further than to emphasize the doctrine of the polyphyletic origin of language—the probability appearing to be that, regarded as types, both the isolating and the polysynthetic are equally archaic, or, at all events, that they have been of equally independent growth. In this connection I adduced the hypothesis of Dr. Hale, to the effect that the many apparently independent tongues which are spoken by different native tribes of the New World, may have been in large part due to the inventions of accidentally isolated children. The curious correlation between multiplicity of independent tongues and districts favourable to the life of unprotected children—in Africa as well as in America—seemed to support this hypothesis ; while good evidence was given to show that children, if left much alone, do invent for themselves languages which have little or no resemblance to that of their parents.

Without recapitulating all that was said upon the phases and causes of linguistic evolution in its various lines of descent, it will be enough to remind the reader that in every case the result of philological inquiry is here the same— namely, to find that languages become simpler in their structure the further they are traced backwards, until we arrive at their so-called "roots." These are sometimes represented as the mysterious first principles of language, or even as the aboriginal *data* whose origin is inexplicable. As a matter of fact, however, these roots are nothing more than the ultimate results of philological analysis : in no other sense than this can they be supposed "primary." Seeing, then, that these roots represent the materials of language up to the place where the evolution of language no longer admits of being clearly traced, it is evident that their antecedents, whatever they may have been, necessarily lie beyond the reach of philological demonstration, as distinguished from philological inference. This, of course, is what an evolutionist knows antecedently *must be the case somewhere* in the course of any inquiry touching the process of evolution, wherever he may have occasion to trace it. For the further he is able to trace it, the nearer must he be coming to the place where the very material which he is investigating has taken its origin; and as it is this material itself which furnishes the evidences of evolution, when it has been traced back to its own origin, the inquiry reaches a vanishing point. Adopting the customary illustration of a tree, we might say that when a philologist has traced the development of the leaves from the twigs, the twigs from the branches, the branches from the stems, and the stems from the roots, he has given to the evolutionist all the evidence of evolution which in this particular line of inquiry is antecedently possible. The germ of ideation out of which the roots developed must obviously lie beyond the reach of the philologist as such ; and if any light is to be thrown upon the nature of this germ, or if any evidence is to be yielded of the phases whereby the germ gave origin to the roots, this must be done by some other lines of inquiry finding similar germs giving rise to similar products elsewhere. In the present instance, the only place where we can look for such parallel processes of evolution is in the case of the growing child, which I have already considered.

Here, then, we are in the presence of exactly the same distinction with regard to the origin of Language, as we were at the beginning of this treatise with regard to the origin of Man. For we there saw that, while we have the most cogent historical proof of the principles of evolution having governed the progress of civilization, we have no such direct proof of the descent of man from a brutal ancestry. And here likewise we find that, so long as the light of philology is able to guide us, there can be no doubt that the principles of evolution have determined the gradual development of languages, in a manner strictly analogous to that in which they have determined the ever-increasing refinement and complexity of social organizations. Now, in the latter case we saw that such direct evidence of evolution from lower to higher levels of culture renders it well-nigh certain that the method must have extended backwards beyond the historical period ; and hence that such direct evidence of evolution uniformly pervading the historical period in itself furnishes a strong *primâ facie* presumption that this period was itself reached by means of a similarly gradual development of human faculty. And thus, also, it is in the case of language. If philology is able to prove the fact of evolution in all known languages as far back as the primitive roots out of which they have severally grown, the presumption becomes exceedingly strong that these earliest and simplest elements, like their later and more complex products, were the result of a natural growth. Or, in the words already quoted from Geiger, we cannot forbear concluding that language must once have had no existence at all. Nevertheless, it is important to distinguish between demonstrated fact and speculative inference, however strong ; and, therefore, I began by stating the stages of evolution through which languages are now known to have passed from the root-stage upwards. Having done this, I proceeded to consider the question touching the origin of these roots themselves.

First, as to their number, we found that the outside esti- mate, in the younger days of philological research, gave one thousand as a fair average of the roots which go to feed any living language; but that this estimate might now be safely reduced by three-fourths. Indeed, in his latest work, Professor Max Müller professes to have reduced the roots of Sanskrit to as low a number as 121, and thinks that even this is excessive. Regarding the character of roots, we saw that some philologists look upon them as the actual words which were used by the pre-historic speakers, who, therefore, "talked with one another in single syllables, indicative of ideas of prime importance, but wanting all designation of their rela- tions." * On the other hand, it is now the generally accepted belief, that "roots are the phonetic and significant types discovered by the analysis of the comparative philologist as common to a group of allied words," †—or, as it were, composite phonograms of families of words long since extinct as individuals. We saw, however, that this difference of opinion among philologists does not affect the present inquiry, seeing that even the phonetic-type theory does not question that the unknown words out of the composition of which a root is now extracted must have been genetically allied with one another, and exhibited the closeness of their kinship by a close similarity of their sounds.

A much more important question for us is the character of these roots with respect to their significance. In this con- nection we found that they indicate what Professor Max Müller calls "general ideas," or "concepts;" bear testimony to an already and, comparatively speaking, advanced stage of social culture; are all expressive either of actions or states; and betray no signs of imitative origin. Taking each of these characters separately, we found that although all the 121 roots of Sanskrit are expressive of general ideas, the order of

* Whitney.                    † Saycc.

generality is so low as for the most part to belong to that which I had previously called "lower concepts," or "named recepts." Next, that they all bear intrinsic testimony to their own comparatively recent origin, and, therefore, are "primitive" only in the sense of representing the last result of philological analysis: they certainly are very far from primitive in the sense of being aboriginal. Again, that they are all of the nature of verbs was shown to be easily explicable; and, lastly, the fact that none of them betray any imitative source is not to be wondered at, even on the supposition that onomatopœia entered largely into the composition of aboriginal speech. For, on the one hand, we saw that in the struggle for existence among aboriginal and early words, those only could have stood any chance of survival—*i.e.* of leaving progeny—which had attained to some degree of connotative extension, or "generality;" and, on the other hand, that in order to do this an onomatopoetic word must first have lost its onomatopoetic significance. A large body of evidence was adduced in support of the onomatopoetic theory, and certain objections which have been advanced against it were, I think, thoroughly controverted. Later on, however, we saw that the question as to the degree in which onomatopœia entered in to the construction of aboriginal speech is really a question of secondary interest to the evolutionist. Whether in the first instance words were all purely arbitrary, all imitative, or some arbitrary and some imitative,—in any case the course of their subsequent evolution would have been the same. By connotative extension in divergent lines, meanings would have been progressively multiplied in those lines through all the progeny of ever-multiplying terms—just in the same way as we find to be the case in "baby-talk," and as philologists have amply proved to be the case with the growth of languages in general.

That speech from the first should have been concerned with the naming of generic ideas, or higher recepts, as well as with particular objects of sense, is what the evolutionist would antecedently expect. It must be remembered that the kind of classification with which recepts are concerned is that which lies nearest to the automatic groupings of sensuous perception : it depends on an absence of any power analytically to distinguish less perceptible points of difference among more conspicuous points of resemblance — or non-essential analogies among essential analogies with which they happen to be frequently associated in experience. On the other hand, the kind of classification with which concepts are concerned is that which lies furthest from the automatic groupings of sensuous perception : it depends on the power of analytically distinguishing between essentials and non-essentials among resemblances which occur associated together in experience. Classification there doubtless is in both cases ; but in the one it is due to the obviousness of analogies, while in the other it is due to the mental dissociation of analogies as apparent and real. Or else, in the one case it is due to constancy of association in experience of the objects, attributes, actions, &c., classified ; while in the other case it is due to a conscious disregard of such association.

Now, if we remember these things, we can no longer wonder that the palæontology of speech should prove early roots to have been expressive of "generic," as distinguished from "general" ideas. The naming of actions and processes so habitual, or so immediately apparent to perception, as those to which the "121 concepts" tabulated by Professor Max Müller refer, does not betoken an order of ideation very much higher than the pre-conceptual, in virtue of which a young child is able to give expression to its higher receptual life, prior to the advent of self-consciousness. In view of these considerations, my only wonder is that the 121 root-words do not present *better* evidence of conceptual thought. This, however, only shows how comparatively small a part self-conscious reflection need play in the practical life of early man, even when so far removed from the really "primitive" condition of hitherto wordless man as was that of the pastoral people who have left this record of ideation in the roots of Aryan speech.

After having thus explained the absence of words significant of "particular ideas" among the roots of existing language, as well as the generic character of those which the struggle for existence has permitted to come down to us, we went on to consider sundry other corroborations of our previous analysis which are yielded by the science of philology. First we saw that this science has definitely proved two general facts with regard to the growth of predication— namely, that in all the still existing radical languages there is no distinction between noun, adjective, verb, or particle ; and that the structure of all other languages shows this to have been the primitive condition of language-structure in general: "every noun and every verb was originally by itself a complete sentence," consisting of a subject and predicate fused into one—or rather, let us say, not yet differentiated into the *two*, much less into the *three* parts which now go to constitute the fully evolved structure of a proposition. Now, this form of predication is "condensed" only because it is undeveloped ; it is the undifferentiated protoplasm of pre- dication, wherein the "parts of speech" as yet have no exist- ence. And just as this, the earliest stage of predication, is distinctive of the pre-conceptual stage of ideation in a child, so it is of the pre-conceptual ideation of the race. Abundant evidence was therefore given of the gradual evolution of pre- dicative utterance, *pari passu* with conceptual thought— evidence which is woven through the whole warp and woof of every language which is now spoken by man. In par- ticular, we saw that pronouns were originally words indicative of space relations, and strongly suggestive of accompany- ing acts of pointing—"I" being equivalent to "this one," "He" to "that one," &c. Moreover, just as the young child begins by speaking of itself in the third person, so "Man regarded himself as an object before he learnt to regard himself as a subject,"[*] as is proved by the fact that "the objective cases of the personal as well as of the other pronouns, are always older than the subjective."[†] Pronominal

[*] Farrar.　　　　　[†] Garnett.

elements afterwards became affixed to nouns and verbs, when these began to be differentiated from one another ; and thus various applications of a primitive and highly generalized noun or verb were rendered by means of these elements, which, as even Professor Max Müller allows, " must be considered as remnants of the earliest and almost pantomimic phase of language, in which language was hardly as yet what we mean by language, namely *logos*, a gathering, but only a pointing." Similarly, Professor Sayce remarks of this stage in the evolution of predicative utterance—which, be it observed, is precisely analogous to that occupied by a young child whose highly generalized words require to be assisted by gestures—" It is certain that there was a time in the history of speech when articulate or semi-articulate sounds uttered by primitive man were made the significant representations of thought by the gestures with which they were accompanied : and this complex of sound and gesture—a complex in which, be it remembered, the sound had no meaning apart from the gesture—was the earliest sentence." Thus it was that " grammar has grown out of gesture "—different parts of speech, with the subsequent commencements of declension, conjugation, &c., being all so many children of gesticulation : but when in subsequent ages the parent was devoured by this youthful progeny, they continued to pursue an independent growth in more or less divergent lines of linguistic development.

For instance, we have abundant evidence to prove that, even after articulate language had gained a firm footing, there was no distinction between the nominative and genitive cases of substantives, nor between these and adjectives, nor even between any words as subject-words and predicatewords. All these three grammatical relations required to be expressed in the same way, namely, by a mere apposition of the generalized terms themselves. In course of time, however, these three grammatical differentiations were effected by conventional changes of position between the words apposed, in some cases the form of predication being A B, and that of attribution or possession B A, while in other branches of language-growth the reverse order has obtained. Eventually, however, "these primitive contrivances for distinguishing between the predicate, the attribute, and the genitive, when the three ideas had in course of ages been evolved by the mind of the speaker, gradually gave way to the later and more refined machinery of suffixes, auxiliaries, and the like." *

And so it is with all the other so-called "parts of speech," in those languages which, in having passed beyond the primitive stage, have developed parts of speech at all. "These are the very broadest outlines of the process by which conceptual roots were predicated, by which they came under the sway of the categories—became substantives, adjectives, adverbs, and verbs, or by whatever other names the results thus obtained may be described. The minute details of this process, and the marvellous results obtained by it, can be studied in the grammar of every language or family of languages." † Thus, philology is able to trace back, stage by stage, the form of predication as it occurs in the most highly developed, or inflective language, to that earliest stage of language in general, which I have called the indicative.

Many other authorities having been quoted in support of these general statements, and also for the purpose of tracing the evolution of predicative utterance in more detail, I proceeded to give illustrations of different phases of its development in the still existing languages of savages ; and thus proved that they, no less than primitive man, are unable to "supply the blank form of a judgment," or to furnish what my opponents regard as the criterion of human faculty. Therefore, the only policy which can possibly remain for these opponents to take up, is that of abandoning their Aristotelian position : no longer to take their stand upon the grounds of purely *formal* predication as this happens to have been developed in the Indo-European branch of language ; but altogether upon those of *material* predication, or,

* Sayce.              † Max Müller.

28

as I may say, upon the meaning or substance of a judgment, as distinguished from its grammar or accidents.

In other words, it may possibly still be argued that, although the issue is now thrown back from the "blank form" of predication on which my opponents have hitherto relied, to the hard fact of predication itself, this hard fact still remains. Even though I have shown that in the absence of any parts of speech predication requires to be conducted in a most inefficient manner ; still, it may be said, predication *is* conducted, and *must be* conducted—for assuredly it is only in order to conduct it that speech can ever have existed at all.

Now, I showed that if my opponents do not adopt this change of position, their argument is at an end. For I proved that, after all the foregoing evidence, there is no longer any possibility of question touching the continuity of growth between the predicative germ in a sentence-word, and the fully evolved structure of a formal proposition. But, on the other hand, I next showed that this change of position, even if it were made, could be of no avail. For, if the term "predication" be thus extended to a "sentence-word," it thereby becomes deprived of that distinctive meaning upon which alone the whole argument of my adversaries is reared : it is conceded that no distinction obtains between speaking and pointing: the predicative phase of language has been identified with the indicative : man and brute are acknowledged to be "brothers." That is to say, if it be maintained that the indicative signs of the infant child or the primitive man are predicative, no shadow of a reason can be assigned for withholding this designation from the indicative signs of the lower animals. On the other hand, if this term be denied to both, its application to the case of spoken language in its fully evolved form must be understood to signify but a difference of phase or degree, seeing that the one order of sign-making has been now so completely proved to be but the genetic and improved descendant of the other. In short, the truth obviously is that we have *a proved continuity of development between all stages of the sign-making faculty ;* and, therefore, that any attempt to draw between one and another of them a distinction of kind has been shown to be impossible.

The conclusions thus reached at the close of Chapter XIV. with regard to the philology of predication were greatly strengthened by additional facts which were immediately adduced in the next Chapter with regard to the philology of conception. Here the object was to throw the independent light of philology upon a point which had already been considered as a matter of psychology, namely, the passage of receptual denotation into conceptual denomination. This is a point which had previously been considered only with reference to the individual: it had now to be considered with reference to the race.

First it was shown that, owing to the young child being surrounded by an already constructed grammar of predicative forms, the earlier phases in the evolution of speech are greatly foreshortened in the ontogeny of mankind, as compared with what the study of language shows them to have been in the phylogeny. Gesture-signs are rapidly starved out when a child of to-day first begins to speak, and so to learn the use of grammatical forms. But early man was under the necessity of elaborating his grammar out of his gesture-signs—and this at the same time as he was also coining his sentence-words. Therefore, while the acquisition of names and forms of speech by infantile man must have depended in chief part upon gestures and grimace, this acquisition by the infantile child is actively inimical to both.

Next we saw that the philological doctrine of " sentence-words " threw considerable additional light on my psychological distinction between ideas as general and generic. For a sentence-word is the expression of an idea hitherto *generalized*, that is to say *undifferentiated*. Such an idea, as we now know, stands at the antipodes of thought from one which is due to what is called a *generalization*—that is to say, a conceptual synthesis of the results of a previous analysis. And the doctrine of sentence-words recognizes an immense historical interval (corresponding with the immense psychological interval) between the generic and the general orders of ideation.

Again, we saw that in all essential particulars the semiotic construction of this the most primitive mode of articulate communication which has been preserved in the archæology of spoken language, bears a precise resemblance to that which occurs in the natural language of gesture. As we saw, " gesture-language has no grammar properly so called ; " and we traced in considerable detail the analogies—so singularly numerous and exact—between the forms of sentences as now revealed in gesture and as they first emerged in the early days of speech. In other words, the earliest record that speech is able to yield as to the nature of its own origin, clearly reveals to us this origin as emerging from the yet more primitive language of tone and gesture. For this is the only available explanation of their close family resemblance in the matter of syntax.

Furthermore, we have seen that in gesture language, as in the forms of primitive speech now preserved in roots, the purposes of predication are largely furthered by the mere apposition of denotative terms. A generalized term of this kind (which as yet is neither noun, adjective, nor verb), when brought into apposition with another of the same kind, serves to convey an idea of relationship between them, or to state something of the one by means of the other. Yet apposition of this kind need betoken no truly conceptual thought. As we have already seen, the laws of merely sensuous association are sufficient to insure that when the objects, qualities, or events, which the terms severally denote, happen to occur together in Nature, they *must* be thus brought into corresponding apposition by the mind : it is the logic of events which inevitably guides such pre-conceptual utterance into a statement of the truth that is perceived : the truth is *received into* the mind, not *conceived by* it. And it is obvious how repeated statements of truth thus delivered in receptual ideation, lead onwards to conceptual ideation, or to statements of truth as true.

Now, if all this has been the case, it is obvious that aboriginal words can have referred only to matters of purely receptual significance—*i.e.* "to those physical acts and qualities which are directly apprehensible by the senses." Accordingly, we find in all the earliest root-words, which the science of philology has unearthed, unquestionable and unquestioned evidence of "fundamental metaphor," or of a conceptual extension of terms which were previously of no more than receptual significance. Indeed, as Professor Whitney says, "so pervading is it, that we never regard ourselves as having read the history of any intellectual or moral term till we have traced it back to its physical origin." Without repeating all that I have so recently said upon this matter, it will be enough once more to insist on the general conclusions to which it led—namely, psychological analysis has already shown us the psychological priority of the recept ; and now philological research most strikingly corroborates this analysis by actually finding the recept in the body of every concept.

Lastly, I took a brief survey of the languages now spoken by many widely separated race₋ of savages, in order to show the extreme deficiency of conceptual ideation that is thus represented. In the result, we saw that what Archdeacon Farrar calls "the hopeless poverty of the power of abstraction" is so surprising, that the most ardent evolutionist could not well have desired a more significant intermediary between the pre-conceptual intelligence of *Homo alalus*, and the conceptual thought of *Homo sapiens.*

Having thus concluded the Philology of our subject, I proceeded, in the last chapter, to consider the probable steps of the transition from receptual to conceptual ideation in the race.

First I dealt with a view which has been put forward on this matter by certain German philologists, to the effect that speech originated in wholly meaningless sounds, which in the first instance were due to merely physiological conditions.

By repeated association with the circumstances under which they were uttered, these articulate sounds are supposed to have acquired, as it were automatically, a semiotic value. The answer to this hypothesis, however, evidently is, that it ignores the whole problem which stands to be solved— namely, the genesis of those powers of ideation which first put a soul of meaning into the previously insignificant sounds. That is to say, it begs the whole question which stands for solution, and, therefore, furnishes no explanation whatsoever of the difference which has arisen between man and brute. Nevertheless, the principles set forth in this the largest possible extension of the so-called interjectional theory, are, I believe, sound enough in themselves : it is only the premiss from which in this instance they start that is untrue. This premiss is that aboriginal man presented no rudiments of the sign-making faculty, and, therefore, that this faculty itself required to be created *de novo* by accidental associations of sounds with things. But we have seen, as a matter of fact, that this must have been very far from having been the case ; and, therefore, while recognizing such elements of truth as the "purely physiological" hypothesis in question presents, I rejected it as in itself not even approaching a full explanation of the origin of speech.

Next I dealt with the hypothesis that was briefly sketched by Mr. Darwin. Premising, as Geiger points out, that the presumably superior sense of sight, by fastening attention upon the movements of the mouth in vocal sign-making, must have given our simian ancestry an advantage over other species of quadrumana in the matter of associating sounds with receptual ideas ; we next endeavoured to imagine an anthropoid ape, social in habits, sagacious in mind, and accustomed to use its voice extensively as an organ of sign-making, after the manner of social quadrumana in general. Such an animal might well have distanced all others in the matter of making signs, and even proceeded far enough to use sounds in association with gestures, as " sentence-words " —*i.e.* as indicative of such highly generalized recepts as the presence of danger, &c.,—even if it did not go the length of making denotative sounds, after the manner of talking-birds. Moreover, as Mr. Darwin has pointed out, there is a strong probability that this simian ancestor of mankind was accustomed to use its voice in musical cadences, "as do some of the gibbon-apes at the present day ;" and this habit might have laid the basis for that semiotic interruption of vocal sounds in which consists the essence of articulation.

My own theory of the matter, however, is slightly different to this. For, while accepting all that goes to constitute the substance of Mr. Darwin's suggestion, I think it is almost certain that the faculty of articulate sign-making was a product of much later evolution, so that the creature who first presented this faculty must have already been more human than "ape-like." This *Homo alalus* stands before the mind's eye as an almost brutal object, indeed ; yet still, erect in attitude, shaping flints to serve as tools and weapons, living in tribes or societies, and able in no small degree to communicate the logic of his recepts by means of gesture-signs, facial expressions, and vocal tones. From such an origin, the subsequent evolution of sign-making faculty in the direction of articulate sounds would be an even more easy matter to imagine than it was under the previous hypothesis. Having traced the probable course of this evolution, as inferred by the aid of sundry analogies ; and having dwelt upon the remarkable significance in this connection of the inarticulate sounds which still survive as so-called "clicks" in the lowly-formed languages of Africa ; I went on to detail sundry considerations which seemed to render probable the prolonged existence of the imaginary being in question— traced the presumable phases of his subsequent evolution, and met the objection which might be raised on the score of *Homo alalus* being *Homo postulatus*.

In conclusion, however, I pointed out that whatever might be the truth as touching the time when the faculty of articulation arose, the course of mental evolution, after it did arise, must have been the same. Without again repeating the sketch which I gave of what this course must have been, it will be enough to say, in the most general terms, that I believe it began with sentence-words in association with gesture-signs; that these acted and reacted on one another to the higher elaboration of both; that denotative names, for the most part of onomatopoetic origin, rapidly underwent connotative extensions; that from being often and necessarily used in apposition, nascent predications arose; that these gave origin, in later times, to the grammatical distinctions between adjectives and genitive cases on the one hand, and predicative words on the other; that likewise gesture-signs were largely concerned in the origin of other grammatical forms, especially of pronominal elements, many of which afterwards went to constitute the material out of which the forms of declension and conjugation were developed; but that although pronouns were thus among the earliest words which were differentiated by mankind as separate parts of speech, it was not until late in the day that any pronouns were used especially indicative of the first person. The significance of this latter fact was shown to be highly important. We have already seen that the whole distinction between man and brute resides in the presence or absence of conceptual thought, which, in turn, is but an expression of the presence or absence of self-consciousness. Consequently, the whole of this treatise has been concerned with the question whether we have here to do with a distinction of kind or of degree—of origin or of development. In the case of the individual, there can be no doubt that it is a distinction of degree, or development; and I had previously shown that in this case the phase of development in question is marked by a change of phraseology—a discarding of objective terms for the adoption of subjective when the speaker has occasion to speak of self. And now I showed that in the fact here before us we have a precisely analogous proof: in exactly the same way as psychology marks for us "the transition in the individual," philology marks for us "the transition in the race."

In the foregoing *résumé* of the present instalment of my work I have aimed only at giving an outline sketch of the main features. And even these main features have been so much abbreviated that it is questionable whether more harm than good will not have been done to my argument by so imperfect a summary of it. Nevertheless, as a general result, I think that two things must now have been rendered apparent to every impartial mind. First, that the opponents of evolution have conspicuously failed to discharge their *onus probandi*, or to justify the allegation that the human mind constitutes a great and unique exception to the otherwise uniform law of evolution. Second, that not only is this allegation highly improbable *a priori*, and incapable of proof *a posteriori*, but that all the evidence that can possibly be held to bear upon the subject makes directly on the side of its disproof. The only semblance of an argument to be adduced in its favour rests upon the distinction between ideation as conceptual and non-conceptual. That such a distinction exists I freely admit ; but that it is a distinction of kind I emphatically deny. For I have shown that the comparatively few writers who still continue to regard it as such, found their arguments on a psychological analysis which is of a demonstrably imperfect character ; that no one of them has ever paid any attention at all to the actual process of psychogenesis as this occurs in a growing child ; and that, with the exception of Professor Max Müller, the same has to be said with regard to their attitude towards the "witness of philology." Touching the psychogenesis of a child, I have shown that there is unquestionable demonstration of a gradual and uninterrupted passage from the one order of ideation to the other ; that so long as the child's intelligence is moving only in the non-conceptual sphere, it is not distinguishable in any one feature of psychological import from the intelligence of the higher mammalia ; that when it begins to assume the attributes of conceptual ideation, the process depends on the development of true self-consciousness out of the materials supplied by that form of pre-existing or receptual self-consciousness which the infant shares with the lower animals ;

that the condition to this advance in mental evolution is given by a perceptibly progressive development of those powers of denotative and connotative utterance which are found as far down in the .psychological scale as the talking birds ; that in the growing intelligence of a child we have thus as complete a history of " ontogeny," in its relation to "phylogeny," as that upon which the embryologist is accustomed to rely when he reads the morphological history of a species in the epitome which is furnished by the development of an individual ; and, therefore, that those are without excuse who, elsewhere adopting the principles of evolution, have gratuitously ignored the direct evidence of psychological transmutation which is thus furnished by the life-history of every individual human being.

Again, as regards the independent witness of philology, if we were to rely on authority alone, the halting and often contradictory opinions which from time to time have been expressed by Professor Max Müller with reference to our subject, are greatly outweighed by those of all his brother philologists. But, without in any way appealing to authority further than to accept matters of fact on which all philo-logists are agreed, I have purposely given Professor Max Müller an even more representative place than any of the others, fully stated the nature of his objections, and sup-plied what appears to me abundantly sufficient answers. So far as I can understand the reasons of his dissent from conclusions which his own admirable work has materi-ally helped to support, they appear to arise from the following grounds. First, a want of clearness with regard to the principles of evolution in general : * second, a failure

* See especially *Science of Thought*, chaps. ii. and iv. The following quotations may suffice to justify this statement. "If once a genus has been rightly recognized as such, it seems to me self-contradictory to admit that it could ever give rise to another genus. . . . Once a sheep always a sheep, once an ape always an ape, once a man always a man. . . . What seems to me simply irrational is to look for a fossil ape as the father of a fossil man. . . . Why should it be the settled or ready-made Pithecanthropus who became the father of the first man, though everywhere else in nature what has once become settled remains settled,

clearly or constantly to recognize that the roots of Aryan speech are demonstrably very far from primitive in the sense of being aboriginal : third, a want of discrimination between ideas as general and generic, or synthetic and unanalytical : fourth, the gratuitous and demonstrably false assumption that in order to name a mind must first conceive. Of these several grounds from which his dissent appears to spring, the last is perhaps the most important, seeing that it is the one upon which he most expressly rears his objections. But if I have proved anything, I have proved that there is a power of affixing verbal or other signs as marks of merely receptual associations, and that this power is *invariably* antecedent to the origin of conceptual utterance in the only case where this origin admits of being directly observed—*i.e.*, in the psychogenesis of a child. Again, in the case of pre-historic man, so far as the palæontology of speech furnishes evidence upon the subject, this makes altogether in favour of the view that in the race, as in the individual, denotation preceded denomination, as antecedent and consequent. Nay, I doubt whether Max Müller himself would disagree with Geiger where the latter tersely says, in a passage hitherto unquoted, "Why is it that the further we trace words backwards the less meaning do they present ?  I know not of any other answer to be given than that the further they go back the less conceptuality do they betoken." *  Nor can he refuse to admit, with the same

---

or, if it varies, it varies within definite limits only ? (pp. 212–215). . . . If the germ of a man never develops into an ape, nor the germ of an ape into a man, why should the full-grown ape have developed into a man ? (p. 117). . . . Let us now see what Darwin himself has to say in support of his opinion that man does not date from the same period which marks the beginning of organic life on earth— that he has not an ancestor of his own, like the other great families of living beings, but that he had to wait till the mammals had reached a high degree of development, and that he then stepped into the world as the young or as the child of an ape " (p. 160), &c., &c.  So far as can be gathered from these, and other statements to the same effect, it does not appear that Professor Max Müller can ever have quite understood the theory of evolution, even in its application to plants and animals. For these are not criticisms upon that theory : they are failures to appreciate in what it is that the theory itself consists.

* *Ursprung der Sprache*, s. 84.

authority, that " conceptual thought (*Begriff*) allows itself to be traced backwards into an ever narrowing circle, and inevitably tends to a point where there is no longer either thought or speech." * But if these things cannot be denied by Max Müller himself, I am at a loss to understand why he should part company with other philologists with regard to the origin of conceptual terms. With them he asserts that there can be no concepts without words (spoken or otherwise), and with them he maintains that when the meanings of words are traced back as far as philology can trace them, they obviously tend to the vanishing point of which Geiger speaks. Yet, merely on the ground that this vanishing point can never be actually reached by the investigations of philology—*i.e.*, that words cannot record the history of their own birth,—he stands out for an interruption of the principle of continuity at the place where words originate. A position so unsatisfactory I can only explain by supposing that he has unconsciously fallen into the fallacy of concluding that because all A is B, therefore all B is A. Finding that there can be no concepts without names, he concludes that there can be no names without concepts.† And on the basis of such a conclusion he naturally finds it impossible to explain how either names or concepts could have had priority in time : both, it seems, must have been of contemporaneous origin ; and, if this were so,

---

* *Ursprung der Sprache,* s. 119.

† It would be no answer to say that by "names" he means only signs of ideas which present a conceptual value—or, in other words, that he would refuse to recognize as a name what I have called a denotative sign. For the question here is not one of terminology, but of psychology. I care not by what terms we designate these different sorts of signs ; the question is whether or not they differ from one another in kind. If the term "name" is expressly reserved for signs of conceptual origin, it would be no argument, upon the basis of this definition, to say that there cannot be names without concepts ; for, in terms of the definition, this would merely be to enunciate a truism : it would be merely to say that without concepts there can be no concepts, nor, *à fortiori*, the signs of them. In short, the issue is by no means one as to a definition of terms ; it is the plain question whether or not a non-conceptual sign is the precursor of a conceptual one. And this is the question which I cannot find that Max Müller has adequately faced.

it is manifestly impossible to account for the natural genesis of either. But the whole of this trouble is imaginary. Once discard the plainly illogical inference that because names are necessary to concepts, therefore concepts are necessary to names, and the difficulty is at an end. Now, I have proved, *ad nauseam*, that there are names and names : names denotative, and names denominative; names receptual, as well as names conceptual. Even if we had not had the case of the growing child actually to prove the process—a case which he, in common with all my other opponents, in this connexion ignores,—on general grounds alone, and especially from our observations on the lower animals, we might have been practically certain that the faculty of sign-making *must* have preceded that of *thinking the signs*. And whether these pre-conceptual signs were made by gesture, grimace, intonation, articulation, or all combined, clearly no difference would arise so· far as any question of their influence on psychogenesis is concerned. As a matter of fact, we happen to know that the semiotic artifice of articulating vocal tones for purposes of denotation, dates back so far as to bring us within philologically measurable distance of the origin of denomination, or conceptual thought—although we have seen good reason to conclude that before that time tone, gesture, and grimace must have been much more extensively employed in sign-making by aboriginal man than they now are by any of the lower animals. So that, upon the whole, unless it can be shown that my distinction between denotation and denomination is untenable—unless, for instance, it can be shown that an infant requires to think of names as such before it can learn to utter them,—then I submit that no shadow of a difficulty lies against the theory of evolution in the domain of philology. While, on the other hand, all the special facts as well as all the general principles hitherto revealed by this science make entirely for the conclusion, that pre-conceptual denotation laid the psychological conditions which were necessary for the subsequent growth of conceptual denomination ; and, therefore, yet once again to quote the high authority of Geiger, "Speech created Reason ; before its advent mankind was reasonless." *

And if this is true of philology, assuredly it is no less true of psychology. For " the development of speech is only a copy of that chain of processes, which began with the dawn of [human] consciousness, and eventually ends in the construction of the most abstract idea." † Unless, therefore, it can be shown that my distinction between ideation as receptual and conceptual is invalid, I know not how my opponents are to meet the results of the foregoing analysis. Yet, if this distinction should be denied, not only would they require to construct the science of psychology anew ; they would place themselves in the curious position of repudiating the very distinction on which their whole argument is founded. For I have everywhere been careful to place it beyond question that what I have called receptual ideation, in all its degrees, is identical with that which is recognized by my opponents as non-conceptual ; and as carefully have I everywhere shown that with them I fully recognize the psychological difference between this order of ideation and that which is conceptual. The only point in dispute, therefore, is as to the possibility of a natural transition from the one to the other. It is for them to show the impossibility. This they have hitherto most conspicuously failed to do. On the other hand, I now claim to have established the possibility beyond the reach of a reasonable question. For I claim to have shown that the *probability* of such a transition having previously occurred in the race, as it now occurs in every individual, is a probability that has been raised tower-like by the accumulated knowledge of the nineteenth century. Or, to vary the metaphor, this probability has been as a torrent, gaining in strength and volume as it is successively fed by

---

* *Ursprung der Sprache,* s. 91. The exact words are, "Die Sprache hat die Vernunft erschaffen : vor ihr war der Mensch vernunftlos." It is needless to observe that the word which I have rendered by its English equivalent " Reason " is here used in the sense of conceptual thought.

† Wundt, *Vorlesungen, &c.,* ii. 282.

facts and principles poured into it by the advance of many sciences.

Of course it is always easy to withhold assent from a probability, however strong : " My belief," it may be said, "is not to be wooed ; it shall only be compelled." Indeed, a man may even pride himself on the severity of his requirements in this respect ; and in popular writings we often find it taken for granted that any scientific doctrine is then only entitled to be regarded as scientific when it has been demonstrated. But in science, as in other things, belief ought to be proportionate to evidence ; and although for this very reason we should ever strive for the attainment of better evidence, scientific caution of such a kind must not be confused with a merely ignorant demand for impossible evidence. Actually to demonstrate the transition from non-conceptual to conceptual ideation in the race, as it is every day demonstrated in the individual, would plainly require the impossible condition that conceptual thought should have observed its own origin. To demand any demonstrative proof of the transition in the race would therefore be antecedently absurd. But if, as Bishop Butler says, " probability is the very guide of life," assuredly no less is it the very guide of science ; and here, I submit, we are in the presence of a probability so irresistible that to withhold from it the embrace of conviction would be no longer indicative of scientific caution, but of scientific incapacity. For if, as I am assuming, we already accept the theory of evolution as applicable throughout the length and breadth of the realm organic, it appears to me that we have positively *better* reasons for accepting it as applicable to the length and breadth of the realm mental. In other words, looking to all that has now been said, I cannot help feeling that there is actually better evidence of a psychological transition from the brute to the man, than there is of a morphological transition from one organic form to another, in any of the still numerous instances where the intermediate links do not happen to have been preserved. Thus, for example, in my opinion an evolutionist of to-day who seeks to constitute the human mind a great exception to the otherwise uniform principle of genetic continuity, has an even more hopeless case than he would have were he to argue that a similar exception ought to be made with regard to the structure of the worm-like creature Balanoglossus.

If this comparison should appear to betray any extravagant estimate on my part of the cogency of the evidence which has thus far been presented, I will now in conclusion ask it to be remembered that my case is not yet concluded. For hitherto I have almost entirely abstained from considering the mental condition of *savages.* The reason why this important branch of my subject has not been touched is because I reserve it for the next instalment of my work. But when we leave the groundwork of psychological principles on which up to this point we have been engaged, and advance to the wider field of anthropological research in general, we shall find much additional evidence of a more concrete kind, which almost uniformly tends to substantiate the conclusions already gained. The corroboration thus afforded is indeed, to my thinking, superfluous; and, therefore, will not be adduced in this connection. Nevertheless, while tracing the principles of mental evolution from the lowest levels which are actually occupied by existing man, we shall find that no small light is incidentally thrown upon the demonstrably still more primitive intelligence of pre-historic man. Thus shall we find that we are led back by continuous stages to a state of still human ideation, which brings us into contact almost painfully close with that of the higher apes. This, indeed, is a side of the general question which my opponents are prone to ignore— just as they ignore the parallel side which has to do with the psychogenesis of a child. And, of course, when they thus ignore both the child and the savage, so as directly to contrast the adult psychology of civilized man with that of the lower animals, it is easy to show an enormous difference. But where the question is as to whether this is a difference of degree or of kind, the absurdity of disregarding the intermediate phases which present themselves to actual observation is surely too obvious for comment. At all events I think it may be safely promised, that when we come to consider the case of savages, and through them the case of pre historic man, we shall find that, in the great interval which lies between such grades of mental evolution and our own, we are brought far on the way towards bridging the psychological distance which separates the gorilla from the gentleman.

# INDEX.

# Classics In
# Child Development

*An Arno Press Collection*

Baldwin, James Mark. **Thought and Things.** Four vols. in two. 1906-1915

Blatz, W[illiam] E[met], et al. **Collected Studies on the Dionne Quintuplets.** 1937

Bühler, Charlotte. **The First Year of Life.** 1930

Bühler, Karl. **The Mental Development of the Child.** 1930

Claparède, Ed[ouard]. **Experimental Pedagogy and the Psychology of the Child.** 1911

**Factors Determining Intellectual Attainment.** 1975

**First Notes by Observant Parents.** 1975

Freud, Anna. **Introduction to the Technic of Child Analysis.** 1928

Gesell, Arnold, et al. **Biographies of Child Development.** 1939

Goodenough, Florence L. **Measurement of Intelligence By Drawings.** 1926

Griffiths, Ruth. **A Study of Imagination in Early Childhood and Its Function in Mental Development.** 1918

Hall, G. Stanley and Some of His Pupils. **Aspects of Child Life and Education.** 1907

Hartshorne, Hugh and Mark May. **Studies in the Nature of Character. Vol. I: Studies in Deceit; Book One, General Methods and Results.** 1928

Hogan, Louise E. **A Study of a Child.** 1898

Hollingworth, Leta S. **Children Above 180 IQ, Stanford Binet:** Origins and Development. 1942

Kluver, Heinrich. **An Experimental Study of the Eidetic Type.** 1926

Lamson, Mary Swift. **Life and Education of Laura Dewey Bridgman, the Deaf, Dumb and Blind Girl.** 1881

Lewis, M[orris] M[ichael]. **Infant Speech:** A Study of the Beginnings of Language. 1936

McGraw, Myrtle B. **Growth: A Study of Johnny and Jimmy.** 1935

**Monographs on Infancy.** 1975

O'Shea, M. V., editor. **The Child: His Nature and His Needs.** 1925

Perez, Bernard. **The First Three Years of Childhood.** 1888

Romanes, George John. **Mental Evolution in Man:** Origin of Human Faculty. 1889

Shinn, Milicent Washburn. **The Biography of a Baby.** 1900

Stern, William. **Psychology of Early Childhood Up to the Sixth Year of Age.** 1924

**Studies of Play.** 1975

Terman, Lewis M. **Genius and Stupidity:** A Study of Some of the Intellectual Processes of Seven "Bright" and Seven "Stupid" Boys. 1906

Terman, Lewis M. **The Measurement of Intelligence.** 1916

Thorndike, Edward Lee. **Notes on Child Study.** 1901

Wilson, Louis N., compiler. **Bibliography of Child Study.** 1898-1912

[Witte, Karl Heinrich Gottfried]. **The Education of Karl Witte,** Or the Training of the Child. 1914